The Third Chinese R
Civil War, 1945–49

This book examines the Third Chinese Revolutionary Civil War of 1945–49, which resulted in the victory of the Chinese Communist Party (CCP) over Chiang Kaishek and the Guomindang (GMD) and the founding of the People's Republic of China (PRC) in 1949. It provides a military and strategic history of how the CCP waged and ultimately won the war, the transformation of its armed forces, and how the Communist leaders interacted with each other.

Whereas most explanations of the CCP's eventual victory focus on the Sino-Japanese War of 1937–45, when the revolution was supposedly won as a result of the Communists' invention of "peasant nationalism," this book shows that the outcome of the revolution was not a foregone conclusion in 1945. It explains how the eventual victory of the Communists resulted from important strategic decisions taken on both sides, in particular the remarkable transformation of the Communist army from an insurgent / guerrilla force into a conventional army. The book also explores how the hierarchy of the People's Republic of China developed during the war. It shows how Mao's power was based as much on his military acumen as his political thought, above all his role in formulating and implementing a successful military strategy in the war of 1945–49.

It also describes how other important figures, such as Lin Biao, Deng Xiaoping, Nie Rongzhen, Liu Shaoqi, and Chen Yi, made their reputations during the conflict, and reveals the inner workings of the First generation political-military elite of the PRC. Overall, this book is an important resource for anyone seeking to understand the origins and early history of the People's Republic of China, the Chinese Communist Party and the People's Liberation Army.

Christopher R. Lew is a senior strategic analyst for the US Department of Defense, and a Captain in the reserve component of the US Army. He has a Ph.D in History from the University of Pennsylvania – his focus is on Chinese Military history and thought.

Asian States and Empires
Edited by Peter Lorge
Vanderbilt University

The importance of Asia will continue to grow in the twenty-first century, but remarkably little is available in English on the history of the polities that constitute this critical area. Most current work on Asia is hindered by the extremely limited state of knowledge of the Asian past in general, and the history of Asian states and empires in particular. *Asian States and Empires* is a book series that will provide detailed accounts of the history of states and empires across Asia from earliest times until the present. It aims to explain and describe the formation, maintenance and collapse of Asian states and empires, and the means by which this was accomplished, making available the history of more than half the world's population at a level of detail comparable to the history of Western polities. In so doing, it will demonstrate that Asian peoples and civilizations had their own histories apart from the West, and provide the basis for understanding contemporary Asia in terms of its actual histories, rather than broad generalizations informed by Western categories of knowledge.

**1 The Third Chinese Revolutionary
Civil War, 1945–49**
An analysis of Communist strategy
and leadership
Christopher R. Lew

The Third Chinese Revolutionary Civil War, 1945–49

An analysis of Communist strategy and leadership

Christopher R. Lew

LONDON AND NEW YORK

First published 2009 by Routledge
2 Park Square, Milton Park, Abingdon, Oxon, OX14 4RN

Simultaneously published in the USA and Canada
by Routledge
605 Third Avenue, New York, NY 10017

First issued in paperback 2011

Routledge is an imprint of the Taylor & Francis Group, an informa business

© 2009 Christopher R. Lew

Typeset in Times New Roman by Pindar NZ, Auckland, New Zealand

British Library Cataloguing in Publication Data
A catalogue record for this book is available from the British Library

Library of Congress Cataloging-in-Publication Data
A catalog record for this book has been requested

ISBN 13: 978-0-415-67386-0 (pbk)
ISBN 13: 978-0-415-77730-8 (hbk)

Contents

List of figures   vi
Preface   vii
Acknowledgments   ix
Introduction   xi

1 Setting the stage   1

2 "March on the North, Defend in the South"
   (August 1945–June 1946)   16

3 The Guomindang high tide (June 1946–June 1947)   40

4 The turning point (July 1947–August 1948)   74

5 Three crucibles of victory   103

   Conclusion   134

Notes   153
Bibliography   180
Index   197

List of figures

1.1   1945: Map of China   1
2.1   1945: Postwar scramble   17
2.2   1945: March on the North   21
3.1   1946–47: General and Strong Point offensives   42
3.2   1945–46: Communist counterattack in the west   51
3.3   1947: The fall of Yan'an   62
3.4   1946–47: The struggle for northeast China   67
4.1   1947: Turning the tide   75
4.2   1947: Seizing the initiative in north and northeast China   89
5.1   1948: The Liaoshen and Beiping Campaigns   107
5.2   1948: The Ji'nan and Huaihai Campaigns   114
5.3   1949: Carry the revolution to the end   129

Preface

This study originated from a casual conversation with the head of my graduate committee, Arthur Waldron, about how astounding it was that some of the largest battles on the Asian mainland in the 20th century had been virtually ignored in the existing body of scholarship. The battles we spoke about were the Liaoshen, Huaihai, and Pingjin Campaigns which were the culmination of the Third Chinese Revolutionary Civil War or, as it is more commonly known in the People's Republic of China (PRC), the Liberation War (1945–1949). Having already decided to focus on military history, I found this question arising frequently during the rest of my studies at the University of Pennsylvania.

As I prepared for my exams and studied the People's Liberation Army's (PLA) role in the Cultural Revolution and the Korean War, I grew even more intrigued about how the Communists came to power in the first place and the lives of the party's military elite before palace intrigues and purges ensued. As a soldier, I was also inclined to wonder who men like Peng Dehuai and Lin Biao really were. I felt that the existing literature in English identified them more for their political travails rather than their military exploits. Those same sources also dealt with these men and their peers as middle aged or elderly pawns being swept away by the course of events – not the decision-makers or masters of their own fates that they had been as young revolutionaries. I also had the creeping suspicion that other people besides Mao Zedong played a role in developing Communist military strategy between the Long March and the founding of the PRC – an assessment that is not always apparent in the current body of scholarship.

These were the challenges I faced when I started researching my dissertation, which eventually evolved into this book. Still planning to focus only on the three aforementioned battles, I was largely stymied in my attempts to piece together information from works in English. However, the sources I was able to find pointed in two completely different directions. One strain seemed to suggest that I was wasting my time because Communist strategy was of little significance in light of the socioeconomic factors and Nationalist or Guomindang (GMD) incompetence. Other works, however, suggested that the war and the personalities involved were complicated and underwent an evolutionary process that finally culminated in an overwhelming victory in 1949.

In the end, it was a combination of both views which made me realize that there was much more to the story than just the three campaigns – no matter how large or how many men they involved. As I began to look at the war as a whole, it became clear that as important as Liaoshen, Huaihai, and Pingjin were, an even more critical story was how the Communists were in the position to even fight, much less win, those battles. This became the new focus of my study as I prepared to travel to the PRC to conduct my research.

Basing myself in Nanjing, a city I had never visited before, I started at the Second Historical Archives of China and eventually made my way to Nanjing University as a visiting scholar. After four months of compiling data, including sitting in a corner of Nanjing University library with a flatbed scanner for days on end scanning in non-circulating collections of dispatches and selected compositions of high-ranking Chinese Communist Party officials, I began the arduous process of translating and arranging the data. Between morning runs at Nanjing and/or Nanjing Normal University and cramming down *xiaolong bao*[1] for breakfast and lunch, I produced a first draft in little over a month.

It was only after I came up for air and took a step away from the draft that I realized the magnitude of the subject and how engaging the story really was. The narrative almost wrote itself and even though I knew the ending, many times I wondered how the events turned out the way they actually did. Like a novel or a cliffhanger, every campaign, strategy and counterstrategy led to multiple, branching paths of what ifs and what could have been. It was at this point that the real crux of this study emerged – that the result which hindsight had deemed to be so inevitable, so predetermined, was nothing of the sort. In pure military and strategic terms, what the Communists achieved was nothing short of incredible.

After my return to the United States in the fall of 2004, I completed my revisions and eventually defended my dissertation three days before deploying to Iraq with the 2nd Brigade Combat Team of the 28th Infantry Division in February 2005. After a year-and-a-half hiatus from academia, I returned and began the process of turning my dissertation into a book. Thanks to Peter Lorge, my manuscript found its way to Routledge in the spring of 2008.

Acknowledgments

This book would not have been possible without the wise mentorship of my graduate committee at the University of Pennsylvania: Arthur Waldron, Matthew Sommer, and Fredrick Dickinson. Instead of letting me restrict myself to a purely tactical or operational analysis, which I may have been inclined to do on my own, I was challenged to think broadly and explore the intellectual aspect of strategy and its integration into the political-military framework. This influence led me to expand the book from its narrow focus on campaigns to the larger question of how the war was won and why it mattered.

For taking time from their busy professional careers to read through portions or the entirety of this book before publication in 2008, I owe a great deal of thanks to Christen Ritter and Clinton Ohlers. I still consider it one of the proudest moments in my life to have walked across the stage with them to receive our doctorates together – a situation only made possible by my stint in the "sand box" which prevented my participation in the ceremony two years earlier.

I also extend an equal share of gratitude to Karl and Marilyn Larew who read through the draft of my dissertation before my defense. It was under Professor Karl Larew at Towson University (then Towson State) where I truly learned what it took to be a professional military historian. To Marilyn, I am thankful that she not only introduced me to the field of Chinese military history, but also expanded my frame of thought to think regionally and across a longer span of time.

During my time in China conducting research, I also could not have asked for better friends than Yang Qing (Hans), Yang Ling (Judy), and Tang Xiaolong (Jackie), who helped me with everything from finding an apartment to getting a "real deal" Nanjing meal. This was in addition to the arguably less important tasks of getting into the archives and translating difficult passages and concepts into English.

It was during this same time that I had the privilege of meeting Cary Feldmann, who also took time out of his busy schedule to give me comments on my dissertation. Thankfully, our chance encounter in a Nanjing café was the beginning of a solid friendship – one that was perhaps made stronger by the fact that a Nanjing café was certainly not the strangest place in which our paths would thereafter cross.

To Colonel Darryl Green and Major Joshua Stewart, my battalion commander and company commander respectively in 2004, I owe a debt of honor for their approving a temporary suspension of my reserve obligation with the Maryland Army National Guard so that I could conduct my research in China. Along those same lines, I am beholden to the US Army Center of Military History which awarded me a dissertation fellowship as a civilian – completely divorced and disconnected from my military service – to partially fund my research in China. I considered it a distinct honor and privilege for the fellowship committee to have approved a Chinese military history project despite the fact that a vast majority of these grants are for American military history subjects.

In a less direct way, the existence of this book also owes much to the soldiers, Marines, airmen, sailors, and Iraqis that I served with in Ramadi, Iraq, during my tour of duty in 2005–06. Not only did they help keep me alive, but they reaffirmed my faith in the human spirit and the will to continue the fight in the worst of conditions. In a more scholarly sense, my experience conducting counter-insurgency operations and participating in missions firsthand shaped and informed the analysis within this study. It put a new perspective on the plight of Du Yuming and the GMD to have witnessed firsthand how elusive the "enemy" can be when he is so desired.

Finally, my greatest debt is to my family. To my parents, Robert Lew Jr. and Sophie Lew, who guided me towards a life as an academic by stressing the little things, like teaching me to read before I went to school, to seek the truth when lies were easier, and to place high value on books and the knowledge therein. To my wife, Zazy Lopez-Lew, who quickly became the keystone of my adult life – the true strength of my being, who not only stood by me through my grinding, simultaneous stint at graduate and Officer Candidate schools, but also through long-term separations from 2003 to 2006, including the aforementioned years in China and Iraq. Without her patience, companionship and love, I doubt much of what I achieved or who I am today would have really mattered all that much.

Christopher R. Lew
Laurel, MD
2008

Introduction

It is often said that history is written by the victors. However, in the case of the Third Chinese Revolutionary Civil War (hereafter the Third Chinese Civil War,[1] much of what is known in the West has been written or influenced by the losers. Non-Communist, foreign and Chinese Nationalist Party, or Guomindang (GMD),[2] interpretations currently dominate the discourse in English. Consequently, instead of providing a balanced understanding, the lasting impression is that the war was lost by one side rather than won by the other. To explain this defeat, these treatments have emphasized GMD corruption, ineptitude, and disunity. Admittedly, these were important factors in their defeat. However, they were not necessarily decisive. In reality, the GMD pushed the Chinese Communist Party (CCP) to the brink of defeat more than once during the war. It took more than luck, amorphous social trends, or GMD incompetence to turn the tide. In those desperate hours, it was the decisions made, strategies enacted, and battles won that made the unlikely and the improbable – a Communist victory – come to fruition.

The path to the CCP's victory in 1949 was a long and hard one that began more than two decades earlier. With over fifty years of the People's Republic of China (PRC) imprinted on our contemporary consciousness, it is often easy to forget how improbable a Communist victory really was. From the dark days of the April 12 Incident in 1927, also known as the White Terror, to the Long March of 1933–34, the Communists always had been on the losing end. Even after outlasting the Japanese during World War II, the Communists were nothing more than a regional power. In fact, the CCP had remained clearly at a disadvantage vis-à-vis the GMD up to the start of the Third Chinese Civil War in 1945.

Yet by the spring of 1945, they were in an unprecedented position with a firm foothold in the countryside of north and central China,[3] a large army and relatively few GMD troops to interfere with them. At the same time, because the CCP assumed that the war would continue into 1946, the abrupt surrender of Japan in the fall of 1945 actually created more problems than it solved. With a large amount of territory to defend, an army still transitioning from an irregular to a conventional force, and now a power void in most of the big cities and regions of coastal China, the strategic landscape offered as much ambiguity and danger as it did opportunity. It was at this decisive moment, when both sides were as closely matched as they ever would be in terms of military and political power, that the Third Chinese Civil War began.

The intent of this book is to pick up the narrative from the end of World War II and examine the course of the Third Chinese Civil War from the Communist perspective. This is done by analyzing the successes and failures of CCP strategy, the changing relationships within the party's political and military power structure, and the transformation of the Communist army from an irregular force to a conventional army. As alluded to previously, the GMD's perspective on the war is well known. This book thus seeks to fill in the missing and neglected piece of the story. It is a story that ultimately ends at the rostrum of the Gate of Heaven overlooking Tiananmen Square where Mao Zedong announced the founding of the PRC on October 1, 1949.

In addition, a study of the Third Chinese Civil War from the Communist perspective is not only important in understanding the war itself, but also the very foundation and development of the PRC. During the Third Chinese Civil War, both the CCP and its armed wing, the People's Liberation Army (PLA) – an appellation it would receive in the final year of the conflict – underwent their final and perhaps most important evolution before the founding of the PRC. This period also saw the party settling important internal issues as well, the least of which was the reinforcement of party hierarchy and the emergence of a professional military core. This pantheon of the Communist political-military elite[4] would go on to dominate the party leadership well into the 1990s.

Despite its critical significance for these later developments, the Third Chinese Civil War has been largely neglected as a scholarly topic for a variety of reasons including a lack of sources in the past and the belief that the conflict itself was less important than socioeconomic or political trends. Of the specific works that do exist in English, the most notable and recent include Suzanne Pepper's *Civil War in China* and Odd Arne Westad's *Decisive Encounters*.[5] The former focuses on the politics of the period while the latter examines the political, military, social, and diplomatic conditions of the war. These relatively new works were among the first to make the important claim that the outcome of Third Chinese Civil War hung very much in the balance even as late as the winter of 1948. This claim is a departure from previous interpretations that focused on GMD shortcomings, the fatal weakening of Chiang Kaishek's[6] regime during World War II, and the nascent peasant nationalism which swept away the old order.

Earlier interpretations mainly drew upon primary and secondary source research undertaken in Taiwan after 1949. Most of the primary source materials drew on self-criticisms written by the GMD high command and Chiang himself, who placed the blame for the collapse on international interference, factionalism, and division within the GMD leadership, rather than Communist strategy.[7] As the GMD sought to rebuild and recover on Taiwan after losing the mainland, evoking self-blame also became a political tool – a moral lesson to enforce patriotism and political unity that conveniently substituted for fact. The spirit of the GMD's interpretation came through in Western scholarship as well, including F.F. Liu who specifically blamed the GMD's inability to lead and deploy its army for the defeat.[8]

In the 1960s, a different perspective emerged, one that traced the roots of victory to the 1930s. Chalmers Johnson proposed a groundbreaking theory by citing the

CCP's active appeal to Chinese patriotism and nationalism during the war against Japan as the decisive factor in their victory.[9] Mark Selden and Tetsuya Kataoka supplemented Johnson's theory by noting CCP socioeconomic reform as an additional catalyst for victory.[10] These lines of thought held that the Communists seized the initiative from the GMD and successfully carried forward the revolution and the modernization that the people wanted. Although this interpretation gave considerable credit to the CCP, it assumes that the war was decided well before 1945, thus rendering the battles at Shangdang, the Dabie Mountains or Liaoshen predetermined or, worse, irrelevant.[11]

The near-universal embrace of Johnson, Selden and Kataoka's theory was also fueled by the geopolitical situation at the time. During that era, Communists movements were on the rise and America had become increasingly involved in the so-called Vietnam "quagmire." Some authors became so enamored with Maoist military techniques and nationalist insurgency that they linked the Chinese example to the Viet Cong – a link which was also an implicit criticism of American methods and intentions in Southeast Asia at the time.[12] The idea of an "inevitable" Communist victory made Hanoi's successful reunification of Vietnam appear to further vindicate their theories. Yet, while these assumptions have been since revisited and reconsidered in other studies, our understanding of the Third Chinese Civil War has largely remained static. Only recently, with sources from the PRC becoming more readily available, has a reexamination of this period begun, but it remains incomplete.

Military histories of the Third Chinese Civil War, on the other hand, are few and suffer from scholarly gaps. The main obstacle was the PRC's tight control of information and its closed archives – a factor which has only begun to loosen in the last decade. In light of these challenges, it is only logical that there would be few scholarly and military histories of the war in the West. Those works that do exist were almost exclusively written before the PRC began to publish its archival materials. The most significant such work was a project for the US Army Center of Military History composed by William Whitson in the 1960s.[13] Whitson used extensive GMD primary source materials and featured interviews with soldiers and political leaders who had fled to Taiwan after the Communist victory. In light of the sources now available, however, it is evident that this work, along with Whitson's other studies of Communist military leaders, only tells part of the story. Yet despite being dated and not benefiting from PRC sources, Whitson's works continue to provide an important foundation for studies of the PLA and the Third Chinese Civil War. Students of this period have owed a great deal of gratitude to Whitson's efforts and likely will continue to do so for some time.

The restrictions of yesterday have eased significantly and available sources, both secondary and primary, have proliferated. As Pepper notes in the 1999 revised edition of *Civil War in China*:

> [The] still largely unmined sources on the 1945–1949 period are sufficient to keep scholars busy for years to come, even without direct access to unpublished archival holdings, which have become the foundation for research

on modern China …. One can easily lapse into an old-timer's lament upon contemplating the younger generation, spoiled by its new embarrassment of riches and heedless of how its pioneering forebears spent years scouring the worlds for their precious scraps and fragments.[14]

These new sources include official and semi-official histories that summarize the war, individual units, and key military leaders. Most of these originate from government publishing houses, although some are being produced by private or semi-private companies.[15] Primary source documents, on the other hand, are almost all published by the government agencies that hold the keys to the archives and regulate publication of autobiographies or firsthand accounts. The main problem with all of these sources is that, regardless of the publishing agency, all such literature is subject to government review and censorship. It is difficult to determine how much information has been withheld, but each year the gap between what exists and what is known in the public sphere is slowly narrowing.

One of the interesting dynamics that affects availability of sources is the salutary influence of political turmoil and debate within the PRC. The use of past events to alternatively criticize and rehabilitate various figures increases disclosure. For instance, the various purges and subsequent rehabilitations of Deng Xiaoping revealed a great deal about his life, activities and association with the Central Plains Field Army. Yet these revisions too are subject to bias and omission and some of the most important documents remain either hidden or "lost."

Despite these problems, PRC primary source material still manages to portray the war as by and large a contingent affair. Although the compilation and composition of some of these documents – especially those written in hindsight – tend to be colored by the determinism of Marxist-Leninism and Mao Zedong Thought, this body of literature is surprisingly candid and seemingly genuine. This is mainly because they tend to focus on actual military operations, and even the best revisionist cannot hide lost battles or obscure widely known events that stand in stark contrast to convenient CCP myths. Additionally, the forced introduction of Mao Zedong dialectics is less apparent in recent publications and even the older ones often manage to suggest that events might have turned out differently had battles or events gone against them.

In regard to the discussion and dialogue in secondary source works published in mainland China about the Third Chinese Civil War, most of it focuses on tactical questions and issues exposed by "struggle sessions" against one figure or another. One of the best examples of this is the use of Lin Biao's disagreement with Mao Zedong during the fighting in Manchuria. The incident would serve as a centerpiece of the "Criticize Lin Biao, Criticize Confucius" campaign following Lin's failed coup.[16] Fortunately, many original, unadulterated documents can still be found in flea markets and curiosity shops in China in the form of pamphlets and leaflets issued by the PRC's National Defense University or other government publishing houses during and after the Cultural Revolution. While offering the most revealing glimpses into Communist strategy during the war, they are limited in focus and increasingly hard to find due to age and scarcity.[17] Nonetheless, as the PRC rehabilitates more of its past Communist leaders, there is increasing discussion of the heroic past of the post-1949 "villains" and those that did not fit the Mao-centric paradigm. For instance, Peng Dehuai, the first major victim of Mao's wrath in the Communist era, is now regarded as a true Chinese patriot in both war and peace.[18] Even the controversial Lin Biao is undergoing a minor rehabilitation of sorts with his position as one of the "Ten Marshals of the PLA" restored after a long absence.[19]

By applying the necessary measure of critical analysis to these sources, this book seeks to construct an accurate retelling of how Communist leaders planned and implemented military strategy during the Third Chinese Civil War. Many of our most fundamental assumptions about the PRC currently are based on an incomplete understanding of what occurred during this critical period. Although mainly a military history, this book focuses on the confluence of personalities and ideas, rather than battlefield tactics or combat maneuvers – a subject which deserves its own monograph. This approach will serve to shed light on three major themes: the fact that the CCP's victory was not predetermined, the evolution and strengthening of the Chinese hierarchy leading into the PRC, and the importance of battle in determining the war's final resolution. A further objective is to draw focus on to how the Communist high command thought, mainly by highlighting their decisions and strategies. To do so sheds light not only on the decision-making process but also on how important CCP figures fit into that process and how their experiences during the war shaped their outlook and their position within the party.

Although this book draws on many different works and ideas spanning fifty years, it is the author's intent for it to be a beginning rather than an end. The discussion about the importance of the Third Chinese Civil War – long thought to be dead – is very much alive in the sense that there is still much work to be done. The wealth of data that is now available and the questions that it raises shows that failure to fully understand this period makes our understanding of the PRC and the CCP problematic at best. More than anything else, the author hopes this work will spark the interest and attention the Third Chinese Civil War deserves.

1   Setting the stage

In the spring of 1945, with World War II winding down in the Pacific and Europe, the Communists began planning for postwar China. On April 23, 1945, two weeks before the surrender of Germany and more than three months before the surrender of Japan, the Chinese Communist Party convened the 7th Congress in Yan'an. Almost 20 years had passed since the previous Congress had assembled in Moscow in 1928. In the two intervening decades, the CCP not only had survived its darkest hour in its struggle against the GMD and Japan, but had emerged stronger. On the eve of the 7th National Congress, the CCP claimed a membership of 1.21 million.

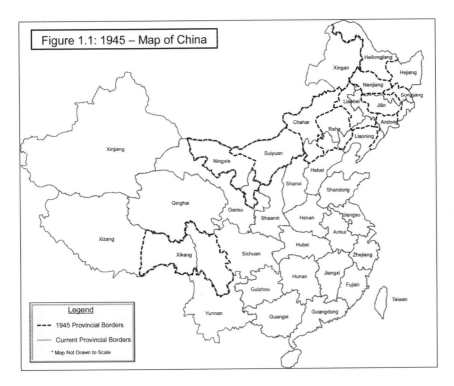

Figure 1.1 1945: Map of China.

Of this 547 regular and 208 non-voting delegates attended the Congress in Yan'an. The party had also created a standing, regular army of 910,000 men and a militia 2,200,000 strong. Although not yet tested in large-scale conventional operations, this so-called 18th Group Army consisted of experienced combat veterans well acquainted with accomplishing missions under great odds and with little modern equipment.

The 18th Group Army derived its name from the forced alliance between the GMD and the CCP, the Second United Front that formed to fight the Japanese. It consisted of the 8th Route Army and the New 4th Army.[1] At its head was Zhu De, the most senior military commander in the Communist ranks. Zhu, in turn, reported to the CCP's Central Military Committee (CMC), of which he was a part. The CMC was technically supposed to report to the GMD high command.[2] However, it did not normally do so because of the remoteness of Yan'an and the poor relationship between Mao Zedong, chairman of the CCP and the CMC, and Chiang Kaishek, president of the GMD. Additionally, in the early days of 18th Group Army, its subordinate armies largely operated independently of each other. For instance, the 8th Route Army had the same commander and staff as the 18th Group Army, whereas a completely different set of personnel commanded the New 4th Army, which was located in another region altogether.

The reason for distinction was mainly due to the fact that the New 4th Army consisted of the collected remains of guerrilla units that had remained behind during the Long March and had continued to fight the GMD in south China.[3] Following Yan'an's guidance in 1937, these units formed the New 4th Army, entered into the Second United Front and turned their guns on the Japanese. Although their commander and political commissar were Communists, unlike the 8th Route Army the New 4th Army was directly under GMD command. This relationship turned sour in late 1941 during the so-called New 4th Army Incident, when Chiang's forces destroyed the headquarters of the army. Most of the army escaped to north Jiangsu, falling back on its bases there and linking up with 8th Route Army units that had expanded east into Hebei and Shandong at the expense of the Japanese. In this way, the New 4th Army Incident proved a blessing in disguise. It allowed the New 4th Army to improve its strategic position and receive reinforcements and supplies from Yan'an.

The movements and development of the 8th Route and New 4th Armies went hand in hand with the creation of so-called Liberated Areas. Pockets of these Communist-administered regions were located in north China[4] and encompassed a total population of 95,500,000 people.[5] As a proto-state, the Liberated Areas represented more successful versions of the Jiangxi Soviet of the previous generation. Many of these had grown and prospered due to the lack of GMD and Japanese presence. As a result, most areas were located outside of the large cities and away from main railroads. These Liberated Areas demonstrated the CCP's growing legitimacy and strength. They also added to the CCP's military capability in terms of industry, logistics, intelligence, and easy access to labor. Territorial control also allowed the Communists to conduct social and political reform, winning them a great deal of support from the general populace.[6]

As CCP strength grew, the strategic situation by the spring of 1945 also looked promising for Yan'an. With solid bases in north China, the Communists were in a superior position to move into strategic areas occupied by the Japanese such as Manchuria and Shandong. History and tradition also favored the CCP; as "conquerors" from the north they were poised to join the ranks of Cao Cao and the Ming emperor Yongle. Only two men had ever unified China from the south. Unfortunately for the Communists, one of those was Chiang and he was prepared to do it all over again as soon as the war ended. The GMD army also had emerged from World War II larger and stronger. It was also well-trained and equipped, thanks to American assistance. Chiang could also call on his wartime alliances with the United States and Great Britain to provide air and naval transport. The international community recognized him as the only legitimate head of the Chinese state, which gave him the sole right to disarm and deal with the defeated Japanese armies and their allies. All these advantages would prove crucial in the postwar struggle. As for the CCP, only the Soviet Union recognized the Communists, although they had won a few supporters in the US thanks to the Dixie Mission. Unfortunately, Moscow also had a vested interested in keeping China divided and weak.

In light of these future challenges, the 7th Congress focused on improving their position vis-à-vis the GMD, not Japan, for the long run. Although they realized the war would soon be over, there was no call to begin mobilization for civil war nor were the Communists interested in speeding up Japan's defeat. In one of his first speeches at the Congress, Mao laid out a broad outline for the defeat of Japan by "mobilizing the masses," "expanding the people's forces, and uniting all the forces of the nation under the CCP."[17] He envisioned seizing Japanese-occupied territory through coordinated armed uprisings from within while the 18th Army Group attacked from without. He also ordered the army to prepare for the defense of the existing Liberated Areas while continuing to expand and modernize. As for GMD-controlled areas, Mao determined the CCP would only conduct political work and, for the time being, permitted no military actions.[8]

Zhu De built on Mao's speeches and went a step further. He declared "mobile" warfare should replace guerrilla warfare.[9] "Mobile" warfare generally referred to using standing, conventional units to fight battles to destroy enemy units, not to capture, hold or defend territory. This pronouncement meant that the 7th Congress was one of the most significant events in the history of the PLA because it was marked the beginning of the end of guerrilla warfare. Zhu's vision for defending the north China Liberated Areas was to conduct an interior line or "mobile" defense with large, professional units. This was a significant change from Mao's earlier policy, which advocated guerrilla warfare as the primary option and "mobile" warfare as a secondary one. However, this did not necessary reflect an independent action on Zhu's part because Mao would have had to approve such a significant change in strategy beforehand. Instead, the shift reflected the new political and military reality of having large amounts of territory and people to protect as well as now having an army capable of defending it. The party also would suffer a significant loss of prestige and public support if the Liberated Areas fell. Yet their strategy of choice illustrated the fact that the Communists anticipated having to give some ground due to the incomplete state of their military reforms and GMD strength. In the end, the survival of the army and the party was still paramount.

To prepare for the new mission, Zhu set a series of goals to modernize and professionalize the army that set the stage for the rest of the Third Chinese Civil War. The first task was a new training regime for the summer of 1945 that focused on improving tactics, leadership and maneuver.[10] At the same time, Zhu oversaw a rapid increase of the army by reorganizing guerrilla elements into regular units. Zhu also tackled tough logistical issues such as the standardization of weapons and creating a domestic production base rather than relying on captured supplies.[11] Driven by his past experience, one of the production items he most emphasized was artillery:[12]

> In battles against enemy and puppet troops and troops of the diehard clique of the [GMD], our fighters often encounter pillboxes and temporary earthworks common in mobile warfare, which keep them from gaining victory.[13]

To this end, Zhu created an Artillery School in Yan'an to train new units. He also decreed that each full-strength regiment was to raise a mortar battery while under-strength regiments were to form a mortar platoon.[14]

While Zhu prepared the 8th Route Army to defend the north China Liberated Areas, Mao had a different vision for south and central China. He dispatched some of his best regular units south to establish guerrilla bases behind enemy lines – the method by which the Communists had secured most of their existing territory. Earlier in October 1944, he had dispatched Wang Zhen's Southern Detachment, a brigade-sized element from the 8th Route Army, along with Li Xiannian's 5th Division from the New 4th Army to create guerrilla bases south of the Yangtze River.[15] A month later, Mao ordered Su Yu's New 4th Army 1st Division also to cross the Yangtze and create a base in Jiangsu and Zhejiang.[16] They were able to do so because Japan was preoccupied with its Kohima and Ichigo campaigns in southeast Asia and in the GMD-occupied areas of south China, respectively. By March 1945, the Southern Detachment was across the Yangtze River establishing a base in north Hunan. In May 1945, after the 7th Congress, Li joined Wang to begin probing Hubei and Jiangxi.[17] Communist guerrilla forces in Guangdong also began expanding northward to link up with these new bases.[18]

Carried out under the guise of continuing the war against Japan by "expanding Communist territory, reducing the occupied zones," the true intent of Mao's policy was to capture strategic areas before the GMD returned. As a directive from the Central Committee of the CCP stated, Communist forces in Henan were to occupy strategic points from which to prepare for a "GMD counterattack within a year or a year and a half."[19] In the 7th Congress, the Communists surmised that even if Chiang decided to counterattack, it would be another year before he could return to Guangzhou, much less north China – more than enough time for them to prepare defenses.[20] The CCP also assumed that Japan would be unable to interfere. In fact, the Communists ordered their new guerrilla forces in south China to "mass its forces and seek battle with the Japanese no matter what the situation."[21] At the same time, the party high command believed the GMD would refrain from attacking out of fear of repeating the New 4th Army Incident and turning the war-weary populace against them.

In late July 1945, with the Pacific war in its final stages, Japanese forces began shortening their lines in China. This included abandoning hinterland possessions like Nanning and strengthening coastal areas, specifically the ports of Shandong. Instead of immediately moving into areas evacuated by the Japanese, Mao continued to stress the need for bases in the countryside, specifically where the four provinces of Hunan, Guangdong, Guangxi, and Jiangxi met.[22] In August, only days before the Japanese surrender, Mao ordered Communist forces in the Central Plains[23] to expand their rural bases into new areas such as the key mountainous regions of the Tongbai and Dabie Mountains.[24] By fortifying these critical locations, the Communists believed they could prevent Chiang from controlling south China. In the event of civil war, he would first have to subdue these regions and would not be able to exert his full strength against the north China Liberated Area.[25]

The strategic developments in the spring and summer of 1945 thus illustrate a two-headed strategy. In north China, where the Communists had already established a mini-state in the midst of a skeletal Japanese occupation, the 8th and New 4th Armies prepared for conventional, defensive operations against the GMD. In south and central China, the CCP sought to create guerrilla bases which would divert GMD troops to the region and hinder, slow, and block Chiang's process of unification. If the plan succeeded, the GMD would have to fight two wars simultaneously – a conventional one in the north and a counterinsurgency in the south. The Communists, however, made a serious miscalculation by assuming that the war against Japan would continue into 1946. The CCP was not the only party guilty of this mistake. The United States, for example, had made the same faulty assessment. Tokyo's abrupt surrender inadvertently destroyed Yan'an's carefully crafted plan to create these two separate fronts. In September 1945, the guerrilla bases in the south were not complete and neither the 8th Route nor New 4th Armies were ready for large-scale fighting. Events took on a frantic pace as Chiang began moving his legions forward. It was indeed a most inopportune moment to have to draft an entirely new strategy.

Cast of characters

As events and strategic plans unfolded from the 7th Congress to the end of World War II, it is important to note that the CCP and the 18th Group Army also underwent a series of organizational changes that significantly affected how the Communists would fight during the Third Chinese Civil War. In terms of personnel, the political-military elite who would go on to win the war and found the PRC emerged during the 7th Congress. Although the *de facto* party hierarchy had already mostly been settled, by electing a new Secretariat and CMC, the 7th Congress made it official. At the same time, the 18th Group Army also began to transform by dropping generic numeric designations and instead formed military districts which had jurisdiction over certain geographical regions. However, while there were no drastic additions or subtractions to the chain of command, the reorganization of the army did entail new promotions and responsibilities. The following section will thus discuss the Communist chain of command and the personalities therein.

Secretariat

The new Central Committee that emerged from the 7th Congress consisted of 44 members and 33 alternates. Approximately 50 percent of these men had military backgrounds. Day-to-day military and political decision-making for the CCP fell to the Secretariat, an elite group drawn from the upper echelon of the Central Committee. On June 19, during the 1st Plenary Session of the 7th National Congress, Mao was reaffirmed as both the Chairman of the CCP and the Secretariat. The other members of this key decision-making organ were vice chairmen Liu Shaoqi, Zhou Enlai, Zhu De, and Secretary Ren Bishi.

While Mao was the paramount leader of the party, he was not the most senior member of the Secretariat. Both Zhu De and Zhou Enlai arguably had more military experience and more impressive revolutionary pedigrees. However, neither had weathered the political infighting as well as Mao, nor they had been as prescient or opportunistic. Zhu's lack of political power may be attributed to his desire to remain a professional soldier, a sentiment seen in his preference for conventional warfare even back to the days of the Jinggang Mountains. For instance, instead of attributing previous failures to "incorrect" political thought, he blamed them on the lack of a proper army and equipment. This proclivity was likely a result of his training as a youth, which included schooling at the Yunnan Military Academy and a stint with Cai Ao's anti-Qing army in southwest China during the 1911 Revolution. After a decade of service with Cai, Zhu attempted to join the CCP but was rejected on the grounds that he was a warlord general. Zhu subsequently traveled to Germany to study military science at the University of Göttingen in 1922.

Zhu finally gained entrance into the CCP after meeting Zhou in Germany. He was expelled from Germany in 1925 after participating in protests, and he spent the next year in the Soviet Union receiving more formal military training. Upon his return, he became an officer in the GMD army and participated in the Northern Expedition. After Chiang's betrayal of the CCP during the April 12 Incident in 1927, he participated in the Nanchang Uprising and co-founded the CCP's first armed force, the predecessor of the PLA. After the GMD counterattack and the failure of the Communist operations in 1927, he eventually commanded the 4th Army with Mao in the Jinggang Mountains.

Despite the myths that arose around this particular partnership, the two rarely agreed on military strategy. While Zhu did recognize guerrilla warfare was the only real option, because of the weakness of the CCP vis-à-vis its enemies,[26] Zhu still wanted to develop conventional units to fight large-scale battles. This may have influenced Zhu to perhaps favor Mao's rival Zhang Guotao during the Long March,[27] a move which may have led to his being supplanted as Mao's preeminent military commander by Peng Dehuai.

After Zhang was defeated by Tibetan and GMD forces, Zhu reunited with

Mao in Yan'an. However, friction over strategy again emerged after the establishment of the Second United Front in 1937. Mao wanted Communist forces to avoid combat and husband their strength, while Zhu wanted to fight the Japanese invaders. Whitson suggests his desire to "defend his potential new empire, adhere to Nationalist orders to prove that the Communists were capable of fighting a large-scale engagement, give heart to defeatists in the despondent Nationalist government, or pursue some other motivation"[28] motivated Zhu to later authorize the Hundred Regiments Campaign without Mao's explicit permission. This would be among Zhu's last major strategic decisions. Soon after the failure of the campaign, Mao launched a rectification campaign. Whether the Chairman's timing was coincidental or in reaction to the Hundred Regiments Campaign is unclear, but afterwards Zhu largely adhered to Mao's line. At the 7th Congress, however, Zhu's view reemerged when conventional warfare became more politically expedient and useful than guerrilla warfare.

In contrast to Mao and Zhu, the third senior member of the Secretariat, Zhou Enlai, did not contribute to military strategy during World War II or the Third Chinese Civil War. While Zhou helped co-found the army and had an extensive record as a political commissar and a strategic planner, he also had a checkered past of military defeats dating back to the April 12 Incident. Politically, however, he was arguably the most senior revolutionary and his personal networks were extensive. For instance, as a worker-student in Europe in the early 1920s, he frequently associated with other Chinese socialists who later played major roles in the Third Chinese Civil War, such as Zhu De, Nie Rongzhen, Chen Yi, and Deng Xiaoping. Upon Zhou's return to China in 1924, he served as deputy director of the political department of the Huangpu Military Academy in Guangzhou, a joint venture between the GMD and the CCP during the First United Front period. Here, he met another set of future Communist military leaders including Lin Biao and Ye Jianying. However, Chiang later removed Zhou in a mini-purge of the Communists shortly before the Northern Expedition.

Zhou was in Shanghai serving as a labor organizer when the Northern Expedition reunified China. After the April 12 Incident, Zhou assumed command of the party's new military department and co-founded the CCP's Red Army during the Nanchang Uprising. In the subsequent Jiangxi Soviet and Long March periods, he eventually sided with Mao and ended up in Yan'an. At that point, Zhou left the day-to-day operations of the party and became the official ambassador of the CCP. He would later spend most of World War II in Chongqing as a liaison to the GMD and the United States. He simultaneously headed the South China Bureau, a position which technically made him a regional governor-general. Yet Zhou's direct influence in strategic affairs was limited and would remain so during the Third Chinese Civil War as well.

In contrast to Zhu and Zhou, Liu Shaoqi was a newcomer to the CCP's upper echelon. Yet by the 7th Congress he had risen to second-in-command of the party and the army – behind only Mao himself. Liu did not have a military background, having dropped out of a military academy during his youth. Instead, his background was with labor agitation and proletariat-based revolution – a product of his training at Moscow's University of the Toilers of the East in the early 1920s. Upon his return to China, he worked with labor and underground organizations in Hubei and Shanghai. He was later elected to the Central Committee in 1927, after the White Terror, and to the Politburo in 1931. During the Jiangxi Soviet era, he served as the Fujian Party Secretary and later participated in the Long March. At the Zunyi Conference, he allied himself with Mao and once in Yan'an, he served as the North China Party Secretary. By this time, Mao's had a great deal of trust in Liu and dispatched him to east China in 1940 to unify the 8th Route and New 4th Armies.

The unification proved a difficult mission as the New 4th Army Incident occurred during his tenure, and the New 4th Army's leadership initially proved to have a mind of its own. Nonetheless, Liu successfully orchestrated the 8th Route Army's expansion into north Jiangsu and reestablished the New 4th Army in central Jiangsu after the New 4th Army Incident. Virtually unknown and unheralded in the West, Liu's strategic acumen and his efforts during this time had a profound effect on how the war in Jiangsu, Anhui and Shandong would develop during the war.[29] It is important to note, however, that Liu was not a military man nor did he claim to be. As fellow Communist An Ziwen noted, "doing armed struggle was not his strong point .... His outstanding talent was providing ideological, political and organizational leadership."[30] Liu returned triumphantly to Yan'an in March 1942 and later vaulted over Zhou and Zhu to become vice chairman of both the CCP and the CMC.[31]

The last member of the Secretariat, Ren Bishi, played little part in strategic planning and was a relative outsider before the 7th Congress. Ren did have the advantage of not being involved in the messy politics of the Jiangxi Soviet because he was stationed with He Long and the 2nd Front Army. During the Long March, Ren served as deputy commander of the 2nd Front Army and, after arriving in Yan'an, became director of the political department of the 8th Route Army. However, Ren's forte was land reform and political issues, and he focused primarily on these throughout the duration of the Third Chinese Civil War. Somewhat of an enigma, Ren died in 1950 shortly after the end of the war.

The Central Military Commission

The new CMC introduced by the 7th Congress had virtually the same leadership as the Secretariat. It had also experienced little turnover since Mao assumed control of it in 1936. Mao served as chairman, Zhu De and Zhou Enlai retained their positions as vice-chairmen and Liu Shaoqi was added in 1945. However, the last three members of the CMC were not part of the Secretariat. This included Peng Dehuai, fourth vice chairman and chief-of-staff; Ye Jianying, the deputy chief-of-staff; and Yang Shangkun, the secretary.[32] Consequently, the leadership of the party and the army remained fused.[33] The military men of the CMC – Zhu, Peng and Ye – administered a separate organ, the Yan'an Headquarters, to deal with issues that concerned only the army itself.

Peng Dehuai represents a delineation of sorts between the political and military aspects of the party, however blurry that line may be. He was a member of the Central Committee but he was not part of the group that formulated and dictated overall CCP strategy. At the same time, he was one of the most influential members of the army. Throughout the war and his career, he readily accepted these limits. A native of Hunan, like Mao, Peng grew up a peasant but shunned that life to join the GMD army at age 16. In 1928, he defected to the CCP to join Mao and Zhu's army at the Jinggang Mountains. A proponent of regular forces and conventional tactics, he has generally been regarded by his peers and outside observers as a pure soldier.[34] Peng was also loyal to a fault and, although he advocated conventional warfare during the Jiangxi Soviet period and the Long March, he remained faithful to Mao. This was especially true during Mao's dangerous confrontation with Zhang Guotao near the end of the Long March. Because of his loyalty, Peng may have displaced Zhu as Mao's favored commander.

Nevertheless, Peng was not above squabbling with Mao over strategy. During World War II, he played a key role in planning and executing the Hundred Regiments Offensive. Whether this affected his relationship with Mao is not clear, but with no large-scale campaigns to plan or battles to fight, Peng gravitated towards more mundane matters such as political work and army building.[35] However, the 7th Congress reenergized him, as it did so many other generals. After his simultaneous appointments to the CMC and to chief-of-staff of the 18th Group Army, he began to plan out Zhu's conventional defense of north China.

The 8th Route Army

The next echelon in the Communist chain of command was the 18th Army Group. Because this group featured the same command staff as the 8th Route Army, both will be discussed at the same time. Zhu De and Peng Dehuai served respectively as commander and deputy commander of both entities. Subordinate to the 8th Route Army were the 115th, 120th, and 129th Divisions, and the Shanxi-Chahar[36]-Hebei (SCH) Military District.[37] The SCH Military District represented a new trend in which the GMD designations disappeared and units were reorganized into military districts.

Arguably the premier unit of the 8th Route Army was the 115th Division in Shandong and Hebei. It featured three future marshals of the PLA: commander Lin Biao, deputy divisional commander Nie Rongzhen, and political commissar Luo Ronghuan. Perhaps the most prominent and controversial was Lin, who attended the Huangpu Military Academy in the mid-1920s. While there he met Zhou and officially joined the CCP. After graduation he served as an officer in the GMD army and quickly rose through the ranks before participating in the Northern Expedition. After the April 12 Incident, Lin escaped to the Jiangxi Soviet and took command of the 1st Army. This command offered his first exposure to Mao, who was then political commissar of the 1st Front Army. Lin's relationship with Mao was less than perfect even during their earlier collaborative years. He frequently criticized Mao during those years, especially during the 5th Encirclement Campaign[38] and the Long March. The Chairman allegedly responded by calling Lin a child and asking,

"How much do you understand?"[39] More critically, Lin also opposed the move into Shaanxi at the end of the Long March. If Lin had pressed his position, he could have severely constrained Mao's actions during the standoff with Zhang Guotao.

In the end, Lin remained loyal and helped lead the remnants of Mao's army to Yan'an. Soon after establishing the new capital, Mao put Lin in charge of the Red Army Japanese Resistance University. After the creation of the Second United Front, Lin returned to active field service by taking command of the new 115th Division. In this capacity he delievered an embarrassing defeat on the Japanese in the battle of Pingxingguan, one of China's few victories in the early stages of the war. In the aftermath of the battle he was injured by friendly fire and was sent to Moscow to receive medical treatment until 1942. After returning to Yan'an, he was assigned to light duty that included a stint assisting Zhou in Chongqing and several teaching assignments. For reasons unknown he did not receive a command during the 7th Congress. One explanation is that there were no new units for someone of his rank to command. Another is that the Communists saw no need to rush him back into service, because there was no real urgency during the 7th Congress. In fact, not until the second month of the Third Chinese Civil War did Lin's name resurface.

The political commissar of the 115th Division was Nie Rongzhen, a senior member of the party and the army. An educated and cosmopolitan figure with a gift for organization, Nie was one of the select few who studied in Europe after World War I. An atypical Communist, he was born to a wealthy landowning family in Sichuan, where he attended middle school in Chongqing with another important military figure, Deng Xiaoping. He traveled extensively and enjoyed ample educational opportunities in his youth. In the 1920s, he went to Europe and worked at the Montargis Rubber Plant and the Creusot (Schneider) Iron and Steel Plant. During this time, he met Chen Yi, Zhou Enlai and Zhu De. Due to their influence, he joined the CCP in 1922. Later on, Nie studied military science at the Soviet Red Army War College in the USSR. He returned to China and served as Zhou's deputy at the Huangpu Military Academy. Nie went on to participate in the Nanchang Uprising and later joined the 1st Front Army as political commissar of Lin Biao's 1st Army.

After the Long March and the institution of the Second United Front, the 1st Army became the 115th Division. At the end of 1942, Nie Rongzhen assumed command of the new SCH Military District to manage Communist expansion into those provinces and solidify CCP control over the heart of the north China plain.[40] He also commanded two conventional units – Yang Dezhi's 2nd Column and Lu Zhengcao's 3rd Column. The latter had been formed out of the remnants of Communist forces ejected from Manchukuo by the Japanese.[41] The column, or *zongdui*, was a unique Communist unit roughly equivalent to a corps in a Western order of battle. At the end of 1944, Mao ordered Nie to begin operations in Suiyuan and Rehe.[42]

The other prominent member of the 115th Division was Luo Ronghuan. Luo had spent his early years as a student activist, first at Qingdao University during the May Fourth period and again at the Sun Zhongshan (Sun Yatsen) University in Nanchang during the early 1920s. He later joined the CCP and was active in recruiting and conducting political work in Hubei during the Northern Expedition.

After the collapse of the First United Front, Luo eventually found his way to the Jiangxi Soviet and served in the political department of Lin Biao's 1st Army. He eventually transferred to the 8th Army right before the Long March, but this unit was destroyed before it could reach Yan'an. Luo made his own way to the new Communist capital where he studied at the Red Army Japanese Resistance University and later served as political commissar of cadre training under Lin Biao. With the onset of the war against Japan and the Second United Front, Luo joined the new 115th Division as the head of the political department.[42] After Nie took on his new assignment with the SCH Military District, Luo assumed the position of political commissar. As the Japanese began to withdraw from the Chinese hinterland in 1944, Luo formed and commanded the Shandong Military Subdistrict to move Communist forces into Shandong. These initial moves before end of World War II provided an important strategic foothold for the coming war against the GMD.

In the west the 120th Division was guarding Yan'an under the command of the legendary He Long. Another Hunan native, He grew up in a poor peasant household, despite the fact that his father was a minor military official during the Qing dynasty. Immortalized as a Robin Hood-like figure whose signature weapon was a meat cleaver, He was one of the more colorful figures to emerge during the warlord era. This made him an unlikely Communist, yet during the Nanchang Uprising he helped found the Red Army. A senior commander on par with Zhu or Peng, He was a proponent of guerrilla or irregular warfare and was a natural ally of Mao. During the Jiangxi Soviet, He's forces were located on the periphery, allowing him to avoid much of the political infighting. Its location also meant his army was the last to join the Long March. As a consequence, He alone was able to bring a nearly intact army to Yan'an – likely the reason He assumed responsibility for protecting the capital.

By the 7th Congress, He concurrently served as commander of the 129th Division, the Shanxi-Suiyuan Military District, and the Shaanxi-Ganxu-Ningxia-Shanxi-Suiyuan United Defense Army (hereafter referred to as the United Defense Army). The first two commands were interchangeable and consisted of regular forces like the 115th Divison and the SCH Military District. The United Defense Army, on the other hand, was made up of five brigades of militia and second echelon troops. It was seen primarily as the last line of defense for the capital.

He's forces were situated between three GMD armies: Yan Xishan[43] in the southwest, Hu Zongnan in the west, and Fu Zuoyi in the east. Fu was the least threatening of the three due to distance and his preoccupation with menacing the Japanese around Beijing. Yan posed a threat insomuch as he considered Shanxi his personal kingdom. However, his relationship with Chiang was strained, and there was hope in Yan'an that he might eventually cooperate with the Communists as Zhang Xueliang had in 1936. Hu, on the other hand, was unquestionably loyal to Chiang and had been specifically assigned to the region to blockade Yan'an. On July 21, 1945, tension between the two sides boiled over when Hu conducted a raid against He's forces northwest of Xi'an in Chunhua county.[44] Although He was able to recover the lost territory and restore the status quo, he had been forced to remove troops overlooking Japanese bases to do so. These events proved to be an ominous portent of things to come.

Liu Bocheng's 129th Division was the last major force in the 8th Route Army. It was based in the Taixing and Taiyue mountains of south Shanxi and south Hebei. The division's main task was to cooperate with Yan while at the same time expanding Communist presence in Shanxi – two tasks that eventually proved to be mutually exclusive. However, if any Communist commander was capable of such a task, it was Liu Bocheng. By 1945, Liu had amassed a military record at least as long and rich as Zhu De's. After attending the Chongqing Military Academy, he joined Sun Yatsen's Revolutionary Party in 1914. While fighting with Sun against warlord armies, he lost an eye and earned his famous moniker the "One-Eyed Dragon." During this period, Liu fought and defeated Zhu, who was then part of Yunnan warlord Long Yun's army. Later, Liu joined the CCP during the First United Front and served as a corps commander in the GMD army during the Northern Expedition. After the April 12th Incident, Liu participated in the Nanchang Uprising and became the first chief-of-staff of the CMC. After a series of defeats, the Communist army went underground and Liu traveled to Moscow to receive more military training. There he mastered Russian and attended the prestigious Frunze Military Academy where he learned conventional, Western-style tactics.

Upon his return to China, Liu served concurrently as chief-of-staff for both the CMC and Mao's 1st Front Army during the defense of the Jiangxi Soviet and the Long March. Like Zhu, Liu's decision to remain with the 4th Front Army when Mao departed for Yan'an likely affected their relationship. Mao and Liu were probably already at odds over Liu's firm support for conventional tactics,[45] expressed in his translation of a Russian textbook on "Combined Arms Tactics"[46] and his commentary on Sunzi's *The Art of War*.[47] Additionally, according to Zhang Guotao, Liu called Mao a pedant and abhorred Mao's preference for micromanaging instead of relying on a general staff.[48] Despite any animosity, Liu's competency, seniority, and training were undeniable. Shortly after arriving in Yan'an, he received command of the 129th Division.

Like Lin's 115th Division, Liu's immediate subordinates were also destined for greater acclaim. Former 4th Front Army commander and future Marshal of the PLA, Xu Xiangqian served as deputy divisional commander. Deng Xiaoping, future paramount leader of the PRC, was the political commissar. Deng's assignment to that particular division was especially fortuitous. His ability to mobilize public support and build a logistical base for the kind of army Liu desired was critical to their later success. In fact the Liu-Deng partnership, as it would be called, became legendary by the end of the Third Chinese Civil War.

Deng was unique in that he was young, the so-called second generation. Yet he was also part of that elite group who studied in Europe and were exposed to socialism after World War I. He joined the CCP in 1924, at age 20, and traveled to Moscow for more schooling. He then returned to China just in time for the Northern Expedition. After participating in the Nanchang Uprising, Deng led a failed uprising in Guangxi before escaping to the Jiangxi Soviet. There he was appointed secretary of the Central Committee and supported Mao's guerrilla line. He remained loyal to Mao throughout the Zunyi Conference and eventually commanded the political department of Lin's 1st Army when Mao's 1st Front Army went to Yan'an. After the outbreak of war with Japan, Deng briefly served as deputy director of the political department for the 8th Route Army under Ren Bishi before transferring to the 129th Division in January 1938.

Xu Xiangqian was a professional military man much like Liu, having attended the Huangpu Military Academy in 1924. He served as a GMD officer during the Northern Expedition and joined the CCP soon after the Nanchang Uprising. However, he did not fall into Mao's inner circle and instead became the commander of the other major Communist Army, the 4th Front Army, with Zhang Guotao as his political commissar. Although their relationship was tempestuous, Xu led the 4th Front Army to Sichuan and founded a new base there to complement the Jiangxi Soviet. During the Long March, Xu made the critical decision not to attack the 1st Front Army when Mao ordered it to proceed to Yan'an. This may have been the reason Mao accepted Xu back into the fold after the GMD destroyed the 4th Front Army. Although this new position, deputy commander of the 129th Division, was a minor demotion, it allowed Xu to return to the battlefield. Xu did not stay with the 129th Division for the duration of World War II. Instead he bounced around the liberated areas, briefly spending time in Shandong building bases with Luo Ronghuan, and later serving as the deputy commander of He's United Defense Army.

The New 4th Army

The New 4th Army was an institution born in defeat and commanded by those who did not participate on the Long March. During the war it was known more for being decapitated in the incident that bore the army's name rather than its spectacular victory at Hongqiao. For these reasons it is easy to overlook the New 4th Army, which, in fact, has been the case – even in PRC literature. Although expertly led, the army produced only one Marshal of the PLA – Chen Yi. His brilliant subordinate Su Yu was denied that honor for unknown reasons. Despite its inauspicious reputation, however, the New 4th Army played a critical role not only in the east China theater, but in northeast China as well.

Chen Yi, the commander of the New 4th Army since the New 4th Army Incident, was a Sichuan native who became a Communist while on the same European work-study program in which so many other future CCP leaders participated. Articulate, erudite and a natural diplomat, Chen was born into a wealthy family and was extremely well-educated, especially so in classical Chinese. Like Nie, he was not a typical Communist, nor did he have a particularly distinctive military background. Nevertheless, he was active in planning the 1927 Autumn Uprising and served as head of the political department of Mao and Zhu's 4th Army in the Jinggang Mountains.

During the Jiangxi Soviet era, he, like many other senior Communist leaders, disagreed with Mao over strategy and tactics. This did not prove to be a serious rift and Chen was apparently a favorite of Mao's due to their shared love of classical poetry.[49] During the 5th Encirclement Campaign, Chen was wounded and could not join the Long March. Instead, he participated in a successful guerilla war, the so-called Three Years War, in south China from 1934–37. After the establishment of the Second United Front, which led to the creation of the New 4th Army, Chen assumed command of the 1st Detachment[50] and also served as assistant political commissar under Xiang Ying. After the New 4th Army Incident, Chen Yi took command while Rao Shushi, a transfer from the 8th Route Army, replaced him as political commissar.

Chen's main subordinate was Su Yu. A Hunan native, he was also born into a Dong family.[51] He joined the CCP in 1926 and immediately entered the Communist Youth Corps. From there, he participated in the Northern Expedition and, after Chiang's betrayal, commanded the security detachment for the nascent Red Army Headquarters during the Nanchang uprising. After participating in the various uprisings and failed offensives in 1927–28, he eventually followed Chen into the Jinggang Mountains to join Mao and Zhu. During the Jiangxi Soviet period, he steadily rose through the ranks. Su stayed behind with Chen during the Long March and helped establish a guerilla base in southern Zhejiang during the Three Years War.

After the creation of the New 4th Army, Su served as deputy commander of Zhang Dingcheng's 2nd Detachment. In this function, he won the New 4th Army's first battle against the Japanese at Weigang on June 16, 1938. Two years later he defeated the GMD at the battle of Hongqiao in 1940. That victory led to Chiang's reprisal, the New 4th Army Incident. After Chen rescued the army and assumed command, he created divisions out of the old "detachment" order of battle. In this new organization, Su took command of the 1st Division (formerly the 1st Detachment) Central Jiangsu Military District.

The core of the New 4th Army was made up of those veterans that fought during the Three Years War. These included Su's aforementioned 1st Division, Luo Binghui's 2nd Division/Huainan Military District, and Zhang Dingcheng's 7th Division. However, after 1939, the army doubled in sized when 8th Route Army generals took command of local guerrilla forces and formed them into regular units. These included Peng Xuefeng's 4th Division/Huaibei Military District, Li Xiannian's 5th Division/Hubei-Henan-Anhui-Hunan-Jiangxi Military District, and Huang Kecheng's 3rd Division/North Jiangsu Military District. Despite the army's growing strength, it remained in a precarious position. For instance, Peng was killed in a skirmish against the GMD in 1944 and was replaced by another Long March veteran Zhang Aiping.[52] Nevertheless, the army continued to seize territory and early in 1945 Li helped Wang Zhen's 359th Brigade cross the Yangtze River to found a base in south China. Although they met with initial success, these bases were still forming when Japan surrendered.

Altogether, the men of the Secretariat, the CMC, and the 8th Route and New 4th Army high command formed the core military leadership of the CCP during the Third Chinese Revolutionary Civil War. They would be responsible for formulating and implementing strategy for this period – the last and culminating phase of the Communist revolution. However, so many personalities with different military backgrounds, levels of experience and even agendas meant that the simple task of conceiving a plan and carrying it out was immensely complicated, even within the strict hierarchy of the CCP's Marxist-Leninist framework. The brief portraits sketched above do not do full justice to who these men were, but do offer a suitable starting point for understanding the various influences and biases that would affect how they viewed strategy and war.

2 "March on the North, Defend in the South" (August 1945–June 1946)

On August 15, 1945, Tokyo announced its surrender. This momentous turn of events changed the political and military landscape of the Chinese mainland overnight. The elimination of Japan as a force on the continent also meant the dissolution of the various puppet governments Tokyo had established in the region. These included Wang Jingwei's National Government of China, Pu Yi's Manchukuo, and Prince Teh Wang's Mongolian Federated Autonomous Government. Their simultaneous collapse created a power vacuum that the GMD and the CCP were both intensely eager to fill – even at the cost of renewing their bitter civil war on the heels of a long Japanese occupation.

The end of the war against Japan was, therefore, not an end at all – it was simply a new beginning. Although hindsight indicates that resumption of the war was probably inevitable, it was not entirely so. There was no doubt that the Chinese people wanted peace, as did the international community. Perhaps even the parties themselves wanted a negotiated end. Yet the situation did not bode well for a peaceful resolution or for coexistence. For the Communists, whose strategy for 1945–46 had been shattered by the sudden end to the war, the days following the Japanese surrender were critical. Their initial maneuvers, conceived on the spot as the events unfolded, would not only determine their survival but also drastically affect the fate of China.

Forging a postwar strategy

After Moscow entered the war against Japan on August 8, 1945 and swept aside the vaunted Kwantung (Guandong) Army, the Secretariat recognized that the war in China would soon end. Unconcerned about the fate of the Japanese home islands or whether or not Tokyo would issue an official surrender, the Secretariat convened a number of emergency meetings to begin rethinking strategy. Almost immediately, they abandoned the idea of relying on their guerrilla bases or a conventional defense of north China. Instead, the CCP ordered their forces to seize as much territory in and around the north China Liberated Areas as quickly as possible. This included the large cities and the major lines of communication – two prizes Japan and its puppet allies previously denied to Communist forces. The Secretariat intended to prevent the GMD from returning and gaining a foothold

Figure 2.1 1945: Postwar scramble.

within the North China Liberated Area.[1] They also hoped to reequip their armies quickly with Japanese armaments and strengthen their numbers by pressing former puppet troops into their own ranks.

This new strategy was called "Protecting the Results of the War,"[2] and it almost immediately ran into problems. For instance, there was no policy on how to react to GMD interference. They also assumed they could disarm Japanese or puppet forces without heavy resistance. Unaware of these flaws, the Communists put the plan into effect. On August 10, Zhu issued the "First General Order of the Yan'an Headquarters" in which he announced the CCP's intent to abide by the Potsdam Declaration – despite the fact that they had not been involved in that diplomatic process – and disarm all Imperial Japanese soldiers and their puppet regimes.[3]

Now that the war with Japan was over and the need for the Second United Front was gone along with it, the CMC made the symbolic move to abandon the unit designations that subordinated their forces to the GMD. He Long's 120th Division became the Shanxi-Suiyuan Field Army/Military District and Liu Bocheng's 129th Division became the Shanxi-Henan-Shandong-Hebei (SHSH) Field Army/Military District.[4] Although named after provinces, these units did not claim to control them entirely. For instance, Liu Bocheng's SHSH Military District was confined mainly to the border areas where the four provinces met. Most of the 115th Division became the Shandong Field Army/Military District under Luo Ronghuan. Those units formerly belonging to the 115th Division, but outside of Shandong, merged with Nie Rongzhen's preexisting SCH Military District. Neither the Shandong nor SCH Military District had field armies, but they each did possess a handful of columns. In addition to regular units, these new military districts could supplement their forces with militia and local levees.

After Zhu issued his first set of general orders, more detailed instructions went out to each region. Units in the north China Liberated Areas were to focus on expansion at all costs. Luo faced the daunting task of securing all of Shandong, which was not only full of Japanese and puppet troops, but would also soon be flooded with GMD troops disembarking from the province's numerous ports. In addition to military operations, he was simultaneously saddled with the responsibility of administering the new territory through the Shandong Bureau.[5] He Long was ordered to secure Shanxi province, including Taiyuan and Datong before either Fu Zuoyi or Yan Xishan attempted the same.[6] Unfortunately for He, both Fu and Yan had mobilized their armies and were already on the march.

Units outside the North China Liberated Area were to support operations in the north. Chen and the New 4th Army (which did not have to change its name, since it was of purely Communist origin) were to capture strategic territory in order to hinder GMD movements into the north China Liberated Areas. Their first task was to attack the Xuzhou in order to sever the Tianjin-Pukou and Longhai railroads,[7] both major transportation arteries.[8] Liu and Deng's SHSH Field Army had similar tasks in Henan and Shanxi, guarding the approaches to the Yellow River and severing the Beiping-Hankou Railroad. In south China, Mao hoped the bases there could conduct guerrilla warfare to slow the GMD onslaught.[9]

Another important decision was to commit troops to northeast China, which was now under Moscow's control. In the "Second General Order of the Yan'an Headquarters," Zhu ordered Li Yunchang, commander of Hebei-Rehe-Liaoning (HRL) Military Sub-District (subordinate to Nie's SCH Military District), to assemble his 1st Column for an immediate march into Liaoning and Jilin. The order also called upon Lu Zhengcao, Zhang Xueshi, and Wan Yi, generals previously in the northeast, to command the next wave of troops that would eventually reinforce Li.[10] The first such unit was the Binghai Detachment (equivalent to a brigade), composed of northeast China natives who had retreated to the Shandong Military District after being expelled by the Japanese. The CMC established a policy that all units headed to northeast China should leave behind their heavy equipment. This was done to increase speed and because they assumed that Japanese equipment or aid from the Soviet Red Army would be forthcoming once the Communists arrived in the region.[11]

However, the CMC gave only vague instructions about what these units were to do once they arrived. For instance, Lu Zhengcao was given verbal orders to "take advantage of the difficulties the GMD would have in getting to the region" and the "short period the Soviet Army would remain in northeast China."[12] On the other hand, written instructions only specified movements. It is important to note that at this point there was no concentrated Communist effort to capture the northeast. On the contrary, dispatches from the CCP high command suggested exploitation of northeast China, like all other sectors, was secondary to the defense of the north China Liberated Areas. Yet these initial steps became increasingly significant for both sides as Manchuria grew in importance.

Friction with the GMD arose as soon as the Communist forces moved to carry out the CMC's orders. On August 10, Chiang's propaganda department declared Zhu's directive a "presumptuous and illegal act" and insisted that only the GMD could disarm Japanese and puppet forces. Zhu wrote an open letter the next day, warning against reigniting civil war and accusing Chiang of delaying the liberation of China for personal gain. Despite their attitude of defiance, the CCP quietly scaled back operations. Between August 13–15, Mao intimated the Communists should begin to focus on capturing the small and medium cities, but not the large ones.[13] On August 22, the Secretariat turned Mao's intimation into policy by ordering all military districts temporarily to avoid the large cities and main railroads. This decision stemmed mainly from the Secretariat's grim assessment that the Soviet Union would not come to their aid if the GMD decided to oust the Communist forces.[14] Complicating the matter was the fact that Chiang had ordered Japanese and puppet forces to defend their positions against any "irregular forces" – i.e. the Communists.

On August 23, Zhou Enlai went to Chongqing to smooth the way for Mao's peace talks with the GMD. The CCP leadership feared conflict was inevitable. Mao, for one, warned repeatedly of Chiang's intent to renew the civil war.[15] In a Central Committee meeting, before following Zhou to Chongqing, Mao expressed little optimism for peace: "Chiang's plan to destroy the CCP had not changed and will not change. Although everyone wants peace, the GMD will not comply and we will have to fight a civil war."[16] Additionally, although both sides were committed to negotiations, this commitment did not preclude fighting. Both believed it was to their advantage to fight for a better bargaining position before and even during the proceedings.

For instance, before leaving, Zhou told He Long to prepare to fight a few "large battles" in central Shanxi and eastern Suiyuan to help the process in Chongqing.[17] On the other side, the pace of the GMD advance was relentless and by the end of August, they had seized 17 cities, including Beiping, Tianjin, Datong, and Taiyuan, and most of the railroads within the north China Liberated Areas. The GMD accomplished this largely by utilizing US naval and air transport to circumvent the nascent guerrilla bases in south China and the Central Plains. As a result, Chiang virtually eviscerated the north China Liberated Areas while still securing most of rich coastal areas of south China.

Mao's strategy was now completely defunct: the guerrilla bases were not ready and even if they had been, there was no enemy to fight. Instead, the best units of the GMD army were either on the doorstep or in the midst of Communist territory. Consequently, the peace talks began under the specter of the imminent isolation and reduction of the Liberated Areas that the Communists had worked so hard to forge during World War II. Clearly, the CCP needed to change its strategy, but with Mao at Chongqing, the responsibility for determining the next step – potentially the most important decision for the future of the CCP – fell to Liu Shaoqi.

"March on the North, Defend in the South"

As events unfolded in early September, Liu Shaoqi, acting chairman of the Central Committee, Secretariat and CMC in Mao's absence, concluded that the army could neither defend the north China Liberated Areas nor could guerrilla bases slow the GMD in south China and the Central Plains. Instead, Liu looked to a completely new direction – northeast China. The advantages there were readily apparent. Its large population, strong industry, and economic potential were the most obvious of them; even more importantly, the area represented an unassailable base surrounded by friendly forces in Mongolia, the Soviet Union, and Korea. On September 11, the CMC ordered Luo Ronghuan to reinforce Li Yunchang's initial penetration into northeast China with another 30,000 troops from the Shandong Military District. Under the command of Xiao Hua, head of the military department's political arm, they were to take the sea route across the Bo Sea to Manchuria. The Shandong Military District would also send another 30,000 men within the month. Doing so made Luo's contribution to the effort in northeast China larger than that of any other military district.

On September 14, the CMC received fresh intelligence from Zeng Kelin, who had led the first units into northeast China after the end of the war (discussed below) and had come to Yan'an to deliver his report in person. His news from the front immediately confirmed the Secretariat's suspicion regarding the boundless opportunities in terms of population, economy, and industry that awaited them there.[18] Shortly thereafter Liu convened a meeting of the CCP high command, including Zhu De, Ren Bishi, Peng Dehuai, Chen Yun, and Peng Zhen.[19] Together, they decided to form the Northeast Bureau with Peng Zhen as secretary and Chen Yun, Cheng Zihua, Wu Jianquan, and Lin Feng as committee members.[20] In the ensuing months, the Secretariat dispatched 20 members and alternates of the Central Committee to the northeast – a full quarter of the entire committee.[21] On September 19, the Secretariat – sans Mao and Zhou – published their new nation-wide strategy.

The plan consisted of three major parts. First, the CCP would build a base in northeast China with aid from the Soviets, Mongolians, and Koreans. In addition to troops already sent by the Shandong Military District, the New 4th Army would also send Huang Kecheng's 3rd Division. Second, the Communists in north China would reorient their defenses to guard the main land approaches into Manchuria rather than defending the entire region. Responsibility for the approaches to Manchuria would fall largely on the newly created Hebei-Rehe-Liaoning (HRL) Military Sub-District, a subordinate of Nie's SCH Military District.[22] Luo Ronghuan would serve as secretary for this new military sub-district while Lin Biao was reactivated to command the military forces. This would be a reunion of sorts between Luo and Lin, although on paper it was a demotion for Luo, who had to leave his position as commander of the Shandong Military District. He Long's Military District and the rest of Nie's Military District were to support this effort by securing west Chahar, north Shanxi, and Suiyuan, thus shoring up the western flank. In effect, this shifted the core of the north China Liberated Area away from Yan'an towards the Communist-held city of Zhangjiakou.

The third element of the plan called on CCP forces in the south to radically shorten their lines. This meant the New 4th Army was now responsible for guarding Shandong while the guerrilla units in south China were to abandon their bases, concentrate into large units, move north, and regroup in three areas: Shandong (to reinforce the now depleted Shandong Military District), central Jiangsu, and the Hebei-Henan-Anhui Liberated Area. This strategy, called "March in the North, Defend in the South," would dominate operations for both sides during first year of the war.[23] "North" referred to northeast China, while "south" generally referred to the region previously described as north China. A day after announcing the new strategy, Mao and Zhou sent a telegram to Yan'an, agreeing with the proposal and the deployments.[24]

Chinese secondary sources generally credit either Mao or Zhu for originating the plan and Liu for implementing it. Documentary evidence, however, strongly indicates that Liu either developed it himself or in conjunction with Zhu. Although Mao had referred to Manchuria as a potential target during the 7th Congress, in the same speech he also identified numerous other areas and specified seizing only

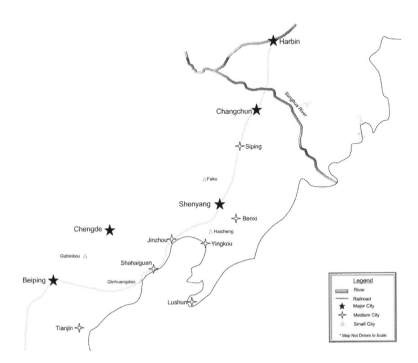

Figure 2.2 1945: March on the North.

the Beiping-Liaoning railroad and part of Liaoning rather than northeast China as a whole.[25] Mao did order units into the region in one of his last telegrams before leaving for Chongqing, but his doing so mirrored Zhu's original plan to dispatch a second wave of troops under Lu Zhengcao and Wan Yi.[26] Most significantly, Mao was not in Yan'an to hear Zeng's report, which proved to be the critical factor in the Communists' commitment to the new strategy.

One could argue that since Zhu did witness the report and because he gave the original orders to move into northeast China following Japan's surrender, the plan was his idea. Yet Zhu had always focused on defending the north China Liberated Areas and it seems unlikely that he would risk so much for the lure of Manchuria. Instead, the plan seems mostly Liu's. Markedly pragmatic, this new strategy bore more than a passing resemblance to his decision to build a base in north Jiangsu, away from both the GMD and the Japanese, in 1940. Most compellingly, the only documentary evidence of the plan was written under Liu's direct guidance. The idea that Mao conceived the entire plan either in the 7th Congress or before leaving for Chongqing, is extremely unlikely.[27] Nonetheless, while it may have been Liu's grand scheme, it was likely vetted by Zhu and Peng, whose superior military knowledge was necessary to make the strategy a reality. The quick consensus and planning cycle (it took less than five days to conceive, draft, and disseminate) suggests that Zhu, Peng, and others were compelled by the plan's promise for regaining the CCP's initiative.

The new plan arguably would place the greatest burden on Nie Rongzhen's SCH Military District, which had to keep the land corridor to Manchuria open while simultaneously fending off large GMD armies in Hebei and Shanxi. To do so, Nie formed two field armies out of his existing resources. He assigned more than half of the SCH Military District to the 2nd Field Army under Xiao Ke, which would provide direct support to Lin Biao's new HRL Military Sub-District. The rest of Nie's troops became the 1st Field Army, which he commanded directly. Nie immediately moved his army west to cooperate with He Long's Shanxi-Suiyuan Field Army[28] in an effort to turn back Fu Zuoyi's 12th War Zone.[29]

However, the situation for the Communists had deteriorated rapidly in Shanxi and Suiyuan since Japan's surrender. By the end of August, Fu had already seized Baotou and Guisui (Hohhot). At the same time, armies from Yan Xishan's 2nd War Zone were also moving into south and central Shanxi, which threatened to sever the main railroads that linked Yan'an with the rest of the north China Liberated Areas. Even more serious was the threat of the two armies joining forces to capture the Communist capital. To prevent this, Nie and He planned to launch a campaign in October to keep Yan and Fu separate.

On the southwest perimeter of the north China Liberated Area, Liu Bocheng's SHSH Military District had to deal not only with Yan's aforementioned thrust but also Sun Lianzhong's armies advancing toward Shanxi from Wuhan. The SHSH Military District was located in perhaps the most strategic area in all of north China. First, it contained four major sections of railroad: Zhengzhou-Taiyuan, Beiping-Hankou, Beiping-Suiyuan and Tianjin-Pukou. Second, it also shared borders with all of the other military districts. Third, unlike all of the other Communist military regions, there was no friendly bordering country or protective geographic feature to restrict the enemy's avenue of approach. Therefore, Liu had to choose to focus on one army or the other when planning his first campaign. His decision to concentrate his forces on Yan would result in the first battle of the Third Chinese Civil War, the Shangdang Campaign.

The opening moves of the skirmish began on August 16, when Yan dispatched 19th Corps commander Shi Zebo and a task force of two divisions from the 19th Corps, three divisions from other units, and various other detachments for a total of 16,000 men[30] to capture Changzhi county in southeast Shanxi. The name Shangdang derives from Changzhi's original appellation in ancient times. For Yan, the area had a moral as well as a strategic value. Yan was eager to reclaim the entire province and potentially build it up as a base from which to renew his rivalry with Chiang. For the Communists, Changzhi was situated between their two large bases in the Taixing and Taiyue Mountains. Recognizing the threat before departing for Chongqing, Mao approved action against Yan despite the warm relations they had enjoyed during the war.[31] By the beginning of September, Liu Bocheng was ready to strike.

In a strategy meeting before the battle, Liu stated that the GMD meant to "kick in the door of the north China Liberated Areas." He believed that his army needed to defend that gate not only to protect the north China Liberated Areas but also to support the effort in northeast China.[32] Both Liu and Deng Xiaoping viewed Sun as the greater strategic threat, but Yan was the more immediate problem and southern Shanxi represented a vulnerable "back door."[33] As a result, Liu and Deng planned to fight first at Shangdang[34] and then immediately turn south to engage Sun. The Shangdang Campaign began on September 10 with the SHSH Military District concentrating 31,000 troops to encircle Changzhi. As the Communists began to close their ring around Shi's force, Yan sent a relief force of over 20,000 men under 7th Army Deputy Commander Peng Yubin to march south from Taiyuan and break the siege.

Liu reacted instantly by concentrating his forces against Peng's relief column while maintaining a screening force at Changzhi. Taken completely by surprise while on the march, Peng's unit surrendered virtually en masse and without much of a fight. The poor performance of this relief column can be attributed largely to the makeshift nature of Yan's army. Unlike Chiang's elite elements, Yan's armies did not benefit from American training or equipment. For all intents and purposes, they were still a warlord army that lacked professionalism and the will to fight. Against a determined enemy like the Communists, they were easily demoralized, outmaneuvered, and rendered ineffective. Now with no hope of relief, Shi attempted to break out on October 8, but like Peng, he was caught on open ground and forced to surrender two days later. Communist sources cite almost equal casualties in battle, approximately 4,000 men. However, the real blow to Yan's army was the fact that the Communist captured 31,000 men, which they added directly to Liu's army through persuasion and coercion.[35] As a result, the Communists actually increased in strength in addition to winning a tactical and strategic victory.

While the actual numbers may be inflated, the fact that large numbers of GMD troops changed sides after capture served as an ominous portent of things to come. Even more devastating for the GMD was that in later battles entire units would defect before or during the fighting. The trend of the GMD army weakening while the Communist army grew stronger played a significant role in Chiang's ultimate defeat. In the aftermath of Shangdang, Liu not only replenished his combat losses but raised entirely new units, not to mention gaining captured equipment and supplies. However, the SHSH Military District would have precious little time to enjoy this victory. On October 10, the army moved east, minus a few units left behind to mop up Shi's failed breakout, and began preparations for the Pinghan (Beiping-Hankou Railroad) Campaign against Sun Lianzhong.[36]

In the meantime, a handover of massive scale was taking place in east China. Luo Ronghuan was moving the bulk of the Shandong Field Army to Manchuria. He was also preparing for his own transfer to the HRL Military Sub-District. Chen Yi, whose New 4th Army would be taking over the Shandong theater, arrived at Luo's headquarters in Linyi on October 4 for the handover. Despite the obvious confusion this reorganization was bound to cause, Chen could at least count on inheriting a relatively stable sector. By late September, Luo's forces had seized a majority of Shandong province. Although they had not been able to capture the large cities of Ji'nan or Qingdao, the Communists did hold the main railroads, including the strategic Tianjin-Pukou line, almost all of the countryside, and smaller cities like Linyi.

Not long after taking command of the Shandong Military District, Chen began to reorganize his various armies and commands which, as per Liu's plan, were to defend a daunting expanse of territory – Anhui, Henan, Jiangsu, Zhejiang, and Shandong. The authority entrusted to Chen likely derived from his past experience and collaboration with Liu before and after the New 4th Army Incident. In place of the old system, Chen established three Military Districts: the Shandong Military District, the Central China Military District (formerly Su Yu's 1st Division and the Jiangsu-Zhejiang Military District), and the Central Plains Military District (Li Xiannian's 5th Division, Wang Zhen's Southern Detachment and the guerrilla bases in Hubei-Henan-Anhui-Hunan-Jiangxi). To command them, Chen combined his New 4th Army headquarters with the remnants of the Shandong Military District headquarters. Perhaps in an effort to distinguish between his regular forces and those still reorganizing, Chen created another echelon – the East China Military District– which included only the Shandong and Central China Military Districts.

While this reorganization helped clarify matters, Chen's problems quickly began to mount. In Shandong, Chen's forces consisted of a handful of regular units that had not gone to Manchuria and local units of questionable quality. Although New 4th Army units were on their way to reinforce the Shandong Military District, these would not arrive until the end of October. In the meantime, Li Xiannian was to speed up the consolidation of his guerrilla forces in the Central Plains to help bolster Chen's position. Mao, who had returned to Yan'an in mid-October, wanted Li's 5th Division to be ready to employ conventional units within the next six months. However, the GMD would not grant Li even that much time, and their rapid advance quickly cut his troops off from the rest of the New 4th Army. The decision to retain this region despite the obvious strategic weaknesses would come back to haunt the Communists in the following year.

The events in the two months following the Japanese surrender clearly presaged the kind of war that awaited the CCP. Although the conflict was now radically different to anything they had ever faced before, Mao seemed almost content in his conceptualization of the problem. For him, the only true difference between the guerilla warfare of yesterday and the mobile warfare of the present was one of mass and concentration. Earlier, dispersion was favorable for avoiding destruction and confusing the enemy, while concentration was useful only in special situations. Now the situation was reversed. Mao believed that concentration to fight "battles of annihilation" was the order of the day.[37] His new perspective appears most clearly in his wholehearted embrace of the "March on the North, Defend in the South" strategy.

The army itself faced unprecedented challenges related to modernization and preparation for conventional warfare. For one, the drastic increase in number of standing units meant that quality as well as command and control quickly became a major problem. Combat leaders who had directed only guerrilla teams or small units now would have to manage thousands of men across vast tracts of territory. Other problems included standardization of equipment – some units required ten or more different calibers of ammunition – and cooperation with other units to avoid friendly fire and establish areas of responsibility. On the tactical level, the Communists also had to figure out how best to combine the guerrilla warfare tenets they knew so well, such as attacking weak points or surrounding and isolating the enemy, with conventional tactics such as the integration of heavy weapons, communication, and maneuvering large units in the field.

The Communist military commanders were well aware of these obstacles and, as outlined in Chapter 1, most had the training necessary to effect the changes. For instance, prior to the Shangdang Campaign, Liu conducted a crash course in professional officer development by issuing a series of instructional dispatches before the battle.[38] Before the Suiyuan Campaign, He Long recognized this was the first time Communist armies of such size would cooperate on such a large scale, requiring a great deal of planning and coordination ahead of time.[39] Meanwhile, Nie stressed tactics and training to compensate for his army's lack of proper equipment and experience fighting in large units.[40] Zhu had tried to address some of these issues after the 7th Congress, but the four months since had not been enough time to complete the transformation. As a result, the Communists faced the difficult prospect of suffering through "growing pains" while simultaneously fighting for their lives.

March on the North

While the Communist army maneuvered to implement Liu's "March on the North, Defend in the South," Mao and Chiang hammered out the October 10 Agreement. This pact laid out each side's sphere of influence which generally adhered to the status quo. However, the status of major unclaimed regions was left undecided.

One of these was northeast China, possibly an intentional omission by both sides. By then, the CCP had already decided to make a bid for the northeast and the GMD would follow, hoping not just to capture Manchuria's resources for itself but also to catch and destroy a large Communist army. This goal put Chiang in a quandary because he lacked the forces to advance everywhere in strength – a flaw clearly exposed in the Shangdang Campaign. Nonetheless, his American-trained divisions had proved effective in capturing the cities, securing railroads, and deterring Communist attacks. Therefore, Chiang decided to send a large group of these elite units to Manchuria by sea and air. By the end of August alone, he had dispatched 150,000 soldiers to the region.[41]

Chiang's countermeasure meant that Yan'an also would have to fight if the "March on the North, Defend in the South" strategy were to come to fruition. Yet to do so by either conventional or guerilla methods posed worrisome obstacles. Conventional warfare would be difficult, if not impossible, due to the CCP's qualitative and quantitative disadvantages. Guerrilla tactics were also out of the question because the Communists lacked an established base in Manchuria; building one would take time. The lack of a guerilla base was due to Japan's success in repelling all previous CCP incursions into the region.[42] For instance, the Manchurian Provincial Committee, the Northeast Anti-Japanese United Army, and 8th Route Army expeditions were all defeated in rapid succession during World War II.[43] Nevertheless, some senior commanders already on the ground in the northeast dolefully predicted that guerilla warfare eventually might be their only option.[44]

The Secretariat believed they could stall or block the GMD in the north China Liberated Areas long enough for Peng Zhen to seize and retain northeast China through a conventional defense. In an unintentional throwback to Mao and Zhu's strategy in the 7th Congress, "March on the North, Defend in the South" called for a two-front war. Communist forces in north, east, and central China were to employ an interior-line strategy. This would involve trading territory for time and menacing, rather than attempting to capture strategic terrain, while inflicting casualties on the GMD whenever and wherever possible. The army in Manchuria, on the other hand, was to engage in positional warfare, holding both the rich industrial heartland as well as defending the mainland and sea approaches.

The effort to implement this new plan was impressive, especially considering the state of the Communist army. As noted above, Li Yunchang led the first expedition into Manchuria just days after Tokyo's surrender. This force included eight regiments and one battalion of regular CCP troops, two Korean volunteer regiments, and 2,000 local cadres – including four prefecture-level party secretaries.[45] The Koreans led the way under the command of Zeng Kelin, clearing a path for follow-on units by capturing Shanhaiguan and Jinzhou, before moving on to Shenyang.[46] At Shenyang, Li was warmly greeted by the Soviet Red Army, but they did not allow his forces to enter the city. They did, however, permit CCP political apparatus to set up its headquarters in the downtown district at the Liaoning Provincial Museum. In the meantime, the rest of Li's force captured Chengde in Hebei and several medium-sized towns in southwestern Liaoning, including Chaoyang, Lingyuan, and Chifeng.

By the end of August, an estimated 110,000 Communist troops and 20,000 political cadres had arrived in northeast China. However, a large proportion of this so-called Northeast People's Democratic United Army (NPDUA) consisted of local conscripts, bandit, and ex-Wang Jingwei or Manchukuo units – all of dubious quality.[47] Reinforcements from the Shandong Military District were on the way but would not arrive until November.[48] Survivors of earlier Communist expeditions into Manchuria, who had found safe haven in the Soviet Union during the Pacific War, and a handful of units from the other Liberated Areas also filtered into the region, but it would take time for these to coalesce. Consequently, as a CMC report candidly pointed out on November 1, although the Communist army in Manchuria underwent a massive and rapid growth on paper, their combat power remained low.[49]

The "March in the North, Defend in the South" also called for changes to the composition and leadership of the NPDUA. In August, Zhu's original plan was to employ units and commanders who either previously served in Manchuria or were native to the region. That was why Lu Zhengcao was to be the first commander of the NPDUA. Liu's plan modified Zhu's vision by creating the Northeast Bureau, which was led by Peng Zhen and other non-native senior ranking members of the CCP. On October 30, the CMC named Lin Biao as the commander of the NPDUA with Lu and Li Yunchang as his deputies.[50] The decision to transfer Lin from the HRL Military Sub-District to this new assignment may have been Mao's. After returning from Chongqing and observing reports from northeast China, Mao was reputed to have commented: "The army and the leaders are in chaos in the Northeast. Only Lin Biao can unite the party, the government, the army and the people in the Northeast."[51] Peng became political commissar of the NPDUA and Luo Ronghuan was reassigned to deputy political commissar. Xiao Ke, commander of the SCH Military District's 2nd Army, replaced Lin as commander of the HRL Military Sub-District.[52]

The reason for this reorganization stemmed in part from growing recognition of the tremendous political and military challenges the CCP faced in the region. Although the rump Secretariat had discussed some of these beforehand, they had not anticipated their magnitude. The most pressing issue was the lack of supplies and equipment. Soviet aid, contrary to expectations, proved meager and not forthcoming. The equipment the NPDUA did have lacked standardization – a problem endemic to the entire Communist army.[53] As mentioned before, the army also lacked combat power, and although better skilled reinforcements would soon solve this problem, they would also worsen the supply problem. Huang Kecheng, whose 3rd Division had been transferred to the NPDUA, remarked that the forces in northeast China suffered from the seven "no's": no local party organization, no mass activity, no administration, no logistical support, no grain, no economy, and no shoes or clothes.[54] Peng Zhen quoted a traditional saying to describe the situation: "the seas are turbulent, the raging waves crash on the shore."[55]

The Communists also suffered from a crisis in strategy. The socio-economic situation in northeast China was completely different than in north China. For this reason, many cadre and military commanders wanted to abandon Mao's method of mobilizing the rural masses and instead focus on capturing the cities and the industrial base of the region. To deny them to the GMD, Peng Zhen and the Northeast Bureau advocated seizing the three large cities of Shenyang, Changchun, and Harbin as soon as the Soviets left.[56] Called the "Three Large Cities Strategy," this plan represented a radical departure from the party line – one that had not been considered since Li Lisan was driven from power in 1930. Consequently, Mao and the Secretariat were lukewarm about this policy and continued to stress countryside bases.[57] However, because the Soviets continued to deny access to the three large cities, the argument remained academic for the time being.

As the Communists struggled through October with their policy for Manchuria, Chiang's seaborne columns began to arrive. The Soviet Red Army denied them access to Yingkou, citing concerns for GMD safety, while the Communists closed the port of Huludao. As his ships searched for a port, Chiang relied on air transport to reinforce the garrisons that Moscow had previously allowed into in the three large cities. Although small, they were able to dig in and build fortifications while the NPDUA remained outside. On November 5, after almost a month at sea, two corps under Du Yuming disembarked at Qinhuangdao and marched north. Despite the delay, Du's forces arrived in front of the main body of Communist reinforcements. The Secretariat decided that the NPDUA would have to fight and stop Du's advance if the reinforcements were to have any effect at all. For this battle they chose Shanhaiguan, a natural bottleneck where the Great Wall met the sea, the traditional gateway between Manchuria and north China.

Fortunately for the Communists, anticipating the GMD would attempt to land troops, Li Yunchang had already organized defenses at Shanhaiguan and Jinzhou.[58] However, the garrison at Shanhaiguan amounted to only two regiments, a total of 2,300 men. After receiving the CMC order to reinforce Shanhaiguan, Xiao Ke dispatched Li Yunchang and the HRL Military District's 19th Brigade. Yang Guofu, who had passed through Shanhaiguan with a large element on November 1, returned to the city with three regiments, a total of 7,000 men.[59] Yang took command of the forces within the city while Li organized the defense of the town's landward flank. Despite this injection of fresh troops, the Communists remained severely outnumbered by Du's 70,000 man force.

Undaunted, Mao and the CMC began to view the upcoming battle at Shanhaiguan as a potential turning point in the war. Consequently, they diverted more forces to the city wherever they could find troops. Liu Bocheng, who was fighting Sun Lianzhong in the Pinghan Campaign, was to commit the 1st Column by November 13. Huang Kecheng's 3rd Division and Liang Xingqie's 1st Shandong Division, still in Hebei, were ordered to speed their movement to join the battle.[60] Before they could arrive, Du besieged Shanhaiguan and cut it off. Therefore, Huang and Liang were sent around Shanhaiguan to rendezvous at Jinzhou.[61] In the meantime, Liu Qiren's 4,000 man detachment, also en route to northeast China but too far south to intervene, attacked Gubeikou to divert any GMD reinforcements from Beiping.[62]

On November 11, the CMC announced that all other efforts were secondary to the battle developing in Liaoning. To this end, the NPDUA was ordered to mass at Jinzhou to prepare for a decisive encounter with Du's force.[63] With Shanhaiguan cut off, their task now was to delay the GMD while Lin Biao prepared to counterattack from Jinzhou. Mao believed Li and Yang could hold Shanhaiguan for a month or two, despite the odds. These hopes were further buoyed when Yang conducted a successful long-range raid against Du's spearhead unit on November 11.[64]

On November 15, Du began a general attack on Shanhaiguan. Despite disadvantage in numbers and reports of the ferocity of the initial assault, the Secretariat believed the line could hold indefinitely. They had faith that Shanhaiguan's defensive features, which included its city walls, mountains to the west, and the sea to the east would offset the GMD's advantages. This hope proved to be unfounded when Yang was forced to retreat from the city on November 16. Receiving Li's bleak report from the hills overlooking the city, the Secretariat was forced to face reality. On November 17, they ordered Li and Yang to conduct a mobile defense north of Shanhaiguan to allow more time for the counterattack to develop.[65] In the meantime, Lin finally concentrated his forces at Jinzhou on November 19. That same day, the GMD captured Suizhong – a little more than a hundred kilometers south of Jinzhou. As the prospect for a large-scale battle neared, the Soviets forced the political arm of the Northeast Bureau to evacuate from the three large cities. Their official explanation was that they were obligated to assure a peaceful handover of the cities and railroads to Chiang's forces.

Oblivious to these events, and still seeking a decisive battle, on November 19 the Secretariat adopted Peng Zhen's "Three Large Cities Strategy" and rejected a strategy of building countryside bases.[66] However, once they received the latest updates from the Northeast Bureau, the Secretariat was forced to reconsider their decision. Mao was suddenly overcome by illness and, for the second time, an important strategic question fell into Liu Shaoqi's hands. Liu ordered Peng not to interfere with the GMD's entry into the cities or to block the railroads and ports.[67] He also retracted the Secretariat's earlier support for the "Three Large Cities Strategy." This suggests that Mao, who was by now clearly leaning towards conventional warfare and decisive battles, may have been the driving force behind the Secretariat's original acceptance of Peng's urban-based strategy. Furthermore, when Liu was in charge of the party it was clear that the Secretariat opposed Peng's plan, perhaps a case of Liu being more Maoist than Mao.[68]

Liu's new orders for the Northeast Bureau called for building three bases in the countryside. The main base was to be in southwest Manchuria and would be responsible for reestablishing contact with the HRL Military Sub-District and controlling the Beiping-Shenyang railroad. The other two bases would be in southeast Liaoning and north Manchuria (Jilin and Heilongjiang). To meet these objectives, the Northeast Bureau separated to ensure the presence of senior leadership at each location. After leaving Shenyang, Peng Zhen and Luo Ronghuan remained at the southeast Liaoning base, which had its headquarters at Benxi. Lin Biao, Li Fuchun, Lu Zhengcao, and Li Yunchang remained at Jinzhou to direct military affairs. Chen Yun went to the north base in Heilongjiang where he joined Gao Gang and Zhang Wentian. Tao Zhu went to Faku, north of Shenyang, to administer to the southwest Manchuria base.

In the meantime, Du continued his advance towards Jinzhou. Sensing the danger, Lin felt that the NPDUA should "avoid hasty battles" and "abandon Jinzhou, withdraw 2–300 kilometers north in order to let the enemy overextend himself." At that point, he envisioned conducting an ambush or concentrating his entire force on a single GMD unit. It is important to note that Lin had been one of the main proponents of fighting at Shanhaiguan,[69] but after seeing the strength of Du's force and the weakness of his own army first hand, he changed his mind. On November 22, the Northeast Bureau adopted Lin's plan and approved a retreat despite the CMC directives to the contrary.[70] Du captured Jinzhou soon after the Communists evacuated and he advanced another 80 kilometers north to Goubangzi before halting on November 28 to rest and reorganize.

Abandoning Jinzhou was not the only decision the Northeast Bureau undertook against the Secretariat's will. Peng still wanted to apply the "Three Large Cities Strategy" now that Moscow announced it would delay its withdrawal from Manchuria until March of 1946. They did so on Chiang's behalf, who feared the Communists would seize the three large cities before Du's armies could break through. On December 5, Peng proposed destroying the GMD garrisons immediately after the Soviets left.[71] Chen Yun and Luo Ronghuan supported this plan, citing the fact that the socio-economic and demographic conditions in Manchuria meant that holding at least the medium-sized cities was essential to victory.[72] Despite these testimonials, Liu Shaoqi again rejected the plan, arguing that occupying the cities was "impossible," especially without "friendly assistance."[73] Faced with such opposition from Yan'an, Peng backtracked by stating a few days later that capturing the large cities and the Zhongchang railroad (short for China [Zhongguo]–Changchun railroad which linked Harbin with Dalian) was impossible for the time being.[74]

After rejecting Peng's plan for the second time, Liu formed the West Manchuria Sub-Bureau and Military Sub-District to handle base building operations in Liaoning. This was done because of the need to solidify Communist control over the strategic Beiping-Shenyang corridor and because this base area was separated from the rest of the Northeast Bureau.[75] Liu appointed Lin Biao to command this district, along with his responsibilities at the head of the NPDUA. By the end of December, both Liu and Mao, who had by now recovered from his illness, issued definitive policy statements regarding Manchuria. Liu Shaoqi criticized the fact that the NPDUA was too close to the large cities and main railroads, and asserted they should concentrate more on base building rather than menacing the GMD. Mao called on the army to shift focus from operations to political work and for the Northeast Bureau to prepare for a Maoist-style "prolonged" struggle in the Northeast.[76]

After the brief dalliance with "decisive battle" and city-first strategies, the pendulum had swung back. Surprisingly, it was not Mao who had maintained a constant line, rather it was his deputy Liu. Contrary to Mao's reputation as a guerrilla strategist extraordinaire, in the months after Japan's surrender he appeared more than willing to seek large-scale battles and hold territory. Although he would moderate this stance as events unfolded, the chairman's desire for a decisive battle represented a significant turning point in Mao Zedong Thought. He had now passed the point of no return – from here on out, conventional war would be the only path for the CCP.

Defend in the South

As the GMD and CCP maneuvered their forces for the anticlimactic clash at Jinzhou, the other military districts fought the GMD to a standstill in the north China Liberated Areas. In the west, from October 18 to December 14, Nie Rongzhen's 1st Field Army and He Long's Shanxi-Suiyuan Field Army conducted the Suiyuan Campaign. Mao set high goals for the campaign, namely the destruction of Fu Zuoyi's main force and the occupation of Guisui, Baotou, and if possible, Datong.[77] Despite lengthy sieges of Baotou and Guisui, neither city fell, nor did Fu ever expose his main force. However, it is questionable what effect the Communists would have had if they had managed to catch Fu in the field. Nie and He did manage to keep Fu and Yan Xishan apart, as well as consolidate CCP control over eastern Suiyuan and spoil Fu's attack on Zhangjiakou. After voluntarily lifting the siege of Baotou and Guisui, Nie and He ended the Suiyuan Campaign to rest and reorganize their forces.[78]

During the same period, Liu Bocheng's SHSH Military District conducted the Pinghan Campaign to repel Sun Lianzhong in northern Henan. As mentioned before, Liu's army was just coming off its victory at Shangdang. For this campaign, Liu disguised a small blocking force to look like his main force. In this way he was able to draw three GMD corps deep into Henan. Sun, overconfident and eager for a victory, subsequently advanced his force straight into a large-scale Communist ambush. On October 28, Liu struck decisively against the GMD flanks near the town of Handan,[79] encircling the entire force and cutting them off from any support. To compound Sun's problems, Gao Shuxun, deputy commander of the 11th War Zone, led the New 8th GMD Corps and part of the Hebei Militia into the Communist ranks two days later. Their morale shattered by the desertion and Liu's masterful trap, the remaining GMD forces attempted to break out but were routed and cut to pieces in the process.

In the end, Sun lost all three of his corps, but as in Shangdang only a few thousand of these were combat casualties – 17,000 were captured while 10,000 defected with Gao. In the course of two campaigns, Shangdang and Handan, the SHSH Field Army had eliminated – or annihilated in Communist terminology – 10 GMD brigades, just over 31% of the original attacking forces. While they gave ground along their entire front, Liu Bocheng commented that the exchange of 17 "empty" cities for 60,000 GMD troops was acceptable.[80] After their victory at Handan, the SHSH Military District could now rest for the winter, while Yan and Sun licked their wounds and prepared for a new offensive in the spring.

In the East China Military District, the situation was more critical, especially because of its proximity to Chiang's newly reestablished capital at Nanjing. The large ports and well-developed rail network of Zhejiang, Shanghai, and Jiangsu added to the region's importance. The transfer of the majority of the Shandong Military District forces to northeast China also had created a gap that momentarily offered the GMD free access into the north China Liberated Areas. At the end of September, Chiang sought to exploit this opportunity by ordering Wu Huawei's 5th Route Army (three divisions) to secure the Xuzhou-Jinan section of the

Pukou-Tianjin while he used his US air and sea transportation to flood the area with GMD troops. The 5th Route Army was formerly a part of the Wang Jingwei regime and did not represent an elite force. However, Wu did manage to seize Lincheng (now Xuecheng) and Tengxian (now Tengzhou) by October 4.

Part of Wu's success may have been because his offensive inadvertently coincided with the Luo Ronghuan-Chen Yi change of command in Shandong. Mao ordered Chen to recapture these lost portions of the Tianjin-Pukou railroad to prevent the GMD from penetrating any further north.[81] However, Chen's headquarters was still in disarray and he lacked the ability to mass his troops quickly. He also had few resources to call on since most of the units that could have responded were on their way to Manchuria. On October 23, Chen's forces in Shandong comprised the 8th Shandong Division (which consisted of only three regiments), the New 4th Army 9th Brigade, a regiment of local troops (at half-strength with only 600 men) and the newly arrived New 4th Army 5th Brigade (two regiments).[82] Despite his weakness, Chen realized he had only a small window of time before the GMD reinforced and consolidated Wu's penetration. In fact, by the end of October, the GMD had already moved four divisions to Ji'nan (the 12th Corps and two cavalry divisions), the 97th Corps to Lincheng and four divisions to Xuzhou (one division of the 12th Corps, the 51st Corps, and the 8th Cavalry Division).[83]

After Du Yuming captured Shanhaiguan and Lin Biao prepared to launch his counterattack, Mao pressured Chen to attack the GMD in west Shandong to prevent units there from joining the battle at Jinzhou.[84] Thus, in the beginning of November, Chen massed what forces he had on hand to wage the Tianjin-Pukou Campaign. Chen decided to attack first the unreliable 5th Route Army, which was in transit to Ji'nan, and then head northwest to attack Lincheng. Beginning on November 1, Chen's forces easily surrounded and destroyed Wu at Zoucheng in a two-day battle. By November 18, Chen had recaptured Tengxian, destroying another GMD division and severing the Tianjin-Pukou railroad in the process. His main mission accomplished, he proceeded to the next phase of his plan by besieging the 97th Corps at Lincheng at the end of the month. Here, Chen's luck ran out and he was unable to capture the city or reduce its defenses. He maintained the siege for the winter but ceased any further attempts to assault the city.

As Chen and the Shandong Field Army fought to reclaim the Tianjin-Pukou railroad, the rest of the New 4th Army began to readjust to its new mission. The forces from east Anhui, Jiangsu, and Zhejiang coalesced near Hai'an in central Jiangsu, where they fell under Zhang Dingcheng's Central China Military District and Su Yu's Central China Field Army.[85] Su was originally offered command of both elements, but he deferred on the grounds that Zhang was senior to him. The Central China Field Army was 40,000 strong and divided into the 6th, 7th, 8th, and 9th Columns.[86] In Henan, Hubei, Jiangxi, and Hunan, Li Xiannian's 5th Division and elements from guerrilla bases became the Central Plains Military District. Li served as commander and Zheng Lisan the political commissar for both entities. The Central Plains Field Army had only two columns but the injection of irregular troops brought its total strength to 60,000 men.[87] The last reorganization was perhaps the most painful as Chen abandoned the proud New 4th Army appellation and reformed it into the Shandong Field Army. By the beginning of January, the final transfers were complete and the army was 70,000 men strong. It was subdivided into the 1st and 2nd Columns and the 7th and 8th Independent Divisions.[88]

The end of the campaigning season coincided with a new round of peace talks. Special US envoy General George C. Marshall, who had arrived in China in December, formed the American Executive Headquarters for Military Mediation in Beiping to oversee the negotiations between the GMD and CCP. His efforts resulted in a truce set to begin on January 13. However, instead of leading to a gradual winding down of hostilities, both sides frantically attempted to improve their position before the armistice began. For instance, Chiang tried to lift the siege of Lincheng by ordering Feng Zhian's 18th Army Group – which, like the 5th Route Army, was formerly a part of the Wang Jingwei regime – to attack Chen's forces. This plan was initially sidetracked when one of Feng's subordinates, Hao Pengjuan, defected with the 6th Corps (10,000 men) on January 9, 1946. However, Feng still had enough combat power to force Chen to withdraw from Lincheng a day later.

There was also heavy fighting in the southern portion of the vital Beiping-Shenyang corridor. After capturing Jinzhou, Du decided to secure his link with Beiping and Tianjin before continuing north towards Shenyang. He sent a portion of his force to capture Chengde but they were delayed by Communist resistance and only managed to capture Pingquan before the ceasefire. Fu Zuoyi had attempted to support Du's thrust towards Chengde, but the Communists effectively blocked them at the Great Wall passes in north Hebei.[89] These were likely half-hearted attempts as Fu was more intent on securing his western flank. In a surprise attack, he seized Jining shortly before the truce. However, He Long counterattacked and recaptured the city on January 17 – after the truce had already gone into effect. Marshall's attempts to mediate this infraction proved futile.[90] In fact, low-level fighting continued everywhere well into the ceasefire period. From January 14 to the end of April there were a total of 927 incidents in the SHSH Military District alone. This included four attacks involving more than 10,000 men, 40 attacks involving 1,000 or more personnel, and 112 attacks of 100 or more men.[91] Instead of leading to a permanent peace, the truce merely allowed both sides to rest, reorganize and gain strategic advantages before the war's inevitable resumption.

Although the Communists had managed to hold their own in 1945, Chiang was looking to expand the war and increase the scale and intensity of the fighting. He envisioned either forcing the CCP to engage his elite units in large battles – battles which they were not fully prepared to fight – or to stand by and watch the north China Liberated Areas be surrounded, isolated, and destroyed. Mobile defense and interior line tactics had scored notable victories, but had done so against puppet troops and second-tier GMD units. Chiang's US-trained and equipped forces had proved their worth in northeast China and soon would bear against the north China Liberated Areas. The balance of power was also still overwhelmingly in Chiang's favor. In mid-December, the CMC estimated that Chiang still had the equivalent of 54 corps ready to attack.[92] While a negotiated settlement was not necessarily out of the question, realists on both sides saw military force as the only arbiter of permanent peace. If negotiations were to have any real and lasting effect, they would have to come after a victory on the battlefield.

Siping: a second chance at the "decisive" battle

While the truce suspended large-scale fighting, there was no end to troop movements and strategic maneuvers on both sides. Northeast China continued to be the focus of both parties during this period. On January 15, after his failed foray into north Hebei, Du turned east and marched unopposed to Shenyang. In the meantime, the NPDUA continued to expand, blooded but still in one piece after Shanhaiguan and Jinzhou. The army grew in size and quality; regular troops, especially those who arrived from Shandong, now amounted to between one quarter and one third of the total force. The NPDUA was thus renamed the Northeast Democratic United Army (NDUA) – the "People's" appellation was apparently omitted to reflect the army's growing professionalization. Lin reorganized the army into ten infantry brigades, two artillery brigades and a number of independent regiments. It numbered 220,000 men by the beginning of 1946.[93]

By the spring of 1946, the January truce expired without resolution or renewal. Many Communist leaders had anticipated this outcome and saw the "peace" for what it was – a temporary lull. For instance, Zhou Enlai deemed it a time to "consolidate strength, especially in northeast … and north China."[94] The ceasefire was indeed an invaluable time for the Communists to rest, reorganize, and reequip their troops as well as for the high command to reflect on their strategy. Despite this cynicism, the GMD and CCP agreed to a reduction of their respective armies down to a ratio of five to one, a series of resolutions dividing up northeast China, and a timetable for a new constitution. Yet these proved mere illusions as the CCP refused to name delegates to the constitutional congress and both sides continued to move troops into Manchuria. It was thus no real surprise that the spring thaw led to renewed military operations.

During the winter Mao and Liu had adamantly opposed the Northeast Bureau's desire to reinstate the "Three Large Cities" strategy. However, as negotiations ground to a halt, the pendulum began to swing back towards drastic action. On March 17, Mao approved the Northeast Bureau's request to sever the Zhongchang railroad after the Soviets left. In his dispatch to Peng, he specifically cited as the reason for this action Chiang's unwillingness to stop the war and grant the CCP concessions.[95] In response, Huang Kecheng's forces seized Siping,[96] an important rail junction between Shenyang and Changchun. On March 25, the Secretariat unleashed the Northeast Bureau to enact the "Three Large Cities Strategy" immediately after the Soviet Red Army left.[97] While most of the Northeast Bureau was ecstatic, Lin Biao was not. He believed the NDUA was still weak and could not withstand Du's reinforced army. The winter had also been hard on the ill-equipped and ill-organized forces, especially because of cold-related injuries and desertions.[98]

Lin's unwillingness to fight after the battle of Shanhaiguan led to criticism from his peers. Nie called Lin selfish for not joining to fight in Shanhaiguan or to assist Xiao Ke by attacking in Liaoning when Du tried to capture Chengde.[99] Later on, during the Cultural Revolution, Lin's desire to maintain the strength of his army was exalted as an example of his steadfast devotion to Mao Zedong Thought. Peng on the other hand was criticized heavily for his "Three Large City Strategy."[100] This judgment was later reversed again after Lin's attempted coup and death in the 1971 Incident and Deng Xiaoping's rise to power in 1976. Politics aside, Lin's hesitancy appeared to be driven by military concerns – he simply had recognized the limitations of his army and his strategic position.

Yet Lin was also a dutiful soldier, as his record prior to 1945 suggests, and this overrode any personal objections. On April 4, he moved the NDUA's main strength to reinforce Huang Kecheng at Siping. He arrived only three days before the GMD advance units made contact with the Communist defenses. Lin's first defensive line was over 100 kilometers long and consisted of three divisions and two brigades outside of the city and three regiments within Siping. He formed a second defensive line south of Changchun and deployed two columns in east Liaoning to protect the Northeast Bureau in Benxi. These forces were also in position to launch a spoiling attack to draw off GMD forces, if necessary. On April 6, Mao called on the NDUA to "not give an inch of land" in front of Siping, no matter the casualties. Some members of the Northeast Bureau also believed that the "[Secretariat] envisioned [the defense of Siping] as the final battle of the war."[101] However, Lin and Peng were both deeply disturbed by this sentiment and sent a reply to Mao requesting that the focus be on destroying enemy units rather than holding ground. On April 12, Mao backtracked and agreed to this new proposal.[102] This would give them more flexibility to dictate how and when they would fight – a key point of distinction for the upcoming battle.

Du had started his march towards Siping on March 18, which coincided with the Soviet withdrawal. The New 1st Corps, veterans of the Burma Campaign against Japan, advanced along the Zhongchang railroad on a direct line to Siping. The 71st Corps was on the left flank, aimed at the Communist base at Faku, while the 52nd Corps was on the right, with its objective being Benxi and the base at Fushun. In support of this main thrust, the New 6th Corps would first secure the port of Yingkou and then move north to reinforce the 52nd Corps. However, inclement weather and bad roads slowed the approach, and it ran behind schedule. The New 1st Corps did not reach Siping until April 7 and, upon encountering the NDUA defense, Du paused to prepare his attack.

Lin was acutely aware of the number of troops Du had at his disposal. As a result, he proposed waging a delaying campaign rather than a fixed defense to the CMC and the Northeast Bureau. This might have swayed Mao had not Zhou reported the possibility of a breakthrough in his negotiations with the GMD at Chongqing. This caused Mao to abandon caution and he reverted to his earlier tone by declaring that there would be no retreat from Siping. He believed that such a battle would strengthen Zhou's bargaining position with Marshall.[103] Additionally, the die had been cast on the "Three Large Cities" strategy as elements of the NDUA attacked Changchun on April 11, just hours after the Soviets left. Four days later, as Du began his attack on Siping, the Communists overcame the garrison at Changchun. This put two of the three large cities in their hands – Harbin had fallen earlier and without a fight.

To counteract the Communists, Du planned a two-pronged offensive. The northern prong was aimed at drawing as many Communist units as possible into the battle at Siping while the southern prong decapitated the Northeast Bureau by capturing Benxi. At the time, the GMD estimated the NDUA's strength at 300,000 troops, of which only 100,000 were regular troops with adequate weaponry. They accounted for another 100,000 irregulars augmentees – mostly made up of unemployed factory workers.[104] Due to the rapid capture of Faku, Du was able to employ an additional division against Siping. However, Lin arranged an ambush for this unit and on April 15 forced it to retire with heavy casualties. By this time, the Northeast Bureau had committed almost all of its front line strength, 80,000 regular troops, to the defense of Siping.[105] Du launched a general attack on April 18, just as the Communists completed their capture of Changchun.

On April 20, Zheng Tongguo's New 1st Corps fought their way into the western suburbs of Siping. Fierce Communist resistance over the previous two days and stiffening defenses in the urban environment caused Zheng to halt and wait for reinforcements. Despite this foothold within Lin's perimeter, Mao insisted on defending Siping, Changchun, and Benxi to the death. Furthermore, he stated that they had to win a decisive victory at Siping – the old model of destroying enemy forces and then evacuating was completely unacceptable.[106] To this end, Mao ordered that more reinforcements be sent to Siping and that Nie Rongzhen should conduct a diversionary campaign in Rehe.[107]

With the Communist high command fixed on Siping, Du began to unfold the other part of his plan. His forces quickly captured Benxi and drove the NDUA out of east Liaoning by the beginning of May. After this success, the New 6th Corps boarded trains and moved north to reinforce Du at Siping. Their arrival allowed the GMD to envelop the Communist's left flank, which was guarded by Huang Kecheng's 3rd Division. Huang wrote to Lin on May 12 calling for a general withdrawal, but after receiving no answer he forwarded the proposal directly to the Northeast Bureau and the CMC. He would not receive a response until fourteen years later, in conversation with Mao at Lushan. During that time, Huang had commented that Lin made a serious mistake by fighting too long at Siping. Mao asserted there was no error – the decision to delay had been his all along.[108] Luckily for the NDUA, the Chairman did not wait too long. On May 19, Mao allowed Lin to withdraw from Siping – which Lin did immediately, barely escaping certain encirclement and destruction.[109]

After the retreat from Siping, Peng Zhen, recently removed from Benxi, and Luo Ronghuan, roused from a brief convalescent stay at a Russian hospital in Dalian, convened a meeting with Lin. Although Mao had ordered a defense of Changchun,[110] the three senior CCP members in Manchuria all agreed that the army was in no shape to fight. The Communist after action reports cited 8,000 casualties, probably reflecting only the killed or wounded. The GMD report of 40,000 NDUA casualties probably takes into account desertions and captured soldiers – numbers which Communists records do not admit. The GMD also notes the mass desertion of the NDUA's 100,000 man irregular force.[111] When these are taken into account, CCP losses were almost twice those suffered by the GMD at either Shangdang or Handan. In light of this setback, Lin, Luo and Peng defied Mao and withdrew the NDUA to Chen Yun's base in Heilongjiang after only a brief delaying action south of Changchun.

Sensing his advantage, Du pursued the NDUA doggedly. He captured Gongzhuling on May 21 and Changchun two days later. On May 25, four Communists regiments fought a desperate but successful rearguard action at the Songhua River – the last major geographical obstacle between the GMD and Harbin. This holding action bought time for the bulk of the NDUA to cross the river safely. After holding off Du's advanced elements, the remaining defenders crossed and blew up the bridge. The Communists occupied the high ground on the north bank and waited for the inevitable GMD attack. In the first few days of June, a handful of GMD units did probe the defenses by crossing the river and seizing some of the heights. However, they advanced no further than that. In the meantime, Lin and the Northeast Bureau stopped in Harbin, but they expected Du soon to cross the Songhua River in strength. They were prepared to retreat further north,[112] perhaps as far as the Soviet Union. Fortunately, this never occurred and Du's forces remained in place.

Multiple factors contributed to the GMD's decision to halt on the south bank of the Songhua River. The first was a surprise attack by Wu Kehua's 3rd Column, which Lin had positioned in east Liaoning to guard Benxi and threaten Du's rear. Wu's capture of Anshan on May 25 and the defection of the Haicheng garrison three days later actually cut Du off from his main supply port at Yingkou. This forced Du to divert forces from Jilin to drive off Wu and recapture the lost cities. To make matters worse, GMD units that were earmarked to reinforce him were tied down in Shandong and Jiangsu due to a spoiling attack by Chen Yi's East China Military District.[113] The second factor was Chiang's decision to agree to a truce negotiated by Marshall on June 10. Chiang later bitterly regretted having ever accepted this:

> If the Government had concentrated its military forces and taken action against the Communist troops for their violations of the cease-fire agreement of January 1946, even at the risk of provoking an all-out war, it could have won.[114]

Yet, at the time, Chiang had good reason to believe that he had the advantage. Siping appeared to be an important, if not decisive victory. He also held the important industrial and urban areas of Manchuria – areas which many of the Communists believed were essential to victory – and advancing any further north might have caused friction with Moscow.[115] There were also sound military reasons for not continuing the pursuit. Du's army was overextended, as the fall of Anshan and Haicheng illustrated. Lin was also looking for an opportunity to strike and might well have found one had Du crossed the Songhua.[116] For the time being, the GMD possessed a commanding strategic position and Lin's battered army in the distant wilds of Heilongjiang had been rendered virtually irrelevant.

On June 16, Lin replaced Peng as secretary of the Northeast Bureau. Peng was demoted to second-in-command, with Chen Yun, Gao Gang, and Luo Ronghuan promoted to deputy party secretaries (all four of these men also served as political commissars for the NDUA). Due to the turn of events, even the most ardent supporters of the "Three Large Cities" strategy were now intent on building bases in the countryside.[117] While the NDUA was still strong on paper, with over 300,000 troops,[118] it was spread out in three major concentrations – in the mountains on the Korean border, in west Liaoning and Harbin. The army still consisted predominantly of bandits and former Manchukuo Army units, and there had been precious little time to integrate and indoctrinate them into the Communist ranks.

The chaos of the retreat to Harbin had only compounded these problems. Huang Kecheng estimated total casualties during the battle and the retreat at as many as 15,000 men – much lower than the GMD figure, but Huang likely was accounting only for the regular troops. During the march, the units had scattered across the entire region, and even those who completed the retreat were mixed with other units and in a state of disarray. This made command and control nearly impossible. For instance, of the four brigades previously assigned to the west Manchuria base, only two were able to return to their original home. One ended up joining Lin in Heilongjiang and the other retreated to east Liaoning to join Wu Kehua.[119] For this reason, the ceasefire and the GMD inability to pursue the NDUA further north probably saved the Northeast Bureau and potentially cost the GMD the war.

The evolution of Communist strategy in the first ten months of the Third Revolutionary Civil War did not follow a straight path nor was it even a qualified success. In fact, by the middle of 1946, it appeared to have been a failure. However, they had survived the GMD's first assault and this alone was a minor accomplishment. The CCP's reliance on an opportunistic land grab, the so-called "Protect the Results of the War against Japan" approach, had paid dividends in the first few months of the war. They were able to consolidate a good deal of territory in north China and create a nearly contiguous entity out of the preexisting disconnected enclaves and Liberated Areas. The Communist army had also made rapid improvements and significant steps toward professionalization, as seen in their success against the Japanese, puppet army troops, and non-elite GMD units.

However, it was clear that simply defending and consolidating the north China countryside would not guarantee survival of the CCP, especially with the GMD holding the cities and railways. Consequently, the "March on the North, Defend in the South" plan emerged – an audacious attempt to shift the balance of the war and the strategic landscape. Although fundamentally sound, the plan ran into two major problems. First, the Communists had not anticipated the problems they would face building a base of support in northeast China. Second, they had not planned on Chiang's decision to dispatch some of his best units to the region. As a result, the Northeast Bureau implemented the "Three Large Cities" strategy, a subset of "March on the North, Defend in the South." Although a complete reversal of traditional Maoist techniques, Mao largely came to agree with the plan and held onto it almost past the point of practicality.

Unfortunately, the Communist defeat at the Battle of Siping meant the end of the "March on the North, Defend in the South" strategy. Instead, the Communists settled in for long-term operations in the region and looked to other military districts to turn the tide. Although the Marshall truce gave them some breathing room, few Communists believed it would last and they would soon be proven correct. The failure to take Manchuria rapidly and establish a safe rear base area for the north China Liberated Area left the Communists in the same situation as they were at the end of the World War II, only now weaker and lacking the initiative. To their credit, they still held the main entry points into the north China Liberated Areas along the Yellow River, and the main Communist armies were still largely intact. However, Chiang Kaishek had yet to commit his elite, American-trained and equipped forces, except in northeast China where they had clearly demonstrated their superiority. The fact that these forces were now moving to the front and bolstering the rest of the GMD army was an ominous sign for Yan'an. With a general attack on the north China Liberated Area likely in the works, the Communist high command would have to conceive and implement a completely new nationwide strategy – for the second time since the end of World War II.

3 The Guomindang high tide (June 1946–June 1947)

The June truce arranged by Marshall lasted long enough for Chiang to present his proposal for the disputed areas. Zhou Enlai returned to Yan'an on June 7 to deliver it in person to the Secretariat. Unfortunately for the CCP, this new "plan for peace" amounted to little more than an ultimatum. Chiang's proposal called for the CCP to withdraw from the Central Plains, Chengde, east Hebei, west Liaoning, and the entire Ji'nan-Jiaodong railroad.[1] If accepted, it would have resulted in the severing of the connection between the north China Liberated Areas and northeast China, as well as splitting the Shandong Military District in two. In return, Nanjing would recognize Communist authority in the far north of Manchuria as well as the districts in Shandong and Shanxi the Communists had seized during Chen Yi and Liu Bocheng's campaigns in 1945. Zhou commented that "[Chiang's] intention was to restrict [the CCP] to these few regions, cut [the CCP] off completely and then annihilate [the CCP]."[2] Mao reputedly lost more than one night of sleep over the decision, but in the end he rejected the terms. The CCP issued a counterproposal on June 21, but Chiang replied five days later by launching the General Offensive – an attack against the Communist bases in the Central Plains and the along southern perimeter of the north China Liberated Areas.

At the same time, the Secretariat was also in the process of modifying their political and social policies. While it is beyond the scope of this book to deal with these issues in depth, they reflected a move towards total war mobilization. For instance, on May 4, Liu Shaoqi called for radical land reform that included land confiscation and redistribution.[3] In terms of military implications, such policies would grant the Communists increased access to manpower as well as solidify their support for the coming conflict. Even as observers in GMD areas later observed, these efforts did go on to pay huge logistical dividends:

> Because the Communist armies have changed production relations and social and economic organization in the liberated areas, they have been able to establish the new social order they need. Grain requisitions, military conscription and self-defense can therefore be carried out with a high degree of effectiveness. There is no need to use excessive military force to defend the villages and towns they control.[4]

At a grassroots level, the effect was also significant:

> After the farmer receives his share of land, he will naturally think that the only way to preserve his share of land is to follow the CCP to the very end. As a matter of fact, farmers are fearful of measures of revenge from the landlords, and it is highly probably that they will plunge in with the CCP.[5]

The Northeast Bureau, in particular, benefited from these policies in their effort to win support where the Communists traditionally had not met with success. Although they had access to a considerable amount of land that could be redistributed without alienating the predominant landlord class,[6] they had no connection or influence with the peasants. At the same time, the NDUA's logistical needs were massive,[7] and its demand for more supplies threatened to accelerate the land redistribution efforts and unravel the political progress that the Communists had already made. This reflected the reason why Peng and the Northeast Bureau had argued earlier on that Manchuria was a special case and required different policies than the rest of China.

Unfortunately, Yan'an and Harbin did not agree on how to build a base in northeast China. For instance, the Secretariat stressed moderation while the Northeast Bureau made stringent demands on the people for taxes, service, and resources. To compensate for these increased burdens, the local cadre increased the speed and scale of land and resource redistribution, radicalizing the entire process and leading to less than desirable results in many areas. These results included violence, opportunism, theft, and alienation of all but the poorest classes – a condition which later became known euphemistically as "raw" or "uncooked rice."[8] In addition, the CCP also formed its own administration, the Northeast Administrative Committee (NAC), for the areas in Manchuria it controlled, which they claimed the January truce talks allowed. Despite this new layer of bureaucracy, Lin Biao remained the Communists' supreme political and military personality in the region.

The changes in terms of administration, land reform, and socio-economic policies reflected the fact that the CCP was preparing to engage in total war. The idea of fighting for a better bargaining position in the peace talks was now over. For these reasons, many historians cite this period as the formal end of the Second United Front and the resumption of the Chinese Civil War. However, it is inaccurate to date the resumption of GMD–CCP hostilities strictly to June 26, 1946, especially considering the battles at Shangdang, Handan, and Siping. Nonetheless, this date does signify that an entirely different kind of war than the one waged unofficially since August 1945 had now begun.

The first phase of the GMD General Offensive fell on Li Xiannian's Central Plains Military District. No longer a guerrilla or irregular force, Li's army could no longer melt away into the countryside. Instead, it now faced being surrounded and destroyed by 10 GMD divisions. The Communist high command had foreseen this peril. In May 1946, Mao pointed out that the Central Plains was in mortal danger now that civil war was unavoidable.[9] For this reason, he instructed Li to prepare an escape, but stopped short of ordering a withdrawal before Chiang broke the truce.[10]

Figure 3.1 1946–47: General and Strong Point offensives.

In June, when Chiang moved to attack, Mao finally ordered Li to break out and retreat to the north China Liberated Areas. To support this effort, Mao proposed that the SHSH and East China Military Districts launch a large-scale spoiling attack into Jiangsu, Anhui, and eastern Henan to draw off GMD troops and recapture territory lost when the Communists contracted their lines as per the "March on the North, Defend in the South" strategy. He also ordered He Long and Nie Rongzhen to attack Yan's army to prevent him from intervening or taking advantage of the situation to move into south Shanxi.[11]

Mao envisioned these campaigns as repeats of Liu Bocheng's Shangdang and Handan campaigns. By employing mobile warfare tactics, he saw them drawing in and isolating individual GMD units through diversionary attacks, stealth, and deception before destroying them with overwhelming numbers. At the same time, Mao reversed his earlier advocacy of positional defense:

> … the temporary abandonment of certain places or cities is not only unavoidable but also necessary. Certain places or cities should be temporarily abandoned in order to win final victory, which would otherwise be impossible.[12]

This reversal was important because it settled an important tactical question that may have otherwise confused field commanders. During World War II, this had been a problem because confusion over whether mobile or guerrilla warfare was the preferred method had significantly hindered the field armies after the Hundred

Regiments Campaign of 1940. Yet, despite Mao's pronouncement on operations and tactics, the Communists' armed forces were still fundamentally inferior to the GMD armies. Mao's desire that they take the offensive would thus not only compound their existing difficulties but create new ones as Chiang's elite units led the assault and untrained Communist units were thrust into the fury of full-scale combat.

Despite the risks involved and the dangerous precedent set at Shanhaiguan and Siping, the military district commanders involved in Mao's counterattack plan all agreed with the general concept. In east China, the Shandong Field Army would provide the main effort with an attack on Xuzhou and Bengbu. Liu Bocheng's SHSH Field Army would support these efforts by attacking east Henan and cutting off the Longhai railroad. Su Yu's Central China Field Army would also provide support by attacking the Bengbu-Pukou railroad and block any potential reinforcements from Nanjing. However, Su was not comfortable with this mission. From his standpoint, his forces were insufficient to simultaneously maintain his defense line in Jiangsu, on the north bank of the Yangtze River, and conduct operations in Anhui. As Mao's order called on him to commit his main strength to Anhui,[13] he believed doing so would inevitably force him to abandon Jiangsu.

Consequently, on June 27, Su wrote to Chen Yi, his commander, and the CMC, offering two counterproposals. The first was to avoid deploying into Anhui at all and instead concentrate his forces in the Jiangsu cities of Yangzhou and Taizhou. By doing so, Su could simultaneously protect central Jiangsu and menace Nanjing and the Tianjin-Pukou railroad. In the end, this would allow him to support Chen's attack on Xuzhou while at the same time keep his field army closer to its home base. His alternate plan was to wait until the GMD began to send forces from Nanjing to reinforce Xuzhou, before moving the Central China Field Army into Anhui. In this way, there would be no threat to central Jiangsu and Su stood a better chance of ambushing the GMD on the march.[14] Before Yan'an provided an answer, Chen completed his own plan of attack and designated July 15 as the start date. In the end, Su's viewpoint won out and before the end of June, the CMC agreed with Su and canceled his portion of the plan.[15] After further consideration, Mao abandoned the counterattack in East China altogether on July 4. Instead, he ordered Liu Bocheng and Chen Yi to "fight a few battles on interior lines" and afterwards plan for a new offensive when the time was right.[16] This cautious approach largely would guide CCP strategy in east and central China for the rest of 1946.

Su's actions at this time have largely been recognized as having swayed Mao from undertaking a counteroffensive that probably would have ended in an irretrievable disaster.[17] Su not only believed that his army lacked the experience and the expertise to sustain such an operation, but that they also would be striking the elite forces Chiang had massed for the General Offensive. Yet Su was probably just one factor, albeit a very influential one, in the decision to abandon the counteroffensive. Intelligence reports coming from the frontlines probably also swayed Mao, as likely did Zhou Enlai's dispatches from Shanghai – where Zhou was continuing negotiations with Marshall and the GMD. These reports also confirmed that Chiang was assembling his best units in the very area where Liu and Chen were to conduct their attack.

At this juncture, the CCP made the important decision to abandon temporarily attempts to reclaim lost territory or attack GMD-controlled regions. Instead, they would focus mainly on isolating and destroying enemy units through conventional tactics in order to wear down the General Offensive and overstretch Chiang's forces. However, to do so meant that a tight, overarching, centrally controlled strategy was no longer in effect. The fate of the party now lay at the operational level, where tactical prowess and local conditions dictated events. This was a dangerous reversal of priorities, and it meant that the initiative was now fully in the hands of the GMD.

The General Offensive in the Central Plains and east China

As the Secretariat and regional commanders wrestled over how to respond to the General Offensive, the Central Plains Military District commanders also debated their next course of action. On June 14, Li Xiannian's political commissar, Zheng Weisan, wrote a telegram to the CMC informing them that two schools of thought existed within the Central Plains Military District high command: either withdraw to north China or remain in place and fight a guerrilla war. Yan'an's response favored the first option but conceded that guerrilla warfare was acceptable as a last-case scenario. In the end, Li Xiannian decided to divide his forces into three elements. The main force, which included the Central Plains Bureau and Wang Zhen's 359th Brigade, would march northwest towards Shaanxi. The second force would remain behind to conduct guerrilla warfare.[18] The third column, composed mainly of the 1st Brigade under Pi Dingjun, would conduct a rearguard action and then move east to join Su Yu and the Central China Military District. Mao's decision to abandon the counteroffensive in Xuzhou meant that Li would have to breakout of the GMD encirclement unaided.

On the GMD side, Liu Zhi's Zhengzhou Pacification Command, which was reinforced with the Wuhan Pacification Command, was responsible for destroying the Central Plains Military District. On June 20, Liu Zhi launched his attack, but Li and Wang deftly avoided the GMD forces. After almost a month of evasion and countermarches, Li's main body reached southern Shaanxi on July 17. Three days later, Pi's column also reached safety and linked up with Su. The breakout was largely complete, but from there the forces further separated to reestablish themselves in their new regions. Wang had led his brigade to Yan'an by the end of August, almost two full years after departing in 1944 to found bases in south China. The retreat north ultimately cost the 359th Brigade two-thirds of its original strength, but Wang, who already had a stellar reputation due to his earlier success in reclaiming the Nanniwan wasteland of Shaanxi, was heralded as a hero for his part in the operation. Equally celebrated, Li remained south of Xi'an at the junction point of Shaanxi, Henan, and Hubei to keep the door open for follow-on units and to pin down Hu Zongnan, commander of the 1st War Zone in Xi'an and deputy commander of Liu's Zhengzhou Pacification Command.

As Liu Zhi lost his quarry in the Central Plains, Xue Yue and his Xuzhou Pacification Command began their part of the offensive by attacking Su's Central

China Military District. It was a two-pronged offensive meant to encircle the Communists to force them either into a decisive battle or drive them from Jiangsu. The northern pincer involved GMD forces attacking out of Qingdao to secure the Ji'nan-Jiaodong railroad and the area around the Jiaozhou Bay. The southern pincer was aimed at dislodging Su Yu from his defense line on the north bank of the Yangtze River running from Yangzhou to Nantong. For this portion, Tang Enbo, one of Chiang's most capable generals, employed five divisions and an independent brigade, a total of 120,000 men, from the 1st Pacification District against Su's 19 regiments of 30,000 men.

On the outset, Tang seized the strategic advantage by crossing the Yangtze south of Taizhou, outflanking Su's defense line. However, Su recovered quickly and ambushed Tang's advanced units at Xuanjiabao and Taixing on July 13. This began the first of seven battles that became known formally as the Central Jiangsu Campaign, but were quickly heralded as the "Seven Battles, Seven Victories" in Communist propaganda. Already well-respected due to his success with the New 4th Army, Su's "seven victories" in the face of great odds made him a legend.

Mao now believed his generals had won him an opportunity to strike back. On July 19, he revisited earlier themes for a counteroffensive.[19] With Su tying down Tang in Jiangsu and Liu Zhi's forces still in pursuit of Wang and Li, Mao wanted the SHSH and Shandong Field Armies to attack the center and drive a wedge between these two forces. Chen Yi immediately agreed and massed his field army in south Shandong. By doing so, he exposed the Ji'nan-Jiaodong railroad to the northern pincer of Xue's offensive – a sacrifice Chen was apparently willing to make. However, even as he prepared for the attack, changes in the strategic situation in Jiangsu and Anhui rendered the entire plan impractical.

At the end of July, Liu Zhi ordered the 5th Corps, an elite unit under Qiu Qingquan, to attack the Huainan Military Sub-District of the Central China Military District. Situated in central Anhui, the sub-district was in a key strategic location because it threatened both the provincial capital of Bengbu and the Tianjin-Pukou railroad. It was also highly vulnerable because the railroad separated it from the rest of the Central China Military District. Zhou Junming commanded both the Huainan Military Sub-District and its forces, the 2nd Division and the 1st Brigade – recently arrived after the Central Plains breakout. Realizing he could not defeat Qiu, Zhou withdrew to Huaian, the headquarters of the Central China Military District. To make matters worse, despite his tactical successes, Su was being slowly driven from his Yangtze River defense line. On August 3, Haian, the keystone of Su's defense line, fell, forcing him to withdraw the Central China Field Army to central Jiangsu.

The abandonment of the Huainan Military Sub-District and the Yangtze River defense line meant that Su's earlier arguments against conducting operations in Anhui were now null. Chen Yi thus proposed that Su support the Shandong Field Army's attack against Xuzhou by severing the Pukou-Bengbu section of the Tianjin-Pukou railroad. If implemented, this plan would have largely mirrored Mao's proposal in late June, suggesting that Chen was eager for a fight and had been disappointed by the cancellation of the larger offensive. However, Su instead advocated continuing the fight in central Jiangsu, which he clearly believed to be a critical region.[20] Like Chen, who may have longed to reclaim Anhui because of his past experience in the Three Years War and with the New 4th Army, Su also may have wanted to cling to those areas in Jiangsu he had fought so hard to seize during World War II. Su again reminded the Secretariat that the Central China Field Army was still incapable of severing the rail line and would be better employed in their current positions.[21] Mao agreed with Su, so much so in fact that he anticipated the imminent recapture of Nantong, a key city on the north bank of the Yangtze River and one of the strong points of Su's old Yangtze River defense line.[22] Although Chen was nominally in charge of both field armies, and could have pressed his point to Mao and the CMC, he acquiesced. It is evident from this and other exchanges that he either had little direct control over the operations of the Central China Military District or he had complete trust in Su. In light of their long and fruitful relationship, the latter was probably more likely. However, Chen did reflect later that his lack of control over Su during this phase had a detrimental effect on the chain of command and on implementing a unified strategy.[23]

Lacking a Central China Field Army supporting attack, Chen scaled back his own offensive. His objective now was simply to break up the Xuzhou Pacification Command's thrust towards Shandong, rather than recapture any territory. On July 27, the Shandong Field Army ambushed the Reorganized 69th Division[24] southeast of Xuzhou and inflicted heavy casualties. As the 69th Division withdrew, Chen boldly moved south, slipping through a gap in the GMD lines, to attack Sixian, an important road junction which, if captured, would have stalled Xue's attack. There, Chen encountered units from Li Zongren and Bai Chongxi's infamous Guangxi clique, a warlord element which joined Chiang Kaishek and the GMD in the 1920s. Guangxi units were highly regarded by the Communists due to their fierce reputation[25] and Mao expressed concern about engaging them on August 3. Instead, he proposed that the Shandong Field Army seek battle elsewhere, but by then the battle had already begun.[26] Mao's premonition proved well founded and, after a series of bloody assaults on the 172nd Division, the Communists withdrew in defeat on August 9. The withdrawl ended Chen's hopes for pursuing an offensive deeper into Anhui.

While the Shandong Field Army retreated into north Jiangsu and Shandong, Liu Bocheng launched the Longhai Campaign on August 10. For this operation, the Secretariat envisioned the SHSH Field Army making a feint towards north Anhui and east Henan to stall Liu Zhi's consolidation of the Central Plains and threaten Xue Yue's flank.[27] Liu Bocheng's plan of attack was first to seize the Kaifeng-Xuzhou portion of the Longhai Railroad and then ambush any GMD reinforcements sent to dislodge him. With GMD reserves in the region thus tapped, he then planned to move south and fulfill Mao's desire for a sustained attack against the enemy's rear areas. However, after less than two weeks of fighting, Liu was outmaneuvered by the GMD reinforcements he had hoped to ambush and was forced to withdraw.[28] Although the SHSH Field Army failed to attain most of its main objectives, the campaign had been successful in drawing forces away from both Jiangsu and the Central Plains.

Indeed, by the time the SHSH Field Army withdrew from the Longhai Railroad, Wang Zhen and Li Xiannian were both safe in Shaanxi. Liu's offensive may have very well been the critical factor, as Hu Zongnan was forced to suspend the pursuit to recapture the vital east-west railroad. The Longhai Campaign may also have assisted Su, as he waged the last of the so-called "Seven Battles, Seven Victories," by denying Tang Enbo further reinforcements. In frustration, Tang attempted to break through Su's central Jiangsu defense line with an amphibious assault across the Grand Canal. On August 25, the Central China Field Army repelled this last-ditch effort, forcing Tang to withdraw. Adding insult to injury, Su was able to move south and recover much of his original defense line along the north bank of the Yangtze River.

Although strategically inconclusive, with the exception of Su's victory, the CCP had generally fought the GMD to a standstill in this first round of the General Offensive. Despite the lack of headway, Chiang ordered his forces to renew the attack in east and central China in the end of August. This new assault represented a much more coordinated operation and threatened to flood the east China region with GMD troops. In the west, Liu Ruming's 4th Pacification District from Liu Zhi's Zhengzhou Pacification Command, were to capture northeast Henan and southwest Shandong. In the east, Xue's Xuzhou Pacification Command attacked along three routes. The main thrust would be delivered by Li Yannian, who was to attack across the Grand Canal from Xuzhou to seize Huaian and Huaiyang. Li's forces were divided into three portions. He commanded the element in the center that was to sever Su's main line of communication – the Lianyungang-Haian highway. On his left flank, Feng Zhian was to capture Taierzhuang in south Shandong to pressure the Shandong Field Army. On the right flank, Tang Enbo would attempt to pin down or force the Central China Field Army to retreat from the Yangtze River.

The first clash of this renewed offensive occurred on September 3 at Dingtao in southwest Shandong between Liu Ruming and Liu Bocheng. Employing his now standard ambush techniques, Liu Bocheng pounced on the 3rd Division, which had broken off from the main column, and in a five-day battle annihilated it. This defeat cost Liu Zhi his job[29] but it did not stop Liu Ruming's advance into Shandong. At this time, Li Yannian approached the west bank of the Grand Canal. Both Mao and Su wanted the Shandong Field Army to intercept the GMD before they reached the canal, fearing that Li would be unstoppable once his forces crossed. They believed that the Central China Field Army could win another victory against Tang Enbo before Su would have to move north to assist Chen.[30]

However, Chen and the Shandong Field Army desperately needed Su's reinforcements and could not defend south Shandong from Feng Zhian and Li Yannian at the same time. As mentioned before, Chen had already stripped his defenses overlooking the Ji'nan-Jiaodong railroad to launch his expedition into Anhui. The defeat at Sixian had also hobbled his main unit, the 8th Shandong Division. The bulk of his army was currently in north Jiangsu and only Ye Fei's 1st Column stood between Feng Zhian's army and the Shandong Military District headquarters at Linyi. Consequently, Chen refused to fight a battle west of the Grand Canal and risk being cut off from Shandong altogether. Instead, he massed his forces well east of the canal at Shuyang, which left only a single column from the Central China Field Army to defend its west bank. As feared, Li broke through these thin defenses on September 10 and threatened to advance all of the way to the coast, thereby cutting off the Central China Military District altogether.

Li's progress finally convinced Mao to abandon central Jiangsu and merge Su's forces with the Shandong Field Army.[31] This decision meant that Chen's army could now operate at full strength – the first time he had such a luxury since the "March on the North, Defense in the South" plan went into effect in September 1945. Mao's new strategic vision was for the entire weight of the Shandong and Central China Field Armies to encircle and annihilate Li's army after it crossed the Grand Canal. If they could win a decisive victory against Li, the Secretariat hoped this would force Feng Zhian to halt his drive in south Shandong.[32]

On September 13, Chen formed the Huaiyang Defense Task Force, a provisional force under Tan Zhenlin, the political commissar of the Central China Field Army. Tan's main task was to slow Li while Chen and Su concentrated their forces for a counterattack. The task force included almost the entirety of the Central China Military District forces in Anhui and north Jiangsu – the 9th Column, two brigades (including Pi Dingjun's 1st Brigade), and the 2nd Division. On September 19, Su met with Tan at his headquarters in Huaiyang and together they decided that the Huaiyang Defense Task Force and the Central China Field Army would link up in Lianshui. By that time, Su's army was already withdrawing north with Tang Enbo's forces in close pursuit. On September 23, the CMC officially recognized that the East China Military District would have command authority over both Shandong and Central China Field Armies – a situation which was evidently unclear in the original reorganization. Chen would serve as commander and Su as the deputy commander of this quasi-Army Group.[33]

After capturing Huaiyang on the heels of Tan Zhenlin's withdrawal, Li Yannian dispatched part of his forces south to link up with Tang. His main force captured Yuxing on the east bank of Hongze Lake before stopping to rest and reorganize in the beginning of October. In the meantime, Xue's northern pincer secured most of the Ji'nan-Jiaodong railroad by the end of August. In desperation, Ye Fei's 1st Column, the only significant portion of the Shandong Field Army actually in Shandong, attacked Taian in the beginning of October to draw the GMD forces away from the railroad. However, Feng Zhian's approach forced Ye to abandon the attack and he fell back to defend Linyi. By October 8, these defenses, which were based at Zaozhuang and Fengxian, collapsed and left the way to Linyi wide open. So far, the only impediment for the GMD had been Liu Ruming's failure to break through the SHSH Field Army in southwest Shandong.

Despite the potential for the bulk of his East China Military District to be completely surrounded in north Jiangsu, Chen continued to wait for Su and Tan to concentrate their forces before he reinforced Ye Fei. Despite Li's earlier decision to pause at Yuxing, he still managed to beat the Central China Field Army to Lianshui. Li's 74th Division launched a ferocious attack on the city beginning on October 19. On the first day of the attack the city actually changed hands twice, with the Communists regaining the upper hand by nightfall. Nonetheless, fighting for the town continued unabated until October 26 when the GMD, battered and bloodied, broke off the attack to rest and reorganize. During the battle, Mao grew concerned that Li would break through and warned Chen against "forgetting Shandong for the sake of Jiangsu."[34] However, since Li's main force, the elite 7th Corps, remained uncommitted in Suqian, Chen had to remain in place and was unable to assist either Tan or Ye. Chen also still hoped to fight a large battle in the Huaihai region[35] – the battle that he had wanted since June. Mao grudgingly agreed, primarily because he, like Chen, still wanted the SHSH, Shandong, and Central China Field Armies to conduct a major, joint campaign in the Central Plains in the coming months.[36]

For Chen, the fall of 1946 was extremely frustrating as the conditions for a perfect battle continued to elude him and the latest round of the maneuvers continued to work against him. Feng Zhian renewed his assault in Shandong on October 27 and, a week later, Tang Enbo reinforced him with two additional divisions. Faced with this new threat, Chen finally returned to Linyi with his elite 8th Shandong Division. However, they could not stem the tide against Tang's reinforcements, which featured armored units. In Jiangsu, Su's army had finally arrived and established a defense line anchored on Yancheng, while Tan continued to hold Lianshui against Li. However, with Chen's forces faltering in front of Linyi, Mao ordered Su to seek battle in north Jiangsu to alleviate GMD pressure on Shandong.[37]

Further west, Mao also ordered Liu Bocheng in the beginning of November, to support the efforts in East China by engaging the Zhengzhou Pacification Command and preventing them from reinforcing the Xuzhou Pacification Command. This would first involve an attack into southwest Shandong to tie down forces there and then an immediate attack west into Henan.[38] By now, the SHSH Field Army had forged the reputation of being the most successful unit in the Communist Army – so much so that many GMD units avoided combat with Liu's force. Instead, they were content with simply keeping the SHSH Field Army separate from the East China Military District. In light of their reluctance, Liu planned to draw out GMD forces by attacking Huaxian near Kaifeng on November 19. During the attack, he eliminated a few regular brigades and so-called Peace Preservation units, paramilitary militias established by the GMD to maintain their control over pacified regions. With the GMD defenses on the Longhai Railroad unraveling Wang Zhonglian's Reorganized 26th Corps and Wang Jingjiu's 27th Corps, both elite units with American equipment and training, launched an attack on Liu. These two men and their units became known by the Communists as the "two Wangs." However, the "two Wangs" soon found themselves in a cat-and-mouse chase as Liu withdrew, having accomplished his mission of pulling forces away from the offensive in Shandong.

This so-called Huaxian Campaign finally gave Chen and Su the opportunity they had been looking for to engage Xue Yue on somewhat equal grounds. Mao now allowed Chen to fight the battle he had been seeking since the beginning of the General Offensive. However, he stipulated that if a decisive victory could not be achieved quickly the entire army should immediately withdraw to Shandong.[39]

When the GMD resumed their three-pronged attack in Shandong and Jiangsu, the Communists combined their forces to isolate and destroy Li's forces in the center. The North Jiangsu Campaign, as it became known, saw the combined strength of the Shandong and Central China Field Armies falling upon the 69th Division. After six days of almost non-stop fighting, Chen and Su annihilated the division and effectively ended the threat to Shuyang. However, in the meantime, Li and Tang captured Lianshui and Yancheng, which in effect turned the Communists' flank. After congratulating Chen and Su on their victory, Mao ordered them to focus on defending south Shandong and leave the task of retaking Jiangsu for a later date.[40]

As 1946 closed, the fight for Jiangsu and Anhui was all but over, with the GMD battered but holding the advantage. Despite Communist tactical victories, Chiang's forces had succeeded on a strategic level by eliminating both the Central Plains and the Central China Military Districts. Liu Ruming's march through southwest Shandong had been costly due to SHSH Field Army harassment, but by the end of the year he was on the verge of linking hands with Wang Yaowu's 2nd Pacification District at Ji'nan, and Feng Zhian's 3rd Pacification District in Zaozhuang. Additionally, the GMD controlled most of the Ji'nan-Jiaodong railroad and Qingdao. With their victory at Lianshui and Yancheng, Li Yannian and Tang Enbo had joined forces in north Jiangsu, thus sealing off the southern front. This left the GMD on the verge of surrounding and isolating Chen's entire East China Military District.

Like the Central Plains Military District only months before, the East China Military District now appeared to be caught in a trap. The Communists had inflicted heavy casualties on their adversaries and stalled the advance at key junctures, but these were not enough to stop the overall momentum of the General Offensive. The fact that both East China field armies had survived and that the Communist strength was at least now concentrated in one area was a minor but important consideration. Nonetheless, the loss of the large and prosperous liberated area in Jiangsu was a steep price for the CCP to pay. Having captured key territory in Anhui, Jiangsu, and Shandong in 1946, Chiang could now focus on securing Shandong and winning a decisive battle against Chen and Su in 1947.

The General Offensive in north and northeast China

As the GMD gained the upper hand south of the Yellow River, the north and west perimeter of the north China Liberated Areas also saw its share of combat. Originally assuming that Chiang's General Offensive would extend to this region, Nie Rongzhen and He Long had intended to fight a series of defensive battles before launching counterattacks. Unlike the revolving debate in northeast China, the Secretariat and the generals in northwest China all agreed that holding the large cities and railroads was critical for victory because of geography, demographics, and the general lack of arable land. Called the "Four Cities, Three Railroad" strategy, the main targets were the cities of Datong, Taiyuan, Baoding, and Shijiazhuang and the Datong-Puzhou, Zhengzhou-Taiyuan, and Beiping-Hankou railroads.[41]

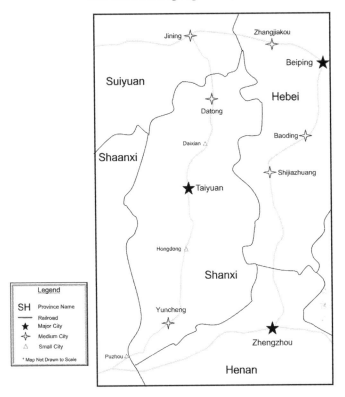

Figure 3.2 1945–46: Communist counterattack in the west.

The focus on capturing cities can be seen in Nie's preparations to increase the acquisition of explosives and his institution of training programs focused on urban warfare.[42] The Communists also saw control of the railroads as the main method to keep the three armies of Yan Xishan, Fu Zuoyi, and Hu Zongnan separate.

In early June, Mao and the CMC decided that there would not be a General Offensive component in Shanxi, and thus ordered He Long's Shanxi-Suiyuan Field Army to attack the Datong-Taiyuan railroad. This would materialize into the North Shanxi Campaign, in which He would strike at weakly defended points on the railroad and menace Yan Xishan's forces. However, one of He's most important planning considerations was to not attract the attention of Fu Zuoyi, whose 12th War Zone in north Hebei and Suiyuan could decisively tip the balance of power in the GMD's favor.[43] He's campaign would also support Li Xiannian's Central Plains breakout. Although Mao would later change his mind regarding the East China Military District's counteroffensive, the plan for an attack in Shanxi went forward unchanged.[44]

He Long formed the North Shanxi Field Army under Suiyuan-Shanxi Military District deputy commander Zhou Shidi specifically for this operation. The North Shanxi Field Army made quick work of the garrisons on the Datong-Taiyuan railroad, but attrition and the pace of their operations soon required reinforcements.

In a decision that would have serious consequences later, He transferred troops previously allocated for blocking Fu Zuoyi to sustain the offensive.[45] Luckily for the Communists, for the time being Fu did not take advantage of He's thin lines. Yan, on the other hand, was also committed to a major offensive in south Shanxi and could not respond to Zhou's attacks. Unable to reinforce his northern flank or repulse the North Shanxi Field Army, Yan struck a defensive stance by contracting his lines around the cities of Taiyuan and Daixian by the end of June. Zhou immediately pursued Yan's forces, encircling Daixian and making preparations to capture it by the end of July.

Yan was willing to withstand the North Shanxi Field Army's siege of Daixian because his priority was to complete a link up with Hu Zongnan in south Shanxi. Fortunately for the Communists, Chen Geng's 4th Column,[46] which was part of the SHSH Military District left behind to guard southern Shanxi, stood between Hu and Yan's armies. This area was strategically vital because it was the only link between Yan'an and the rest of the north China Liberated Areas. On July 11, Hu and Yan began their attack on the 4th Column. Despite winning a tactical victory at Wenxi, Chen could not stop either army. On August 6, Mao ordered Chen to disengage and prepare for a delaying action at Hongdong – the approximate midway point between Yuncheng and Taiyuan.[47]

With Chen tying down the bulk of Yan's army in south Shanxi, the North Shanxi Field Army prepared for an assault on Daixian. At this time, Mao wanted to increase the scope of the campaign by ordering Nie's 1st Field Army to attack the Beiping-Hankou railroad in central Hebei.[48] However, Nie disagreed with this plan because it would separate him from the Shanxi-Suiyuan Military District, making them weak in two places instead of strong in one. Alternately, Nie proposed that the Communists attack Datong to complement He's attack on Daixian. Afterwards, both armies could move south together and carry out Mao's plan to sever the Beiping-Hankou railroad.[49] Mao had originally opposed attacking Datong out of fear that it would invite Fu's intervention,[50] but Zhou and Geng's success had convinced Mao that it was now feasible. At first, he believed that He could seize the city with his own forces alone, but with the North Shanxi Field Army spread out in east Suiyuan and still besieging Daixian, it was clear Nie's forces would be required. In mid-July, Mao and the Secretariat approved this new campaign.[51]

On July 27, He Long repelled a GMD attempt to lift the siege of Daixian. Free from interference, he turned his focus on the town itself three days later. However, the bloody repulse of three large-scale frontal attacks forced He Long to call an end to the campaign by mid-August. This exposed the Communists' lack of experience in reducing fortifications – a mistake that Nie did not plan to repeat at Datong. Starting on the same day as He's attack, Nie's 1st Field Army encircled the city in a five-day operation, but failed to catch the garrison before it withdrew to its defenses. After hard fighting, the Communists penetrated the suburbs and began tightening the ring around Datong. Patiently drawing his units closer, Nie took almost a full month to reach the city walls. During this time, he deployed his artillery in siege positions and ordered sapping trenches created to reduce the open ground between his lines and the city walls. Despite these preparations, he still made little progress.

Although the Communists had not broken through, the situation in Datong grew increasingly desperate. Yet despite this, Yan did not march north to relieve the garrison and instead was preparing to renew his attacks on Chen Geng. Even if he had sent forces north, the North Shanxi Field Army guarded the way to Datong. Fu Zuoyi had refused to intervene, but sensing a crisis, Chiang personally intervened and granted Fu jurisdiction over Datong.[52] Now responsible for the city, Fu sent out a relief force in early September. Astutely assuming that Nie would attempt to ambush him, Fu attacked the 1st Field Army's headquarters at Jining instead of proceeding directly to Datong. Mao saw this as an opportunity to destroy the GMD army in the field,[53] but Fu moved too quickly for the Communists to react. Jining fell on September 13, forcing Nie to lift the siege before Fu trapped the 1st Field Army outside of Datong.

After securing Datong, Fu did not pursue Nie. Instead, he turned east towards Zhangjiakou. In Hebei, the Communists had also suffered a series of setbacks since the beginning of the General Offensive, including the loss of Chengde at the end of August. This not only severed a critical link to northeast China, but it also freed up Sun Lianzhong's 11th War Zone to conduct operations in west Hebei and Shanxi. At the time, Nie had overestimated the problems the GMD would face in Hebei and had transferred the 1st Column from Rehe to assist in the siege of Datong. This miscalculation meant that Communist forces in Zhangjiakou – the so-called strategic center of the north China Liberated Area – were in danger of being surrounded and annihilated. In telegrams to the Secretariat, Nie advocated abandoning the city.[54] The Communist high command agreed to this proposal[55] and, in effect, conceded their last physical link to Lin Biao's forces in northeast China.

To try to delay the enemy long enough to evacuate Zhangjiakou, Nie ordered Xiao Ke to employ local SCH Military District units to slow the GMD advance. Assuming that Fu would consolidate his gains in Datong and northern Shanxi, Xiao placed most of his army east of Zhangjiakou to guard against Sun Lianzhong's approach. Nie also positioned a smaller element along the Beiping-Hankou railroad under 3rd Column commander Yang Chengwu to block enemy reinforcements from Wuhan and to possibly draw Fu in that direction. This deployment left Zhangjiakou's western flank virtually undefended. However, Nie's gamble worked because Fu did not begin a determined drive on Zhangjiakou until the beginning of October. By then, Xiao had held off Sun's 34th Army Group long enough for the Communists to evacuate the city. Although he avoided catastrophe, Nie had suffered a serious defeat. He had lost his hold on east Hebei and was unable to destroy or inflict heavy casualties on any GMD unit. Yang Chengwu did score a minor success by severing the Beiping-Hankou railway, but this did not make up for the fact that the GMD had captured another piece of the north China Liberated Areas.

The situation was not any better further west as Chen Geng and He Long braced for a major attack from Hu Zongnan and Yan Xishan, who had finally joined forces in the late summer. The threat of Yan'an being cut off and overrun was now a reality and the CMC began preparations for its defense.[56] The GMD recognized their success and began premature celebrations. Fu and Sun were promoted and received independent commands – the Zhangyuan and Baoding Pacification Commands respectively. Chiang also used the victory to convene the National Assembly and draft a new constitution. He also considered launching an offensive against Yang Chengwu on the Beiping-Hankou railroad in an effort to win another big victory before the Assembly convened. However, Chiang's regional commander in Beiping, Li Zongren, talked him out of it on grounds that it would only overextend their forces and make them vulnerable.[57] As a result, Chiang agreed to allow Fu and Sun to rest their forces and instead looked to northeast China for his next campaign.

In the months after the battle of Siping, the Manchurian battlefield had been relatively quiet. Part of the reason for this was that Du had ignored the NDUA in favor of conducting campaigns in Hebei in order to consolidate his lines of communications. In August, Du's elite units, the 13th and 53rd Corps, attacked Communist forces monitoring the Beiping-Shenyang railway. It was at precisely this time that Chengde fell and Xiao Ke's 2nd Army was forced west to defend Zhangjiakou. This left Cheng Zihua's HRL Military Sub-District cut off from the rest of the SCH Military District. To reflect the new reality and improve command and control, Nie reassigned Cheng to Lin Biao and the NDUA.

On July 7, the Northeast Bureau adopted a resolution by Chen Yun that laid out a plan for a protracted struggle against an enemy who would only grow stronger with time.[58] This plan rejected pitched battles with the GMD and instead called on the NDUA to conduct political work. This would mostly take the form of bandit suppression, restoration of law and order, training the army, and raising more troops. However, this strategy assumed that Nie's SCH Military District would be able to maintain a land bridge to northeast China. When the GMD severed that link in the fall, Du moved his forces back to Manchuria in October to eliminate the Liaodong Military Sub-District in east Liaoning. Recognizing the danger, the Northeast Bureau ordered the Liaodong Military Sub-District to withdraw. They dispatched Chen Yun to assist in the process.[59]

However, Mao wanted the NPUA to inflict casualties on Du's forces in south Manchuria and launch a large-scale counterattack sometime during the winter. He based his plan on the assumption that Chiang's General Offensive was running out of momentum and that a turning point was imminent.[60] Complying with these orders, Lin stopped the withdrawal and instead ordered Xiao Hua, political commissar of the Liaodong Military Subdistrict to seek an opportunity to engage Du. This came to fruition on November 2 when Xiao's forces destroyed the 25th Division. Viewing this as the opportunity he had been waiting for, Mao proposed that Lin commit his troops in Heilongjiang to the fight.[61] However, the cold weather and exhausting marches had drained the strength of the Communist forces in Manchuria. On November 7, for instance, the 4th Division reported that their forces were combat-ineffective with only 60 percent of its draught animals left and its soldiers completely exhausted.[62]

The Northeast Bureau also realized that committing troops prematurely would be disastrous. For instance, Gao Gang, third political commissar of the NPUA, opposed fighting in west Liaoning because he believed the GMD's plan was for the Communists to overextend themselves to the point where they could be destroyed piecemeal.[63] Lin thus decided against expanding the campaign and, at the end of November, ordered Xiao to destroy the railroad between Changchun and Siping and withdraw east.[64] By the end of the year, Xiao had safely retreated to Linjiang and the Changbai Mountains on the Yalu River. Although they were in a superior defensive position, the Liaodong Military Sub-District could no longer threaten GMD forces in the lowlands of the Manchurian plain. As a result, Du had gained control of the railroads as well as unfettered access to the ports of the Liaoning peninsula, almost by default.

The success of Du's offensive in southern Manchuria brought an end to GMD operations in 1946. This also marked the end of Chiang's General Offensive, as Mao had predicted. However, unlike Mao's forecast, the Communists were in no position to strike back. In fact, they faced the very situation that they would have faced had they accepted Chiang's ultimatum – namely, the division and isolation of the north China Liberated Areas. For this reason, the General Offensive had largely been a political and strategic success for Nanjing. The elimination of the Central Plains and Central China Military Districts, as well as the Liaodong and the HRL Military Sub-Districts were significant victories. The only real blemish was the survival of the Communist field armies. While relatively minor at the time, this would become increasingly important as the war went on. Despite the disappointment of losing the territory they had fought so hard for during World War II, the Communist armies were gaining valuable experience and confidence. Soon, this would translate into the ability to meet their adversaries on an equal footing.

The fateful decision: the GMD Strong Point Strategy in Shandong

By the beginning of 1947, the Communists had lost ground on all fronts. This was due in part to their choice to employ an interior line defense strategy, but one should not overlook the fact that at some critical points the GMD had outmaneuvered and outfought them. Zhou Enlai estimated that in 1946, Chiang had attacked the Liberated Areas with 218 divisions or 90 percent of his total strength, and had captured 179,000 square kilometers and 165 cities.[65] In return, the CCP claimed the annihilation of 40 to 50 GMD brigades. Although Zhou believed that with their current tactics they could destroy another 40 to 60 brigades in another six months to a year, he admitted that without a change in the strategic situation, this period would be "tense."[66] Zhu De offered a more optimistic appraisal, viewing the destruction of another 45 brigades as a critical step in stopping the GMD offensive and recovering their territory.[67]

Mao agreed with these assessments and stood firmly by the concept of a strategic defense based on interior lines. He assessed that the GMD had no appreciable reserve and their overextension would soon become fatal.[68] Mao stated this belief as early as October 1946, just before the fall of Zhangjiakou.[69] Despite setbacks,

Mao continued to push his units to seek battle, as seen in his reversal of the Northeast Bureau's decision regarding the abandonment of the Liaodong Military Sub-District. Peng Dehuai supported Mao and stated that the time for a strategic counterattack would soon be at hand. From November 1946 to January 1947, he sent a number of telegrams to the various military districts, focusing on production, logistics, and planning in anticipation of this counterattack.[70]

While the Communists mulled over their next move, Chiang began preparations to finish the war. Thinking that he had secured Shanxi, Suiyuan, Chahar, Anhui, Rehe, and the Central Plains, as well as a majority of Jiangsu, Hebei, and Manchuria, Chiang believed the conclusion of the long civil war was within his grasp. In light of the accomplishments of the General Offensive, it was not unrealistic to believe that one or two more GMD victories could have achieved this goal. For the next phase, Chiang transferred the bulk of his elite forces into two theaters, Shandong and Shaanxi. The concept of this so-called Strong Point Offensive was two large-scale pincer maneuvers that would first destroy the Communists on the east and west flanks, followed by a converging attack on the center. The attack in the east would be a continuation of Li Yannian, Tang Enbo, and Feng Zhian's attacks against the East China Military District which had begun in June with the General Offensive. The western pincer was aimed at capturing Yan'an and destroying the CCP's political apparatus. The intent appeared to be focused on winning a political victory in the west and a military one in the east. If it had been successful, this so-called Strong Point Offensive may very well have ended the war in 1947. In fact, it would come tantalizingly close to succeeding, except for its one fatal flaw – overextension. Almost serendipitous in the way it played into Mao and Peng's counterstrategy of attacking areas Chiang believed were safe, the Strong Point Offensive would ultimately be defeated because of the assumptions Chiang had made about the other theaters.

The heaviest campaigning would be in Shandong, where three Communist field armies (two being equal to a European-style army and one roughly equal to a corps) faced the combined forces of two GMD Pacification Commands (each containing one or more Army Groups) – a ratio of nearly three to one in favor of the GMD. Not only were the Communists outnumbered, they were also geographically separated. While the Shandong and Central China Field Armies had joined by December 1946, the SHSH Field Army was in southwest Shandong on the other side of the GMD army. The Shandong Field Army headquarters at Linyi was also still under threat from multiple directions and Chen did not appear to be rushing to reinforce it. Neither did he seem intent on regaining contact with Liu Bocheng. Instead, Chen and Su planned to engage Li Yannian in another battle in north Jiangsu, with their priorities on seizing the initiative and not surrendering any more Communist territory.

The East China Military District plan was to destroy the 74th Division near Shuyang. Although Mao was concerned about Shandong, he acquiesced to Chen and Su by allowing them to continue the fight in Jiangsu.[71] However, on December 22, Zhang Yunyi, deputy commander of the Shandong Field Army, and his chief of staff, Chen Shiju, made a desperate request to the CMC for reinforcements at Linyi. This breach of the chain of command resulted in Zhang and Chen Shiju receiving a serious rebuke from an irate Chen Yi.[72] However, this incident and the fact that the 74th Division would remain in place for the time being finally convinced Chen to abandon his obsession with a counterattack in Jiangsu and Anhui. With Mao's consent, he decided on December 24 to move the main strength of the Shandong Field Army to south Shandong.[73] Mao further proposed that the Central China Field Army should also abandon north Jiangsu if they could help effect a decisive victory in Shandong.[74]

In south Shandong, Ma Liwu's Reorganized 26th Division, the "Fast" Column of armor that had been unstoppable in the previous months, led the assault toward Linyi. The Secretariat specifically earmarked this unit for destruction, no matter the cost. Due to poor GMD cooperation and control, such an opportunity presented itself in early January. The division was dangerously overextended and isolated thanks to the fact that its supporting units, the 11th and 69th Divisions, had been driven away during early battles. To make matters worse, Xue Yue had not allowed Ma to withdraw or shorten his lines. Gathering units from both field armies, Chen attacked the Reorganized 26th Division with overwhelming force. On January 2, after surrounding and isolating Ma's division, the attack commenced. After two days of intense fighting that often involved the flesh of Communist soldiers cast against the steel of GMD tanks, weight of numbers finally overran the "Fast" Column. Having captured many armored vehicles during the fighting, the East China Military District would be one of the first Communist elements to field an armored unit.

Believing this may have been a decisive battle, Mao proposed that Chen attack Fengxian, Zaozhuang, Taierzhuang, Lincheng, and Chaozhuang to virtually drive the GMD from south Shandong. In order to generate sufficient combat power, Mao again proposed abandoning north Jiangsu.[75] In this case, Chen was less ambitious than Mao and instead attacked only Fengxian and Zaozhuang, in what was called the South Shandong Campaign. While Mao approved of the plan, he again emphasized the relative unimportance of holding north Jiangsu.[76] This point of contention was becoming more pronounced and it marked a considerable difference of opinion. The Secretariat was fully convinced that mobile warfare was the only viable strategy, but Chen and Su continued to cling to the hope that they could not only defend their territory but reclaim lost portions in the near future. By January 20, Chen used forces on hand to capture his two objectives and destroy their garrisons. Afterwards, he withdrew his army to rest and reorganize.

While Chen waged the South Shandong Campaign, Liu Bocheng launched his own campaign to tie down the Zhengzhou Pacification Command and prevent it from intervening in Shandong. In December, Liu engaged the 5th Corps to force Chiang to dispatch troops from south Shandong, but the GMD were not accommodating.[77] Consequently, Mao proposed that Liu seek battle further south and possibly recapture lost territory in the process.[78] Liu accepted this guidance and used it to plan the Juye-Jinxiang-Yutai (Jujinyu) Campaign. Beginning on December 22, the operation continued into late January as Liu's forces seized Liaocheng and Juye before stopping to await the inevitable GMD counterattack.

Liu Ruming led the first relief column, which included elements of the 88th Division and the 4th Peace Preservation Corps Column, as well as some of his own troops from southwest Shandong. Liu Ruming, learning nothing from the past year of fighting, rushed headlong into a Communist trap. Despite Liu Ruming's blunder, Liu Bocheng was able to surround and inflict heavy casualties only on the spearhead GMD units. By January 16, the "two Wangs" again intervened and forced Liu Bocheng to end the campaign. Having accomplished his primary task of diverting GMD troops from Shandong, Liu subsequently led the "two Wangs" on another fruitless chase through Henan.

After escaping the "two Wangs," Mao proposed that Liu double back and take advantage of territory the "two Wangs" had left exposed and undefended, especially around the Longhai railroad and the Central Plains. Mao also hoped that Liu could lure the "two Wangs" into the flat and open country of Henan where, aided by their familiarity with the terrain, the Communists could employ mobile warfare to destroy the GMD army.[79] Liu agreed to this plan and divided his army into two. The first part would fall under his direct command and he employed it against the Longhai railroad. Deng Xiaoping commanded the other part and his mission was to march south of the railroad and create a new base in the Central Plains. On January 24, the SHSH Field Army began its attack, forcing the "two Wangs" to separate and pursue Liu and Deng separately. However, the Communists would have to abandon their grand plan at the end of January when the Xuzhou Pacification Command resumed its offensive against Chen Yi. To prevent Wang Jingjiu from returning to Shandong, Liu recombined his army to begin a large-scale blocking action. In the end, he was only able to tie down one corps – the rest of Wang Jingjiu's army made it to Shandong unimpeded.

Between the end of the South Shandong Campaign and Xue's new offensive, Chen used the lull to restructure his army. He combined the Shandong and Central China Field Armies into the new East China Field Army. This new chain of command further streamlined and unified his ability to command units in the region. In addition, while previously it may have been practical to have separate commands in different theaters, there was no need to now, since Shandong was to be the East China Field Army's only battlefield. Although Chen remained in charge of both the East China Military District and the Field Army, the command structure for those two entities reflected their different priorities. While the military district consisted of former Shandong Military District and New 4th Army personnel, the Field Army consisted of Central China Military District personnel. This included Su Yu as deputy commander and Tan Zhenlin as deputy political commissar. Chen served as both commander and first political commisar of the army.

The new East China Field Army consisted of nine columns, which in turn were divided into three or more divisions each. This reorganization mirrored the trend of professionalization that was also occurring in the other Communist field armies. Strength varied among these units as the 1st, 2nd, 7th, 8th, and 12th Columns had 23,000 to 50,000 men, while the 3rd, 6th, 10th, and 11th Columns all had less than 20,000 men each. The formations also had different levels of experience, which one could discern from their lineage. The 1st and 4th Columns, for instance, went unchanged from their original forms as the 1st and 4th Columns of the Shandong Field Army. In some cases, units absorbed or merged with each other to bring them to full strength, like the 2nd Shandong Column and the 9th Central China Column, combining to become the new 2nd East China Column. The rest were either redesignated and augmented – such as the New 4th Army 7th Division expanding to become the 7th Column – or were built upon the remnants of standing units. All of the columns had been reinforced in some way, either with captured GMD troops or local/irregular units raised to a regular status. The Communists also had a policy of mixing old soldiers with new ones in order to both control the new troops and indoctrinate them. Meanwhile, the trend of GMD defections was increasing thanks to persuasive Communist political tactics, as well as better treatment and pay.

There would be precious little time for Chen's reorganization to go into effect as Xue Yue's forces attacked simultaneously from the north and south on January 31. In the south, Ou Zhen's Reorganized 19th Corps was augmented to a total strength of seven divisions while Li Xianzhou, deputy commander of the 2nd Pacification District, led nine divisions out of Ji'nan. At the same time, the Zhengzhou Pacification Command deployed to prevent the SHSH Field Army from coming to Chen's assistance. This combination of numbers and coordination marked the beginning of a new, dangerous period for Chen Yi's forces. Previously, he could count on ponderous, unimaginative GMD maneuvers and an ineffectual and often feuding high command that allowed subordinate units to lose contact with each other and become isolated. Now, it appeared as though the GMD was finally on the verge of conducting an effective, unified operation.

For instance, Su planned to first pin down Ou in the center and then mass on one of his units on the flank when GMD cohesion began to break down.[80] Unfortunately, the GMD did not offer such an opportunity and instead maintained close ranks and tight command and control. As a result, on February 4, the Secretariat ordered Chen to begin preparations to abandon Linyi.[81] Ou reached Linyi on February 12 and, after a three-day siege, the city fell. By that time, the Communists had already evacuated both their political and military apparatus. Spurred on by their victory, Chen Cheng, chief of staff of the GMD army, ordered Ou and Li to advance quickly and trap the Communists in the Yimeng Mountain district. Wang Yaowu, commander of the 2nd Pacification Zone, was concerned that the East China Field Army was preparing to ambush Li. This was exactly Su's plan after failing to stop Ou outside of Linyi. Despite Wang's protests, Chiang and Chen Cheng ordered the attack to continue.[82] By the middle of February, Li's army had reached Laiwu, east of Taian, and had indeed, as Wang feared, marched into an ambush.

After abandoning Linyi, Chen Yi secreted four columns to Laiwu, where they joined three columns he had previously positioned there. With seven columns, the East China Field Army could meet Li's army on an equal basis. On February 15, the Communists deployed for the attack, and the GMD forces reacted by shortening their lines. However, they did not respond quickly enough to prevent the East China Field Army columns from moving between Li's units. Five days later, Chen ordered a general attack, easily eviscerating Li's lines and cutting him off from Ji'nan. Wang lacked the forces to intervene anyway, which meant that the only potential relief was either in Xuzhou or from Ou Zhen, who was still mopping up around Linyi. The Communists, on the other hand, piled on reinforcements and exerted unrelenting pressure on Li's rapidly shrinking perimeter.

By February 23, the situation grew critical and Wang ordered Li to attempt an escape. During the breakout, Li was wounded and his army relapsed into chaos. By evening, Su had annihilated any remaining resistance. This stunning victory, called the Laiwu Campaign, not only immediately helped redress the Communists' numerical and strategic disadvantages, but also eliminated the bulk of Wang's 2nd Pacification District's forces in a single blow. Now, Ji'nan was virtually defenseless and there were no significant GMD forces in west or north Shandong. In the space of a week, the East China Field Army had completely reversed its situation.

The defeat shook the confidence of both the Xuzhou Pacification Command and Chiang in Nanjing. Although they had captured Linyi and forced Chen to abandon south Shandong, the destruction of the bulk of the Ji'nan garrison at Laiwu was a serious blow. Ou Zhen suspended his advance out of fear of also being surrounded and destroyed. Chiang responded to the disaster at Laiwu by eliminating the Zhengzhou and Xuzhou Pacification Commands. In their place, he created a single command – the Army General Headquarters at Xuzhou, under Gu Zhutong. Now, a single authority controlled the 24 reorganized divisions in Henan, Anhui, Jiangsu, and Shandong. To deal with Chen, Gu divided his units into three armies: the 1st Army on the right, under Tang Enbo (six divisions near Linyi), the 2nd Army on the left, under Wang Jingjiu (one regular corps and three reorganized divisions north of Jining), and the 3rd Army in the center, under Ou Zhen (five reorganized divisions near Tengxian).

The GMD reorganization took almost a month, giving Chen Yi an opportunity to rest his forces. After the Laiwu Campaign, Chen withdrew the East China Field Army to Zibo and relocated his headquarters to the quarries east of Zichuan. By seizing Zibo, he also severed the Jiaodong-Ji'nan railway, which the GMD had left undefended. By the end of March, Gu began a new offensive intent on recapturing Laiwu. On March 28, Su sent three columns in a feint towards Ji'nan in an attempt to force Tang Enbo to extend his left wing to intercept him. In the meantime, Su's main effort, consisting of five columns, was ready to cut off and destroy any forces Tang sent out. Unfortunately, the diversionary force was discovered and subjected to heavy air attack on April 3. This allowed Tang to ignore them and continue his march without creating gaps in his line. Su formed another three-column task force to attack the 72nd Division at Taian on April 22 in an effort to draw Tang in that direction. However, the assault failed to persuade Tang to intervene; instead, he continued to move forward while maintaining contact with Ou. While this allowed Su to destroy the 72nd Division and capture Taian four days later, the GMD offensive continued on its relentless path to push the Communists into the sea.

Unable to force the GMD to detach forces and break ranks, Chen and Su settled for blocking and delaying the advance. While a small force held the GMD at Mengyang for a week, Chen Shiju, whose three-column task force had just captured Taian, swung south to begin raiding the GMD rear areas. These actions momentarily stalled the attack and Su used this opportunity to try to again induce Tang into battle. In the end, reinforcements from Wang Jingjiu's 2nd Army forced Su to abandon the attempt. Faced with their failure to produce a large battle on their terms, Chen and Su proposed detaching two columns to reinforce Chen Shiju in south. However, Mao disagreed with the idea of breaking up the field army and instead instructed them to remain "patient" and seek battle in Laiwu or north of the Jiaodong-Ji'nan railroad.[83] On May 10, that opportunity finally presented itself as Tang ordered the Reorganized 25th and 74th Divisions to move east out of recently captured Mengyang towards Menglianggu.

Mao wanted the East China Field Army to attack immediately,[84] but Su recognized that the Reorganized 74th Division was an elite unit with advanced equipment and superior training. Its commander, Zhang Lingfu, was also well respected within the Communist ranks and had been responsible for many of the GMD victories in Shandong. Nevertheless, Su realized that this opportunity might not come again and ordered his forces to attack Zhang on May 13. Aware of the danger, Zhang stopped and tried to close ranks with the Reorganized 25th Division. They were only three miles away from each other when Su's forces completed the encirclement. By employing almost his full strength against the elite unit, Su reduced and then destroyed Zhang's force by May 16. True to their reputation, the Reorganized 74th Division had, by and large, fought to the death. Zhang himself was killed in battle[85] and the division suffered 15,000 casualties during the fighting. Only 5,000 soldiers surrendered and were later integrated into the Communists ranks. However, many of these returned to the GMD army at the first opportunity.[86] A further testament to Zhang's unit was the fact that the fight had also consumed most of the East China Field Army's supplies as well as exhausting many of its frontline units. For this reason, Chen and Su withdrew rather than risk prolonging the campaign by engaging the Reorganized 25th Division.

The victory at Menglianggu was an important Communist success. For the first time, a Communist field army had engaged an elite GMD unit and defeated it soundly, although they suffered heavy casualties and had to literally flood the battlefield with troops – as they had earlier against Ma Liwu's tanks. After the disaster, Gu Zhutong suspended the offensive immediately and the GMD again reorganized and reinforced the units in the region. This resulted in a two-month pause on the Shandong battlefield. Chiang's Strong Point Offensive in east China had won him significant territory in north Jiangsu and south Shandong, but at the cost of losing an army in Ji'nan, a regular division, and an elite reorganized division. Nonetheless, he had further separated the East China and SHSH Field Army, as well further reduced the north China Liberated Area. Despite Chiang's losses, the strategy of securing the eastern flank, either by trapping Chen's army in east Shandong or forcing it across the Yellow River into Hebei or northwest Shandong, also appeared to be working. However, perhaps even more significant was the growing strength of the East China Field Army and its newfound ability to engage and destroy Chiang's best units on the battlefield.

Ultimately, the success of the Strong Point Offensive was still in the balance. For the Communists, a single tactical defeat or a Pyrrhic victory might well mean the end of the East China Field Army. They were also running out of room to retreat, which would force them to either disperse or stand and fight under disadvantageous circumstances. Yet, on the other side, time did not necessarily favor the GMD either. Attrition and overextension was having its effect. Gu Zhutong's forces either had to destroy the East China Field Army outright or face the prospect of trying to keep it contained indefinitely. Consequently, the fate of the Shandong theater was yet to be decided. In the end, it would take events in other regions to finally tip the balance.

The fateful decision part two: the GMD Strong Point Strategy in Shaanxi

As Chiang's attack in east China began to corner the East China Field Army in Shandong, Hu Zongnan was promoted to command the new Xi'an Pacification Command and began the second component of the Strong Point Offensive in March. This component consisted of a straight-forward attack up the spine of Shaanxi

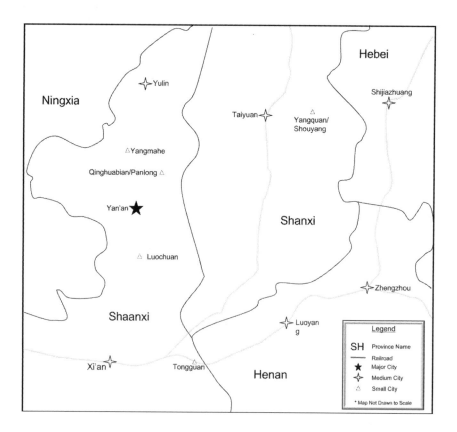

Figure 3.3 1947: The fall of Yan'an.

toward Yan'an. Hu intended to draw out He Long's Shanxi-Suiyuan Field Army and United Defense Army, which would likely respond to the threat by defending the capital. The attack would also serve the secondary purpose of allowing Fu Zuoyi and Yan Xishan to concentrate their forces on the SCH and SHSH Field Armies.[87] Politically, Chiang also hoped to win prestige by capturing the Communist capital and possibly detaining, or at least displacing, the CCP leadership.

The Secretariat and the CMC – mostly under the supervision of Peng Dehuai – had foreseen this eventuality and had begun planning the defense of Yan'an since October 1946. He Long's Shanxi-Suiyuan Field Army was slated to lead the defense. After the fall of Zhangjiakou, He reorganized and streamlined his army into three columns. The Shanxi-Suiyuan Field Army deputy commander, Zhang Zongxun, Wang Zhen (reassigned to the Shanxi-Suiyuan Military District not long after the Central Plains breakout), and Xu Guangda led the 1st, 2nd, and 3rd Columns, respectively. However, unlike the larger East China Field Army, these columns were equivalent to weak divisions and consisted of two full-strength brigades each.[88] The United Defense Army, currently under the command of Wang Shitai in the absence of its official commander, He Long, was also available to reinforce the Shanxi-Suiyuan Field Army. Although they had little combat power to offer, they had recently received unexpected reinforcements from He Yingduo, deputy commander of the GMD's Shaanxi Peace Preservation Corps, who defected with 2,100 troops. These were subsequently reorganized into the 6th Cavalry Division.[89]

In October, Peng ordered the Shanxi-Suiyuan Field Army's 1st Column to supplement the defenses of Yan'an while the 3rd Column went to Suiyuan to conduct a guerrilla warfare campaign against Fu.[90] In November, as it became clear that Hu was preparing to attack Shaanxi, Peng ordered Yang Dezhi's 1st Column to detach from the SCH Military District to join the Yan'an garrison. He also ordered Chen Geng's 4th Column to immediately begin delaying operations against Hu in south Shanxi and south Shaanxi. For this operation, Chen's 4th Column was reinforced with the Shanxi-Suiyuan 1st Column.[91] At the end of November, Mao ordered Chen to launch an attack in the Luliang District in south Shanxi to prevent the GMD from transferring forces from there into Shaanxi.[92] However, before the 4th Column could start the campaign, Hu crossed the Yellow River and began his march towards Yan'an. Peng subsequently took direct control of the 4th Column and ordered it to leave the SHSH Military District, its parent command, to pursue Hu. He also transferred Wang Zhen's Shanxi-Suiyuan 3rd Column to Chen's command, effectively promoting his force to the size of an army.

As a result of this reorganization, Hu now faced a significant Communist force. When he had started his offensive in March, Shaanxi had been devoid of enemy conventional units. However, the new forces Peng assembled were not in position to engage or slow his progress. As mentioned above, Chen's 4th Column was behind Hu's army and only the Shanxi-Suiyuan 1st and 3rd Columns, and the United Defense Army – approximately 25,000 troops – were between Hu and the capital. On the other hand, Nanjing employed three armies to converge on Yan'an: Ma Hongkui and Ma Bufang, or the "two Mas," in the west, Deng Yushan in the north, and Hu Zongnan from the south. Hu alone had 240,000 troops at his disposal and, due to his relationship with Chiang, his armies were at full strength with first-class equipment. Zhang Zongxun moved the 1st Column south to delay Hu, but he quickly suffered heavy casualties and retreated without appreciably delaying Hu's advance. By March 10, GMD forces captured Luochuan, less than a hundred kilometers south of Yan'an.

As the threat to Yan'an grew more pressing, the Communist high command underwent a slight reorganization. Peng Dehuai took personal command of Yan'an's defense, which was more practical than relying on Chen Geng, who was still in south Shaanxi and in no position to coordinate the defenses. Zhou Enlai replaced Peng as CMC chief-of-staff while Ren Bishi took over Zhou's duties of handling the Secretariat's day-to-day functions. On March 16, the Peng assumed command of the newly formed Northwest Field Army[93] which consisted of the 1st and 3rd Columns of the Shanxi-Suiyuan Field Army and the United Defense Army. At that time, the 1st Column was in the midst of self-criticism for their earlier defeat, but Peng ordered them to return to the fight and buy him more time to organize the defense.

Assessing that their forces were insufficient to stop Hu, the CMC made the fateful decision to abandon Yan'an. Peng's task thus changed from defense to delay – he would engage Hu long enough for Mao and the rest of political apparatus to escape.[94] As per this new directive, the 4th Column was to abandon its attempts to move to Yan'an and instead they were to support the rearguard action by attacking Hu's rear areas in the vicinity of the Tongguan-Luoyang railroad. Hu's army reached the outskirts of Yan'an on March 13, but Mao did not personally evacuate the city until three days later when GMD forces were already within artillery range of the airfield. Giving orders to "sweep the house clean but leave the furniture undamaged,"[95] Mao boarded a plane and left the capital he had founded in the darkest days of the revolution. The city quietly fell the next day.

The capture of Yan'an was a highly symbolic victory for the GMD. Even for the Communists, who had professed many times that retaining cities was not important, it was a significant psychological blow. However, there would be no time to dwell on this as Hu continued his advance north. Conscious of this pursuit, the Secretariat decided to split into two parts. Mao, Zhou, and Ren Bishi would remain in northern Shaanxi under the protection of Peng's army while Liu Shaoqi, Zhu De, and most of the Central Committee were to proceed to Nie's SCH Military District to establish the Work Committee. The idea was for Mao to serve as a moving target, a decoy of sorts, which would attract GMD troops and attention, while Liu and Zhu resettled under Nie's protection to administer the Liberated Areas and continue the day-to-day political and military work of the CCP. However, despite the fact that he would be playing the bait, Mao asserted that he and Zhou would maintain control over the CMC and strategy.

In the meantime, Peng sought to slow Hu's relentless pursuit. His plan was to withdraw the bulk of his forces northeast to Qinghuabian, while baiting Hu with a smaller force in the northwest. Hu fell for the ruse, sending two divisions northwest towards Ansai, but dispatching only the 31st Brigade to Qinghuabian. Peng attacked this unit twice, destroying one of its regiments and capturing the brigade commander on March 25. Hu responded by sending two reorganized corps (11 brigades in total) to circumvent Qinghuabian and seize the ferry sites on the Yellow River, thus cutting off the Northwest Field Army's escape route east. Despite the danger, Mao believed that Chen Geng's operations in south Shaanxi would soon force Hu to stop on the account of lack of supplies and for fear of being cut off from his base.[96] For this reason, Mao wanted Peng to attack Hu immediately. Peng disagreed, citing his numerical inferiority, and argued that it would be better to wait until Chen's attacks actually began to have an effect.[97] Mao was persuaded by Peng's counterpoints and conceded.

However, Mao would not have to wait long. Peng found his opportunity on April 14 when he ambushed and destroyed the 135th Brigade at Yangmahe. Following up his success, over the next three weeks he conducted a series of highly-successful operations, ending with the destruction of the 167th Brigade at Panlong. Capitalizing on Hu's strung out forces, their overconfidence, and the fact that they had not been able to fortify any of their newly-won ground, Peng stole the initiative and stopped the GMD offensive in its tracks. After these defeats, Hu shortened his lines to make his individual units more difficult to attack. Peng responded by withdrawing his forces to rest, reorganize, and resupply off captured GMD materiel. The latter consideration was especially important because the Northwest Field Army was the worst equipped force in the Communist order of battle due to their geographic isolation. They would, in fact, remain so during the course of the entire war.

In the space of a month and a half, Peng had secured the survival of his army, inflicted casualties on the GMD, and was no longer fighting for his life. Much as Chen Yi and Su Yu had done in Shandong, the Communists had given up territory – in this case the capital – but retained their combat power. Although the battles in this sector were small in scale and the GMD casualties relatively light, the mere survival of the Northwest Field Army meant that Shaanxi would not be a quiet sector – the goal which Chiang had hoped for when he instituted the Strong Point Offensive. Much like Gu Zhutong's forces in Shandong, Hu would have to continue the fight and would probably require more reinforcements – troops which Chiang was increasingly finding harder to come by.

Nonetheless, the fall of Yan'an produced many question marks both for international observers and even within the CCP itself. Mao did his best to answer these questions by explaining away the loss as a necessary step in the larger strategic picture. He also went so far as to say that it was a vindication of their policy of drawing out the GMD armies and forcing them to overextend their forces.[98] He compared the situation to a mushroom to illustrate the idea that the GMD offensive was continually expanding while its base of support remained narrow.[99] The climate and terrain of Shaanxi also contributed to this strategy because of how they exacerbated attrition and complicated logistics. In the middle of April, Mao stated that Peng's mission was to "keep the enemy on the run," "tire him out completely, reduce his food supplies and then look for an opportunity to destroy him." For this reason, Mao instructed the Northwest Field Army to avoid the GMD base at Yulin and the roads between Yan'an and Xi'an. He argued that attacking these would only force Hu to shorten his lines of communication, a move which, in turn, would alleviate his logistical problems.[100]

By the summer of 1947, it was clear that the Communists had weathered the worst of the GMD offensive in Shaanxi and Shandong. However, survival had not come without losses to both their prestige and position in North China. Chiang had gambled that he could tip the balance by either winning a decisive battle or achieving large-scale territorial gains. However, his armies had failed to attain the former and achieving the latter had resulted in a whole new set of problems. In the end, the Strong Point Offensive had created stalemate, not victory. As a result, it would be operations in the sectors that Chiang had already deemed safe – Manchuria and north China – that would ultimately determine how successful the strategy really was. These operations would also decide which side would dictate the next phase of the war.

Combating the Strong Point offensive

By the end of 1946, Du Yuming had secured most of south Manchuria, forcing the Communist administration in that area, the Liaodong Military Sub-District, to retreat to Linjiang on the border with Korea. Fearing Linjiang's vulnerability, elements within Liaodong and the Northeast Bureau considered abandoning the sub-district altogether. Chen Yun, political commissar of the Liaodong Military Sub-District and secretary of the Liaodong Bureau, and Xiao Jingguang, commander of the Liaodong Military Sub-District, both disagreed. They believed that maintaining a presence in Linjiang would disrupt Du's strategy, which was to "first secure the south then attack the north." Chen Yun also envisioned the forces at Linjiang coordinating with Lin's main force in Harbin for a two-pronged attack on Du's army.[101] Lin wholeheartedly agreed with this idea and, with minor modifications, adopted it as his own as the "one point, two front" strategy.[102] Furthermore, Lin expanded the concept by envisioning it evolving into a long-term strategy in which alternating attacks on either front would wear down Du's forces, prevent him from massing at any one point, and eventually shift the balance of power in the region.[103]

Lin put his new strategy into effect in early January by raiding GMD defenses south of the Songhua River. This was timed to assist Chen and Xiao at Linjiang, who were weathering another wave of attacks from Du's army. Eventually, the January raid would become the first of seven separate battles over the course of three months. Deemed the "Three Attacks Across the (Songhua) River, Four Defenses of Linjiang" or the "Three Attacks, Four Defenses" Campaign, it would demonstrate the devastating effectiveness of Lin's strategy.[104] On January 5, the NPUA marched across the frozen Songhua, braving frigid temperatures (negative 40 degrees Celsius) and icy winds. Lin employed almost his entire strength in north Manchuria: three columns (roughly equivalent to divisions), three independent divisions, and three artillery units (of undetermined strength, probably equivalent to regiments).

Sun Liren's Reorganized New 1st Corps, an elite unit which had played a prominent role in defeating the NDUA at Siping, manned the defenses south of

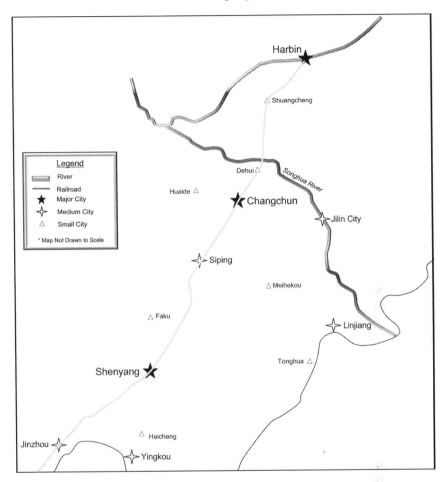

Figure 3.4 1946–47: The struggle for northeast China.

the river. They were not expecting an attack at the time, assuming that the brutal Manchurian winter would preclude any major offensive. Lin's three independent divisions delivered the main attack against the 38th Division at Qitashan while the 6th Column took up position to intercept the relief column. By January 8, the NDUA captured Qitashan and the surrounding area, which caused Sun to deploy forces from Jilin City. Despite the fact that ambushing a relief column was a well-known Communist tactic, the unsuspecting GMD forces marched straight into the jaws of the 6th Column. Although Sun's relief column escaped, albeit with heavy casualties, their defeat removed any immediate threat to Lin's offensive. The NDUA quickly spread out along the south bank and wiped out the Peace Preservation Corps units stationed there. This forced Du to suspend his assault on Linjiang before his entire Songhua River defense line unraveled. As Du's relief forces approached, Lin broke contact and withdrew on January 19.

During this process, the Communists left a path of devastation behind them, destroying bridges, fortifications, railroads, electrical lines, and boats.[105] They also looted large quantities of goods and supplies to refill their own dwindling stores. Surprisingly, aside from the brief skirmish in the beginning of the campaign, the fighting had been relatively light. The GMD estimated correctly that Lin had committed approximately 100,000 troops, but had only used 20,000 of them in actual combat. They also noted that Lin had intentionally avoided pitched battles.[106] Although battle casualties on both sides were roughly equal,[107] and the operation amounted to little more than a raid, the effect on morale for both sides was significant. The Communists had saved the Liaodong Military Sub-District for the time being, while the GMD's confidence in their northern defense network had been shaken.

Despite the embarrassing defeat of his Songhua River defenses, Du remained doggedly committed to his "secure the south first" strategy. In the beginning of February, he again attacked the Linjiang defenses but Xiao turned these back with a counterattack on February 5. Well-placed Communist ambushes and the harsh climate rendered Du's forces ineffective in less than a week. Furious at this setback, Du immediately ordered a new attack on February 16. Lin responded by crossing the Songhua once again, on February 18, to conduct another spoiling raid. This time, the Communists planned to besiege Chengzijie and then ambush a relief column that would likely come from Dehui.[108] This time, however, Sun Liren refused to take the bait and made preparations to withdraw all of his forces to Changchun and prepare a deliberate counterattack.

Sun abandoned Chengzijie on February 22 but the Communists were still able to destroy the 89th Regiment during the breakout. However, most of Sun's forward defenses were able to withdraw before the Communists arrived, leaving only Dehui's 7,000 man garrison as the last sizable GMD strongpoint north of Changchun. Having failed to trap Sun's forces at Chengzijie, the 6th Column instead encircled Dehui. They began a general assault on the town on the last day of February, but a stout defense repulsed the initial Communist assaults. On March 1, Du dispatched Chen Mingren's Reorganized 71st Corps and another division from his attack on Linjiang to help Sun lift the siege of Dehui. His main objective achieved, Lin voluntarily lifted the siege on March 2 and withdrew. Unlike his first raid, however, this time he lingered in the general area with the intent of ambushing any pursuers.

On this occasion, Chiang wanted Du to pursue the NDUA across the Songhua River and destroy the army in north Manchuria once and for all. Reports citing as many as 10,000 Communist casualties at Dehui had led him to believe that the NPUA was crippled. However, Du knew better and instead worked on constructing a new defense line from Changchun to Jilin.[109] He also hoped he could finally capture Linjiang before the NPUA in Heilongjiang could reorganize and conduct another raid. Realizing that Du was retreating rather than advancing, Lin tried to catch the GMD before they fell in on their new defense line. On March 11, the Communists managed to catch elements of the 87th and 88th Divisions near Meijiatun on the road from Kaoshantun to Nongan. After two days of fighting, the NDUA inflicted a total of 7,000 casualties and had besieged the remnants of the

87th Division at Nongan. As feared, this forced Du to suspend his third attack on Linjiang and transfer the Reorganized New 6th Corps and the 13th Corps to repair the situation in the north. As these approached, on March 16 Lin ordered his forces to withdraw, repeating the pattern that by now had become almost ritual.

However, instead of returning to the status quo, Xiao Jingguang capitalized on the situation by opening up another front in south Manchuria. He dispatched elements of the 3rd and 4th Columns to cut off the Tonghua-Shenyang railroad and besiege the 195th Division at Tonghua. Consequently, by the spring of 1947, five months of GMD campaigning had been almost completely nullified. Yet Du remained committed to his plan, and now that the forces of the Liaodong Military Sub-District were no longer concentrated at Linjiang, he believed his chance had arrived. Du ordered his deputy commander, Zheng Dongguo, to lead one last offensive on Linjiang at the end of March. Du transferred the Reorganized New 6th and 13th Corps to assist Zheng's attack. At this time, there were only four Communist divisions, approximately 24,000 men, guarding Linjiang. Despite this advantage, Du's subordinate commanders played into the Communists hands by using the same avenues of approach as in prior offensives. Consequently, the result was same. On April 2, Xiao's forces ambushed and destroyed the 89th Division, effectively turning back the assault.

As the GMD position in Manchuria continued to erode, Lin planned to build on the success of the "Three Attacks, Four Defenses" to launch the Summer Offensive. On April 8, he moved his headquarters out of Harbin to Shuangcheng to be closer to the front. On May 5, he convened a meeting of the Northeast Bureau to announce a change of strategy. Instead of conducting long-term, base-building operations, Lin envisioned launching a large-scale counterattack and eventually seeking a decisive battle.[110] Thus, in less than a year, Communist strategy in northeast China had come full circle. Sensing that the tables were beginning to turn on the GMD, Du requested reinforcements from Nanjing. However, as Chiang was completely dedicated to his strongpoint strategy, he refused to dispatch any more troops to Manchuria. His instruction to Du was to "find your own solution to your problems."[111]

On May 8, the NDUA launched the Summer Offensive. Lin divided his forces in north Manchuria into two parts. The first part consisted of three columns and two independent divisions. The second part, called the East Army, was made up of the elite 6th Column and two independent divisions. Employing their standard tactics, the larger element attacked Huaide with the intent of ambushing the relief column. On May 17, they destroyed the already battered 88th Division and forced the rest of the garrison to withdraw to Changchun and Siping. The East Army, on the other hand, was actually the main effort, since it was responsible for securing a line of communication with the Liaodong Military Sub-District. Infiltrating the GMD defenses east of Jilin City, they made contact with the Liaodong Military Sub-District, cleared the area of GMD garrisons, and severed the Jilin-Shenyang railroad.[112] The Liaodong Military Sub-District also participated in the offensive. By May 20, Xiao's forces had surrounded the 184th Division at the railroad junction of Meihekou. After a series of attacks, the 4th Column captured the town on May 28, effectively bringing the campaign to an end.

The Summer Offensive was a complete success. Not only had Lin finally re-established contact with the Liaodong Military Sub-District, he had also forced Du, who simply lacked the combat power to oppose these moves, to contract his defenses in north and east Manchuria to defend only the large cities and the railroads. Lin decided to capitalize on this by capturing Siping, which would separate Du's two largest garrisons at Changchun and Shenyang. Deploying his largest force to date, Lin massed three columns (consisting of seven divisions) and five artillery battalions for the attack. Li Tianyou's 1st Column would conduct the main assault while the rest of the army deployed to block reinforcements from Shenyang or Changchun.

Du, on the other hand, had reorganized his army into six "mobile field groups." These consisted of two to three divisions with integrated air support. While half of these were tied down in a static defense of Siping, Changchun, and Jilin City, the other three were ready to move at any time. Du decided to place them in two areas: west Liaoning, which would protect his lines of communication with Beiping and Nanjing, and Siping, which was already under siege by Lin's forces.[113] By doing so, Du effectively abandoned southeast Manchuria, surrendering the initiative and now becoming completely reactive to the Communists.

The NDUA began to reduce the strong points outside of Siping beginning on June 11. After completing this task three days later, they launched a general attack on the city. At Siping, Chen Mingren commanded the 87th and 54th Divisions – approximately 29,000 men. They were entrenched in strong positions inside the city and used these to great effect. The first Communist waves suffered devastating casualties. Although the Northeast Bureau instructed their forces to dig sapping trenches and employ explosives against enemy strong points, they made little effect on Chen's defenses.[114] The two primary reasons for the lack of progress were ineffective Communist fire support – Lin had only allocated 70 guns to the siege – and GMD air superiority.[115] Despite these disadvantages, the NPUA forces did manage to break into the city on two separate occasions. After violent street-to-street fighting, Chen threw back the Communists and inflicted heavy casualties each time.[116] By June 19, Lin began to rotate his assault units as they became ineffective because of attrition and exhaustion. Nonetheless, he was set on capturing the city and openly declared his willingness to suffer upwards of 15,000 casualties to do so.[117]

As the siege dragged on, Du finally received reinforcements from Nanjing. On June 17, the 53rd Corps, which had been part of Du's original task force in 1945, boarded trains in Hebei to return to Manchuria. Du also assembled two corps and an additional division out of his existing force to help lift the siege. The Reorganized New 1st Corps in Changchun would also support the operation once the relief column assembled. On June 24, the reinforcements arrived and Du moved to lift the siege of Siping. In the face of this new threat, Lin suspended the assault on Siping and instead sought victory by ambushing the relief force. However, after taking stock of his own available forces, which had been reduced significantly by Chen's stand, Lin decided to end the entire campaign. He withdrew north of the Songhua River on July 1, no doubt haunted by the fact that this was the second defeat he had suffered at Siping in less than a year.

The casualty reports of the battle spoke of the intensity and scale of the fighting at Siping. GMD sources reported over 40,000 Communist casualties in and around Siping,[118] while Communist sources cite a much smaller figure – 13,000 casualties.[119] Even if one takes the smaller figure at face value, this was easily the most costly defeat suffered by Communists in the war to date. The Northeast Bureau did try to claim a moral victory by citing 30,000 GMD casualties, but these were probably inflated. Most of the GMD losses were from the 71st Corps at Siping, which was reduced from its original strength of 20,000 to little over 3,000 remaining effectives by the end of the battle.[120] The Communists did benefit from the fact that Du had been forced to withdraw from southeast Manchuria. The Northeast Bureau claimed to have liberated ten million civilians as well as capturing 36 county seats, 160,000 square kilometers of territory, and 1,250 kilometers of railway during this campaign.[121]

Despite the defeat at the Second Battle of Siping, the NDUA had still made significant strategic gains in the first half of 1947. In fact, Lin had turned the tables on the GMD by achieving strategic parity, or perhaps even ascendancy. Strangely, this turning point was the result of a relatively quiet and prolonged campaign that was capped by a tactical failure. The initiative had slowly swung into the possession of the NDUA while the GMD had squandered their best opportunity to gain total dominance in the region during the winter of 1946–47. In addition to demonstrating an improved capacity to attack and defend against Du's best units, the NDUA had also fully exploited the GMD's overextension and lack of presence in the countryside.

In essence, Lin's "one point, two front" strategy, which was based on exterior lines, had effectively offset Du's interior lines. However, much of this victory should be attributed to superior leadership from Lin, Xiao Jingguang, and Chen Yun, who had decided on a unified strategy as early as October and relentlessly carried it out. Yet, on the other hand, Du was equally as dedicated to his own plan. By all accounts, it was sound and should have worked, but the execution proved lackluster and lethargic. Du's subordinates in particular displayed both poor reactions and lack of determination. The situation in Manchuria in the summer of 1947 was far from irretrievable for the GMD, but, considering the dire straits of the Northeast Bureau only six months before, the reversal of fortune was both significant and striking.

A similar strategic transformation was taking place in north China as Nie Rongzhen's SCH Military District took the offensive for the first time since the disastrous siege of Datong in 1946. Up to this point, the only strategic advantage they maintained was their hold on the Beiping-Hankou railroad near Baoding. However, on January 25, Mao called on them emulate the other military districts and seek battles of annihilation.[122] Nie demurred despite two more proposals from Mao in February and March. Finally, at the end of March, Nie decided to launch the Zhengzhou-Taiyuan (Zhengtai) Campaign. Part of the reason for this may have been that Nie was under pressure to dispatch Yang Dezhi's 1st Column to help defend Yan'an. Nie managed to retain the unit but only temporarily. Mao agreed to allow the 1st Column to remain with Nie during the Zhengtai Campaign, but afterwards it was to join the Northwest Field Army. Mao furthermore ordered Nie to expedite the campaign so that the transfer could occur as soon as possible.[123]

Nie's Zhengtai Campaign came about because of Li Zongren and the Beiping Field Headquarters' decision to seize the Daqing River valley in west Hebei. To do so, Li had contracted his lines and reinforced certain garrisons. However, this did not include Shijiazhuang and, as a result, there were only three divisions from Sun Lianzhong's army in defense of that city and the important Zhengzhou-Taiyuan railroad in southwest Hebei. Therefore, Nie's campaign sought to exploit this weakness by severing the railroad and then preparing an ambush for any reinforcements. An additional calculation on Nie's part was the fact that the nearest GMD reinforcements would have to come from Yan Xishan's Taiyuan Pacification Command. However, since Yan did not get along with Sun Lianzhong, Nie predicted that reinforcements from that region would not be forthcoming.[124]

On April 9, Nie deployed his forces for the attack. One part focused on securing the railroad east of Shijiazhuang while the other attempted to lure the city's garrison, the 3rd Corps, out of its defenses. In the meantime, Li's main force crossed the Daqing River and began its own offensive. This led to a debate within the SCH Field Army headquarters over whether to continue the Zhengtai Campaign or to respond to the Daqing incursion. Nie opposed the later option, instead citing the need to maintain the initiative and continue the current campaign. Mao agreed with Nie's viewpoint[125] and that decided the issue.

Although the 3rd Corps did not take the SCH Field Army's bait, the Communists had still managed to isolate Shijiazhuang by cutting the railroads and surrounding the city. Having met this first objective, Nie moved the majority of his army west to attack his main target, the Zhengzhou-Taiyuan railroad. These operations took them into Shanxi, which provoked Yan to dispatch Zhao Boshou, commander of the 7th Army, to lead a task force to defend Yangquan and Shouyang, two important industrial centers in east Shanxi. Nie allowed Zhao to enter Yangquan, believing that he could eventually draw out a larger force. In the ensuing week, the SCH Field Army captured a number of smaller towns around Yangquan and threatened Taiyuan with a number of long-range raids. Fearing more attacks, Yan deployed the full weight of the 7th and 8th Army to reinforce Yangquan. Nie quickly redeployed his forces to intercept this new relief column. Although unable to destroy it completely, he inflicted heavy casualties and forced them to turn back on the evening of May 3. Now with no hope of relief, Zhao broke out of Yangquan the next day. Although he was able to return to Taiyuan successfully, Yan's precious industrial districts as well as the Zhengtai railroad were now in Communist hands.

The General and Strong Point Offensives represented the GMD high tide in that Chiang was in direct control of more parts of China than he arguably ever did. His notable victories in Shandong and Shaanxi had won him his political victory, but he achieved very little strategically. In fact, by switching emphasis away from regions such as northeast China and Hebei during the Strong Point Offensive, Chiang had exposed his forces to a series of attacks which virtually nullified much of his accomplishments during the General Offensive. The Zhengtai Campaign and the Summer Offensive clearly revealed the fact that Chiang's strategic reserve was nearly empty. They also revealed the major problem with the General Offensive – namely the failure to destroy any Communist army or fully "pacify" a region. Consequently, the large-scale strategic and territorial gains won during both offensives transformed into burdens virtually overnight. Nanjing simply lacked the resources to defend them adequately and the forces they did have were dangerously overstretched.

In the end, the General and Strong-Point Offensives represented Chiang's best chance to win the Third Chinese Civil War. Yet the failure of these campaigns to achieve the desired result was not decisive in itself. The CCP merely achieved strategic parity, not necessarily ascendancy. The Communists still had to find a way to counterattack and force the GMD on the defensive. Traditionally, this transition was not an easy one for any army to make, especially one that had just recently embraced conventional tactics. It was quite possible that the Communists' attempts to assail GMD holdings would also end in disappointment. However, this would have to be their next move, whether they were ready for it or not. With the war in balance, the Communists would have to make plans to strike back and carry the war into GMD-held territory.

4   The turning point
(July 1947–August 1948)

The immediate fallout of the Strong Point Offensive was to create a situation in north China that held certain parallels to World War II. The GMD now possessed the coastline and all of the major cities and railroads from Shaanxi to Shandong. However, by capturing this extensive stretch of territory, they made it more difficult for their armies to engage the mobile Communist armies. Most of the GMD soldiers were now tied up in garrison duty, either in the cities or on the rail lines. For instance, Communist intelligence calculated that despite the fact that Chiang had 30 divisions in the SCH Military District, he could muster only two corps at any given time.[1] The same was true for Du Yuming, who had to abandon entire areas of Manchuria to lift the siege of Siping. Even in areas where the Strong Point Offensive took place, i.e. Shaanxi and Shandong, GMD generals had to take creative measures to generate sufficient combat power, often stripping defenses from other regions to do so.

Chiang recognized the scale of these problems and knew he would need more resources to continue the war. Therefore, to put the country on a total war footing he pushed the General Mobilization Bill through the legislature, and officially outlawed the CCP on July 4, 1947. Nanjing's propaganda and political departments also tried to build public support for prolonging and escalating the war. For instance, they manufactured a close link between the CCP and the Soviet Union to generate an "exterior" threat, which had so galvanized the country during World War II.[2] However, these attempts were largely ineffective and the general populace remained unresponsive. As for the battlefield, Chiang announced that the Strong Point Offensive would be replaced by "moving on a broad front in selected areas."[3] This did not reflect an abandonment of his original scheme, rather it was a tactical adjustment. The new strategy was meant to minimize casualties by denying the Communists the chance to isolate and destroy scattered units. Xue Yue had employed this strategy in Shandong during the spring, although his defeat at Menglianggu demonstrated that the GMD still had problems applying it.

In response to Chiang's political attacks, the Communists continued to claim that theirs was a war of self-defense. The General and Strong Point Offensives had only further fueled this propaganda effort. The Communists also actively courted independent political parties that Chiang had alienated. Yet, despite the benign image it attempted to project, the CCP was unswervingly fixed on taking the war into GMD-controlled areas. Consequently, many hard decisions and campaigns awaited the Communists before they could even begin to challenge Nanjing's authority on a national scale.

Breaking the deadlock: one thousand *li*[4] to the Dabie Mountains

For both sides, the end of the Strong Point Offensive marked the beginning of a new phase. For the GMD, the chance to end the war in one stroke had vanished and they now looked to consolidate their gains and prepare for a protracted war. This shift meant that the CCP strategy of encouraging GMD overextension and conducting an interior line defense had also run its course. For Mao, the next step was to launch a counterattack to reclaim the territory lost in the previous year. However, who would conduct such an attack and where it should fall was still in question. Perhaps even more critical was whether or not the strategy was even feasible.

While no one in the Communist high command denied the eventual need for a counterattack, there was considerable disagreement over the mechanics and timing. Mao had lobbied for such a counterattack on numerous occasions in 1946, only to have his generals convince him otherwise. Chen Yi had also wanted to strike

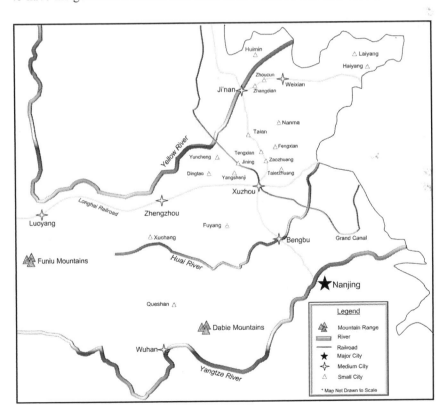

Figure 4.1 1947: Turning the tide.

back in his own sector, only to be thwarted by the pace of the GMD offensive. In the summer of 1947, with the Strong Point Offensive waning, Mao again brought up the idea of a large-scale strategic offensive. However, Lin Biao's Summer Offensive, especially his bloody repulse at Siping, offered a preview of what the Communists were likely to encounter once they switched to the attack. However, Mao overlooked this particular concern and increasingly believed that the war could be won by building bases and political support. The path to victory ran through Chiang's center of power in south China and the Yangtze River delta. For this reason, the CCP counterstroke would have to take place in the Central Plains or east China.

Due to Chen Yi's precarious situation in Shandong, the burden of the new offensive fell almost by default on Liu Bocheng, Deng Xiaoping, and the SHSH Field Army. In a series of telegrams at the beginning of May, Mao proposed that Liu consider launching a counterattack in the Central Plains against Chiang's operations north of the Yellow River.[5] At this time, Liu could not address the request because he was engaged in the North Henan Campaign, which was meant to relieve GMD pressure on the Northwest Field Army. Nonetheless, Mao continued to press the issue and proposed that Liu undertake the offensive after his current campaign concluded. He actually offered up four different proposals, with one of these identifying the Dabie Mountains as a potential base from which the SHSH Field Army could conduct operations against the GMD rear areas.

On May 25, Liu called off the North Henan Campaign after winning a few tactical victories, but failing in his larger task of luring Wang Zhonglian into a decisive battle. Withdrawing to rest and reorganize, Liu and Deng now considered whether they could implement Mao's desired counterattack. On June 10, they convened a strategy meeting with the SHSH Bureau and the SHSH Field Army commanders at Shilinzhen. The representatives from the field army clearly favored staying put, citing the difficulties they likely would face if they moved into a new region.[6] Much as Su Yu had argued in 1946, the officers of the SHSH Field Army raised as concerns the Communists' inability to sustain an offensive far away from their bases and the danger of leaving the liberated areas undefended.

However, Liu, Deng, and SHSH Field Army chief-of-staff Li Da firmly supported the idea of counterattacking into the Central Plains. They presented strong arguments for leaving their current area of operations. For one, Liu and Deng cited the fact that the forces Li Xiannian left behind during the Central Plains breakout in 1946 were still maintaining the old base area.[7] Second, Deng and the SHSH Bureau reported that their current bases might not be able to support the army long-term:

> After fighting on interior lines in the Hebei-Shandong-Henan Border Area for one year ... the number of chickens, swine and draught animals cultivated by the local peasants dropped sharply, as also did the number of trees in the villages. We may well ask whether we can afford to restrict the fighting to the liberated areas. If we were bent on fighting on interior lines for the sake of convenience, we would fall into the enemy's deadly trap.[8]

For Deng, the best way to alleviate this logistical problem was to take advantage of the untapped resources in the Central Plains.

Liu further argued that the offensive would be critical for helping the Communists' overall strategic situation. As Deng recalled Liu saying to the SHSH Field Army high command:

> If we do this, we can draw the enemy to ourselves and make it easier for the other field armies. How can you take hot embers out from under a pot if you are afraid of burning your fingers? Even if we have to make sacrifices, we should not begrudge them.[9]

To describe the GMD's configuration after the Strong Point Offensive, Liu likened it to a "dumbbell" because all of the weight was on the flanks and there was only a thin defense line in the center. After the North Henan Campaign, Liu ordered an extensive reconnaissance of the middle portion of this "dumbbell" and discovered that he faced only four brigades on the south bank of the Yellow River. Part of the reason for this weakness was the GMD's belief that the river itself was a sufficient obstacle. Its defensibility was further enhanced by the efforts to reroute the path of the river, which had been diverted when Chiang destroyed the dams in 1937 to slow the Japanese onslaught. Starting in March, the river began to flow on its original path, north to the Bo Sea instead of south to the Yellow Sea. In addition to further separating the SHSH and East China Military District, this engineering project also turned southwest Shandong and north Jiangsu into a veritable swamp.

In the end, while Mao was the driving force behind a counterattack on the Central Plains, it was Liu and Deng who made it feasible. If either man had rejected the idea, the plan likely would have been aborted. Although other members of the SHSH Field Army and Bureau harbored doubts, the decision had been made. On June 15, the Secretariat issued orders for the SHSH Field Army to cross the Yellow River in southwest Shandong by the end of the month. To this end, the SHSH Bureau appointed Liu, Deng, and Li Xiannian to form a new Central Plains Bureau. Li was also transferred to the SHSH Field Army as deputy commander for the operation.[10]

Before the counterattack, the SHSH Field Army took time to replenish its ranks and reorganize its order of battle. Liu promoted local units to form five new regular columns – the 8th, 9th, 10th, 11th, and 12th Columns – a total of 280,000 men added to the field army. Liu would need these new troops to convince GMD commanders Wang Zhonglian and Liu Ruming that his army was still north of the Yellow River. Leaving his old SHSH base area in the hands of these new columns, Liu secretly shifted his veteran units and headquarters east to the Yellow River. On the night of June 30, he led his army across the river in secret, taking the GMD defenders by surprise. While Chiang ordered all available forces to converge on the bridgehead, Liu began the Southwest Shandong Campaign to destroy this defense line before moving south.[11] Thanks to superior reconnaissance and the rapid river crossing, the SHSH Field Army outflanked the entire 80 kilometer defense line, which put them in prime position to destroy one unit after another with ease.

In the meantime, the East China Military District was to support Liu's campaign by conducting an attack in its own sector. However, despite their victory at Menglianggu two months before, Tang Enbo was now frustrating Chen Yi and Su Yu. Tang had evidently learned from his mistakes and successfully avoided Communist attacks all through May, while still capturing large amounts of territory.[12] Unhappy with this turn of events, Mao criticized Chen and Su in the beginning of June and subtly accused them of relying too much on Liu's army and waiting for the Central Plains counterattack to take action.[13] After another failed attempt to draw Tang into battle in June, Mao admonished them again for excessive caution.[14] Consequently, the East China Field Army was shamed into seeking battle at all costs at the end of June.

Before Chen and Su deployed their forces, Mao reversed himself and instead instructed them to break up the field army and attack the enemy's rear with individual columns.[15] This decision may have arisen because the East China Field Army simply ran out of time to support Liu Bocheng's attack with a large battle. On the other hand, Mao may have realized that he was forcing Chen and Su to initiate a battle they probably could not win. The East China Field Army high command evidently agreed with the instructions because they had proposed the same plan earlier, before Menglianggu. Although Mao's decision to decline their request at that time was vindicated by the rest of the campaign, it appeared as though he had only delayed the inevitable.

On July 1, as Liu's forces crossed the Yellow River, Chen divided the East China Field Army into three parts. The West Army, consisting of the 1st and 4th Columns, was to conduct operations in south Shandong in the vicinity of the old Shandong Military District headquarters of Linyi. The 3rd, 8th and 19th Columns became the Chen-Tang Army, named after its commander and its political commissar, Chen Shiju and Tang Liang. They were to conduct operations in support of the SHSH Field Army. Lastly, Chen Yi and Su commanded the largest formation, consisting of the 2nd, 6th, 7th, and 9th Columns, which were responsible for pinning down Tang's army.[16] On July 8, the Chen-Tang Army captured Taian and Jining before moving west to link up with Liu Bocheng. At the same time, the West Army ejected Feng Zhian's forces from Fengxian and Zaozhuang and then severed the Tianjin-Pukou railroad at Tengxian. Much like Lin Biao's "Three Attacks, Four Defenses" Campaign and the Summer Offensive, by separating and attacking on different fronts, the Communists had completely undone Chiang's grand offensive.

This turn of events forced Gu Zhutong to transfer the two corps and five reorganized divisions from Tang Enbo's broad front offensive to combat the new threat. Hoping to capitalize on the shift of forces, Chen and Su attacked the four-regiment garrison at Nanma on July 18 in an attempt to draw out a relief column.[17] The GMD responded by sending three reorganized divisions that nearly trapped the Communist force. On this occasion, even Communist sources had to admit heavy, uneven losses; official totals cite 21,586 casualties, which was almost twice what they claim to have inflicted on the enemy.[18] Despite these less than desirable results, the battle of Nanma had at least pinned down Tang's forces at the exact time when Liu Bocheng was launching the Southwest Shandong Campaign.

Thus, without any support from Tang, Liu Ruming responded to the SHSH Field Army's crossing of the Yellow River by withdrawing his exposed units into the cities. He ordered his main element in the area, the 55th Division, to withdraw to Yuncheng and defend it to the death to buy time for reinforcements. With their sacrifice they would buy precious little time – the siege that began on July 4 was over only four days later. On July 10, the SHSH Field Army went to the next town, Dingtao, and destroyed the defending brigade there in short order. At this point, the SHSH Field Army had already destroyed half of the GMD defenses in southwest Shandong, and only Wang Jingjiu had been able to send reinforcements. To assure Liu's victory, Mao ordered the East China Field Army to redouble their efforts to prevent Gu from sending reinforcements.[19] However, Wang did not fall for Liu's trap and instead created a defense line at Jinxiang and Jiaxiang. With time against him in this case, Liu was forced to attack before Wang could consolidate his position.

Despite the makeshift nature of Liu's attack, in an impressive demonstration of how much the SHSH Field Army had improved its ability to conduct attacks against prepared positions, the Communists surrounded, isolated, and destroyed two thirds of Wang's force by July 14. This left only the 66th Division, which held the heights at Yangshanji, in the immediate area. Yet, unlike the other two divisions, the 66th Division proved more resilient. Assailed by two full-strength Communist columns, it did not collapse and instead forced Liu to commit reinforcements from his dwindling reserve. Inspired by this stand and probably aware of the importance of not letting the SHSH Field Army break through, Chiang took personal command of the relief effort. Sensing the danger, Mao suggested that Liu abandon the attack on the 66th Division and instead take a different route to the Central Plains.[20] However, Liu did not want to leave an enemy unit behind him and was intent on continuing the battle. The 3rd Column bought him some time by repulsing the first wave of GMD reinforcements – although this was not the force Chiang led. Nonetheless, this was all the time the SHSH Field Army needed and they finally overran the 66th Division on July 27.

Although the Communists had emerged triumphant from the Southwest Shandong Campaign, it had been a costly victory. This price could be measured in casualties – Liu estimated 13,000 men in his report to the CMC[21] – and in time – as the window of opportunity for winning a quick victory and then slipping off into the Central Plains evaporated at Yanshanji. Despite these setbacks, the Secretariat decided on July 19 that the counterattack would proceed and the SHSH Field Army should advance to the Central Plains with minimal delay. In fact, they planned to reinforce Liu with Chen Geng's 4th Column,[22] which was without a mission after the Northwest Field Army abandoned Yan'an. This transfer actually placed Chen under the same chain of command as the end of World War II.[23] The CMC's official order was transmitted on July 23:

> Immediately concentrate on reorganizing the army for 10 or so days and, except for sweeping the routes clean of small enemy units or militia, do not fight on the Longhai railroad, east of the Yellow River and/or the Beiping-

Hankou railroad. Also do not worry about establishing a rear area. In half a month, begin moving to the Dabie Mountains, seize the Dabie Mountain's ten core counties, clear away any GMD militia and start building a base and mass work. Force the enemy to move and engage us there.[24]

Liu and Deng, however, requested more time to replace their losses and reorganize after the battle. They also believed that they could wage another major campaign in southwest Shandong by cooperating with the Chen-Tang and West Armies to ambush the GMD reinforcements still en route to Yangshanji. Despite his desire to move into the Central Plains as soon as possible, Mao agreed with Liu and Deng's proposal.[25]

For this new operation, the availability of the Chen-Tang and West armies added five more columns to the forces available to the Communists. Mao and the CMC ordered Su Yu to leave east Shandong and take command of this combined detachment. Additionally, for this campaign, he would receive orders from the SHSH Field Army instead of the East China Field Army.[26] As Liu prepared his offensive, the first week of August brought heavy rains which threatened to turn the roads to mud, hamper any movement, and cause the Yellow River to overflow. Consequently, Liu cancelled the operation against the GMD relief column, determining that to delay the march south any further might make the whole endeavor impossible. As the courtyard in his own headquarters flooded, Liu ordered his army south and began the long-awaited counterattack. Although Mao was ecstatic, he nonetheless instructed Liu to allow for enough rest to prevent exhaustion and fatigue on the march, to avoid fighting any large battles, and to establish the new base in the Dabie Mountains with the idea of fighting a protracted war.[27]

On August 13, the SHSH Field Army crossed the Longhai Railroad and marched through Anhui toward the Dabie Mountains. Now behind enemy lines, Liu sent word to the CMC to transfer the local forces of the SHSH Military District he had left north of the Yangtze River to Nie Rongzhen's SCH Military District. Facing converging attacks from GMD forces pursuing his army, Liu developed an elaborate plan to deceive them into believing the SHSH Field Army was retreating west over the bend in the Yellow River. He also divided his army to force the GMD to spread out and attack in different directions. Benefiting from the continuous downpour and GMD confusion, which was still prevalent after the battle of Yangshanji, the SHSH Field Army slipped through untouched. By the time the rain stopped on August 16, Liu had completely eluded his adversaries.

However, a potentially greater threat awaited them – the swamps created when the Yellow River returned to its northerly flow. With the GMD looking to catch up and the SHSH Field Army's artillery and vehicles rendered immobile, Liu was forced to destroy his heavy equipment rather than risk the whole army being caught in the open by GMD aircraft or long-range artillery. Although a military necessity, it was a negative blow to morale. Some of the more poignant scenes included soldiers sobbing over the decision to destroy their guns because of the number of their comrades who had died to capture them. Exhausted, demoralized and filthy, the SHSH Field Army would continue its march on foot.

By August 18, the army had cleared the swamps and moved to the next obstacle, the Sha River. Thanks to guerrilla troops in the region, the bridges had been seized ahead of time, allowing the army to cross unimpeded. The Communists repeated this pattern at the Pinghong River. At the Ru River, they ran out of luck as GMD brigades from the New 85th and the 15th Division, a total of 3,000 men, held the south bank. To make matters worse, their pursuers closed to within artillery range of the crossing site and had already begun shelling it with long-range fire. On August 24, under heavy air and artillery attack, the SHSH Field Army forced its way across the Ru River and brushed aside the defenders. Although they managed to escape the closing trap, it was a narrow escape at best. The next day, the main element of the army reached its final major obstacle, the Huai River. Deng commanded the rear guard while Liu led across the first units, who were to sprint ahead to link up with the guerrilla forces in the Dabie Mountains. During the crossing, the GMD again caught up and employed indirect fire on the Communists. As artillery shells began to fall around him, Deng crossed over with the last group of soldiers and joined the main force at the Dabie Mountains on August 27.

To celebrate their triumph, the four columns of the SHSH Field Army that had made the journey south (the 1st, 2nd, 3rd, and 6th) were renamed the Central Plains Field Army – in effect reactivating Li Xiannian's old command. Yet, despite their accomplishment many significant challenges awaited this new army. For one, it had suffered heavily from both attrition and exhaustion, not to mention having to abandon all of its heavy weapons. Second, the GMD would soon arrive to cordon off the Dabie Mountains – a monumental task in itself considering the size of the area and the terrain – and the Communist army was in no condition to oppose them. Third, they had to reconfigure the old Central Plains base to sustain a standing army rather than a guerrilla element. In addition, the vicissitudes of war had reduced the local population, which had once exceeded 200,000, to a fraction of their prewar total.[28] Those who remained were hesitant to support the Communists, fearing GMD reprisals should the army leave again.

To address these unique challenges, Deng drafted a new strategy for developing the region. He composed it on the same day he crossed the Huai River – an act symbolic of his legendary energy and dedication. For the political commissar of the new Central Plains Military District, two major goals needed to be accomplished. First, the Communists had to rebuild their base and support network by demonstrating to the masses that they not only represented a better alternative to the GMD, but that this time they meant to stay. This message would have to be transmitted through good discipline, land reform, public works projects, bandit suppression, and the ruthless destruction of any GMD units in the area. The last was arguably the most important, as Deng warned:

> … we must be aware that unless we wipe out more than ten enemy brigades within six months, we shall not be able to convince the masses that we are here to stay to support their courage to rise up and fight, and as a result we shall encounter even more difficulties.[29]

The second goal seemed at odds with the first. It called on the army to avoid large-scale battles, which it could not win in its current state, while still occupying cities and towns. Deng's compromise was to wage "small battles" to annihilate one or two enemy regiments at a time. During this process, Deng hoped the commanders and soldiers would be able to gain familiarity with the region and build camaraderie with the locals. In all, Deng estimated the process would take six months,[30] a significant investment in time and manpower.

Shortly after the SHSH Field Army arrived in the Dabie Mountains, Mao proclaimed the beginning of the CCP's nationwide offensive in his "Strategy for the Second Year of the War of Liberation."[31] Zhou Enlai confirmed the strategy by asserting that the CCP's military forces were now actively seeking battle in GMD-controlled areas and expanding the size of the Liberated Areas.[32] Cognizant of their precarious hold in the Central Plains, the Secretariat and CMC transferred the SHSH Field Army 10th and 12th Columns, which had been left behind before the Southwest Shandong Campaign, to the Dabie Mountains at the end of September.

The East China Field Army, which had once been the main agent of the Communist war effort, was now to take on a supporting role. As mentioned above, Su Yu's five-column task force (formerly the West and Chen-Tang Armies) was to have conducted a joint campaign with Liu in west Shandong while Chen Yi and Tan Zhenlin tied down Tang Enbo in east Shandong.[33] Before this plan was put into effect, and later cancelled due to the rain, Su requested that Chen Yi take command of the army in west Shandong, with Su as deputy commander.[34] Mao and the CMC approved his request without question. Su may have been concerned that this represented a promotion above Chen Yi, which echoed his previous rejection of a similar promotion in 1945. It is also likely that he was concerned not to recreate the division of command which had hampered the Central China and Shandong Field Armies in 1946.

As per Su's request, Chen moved to west Shandong with another column and the entire task force was renamed the West Army (not to be confused with the earlier and smaller West Army). The forces Chen left behind, consisting of four columns and two independent divisions, were designated the East Army and placed under the command of Xu Shiyou and political commissar Tan Zhenlin. The East China Bureau and Military District headquarters – which Chen Yi still commanded – shifted to Binghai, north of the Yellow River, to facilitate communication between the two armies.[35] However, as mentioned before, these preparations were upset by Liu's decision to proceed directly to the Dabie Mountains, before the rain prevented the movement altogether.

Now the West Army's main task was to support the SHSH Field Army's movements and pin down any potential pursuers.[36] Additionally, before Liu had even reached the Dabie Mountains, Mao was already envisioning them conducting a similar foray into the Central Plains.[37] In many ways, the SHSH Field Army's campaign would serve as a test for future counterattacks. In the second half of August, after Liu had cleared the swamps in southwest Shandong, Su planned to move the West Army into the so-called Huaihai area between the Huai River and the Longhai railroad. There, he planned to occupy a few weakly defended towns, destroy any enemy units in the area and consolidate Liu and Deng's lines of communication with the other military districts. The Secretariat agreed with this course of action, finding it consistent with their counteroffensive strategy.[38]

However, since Su and Chen would not arrive to take command of the West Army until September, Chen Shiju remained at its head for the time being. Unfortunately, his efforts to keep Qiu Qingquan's 5th Corps in southwest Shandong went awry and the 10th Column suffered heavy casualties. Therefore, Chen Shiju ordered the 10th Column to retire north of the Yellow River to refit and reorganize. There, they linked up with Chen Yi, Su Yu, and the 6th Column, who were stuck in Huimin because of the lack of boats. This delay drew criticism from the Secretariat, who ordered them to make all necessary haste to Yuncheng and warned that any delay would endanger the Central Plains counteroffensive.[39] On September 5, Chen, Su, and the two columns finally made their way to Yuncheng. There, they discovered that the GMD had moved their main strength south under the mistaken assumption that the entire West Army, not just one column, had retreated north over the Yellow River. Consequently, Su immediately fell on the unsuspecting 57th Division at Shatuji on September 8 and destroyed it. Qiu's attempt to intervene came too late and, upon word of Shatuji's capture, he withdrew rather than be caught in an ambush.

After the battle of Shatuji, Chiang ordered Tang Enbo to detach Hu Lian's Reorganized 11th Division to make up for the losses of the 57th Division. Unfortunately for Hu, the Communists detected this movement and he soon faced the combined strength of five columns at Tushanji. Despite the disparity in forces, Hu repelled the West Army's attacks and the Communists melted away rather than prolong the fight. After the defeat at Tushanji, Chen and Su decided finally to move south into the Huaihai region, as Su had earlier proposed.[40] On September 27, the West Army split in two for the march south. Once they settled into their new region, they, like Liu and Deng, would spend the rest of 1947 conducting political and work with the masses to forge a new base. Chiang, on the other hand, ignored them and focused on destroying the Central Plains Field Army and Xu Shiyou's East Army in Shandong. In fact, their decision to remove into the Huaihai region may have appeared to be a blessing to Chiang since it meant that the West Army was no longer causing problems for Tang Enbo.

This left Xu Shiyou's East China East Army as the only Communist force in Shandong. They had been under heavy pressure since August when Chiang employed six reorganized divisions under Fan Hanjie to destroy them. The East Army considered evacuating Jiaodong and retreating north, but Chen Yi believed the region was too important an industrial and transportation center to simply abandon. Furthermore, he argued that allowing the GMD to control this region would not only deny war materials to the East China Field Army but could also facilitate Nanjing's ability to reinforce Manchuria by sea.[41] Consequently, the East Army remained in place and conducted the Jiaodong Defense Campaign for the rest of 1947.

Despite raising another column, the East Army was still too weak to effectively surround Fan Hanjie's units and destroy them. By the middle of September, with

Communist casualties increasing and Fan's momentum seemingly unstoppable, Xu sought permission to abandon Jiaodong and conduct operations against the enemy's rear. Mao echoed Chen's earlier arguments and disapproved.[42] Although still unable to win any major victories, Xu succeeded simply by avoiding destruction in September and October. This tenuous stalemate continued until November when Chiang recalled two divisions for use in other theaters. Not only did this slow Fan's attack but it finally opened up an opportunity for an East Army counterattack. While they were unable to block or cause any appreciable damage to the two divisions in transit, the East Army did manage to capture Haiyang and Laiyang. Xu later repulsed an attempt by Fan to recapture Laiyang. This was not only an important tactical victory for the East Army, but it had significant political and strategic implications as well, by demonstrating that even Shandong remained an active battlefield.

As the East China Field Army disrupted Chiang's plan to secure his eastern flank, the Communists began to dispatch more troops into the breach created by the Central Plains counteroffensive. In August, Chen Geng's 4th Column began its own march south. For the attack, the Secretariat promoted the column to full army status and reinforced it with units recently promoted from local to regular status – the 9th Column and two independent brigades. He Long also transferred to Chen's command the 38th Corps, made up of former GMD defectors who had joined the United Defense Army in 1945. Now more than 80,000 strong, the combined forces became the Chen-Xie Army, named after its commander and its political commissar, Xie Fuzhi. In early August, the CMC ordered Chen to cross the Yellow River and attack the Tongguan-Luoyang railroad in conjunction with the Northwest Field Army's attack on Yulin. This would serve to tie down Hu Zongnan and Yan Xishan so that they could not interfere with Liu and Deng's efforts. Although Mao wanted to wait until that operation was completed before planning the next one,[43] it was widely assumed that Chen would then move directly into the Central Plains.

The Communists' plans were upset when heavy rains – the same weather that forced Liu immediately to the Dabie Mountains – impeded Chen Geng's crossing of the Yellow River. It would not occur until August 22, when the waters subsided and the civilian ferries resumed service. Although unable to assist in the SHSH Field Army's march to the Dabie Mountains, Chen continued with the original plan of launching attacks in his sector. Although he secured a number of towns and chased away the GMD garrisons, he did not press his luck against Luoyang's defenses.[44] Instead, Chen began planning an ambush for Hu Zongnan's inevitable counterattack.[45] However, the GMD response, two corps from Hu and Gu Zhutong's provisional East Shaanxi Army (consisting of nine brigades) converged from the east and west and was more than the Chen-Xie Army could adequately handle. Mao thus ordered them to retreat to the Funiu Mountains on the border of Henan and Shaanxi and establish a base similar to the one being built in the Dabie Mountains.[46] To elude his pursuers, Chen dispersed his army to lead Hu on a fruitless chase for almost three months, then he reassembled his army and founded the Henan-Shanxi Military District.

With their flanks secured by Chen Yi's West and Chen-Xie Armies, the Central Plains Field Army could better concentrate on consolidating its position deep behind enemy lines. Although satisfied with Deng's proposal for the Dabie base, Mao also wanted them to consider crossing the Yangtze River and building a base in south China.[47] In many ways Mao's idea was a throwback to his late-1944 to early-1945 strategy of building bases in central and south China. Unlike earlier in the war, Chiang could not ignore or circumvent this growing threat in the Central Plains. Consequently, to crush the penetration he reactivated his old political adversary, Bai Chongxi, from his "ceremonial" post as Defense Minister. Largely credited as the best general the GMD had to offer, Bai was put in command of the new Jiujiang Field Headquarters.[48] This consisted of five reorganized divisions – more than 300,000 men. Some of these forces were drawn from units posted on the Yangtze River, as well as from Gu Zhutong's forces at Xuzhou. Bai's plan was to converge on the Dabie Mountains with the intent of surrounding, containing, and eventually destroying the Central Plains Field Army. The plan had more than a passing resemblance to the Encirclement Campaigns against the Jiangxi Soviet of the 1930s, which was likely intentional.

Thus by the end of 1947 the face of the war had changed. After the dramatic Communist campaigns of the fall, a period of unprecedented calm set in. Having pulled up their stakes and moved hundreds of miles to new territory, the Communists were in the process of rebuilding and reorganizing, rather than seeking battle. The GMD, surprised by the CCP's counterattacks, also required time to deploy their forces in areas they had "pacified" only a year ago. Consequently, the entire strategic situation in central China took on a guerrilla war flavor. This scenario did not bode well for Nanjing, especially on the heels of its two large offensives that had failed to produce a decisive victory. Indeed, the GMD had now lost the initiative completely, not only within individual theaters but on a national scale.

Yet the situation was not completely bleak for Chiang. One of the simplest ways to recover the initiative was to pacify one of the regions that the Communists had emptied for their counteroffensive – much like the Communists had done to Chiang in 1947. Indeed, in Shandong, the main tasks of Xu Shiyou and Tan Zhenlin's East Army was to remain south of the Yellow River and avoid incurring casualties. The intent was simply to deny Chiang control of the province and force him to keep troops there instead of transferring them elsewhere. Tang Enbo renewed his offensive in September and, although he was able to push through to the coast, he could not destroy the East Army. The same was true in Shaanxi, where the Northwest Field Army continued to elude Hu Zongnan's best attempts to destroy it or else force it across the Yellow River into Shanxi. The GMD's continuing inability to secure these flanks by the end of 1947, even after the Communists had made their dramatic counterattack, contributed considerably to their ultimate defeat.

The northeast

While the Central Plains counterattack wrecked the GMD's grand strategy, important battles were also occurring in north and Northeast China. Although not as dramatic as Liu Bocheng's breaching of the Yellow River defenses and his march into enemy territory, both Nie Rongzhen and Lin Biao were also winning the strategic battles in their regions. Not only had they gained considerable ground during their summer offensives, but their adversaries were steadily weakening. While the Communists armies continued to grow stronger and more confident through battle and defections, the GMD armies facing them suffered from poor morale and attrition. To make matters worse for the GMD forces, they would not be reinforced due to the crisis in the Central Plains.

However, there were many in Nanjing who believed they were winning in Manchuria, as evidenced by their successful defense of Siping. In fact, GMD reports from the front claimed crippling Communist losses at Siping and its aftermath. In addition to 40,000 battle casualties, GMD news reports cited 143,000 Communist defections and an additional 94,000 men captured.[49] Another editorial painted an optimistic picture by estimating that Lin had used almost all of his forces during the campaign and still lost.[50] While a portion of these estimates can be attributed to propaganda, it is clear that Nanjing believed they had won a decisive victory. Chiang therefore replaced Du Yuming with Chen Cheng, the GMD army chief-of-staff, not only to inspire the GMD forces in the region but also to give his favorite general the honor of delivering the final blow against Lin's army.

On the Communist side, the Northeast Bureau and the Secretariat viewed the Second Battle of Siping as a major failure. Lin himself offered to write a self-criticism for the setback. He also severely rebuked Li Tianyou, commander of the assault against the city, for deficiencies in tactics and "revolutionary spirit."[51] Peng Zhen was also recalled by the Secretariat in the fall. Ostensibly motivated by the need to have him assist with state-building efforts in north China, it is likely that this transfer was connected to the defeat.[52] In an official summary of the Summer Offensive, the NDUA reported more than 30,000 casualties, almost equal to the GMD claims. This was twice the amount Lin had allowed for as a worst case scenario before the campaign began.[53] Additionally, GMD reports of Communist defections and desertions were not far from the truth, although the numbers appear exaggerated. For instance, on August 8, Deng Hua, commander of the Liaoji Column, stated that none of his divisions had more than 1,900 men and each one had lost an average of 300 men to desertion.[54] Despite the losses, Lin pieced his army back together and reorganized it into standing columns – mainly by combining units and raising local troops to regular status. By September, the NDUA consisted of nine columns (each consisting of three divisions), ten independent divisions, two cavalry divisions, and an artillery division (consisting of four regiments), for a total of 510,000 soldiers.[55]

Despite the setback at Siping, the Communists still maintained a favorable strategic position in Manchuria. Du's decision to withdraw from certain areas had not only allowed the various Communist bases scattered across Manchuria to reunite, but it also meant that the GMD manned a vulnerable salient with its head at Jilin and Changchun in the north, its headquarters at Shenyang, and a thin neck that ended at Shanhaiguan. The area between Shenyang and Shanhaiguan became known as the Liaodong[56]-Shenyang (Liaoshen) corridor. Militarily, this position was untenable because the salient could be pinched off at numerous places. However, the Second Battle of Siping had demonstrated that the GMD still maintained considerable advantages in firepower and that the NDUA was still unable to capture heavily defended cities. GMD air support had proved devastating during the siege of Siping and the Communists had no way to counter these attacks. Air transport provided by Claire Chennault's Civilian Air Transport also provided a constant flow of supplies and reinforcements to the defenders.

As a result, the GMD maintained a strong position in the Northeast in the fall of 1947. The problem for incoming commander Chen Cheng, however, was that the recent Communist offensives had hammered the defenders into a state of passivity. Chen doggedly went to work to restore morale and to address organizational problems that had hounded Du Yuming. One solution was Chen's decision to dispose of redundant political and military organs. Instead, he assumed supreme command of the region, which mirrored how the Northeast Bureau and NDUA operated. Chen also eliminated cliques by transferring problem units, such as Sun Liren's Reorganized New 1st Corps, away from the theater. He also dismissed former Manchukuo officers and units to alleviate problems with defections and espionage. To replace these, Chiang granted him five new divisions and an artillery regiment – bringing his total strength to half a million soldiers.[57] This put him roughly on par with the NDUA in strength as well as in command and control.

However, Chen's strategic situation was still crippled because his forces remained dispersed, guarding the railroads and cities. Consequently, he resolved to take the offensive in October to try to eliminate the threat to at least one of his fronts. The area he chose was Jilin province, where he hoped to drive a wedge between NDUA forces near Siping and in Harbin. After breaking up Lin's forces in this area, he would turn his forces south to destroy the remnants of the NDUA south of the Songhua River.[58]

However, Lin nullified all of this by launching the Autumn Offensive before Chen could act. For this operation, Mao and Lin had agreed to probe the Liaoshen corridor to assess the strength of the GMD defenses near Jinzhou or Shanhaiguan and gauge the effect of cutting the railroad.[59] Cheng Zihua's HRL Military Sub-District employed its two columns to spearhead this attack on September 16. Chen immediately responded by contracting his lines and sending large relief columns to the threatened areas. Although the Communists did not manage to destroy any particular unit, they inflicted heavy casualties on five divisions and disrupted the GMD's defense network in south Manchuria. Before withdrawing on September 30, Cheng's columns also destroyed the railroad, temporarily severing Chen's lines of communication.

As Chen shifted forces south to deal with Cheng, Lin initiated the second phase of the offensive by launching a feint in the north. On October 1, the 3rd Column attacked Weiyuanbao, a town south of Siping. Instead of engaging the NDUA, the GMD pulled back into the cities of Siping, Kaiyuan, and Tieling. This prevented the Communists from attaining their main goal of destroying enemy units. Chiang also ordered Li Zongren to dispatch reinforcements from Beiping to reinforce Chen immediately – a noticeable difference from his earlier dealings with Du Yuming.

Unfortunately for the GMD, the reinforcements would be delayed until the railroad Cheng had destroyed was repaired. This allowed the NDUA to continue their offensive. Finding Chen unwilling to take his bait, Lin shifted the main thrust of his attack to Jilin City. In order to prevent the GMD defenses from contracting their lines around the city itself, the Communists deployed quickly to catch individual units on the move. The 7th Column quickly destroyed four regiments from the 57th Division at Xinlitun on October 9, but the next week it was ambushed by the GMD 195th Division. This forced one of the 7th Column's divisions to retire with heavy casualties. The 4th Column also failed to capture Yingpancun. Although the Independent 4th and 5th Divisions had more success, including capturing Dehui, the NDUA as a whole was not able to prevent the GMD from falling back into a series of strong points that the Communists dared not attack.

On November 9, with Chiang's reinforcements now in Manchuria and no more viable "soft" targets, Lin planned to lay siege to Jilin City and ambush the inevitable relief column.[60] As his main force withdrew north to take up ambush positions, destroying garrisons and rail lines along the way, he left three columns around Jilin City. However, Chen made no effort to relieve the city and with this, the Autumn Offensive ended. For the Communists, the results were mixed. Although CCP sources cite Chen Cheng's army suffering approximately 67,000 casualties and losing 15 county seats,[61] the NDUA had not managed to destroy any units or induce him to fighting a large-scale field battle. The GMD tactic of withdrawing into the cities, where they could rely on static defenses and firepower, had largely foiled the NDUA's offensive.

Mao on the other hand grew enamored with the vulnerability of Chen's lines of communication to north China, as revealed by Cheng Zihua's attack. For instance, during the campaign, Mao believed that after capturing Jilin City – which never materialized – the NDUA should next attack Jinzhou and sever the Beiping-Liaoning railroad permanently.[62] From his telegrams and his perspective of the strategic situation, it was clear Mao wanted to finish the battle for Manchuria as soon as possible, so that the NDUA could be used in north China. Lin disagreed with this plan and saw significant problems in moving the majority of his forces south while leaving GMD units in Changchun and Shenyang in his rear. Instead, he continued to preach his "one point, two front" strategy, rather than Mao's "one-point" strategy.[63] This difference in opinion would become increasingly important through the winter as the NDUA tried to find a way to crack Chen's strong point-based defense scheme that had fought them to a standstill in the fall.

Yet, despite the success of GMD defensive measures during the Autumn Offensive, the second-order effects for Nanjing were all negative. Chen's plans for seizing the initiative with a sudden, well-placed attack were now postponed indefinitely. The Communists still maintained the ability to strike anywhere along the entire perimeter of the salient, and their exploitation of the weak situation in the Liaoshen corridor was especially troubling. Chiang's decision finally to dispatch reinforcements to Manchuria not only illustrated the scale of the problem, but it also weakened the defenses in north China at the exact same time that Nie Rongzhen's SCH Military District was delivering its own fall offensive.

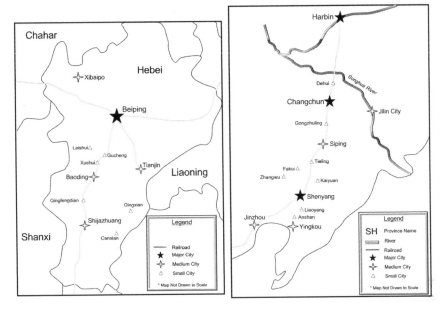

Figure 4.2 1947: Seizing the initiative in north and northeast China.

Qingfengdian and Shijiazhuang

Thanks to its Zhengtai Campaign in the spring of 1947 and the reemergence of the NDUA as a threat, Nie's SCH Military District faced its best strategic situation since 1945. By the summer, they maintained a strong presence in south Hebei and had isolated the large city and railroad junction of Shijiazhuang. This meant that GMD forces in Beiping, Xuzhou, Henan, and Shanxi were unable to coordinate with each other. In the meantime, Liu Shaoqi, Zhu De, and the Work Committee set up their headquarters at Xibaipo, a village in northwest Hebei. While Mao, Zhou, and Ren Bishi continued to direct the war in the critical border regions of Shaanxi, the Central Plains, East China, and Manchuria, Zhu and Liu assumed responsibility for the central regions of Shanxi, Suiyuan, Chahar, and Hebei. Although Mao still maintained overall command authority,[64] the Work Committee began to direct strategy for the SCH Military District. They decided that Nie should seek a large battle of annihilation in the summer to solidify Communist control of the region.

To this end, the Work Committee called for a reorganization of the Shanxi-Chahar-Hebei Military District command structure. While Nie had formed field armies in the past, these were mostly provisional.[65] The Work Committee decided that the SCH Military District should permanently establish a SCH Field Army with Yang Dezhi as commander and Luo Ruiqing as political commissar. This new field army consisted of three columns and an artillery brigade, small in comparison with the East China, Central Plains Field Armies, and the NDUA, but larger than the Shanxi-Suiyuan and Northwest Field Armies.

In the latter half of May, Nie proposed an attack on the Tianjin-Qingcang segment of the Tianjin-Pukou railroad. Although this area contained many waterways, including the Grand Canal, and offered little opportunity for a large battle, Nie argued that it would prove an ample precursor to the battle the Work Committee sought. In fact, he was concerned that his force was not yet ready for the major battles the party leadership desired.[66] Indeed, his plan explicitly avoided engaging regular GMD troops and instead focused on Peace Preservation Corps and garrison units. The Secretariat approved the plan and the attack began on June 12. In three days Yang Dezhi's forces secured Qingxian, Canxian, and Shuiqing, as well as 80 kilometers of the Tianjin-Pukou railroad. In the process, they annihilated the 6th Peace Preservation Corps Detachment and swept aside the 2nd, 3rd, and 8th Detachments. With this accomplished, Nie ended the campaign and withdrew. A week and a half later, Sun Lianzhong recovered the railroad.

Although the results of the Qingcang campaign were limited – as they were designed to be – it served its purposes of preparing the SCH Field Army as well as diluting the GMD defenses. Anxious for a military victory, Zhu and Liu ordered Nie to rest his forces for three days and then launch an even larger attack on the Beiping-Tianjin railroad. Mao agreed and added that Nie's main objective should focus on enticing the large GMD army in the Daqing River region to intervene so that the Communists could annihilate it.[67] Nie agreed with the concept but not the location. He convinced the Secretariat to allow him to attack north of Baoding, which was closer to the Daqing River and his own base of operations outside of Shijiazhuang. On June 25, Yang initiated this North Baoding Campaign. Despite seizing towns and destroying their garrisons, the SCH Field Army's primary target, Gucheng, did not fall. To make matters worse, Li did not dispatch troops from Daqing. Nie was forced to call off the campaign on June 28 after only three days of fighting.

After the North Baoding Campaign, the Shanxi-Chahar-Hebei Field Army rested for two months. Although they had not yet found their "battle of annihilation," the two summer campaigns had served to shape the strategic situation in the Communists' favor. The GMD now faced Communists threats along three fronts: Qingcan in the east, Baoding in the center, and Shijiazhuang in the west. Nie's probing attacks had also confirmed that Sun Lianzhong's Baoding Pacification Command would not receive assistance from other GMD units in the region. As a result, Nie and the Work Committee agreed that the SCH Field Army should seek a large battle with Sun's forces in the fall. Destroying the Baoding Pacification Command would not only be a significant victory in north China, but would also have considerable side effects in the other critical theaters – especially Shandong, Shaanxi, and the Central Plains.

In mid-August, the SCH Field Army made plans to attack Laishui to try to draw out a relief column from Beiping or from the GMD forces operating on the Daqing River. After receiving approval from the Work Committee, Yang launched his attack on the night of September 6. From the very start the offensive encountered problems. Laishui's defenses proved formidable and Yang's forces incurred unexpected casualties while encircling the town and conducting the initial probes. The GMD did oblige by dispatching reinforcements, which allowed Yang to set up an ambush. Unfortunately for the Communists, the relief column slipped through the SCH Field Army's screening force and captured a bridge over the Juma River. This act allowed the GMD troops to circumvent Yang's trap. His plan wrecked, Yang attempted to improvise by attacking the north bank of the Daqing River, the defenses of which had been weakened to lift the siege of Laishui. However, this operation proved ill-fated as Li Zongren's forces easily beat back Yang's makeshift attacks. The SCH Field Army thus retired from the field of battle in abject defeat. During these two actions at Laishui and the Daqing River, the Communists admitted suffering more casualties than they inflicted (6,778 versus 5,278).[68]

Yet the Work Committee judged that this campaign had at least met the primary goal of dispersing the enemy's troop concentrations and isolating his strong points. More critically, Mao and Nie did not criticize Yang and instead stated that the spirit of the maneuvers were correct.[69] The NDUA's aforementioned Autumn Offensive helped the SCH Military District immensely as the GMD transferred five divisions away from north China to help Chen Cheng fend off Lin Biao. After these units departed, Sun Lianzhong was forced to reconfigure his defenses. Unfortunately for him, his most powerful unit, the 3rd Corps, was at Shijiazhuang, isolated amid Communist-controlled territory. The rest of his deployment was spread out across the entire region. His 16th Corps was north of the Daqing River, the 94th Corps was near Laishui, two reorganized divisions guarded Baoding, and the 5th Division held Gucheng and Xushui.[70] In light of this weakness, Nie decided to draw Sun's forces into a battle north of Baoding by attacking the 5th Division with the intent of ambushing a relief column.

On October 11, Yang opened the campaign by besieging Xushui. To lift the siege Sun created a five-division task force drawn from his forces in Laishui and Daqing and placed them under the command of 94th Corps commander Li Wen. The SCH Field Army's 3rd and 4th Columns deployed to delay these forces and seek to exploit any breaks in the lines. However, Li Wen gave the Communists no such opportunity and, after a week of indecisive probing, Nie withdrew these columns to try to draw Li away from Xushui.[71] The GMD force did not take the bait and instead pressed on to lift the siege. At this point, with two columns now out of the fight and a single column at Xushui, Chiang saw an opportunity to trap the entire SCH Field Army. He personally intervened in the battle by ordering Sun to deploy Luo Lirong's 3rd Corps from Shijiazhuang to join in the attack.

Recognizing the danger – and the opportunity – Nie left four brigades to delay Li Wen and maintain the siege of Xushui. He sent the rest of Yang's army on a 100-kilometer forced march to ambush the 3rd Corps. Although the SCH Field Army's staff had earlier considered the possibility that Luo might intervene, Yang ruled it out on the grounds that it would have been foolhardy to try to move through Communist-held territory.[72] Indeed, although Luo only had to cover half the distance that Yang did, Communist militia and guerrilla harassment slowed the 3rd Corps' progress to a crawl. In the space of a critical 36 hours, Yang arrived at ambush positions in front of Luo on the afternoon of October 19. The long-awaited opportunity for a battle of annihilation in the SCH Military District had finally arrived.

On October 20, the 3rd and 4th Columns launched a general attack against the 3rd Corps to pin them down at Qingfengdian – the approximate halfway point between Shijiazhuang and Baoding. The sudden appearance of Communist regular troops blocking the road to Baoding stunned Luo and instead of trying to push through, he stopped in the vicinity of Xinanhe to await reinforcements. This proved fatal as Yang, despite fatigue, ruthlessly launched an attack along Luo's entire perimeter. Unable to create fixed defenses and taken aback by the sudden appearance of so many Communists, the 3rd Corps defenses were steadily reduced until they only included Xinanhe. With 10,000 men now hemmed into a village with a normal population of 400, the 3rd Corps teetered on the point of utter defeat in little less than a day.

In the meantime, Li Wen turned north to assist Luo, but he failed to break through the blocking force at Xushui on October 20–1. Part of the reason for this was Nie's decision to employ four brigades instead of only one at Xushui. His reasoning was that the area was "a flat area, not a pass" and that without sufficient forces, the enemy could "counterattack and surround" his troops.[73] In retrospect, this was the key decision of the battle because Yang was not able to finish off the 3rd Corps until midday on October 22. Had the force been smaller, Li might very well have broken through and rescued the Luo's beleaguered force. In the final tally, the SCH Field Army completely destroyed the 3rd Corps at Qingfengdian – a loss of 13,000 GMD troops – as well as successfully disengaging from Li Wen's 49th Corps at Xushui.

The battle of Qingfengdian was almost instantly decisive, shifting the balance of power in south Hebei to the Communists' favor in just under a week. With the destruction of the 3rd Corps, the garrison at Shijiazhuang now consisted of only the 32nd Division and local troops – less than 25,000 men. Despite its being virtually isolated after the Zhengtai Campaign, Nie had avoided assaulting the city because of strong fortifications and the lack of Communist success in urban warfare – especially his own failure at Datong in 1946. Shijiazhuang's defenses were especially formidable because the Japanese had modernized them during World War II with trench lines both inside and outside the city, networks of barbed wire, mines, tunnels, and electrified wire, not to mention 6,000 pillboxes in the city itself.[74] However, with the destruction of the main GMD force in the region, 3rd Corps, the city was now vulnerable and the garrison undermanned.

However, the strategy for the attack remained in dispute. Mao saw an attack on Shijiazhuang as another opportunity to draw in more GMD reinforcements and destroy them in a field battle.[75] Nie, on the other hand, wanted to capture the city and he believed dealing with the relief columns was a secondary concern. He felt that there would not be any significant reinforcements because Li Wen's force had already been battered and Yan Xishan would not intervene.[76] While Nie did allocate some forces to block any reinforcements, these consisted of small or local units rather than his regular columns. Zhu De wholeheartedly supported seizing Shijiazhuang, which would finally give the Communists a large city of their own to enhance the party's war production capability and prestige. To this end, Zhu stressed the need to protect and exploit commerce and city infrastructure through troop discipline and political work.[77] On the tactical level, Zhu emphasized the importance of artillery, tunnels, and concentration of fire on enemy strong points.[78]

In the beginning of November, Yang began to deploy the SCH Field Army against Shijiazhuang. His first objectives included capturing the Daguncun airfield and Yunpan Ridge, which overlooked the city. After seizing the latter, Nie placed his artillery there and used it to destroy Shijiazhuang's power station. With these shaping operations completed on November 6, the army began its assault on the city walls. Like Nie's earlier siege of Datong, Yang's forces dug sapping trenches under the cover of darkness and beneath a constant barrage of supporting, indirect fire to close the distance to the GMD lines. As a result, the first Communist assaults a few days later were violent and effective. A captured GMD regimental commander commented to his captors:

> Just yesterday evening I saw an extensive plain spreading before our position. The next morning, however, many of your trenches appeared in front of us and communication trenches criss-crossed the whole place. I knew then we were finished.[79]

The sight of Communist troops suddenly appearing and seeking close combat caused the GMD frontline defenders to rapidly collapse.

After penetrating the walls, the Communists rapidly converged on the center of the city. Utilizing small-unit tactics and an abundant amount of hand-held explosives like dynamite and satchel charges to confuse and cut through any strong points, they quickly reduced the defenses at the Stone Bridge, Zhengtai Hotel, and the railway station. The battle was over within a week, with the final pockets of resistance being silenced on November 13. The fall of Shijiazhuang cost Sun another 24,000 men, consolidated the Communists' control over the Beiping-Hankou railway, and, perhaps more importantly, proved they were capable of capturing cities. Yang's forces later completed their victory and solidified their stranglehold on south Hebei by capturing Yuanshi, a city with strong walls and a 4,000 man garrison, on December 13.

On December 1, Zhu De praised the "great significance" of the Shijiazhuang campaign, pointing out the unprecedented tactical and logistical achievements of Nie's army.[80] The most important points he addressed were combined arms and lower echelon leadership. In particular, the use of trenches dug perpendicular to the city walls to close with the enemy was a considerable improvement over the mass human wave attacks employed at the Second Battle of Siping. Zhu also praised the high degree of cooperation between the infantry and artillery. Although the Communists still suffered from shortages in firepower, the SCH Field Army's squad-level assault tactics proved effective against enemy strong points and obstacles. Apparently, one of their keys to success was the ability to make alternate routes and attack the enemy from an unexpected direction by destroying walls or creating tunnels with explosives. Junior and noncommissioned officers also proved their worth by effectively conducting maneuvers and seizing the initiative. All of this demonstrated the increasing professionalism the successful integration of modern equipment into the Communist army. Not just an important victory, the capture of Shijiazhuang marked an important step in the maturation of the army as a whole.

The transformation of the Communist army at the tactical level went hand-in-hand with its strategic successes. While the Central Plains Offensive was perhaps the most significant strategic event of 1947, it could be argued that the clashes at Qingfengdian and Shijiazhuang were the most important battles of the same year. For one, the Communists had not had much success in this region before Qingfengdian, with major defeats at Datong, Jining, Zhangjiakou, and Chengde in 1946, and only limited successes in the first half of 1947. Winning a major field battle and capturing their first large, defended city of the war were important boosts for morale. Also important was the fact that cities were no longer safe havens for the GMD. For instance, Mao directed that cities and strong points should now be taken if weakly defended.[81] Zhu expressed a similar sentiment when he noted that "soon, we will capture a second and a third city the size of Shijiazhuang, and there are many more to come."[82] Lastly, with south Hebei now firmly in Communist control, they had again defeated Chiang's strategy of pacifying a region in order to divert troops elsewhere. Instead, it was the Communists who had secured a region and could now employ one of their field armies to support a region of their choice.

Return to hallowed ground: Third Battle of Siping

At the end of 1947, as Nie began to consolidate his hold on south Hebei and while the East China Field, Central Plains Field, and the Chen-Xie Armies established their respective bases in the Central Plains, Lin Biao launched the Winter Offensive in Manchuria. Part of the reason for this attack was the return of the 17th Army, which Chiang had originally sent to reinforce Chen during the Autumn Offensive, back to north China. This move was the result of Nie's victory at Qingfengdian and Shijiazhuang, which made the SCH Field Army's accomplishment all the more important. Originally, Lin planned a repeat of his earlier attack against Jilin City – a siege followed by an ambush of the relief column.[83] Mao approved a new attack and proposed that the SCH Military District support it by attacking one of the major railroads in Hebei.[84]

However, after reviewing the GMD disposition, Lin decided that southern Manchuria was a better target. He planned to first attack in northwest Liaoning to spread out Chen's defenses and then conduct a widespread offensive against the smaller cities of the Liaoshen corridor including Anshan, Yingkou, and Jinzhou.[85] Waiting for the Liao River to freeze over, the NDUA did not begin deploying until early December.[86] On December 15, the attack began with Communist forces simultaneously investing Fakui, Zhangwu, and Xinlitun. This forced Chen to employ the 22nd Division to relieve Fakui.[87] Although this move was anticipated, the NDUA ambush failed, threatening to unravel the rest of Communists' the siege operations.

Lin decided to abandon the attack on Fakui and shifted his forces west to Zhangwu to reapply the same method of siege and ambush. This time, Chen did not intervene and the town fell on December 28. Believing the main part of the campaign to be over, Lin dispersed his columns, resting some, and ordering others to attack secondary targets.[88] Chen, however, saw that as an opportunity to finally seize the offensive and, on the first day of 1948, he deployed four corps to conduct a large-scale attack into north Liaoning. Lin and his staff immediately drew in their forces and concentrated against the 5th Corps, which had not yet joined the rest of Chen's forces and was relatively isolated.

The two sides met on January 3 when the 5th Corps encountered a Communist blocking force outside of Gongzhutun. The GMD commander, Chen Linda, realized he was being surrounded and sent an urgent request for reinforcements, while attempting to disengage his forces. Chen Linda's requests were ultimately futile as NDUA blocking positions on the north bank of the Liao River and in the hills of the Huangjia district had already cut him off from immediate support. Chen Cheng's response was to "allow" Chen Linda to withdraw, but by then the Communists had completed their encirclement. The 5th Corps attempted to break out but was destroyed in short order on January 7. This effectively ended the counterattack as well as Chen Cheng's tenure as commander in the Northeast. He was ignominiously replaced by Wei Lihuang ten days later. However, the NDUA was not finished and before Wei could even assume command, the 4th and 6th Columns struck deep into the GMD rear. They attacked Liaoyang at the end of the month and captured the city on February 6. In the process, the NDUA destroyed the 54th Division and severed the Zhongchang Railroad south of Shenyang, effectively cutting Wei off from his ports on the Bo Sea.

These successes gave Mao pause, but not because he feared a GMD counterattack. Instead, Mao's concern was that Chiang might withdraw his forces from Manchuria altogether. While this would be a major tactical victory for the Communists, it could endanger operations in the Central Plains if forces from northeast China were reassigned there. In fact, this was exactly what US advisors in Nanjing were already proposing. Mao judged that Chiang had not taken this step because the Communists were still contained north of the Yangtze River and the NDUA had not yet won a major, decisive battle. While Mao supported continuing the current line of operations in Manchuria, he was increasingly wary that Wei might retreat into Hebei of his own volition. Consequently, Mao believed there was a need to surround the entire GMD army and destroy it, rather than simply defeat it. He envisioned a dual pincer attack with the NDUA engaging from the north and the SCH Field Army converging from the south.[89] Yet Lin was not convinced by Mao's reasoning and instead insisted on securing his rear and advancing in an linear fashion. Additionally, Lin thought that as long as Chiang held Changchun, Siping, and Jilin City he would not abandon Manchuria.[90] Therefore, his strategy called for seizing one of those cities in order to draw Wei's army into the open.

Despite this larger strategic discussion, the NDUA's next attacks would be shaping operations focused on isolating Shenyang. Lin's forces captured Fakui and swept away all the GMD garrisons between it and Siping, granting the Communists unimpeded control over western Manchuria. In the south, the 4th and 6th Columns rolled up Liaoyang and Anshan by February 19. The 4th Column then moved south to Yingkou and induced its garrison, the 58th Division, to defect. Taking possession of this critical port on February 26th, the Communists now could concentrate on the cities. Lin's eyes fell on Siping. In addition to its symbolic value,

Siping was the next logical target because its capture would completely isolate Changchun and Jilin City. Additionally, Chen Cheng had stripped its garrison for his offensive in January, leaving only a single division in defense. Wei had yet to address this weakness.

On February 26, the NDUA took another step toward professionalization by becoming the Northeast Field Army.[91] The next day, Lin's forces deployed north of Siping to begin the attack. Three columns under Li Tianyou would be responsible for the assault, while four columns would provide support south of Siping to ambush any relief effort. Smaller units were also deployed to guard the approaches to Jinzhou and Jilin City. However, these blocking forces moved too late to stop the transfer of the Jilin City garrison, the 60th Corps, to Changchun on March 9. Wei's decision to abandon the city took the Communists by surprise, but it did not change their plans for the attack on Siping. Facing them was Peng E's 88th Division, which was an experienced, elite unit. However, the siege and the extended operations in the harsh Manchurian climate had taken their toll on the unit. As Lin employed his artillery to good effect against this city – having learned his lesson from Second Siping – the 88th Division's morale and fighting capacity quickly withered. On March 13, the Northeast Field Army began a general assault. After almost a full day of fighting, the city that for so long had been a thorn in Lin Biao's side finally fell into his hands.

The capture of Siping officially ended the Winter Offensive, and with it went the GMD's best chance to retain anything more than a foothold in Manchuria. In three months of fighting, the Northeast Bandit Suppression Headquarters – which was re-designated upon Wei's arrival – had suffered 156,000 casualties and lost key territory. As in other theaters, most of the captured GMD soldiers were quickly integrated into the Northeast Field Army, furthering the damage to Nanjing. Yet these quantifiable values paled in comparison to the damage done in terms of morale, strategic position, and faith in the government. For instance, a Communist press release estimated that of the total 1,120,000 GMD casualties suffered from August 1946 to August 1947, only 426,000 were killed or wounded in action. The rest had surrendered or defected.[92] This evoked a public outcry in Nanjing about the poor handling of the war, and the loudest critics called for a complete withdrawal from the Northeast.

Yet Chiang would not budge, and he called for an "all-out effort to save Manchuria from the fate of becoming another 'Manchukuo'" and stated that the region was "as vital to China as the head is to the rest of the body." Consequently, Chiang moved four corps north to Changchun and Shenyang in a desperate attempt to repair the situation.[93] He also tried to fix some of the systemic issues that crippled effective GMD political-military cooperation at a national level. This included appointing a new Defense Minister, He Yingchin, and promoting Gu Zhutong to chief-of-staff. They were brought in to try to break down the personal animosity among the GMD generals and enhance centralized control. In one of his first public statements, Gu advocated better treatment and training for the rank and file, increased latitude for field commanders to make decisions, only employing men of proven ability, and an effort to recover the initiative on the battlefield.[94]

In the end, it was a case of too little, too late, at least in regard to northeast China. The fall of Yingkou, Siping, and Jilin City reduced the GMD holdings to Changchun, Shenyang, and the narrow rail connection through the Liaoshen corridor. Any one of these places was vulnerable to attack from any direction and could easily be isolated. This outcome left the Communists in a dominant strategic position in Manchuria, leading many in the CCP high command to start looking forward to the next operation. Mao already anticipated overrunning Wei's army and deploying Lin's powerful Northeast Field Army against Beiping or an objective further south. As with his earlier ideas, he envisioned waging a decisive battle in the spring in which Lin would concentrate his forces at Shanhaiguan or Jinzhou and conduct a massive encirclement campaign to annihilate Wei's army. Again, Lin opposed this scheme and cautioned that long-term operations were needed, including a methodical reduction and capture of Changchun. Fearing Mao's audacious and dangerous flanking maneuver, he believed that capturing Changchun would lead to a much more manageable field battle. He saw an attack on the Liaoshen corridor as unnecessarily risky.

Despite the fact that the Communists possessed the upper hand, Mao and Lin's debate would have to wait. Realistically, Wei's main force had yet to be weakened to a point where the Northeast Field Army could defeat it. Additionally, despite their defeats, the GMD forces were even more concentrated than they were in the past, which offered Lin no opportunity to nibble away at the edges as he had for the past two years. The GMD's new reinforcements and leadership also had the potential of turning the tide. Another major defeat like the Second Battle of Siping, or a Pyrrhic victory at Changchun, in which Lin's army was again decimated, might cast the momentum back into the GMD's favor. Thus, while the tide had turned in northeast China by the end of 1947, the battle would not be decided until 1948.

Chasing the deer in the Central Plains

By the winter of 1947–48, the Central Plains Offensive had radically changed the GMD dispositions and contributed greatly to CCP successes in other regions, most notably north and northeast China. Of the 160 brigades available to the GMD for frontline duty, the Communists estimated that 90 had been tied down by the Central Plains Field Army.[95] However, this also meant that Liu and Deng's forces were under a great deal of pressure. In December, the Central Plains Bureau decided that the only way to avoid collapse was to break out of the ring of GMD forces with one part of the army. In this way, they hoped to divide Bai Chongxi's attention between the base area and a mobile force in the countryside. Although it is a well known military dictum to not divide forces in the face of a superior enemy, the Communists realized that the status quo eventually would be just as risky. For this new plan, Deng, Li Xiannian, and three columns would remain in the Dabie Mountains, while Liu, the Central Plains Bureau, and a single column would break out and conduct operations north of the Huai River. To aid the Central Plains Field Army, Su Yu and Chen Geng would attack in their respective regions to distract the enemy. Mao agreed to the plan on December 9.[96]

The operation began on December 14, with the West Army capturing Xuchang the next day. Over the ensuing week, the Communists gained control of some of the smaller towns and destroyed roads and railroads, forcing Bai to dispatch the Reorganized 3rd and 20th Divisions and the 47th Corps to suppress the new threat. In response to this deployment, Su Yu and Chen Geng decided to concentrate their forces to attack the Reorganized 3rd Division before it joined hands with Bai's reinforcements. After surrounding their target at Jingangsi on Christmas Day, weight of numbers allowed the Communists to deal with the garrison in a single day of fighting. Hoping to capitalize on their success, they attacked the Reorganized 20th Division, which had withdrawn to Queshan, but failed to destroy it. Ending the campaign on the last day of 1947, the operation had succeeded in its main goal of assisting Liu Bocheng and his portion of the Central Plains Field Army in escaping Bai's cordon.

In early January, Mao, Zhou, and Ren Bishi held a secret meeting to plan operations for 1948. Chen Yi, who had traveled to northwest China for another meeting, was the only field commander available to attend. During the course of this session, Mao proposed that Chen send a detachment from the East China Field Army across the Yangtze River to south China. This had been one of Mao's personal projects since 1944, and he had proposed it at least three times in 1947.[97] Previously, Mao's generals had managed to change his mind by citing a wide range of limiting factors, including casualties, lack of supplies, lack of cadre to establish a new base, etc. This time, the idea met with more enthusiasm. After cabling the proposal back to the East China Field Army headquarters, Su Yu replied with two alternatives. The first was to rest for a month and a half and then move south at the end of March. The second was to rest for a month and a half, fight one or two battles, and finally cross the Yangtze in May. Mao approved the first option and ordered the East China Field Army to reorganize for this new strategic offensive.[98]

The East China Field Army, which was already divided into two elements, would now separate into four. Chen Shiju and three columns, the 3rd, 8th, and 10th, were to remain in the Central Plains under the command of Liu Bocheng. Chen Yi and Su Yu would lead the remnants of the West Army, the 1st, 4th, and 6th Columns across the Yangtze River as soon as they were ready.[99] Xu Shiyou's East Army became the Shandong Army and would continue its current line of operations to deny Chiang total control over the province. The last portion would be formed out of Wei Guoqing's 2nd Column, which was to detach from the Shandong Army and join the units the Central China Field Army had left behind to conduct guerrilla operations in 1946. Together, they would form the new North Jiangsu Army.[100] This force would serve the dual functions of providing support to the Central Plains Field Army as well as keeping open a line of communication with Chen and Su's expedition.

Chiang also now saw Shandong as secondary theater. Believing that Fan Hanjie's offensive in the latter half of 1947 had finally secured the area, he dissolved the Jiaodong Army and transferred Fan to serve as deputy commander of the Northeast Bandit Suppression Headquarters under Wei Lihuang. After reinforcing GMD elements in northeast and central China, Chiang left only 13 divisions in Shandong. These were concentrated mainly in the large cities and in defense of the

Jiaodong-Ji'nan and Tianjin-Pukou railroads. He also formed the Xuzhou Bandit Suppression Headquarters, formerly Xue Yue's Xuzhou Pacification Headquarters, under Gu Zhutong, to command GMD forces in the region, which included Shandong and the Longhai, Beiping-Hankou, and Tianjin-Pukou railroads.

With Fan gone, Xu's Shandong Army could finally take the offensive. Since the GMD no longer had the strength to dominate the Jiaodong region, the Secretariat approved Xu's earlier plan to leave the area and conduct attacks behind enemy lines. To do so, they would first sever the Jiaodong-Ji'nan railroad to draw the GMD into northeast Shandong. Afterwards, the Shandong Army could slip into central and west Shandong to coordinate with the rest of the East China Field Army. The eventual plan was for the army to remerge and engage the Xuzhou Pacification Command in early summer in a large battle somewhere in the Huaihai or southwest Shandong. In this way, they could destroy or cripple Gu's forces and thus remove the last major obstacle between Su Yu and the Yangtze River.[101]

Xu's plan of attack was to send one column each to capture Zhoucun and Zhangdian, two towns east of Ji'nan on the Jiaodong-Ji'nan railroad. He would leave his last column behind to block any enemy reinforcements from Qingdao and Yantai. On March 10, the 7th Column surrounded Zhangdian, but the garrison abandoned the city rather than be destroyed. The 32nd Division at Zhoucun was not as lucky, and on March 13, the Communists wiped them out and captured the town. The Shandong Army moved quickly to its next objective, Zizhou, which they captured before Wang Yaowu, commander of the 2nd Pacification District in Ji'nan, could send reinforcements. Wang, believing the next attack would be against his headquarters, ordered Chen Jincheng, commander of the Reorganized 45th Division at Weixian, to transfer two regiments to the Ji'nan garrison. The loss of these troops meant that Chen would have to reduce the size of his perimeter, which included abandoning the high ground surrounding the town. This proved extremely fortuitous for the Communists since Weixian, not Ji'nan, was Xu's next target.

On April 2, local troops from the East China Military District moved ahead of Xu's regular forces to besiege Weixian. Over the next few days, the 7th and 13th Columns arrived and positioned their artillery to reduce Weixian's defenses. Taking a page out of Nie Rongzhen's book, they also began digging sapping trenches for the final assault. In the ensuing two weeks, the 9th Column also arrived. Together, they eliminated most of the GMD strong points outside the city. The final assault began in the early morning hours of April 24 and by dawn the Shandong Army had captured Weixian.

As the Shandong Army severed the Jiaodong-Ji'nan Railroad, the Central Plains Field Army planned to mass its forces north of the Huai River to pave the way for Su Yu's Yangtze River Campaign. In order to do this, however, Liu Bocheng had to extract Deng Xiaoping's army from the Dabie Mountains. He deployed the "two Chens" – Chen Geng and Chen Shiju (who had just recently been detached from the East China Field Army) – to attack the Longhai railroad and assist Deng's breakout. However, at the end of February, they changed their plans when Peng Dehuai's Northwest Field Army destroyed Hu Zongnan's Reorganized 29th Corps at Yichuan. This disaster forced Hu to transfer Pei Changhui's Army from Luoyang to defend Tongguan and Xi'an while he drew on the Xi'an garrison to replace his losses in north Shaanxi. Recognizing that only Qiu Xingxiang's 206th Youth Corps Division now defended Luoyang, the "two Chens" decided, with CMC approval, to join forces and capture Luoyang.[102]

The two Chens employed four columns for the operation, two to attack the city and two to block GMD reinforcements. By March 11, they had surrounded Luoyang and were preparing to assault the city itself. Chiang ordered Bai Chongxi and Hu to send forces to lift the siege, but they were too slow and the city fell on March 14. Two days later, Hu belatedly reached the southern suburbs. He began to surround the city in preparation for a siege. This might have been disastrous for the Communists, who were still in Luoyang, but heavy rain made movement impossible. With the Luo and Yi Rivers uncrossable, Hu could not complete his encirclement and the "two Chens" escaped.

The Luoyang Campaign not only inflicted another damaging blow to GMD morale, but it succeeded in its main goal – assisting Deng's breakout from the Dabie Mountains. However, the battle had been costly for the "two Chens." Casualties were heavy, especially in the 8th Division, which led the assault on Luoyang. This meant that the Communists would not have three full-strength armies available to fight a large-scale battle in the Central Plains. Instead, Mao ordered Chen Geng and Chen Shiju to rest and then move to southeast Henan to await future opportunities. In the meantime, the now combined Central Plains Field Army would conduct a smaller-scale campaign to shape the battlefield.[103] Another consequence of the assault on Luoyang was that the "two Chens" also could not provide any further support to the Northwest Field Army, which now had the upper hand in Shaanxi. Unfazed, Peng Dehuai decided against retaking Yan'an, despite its political value, and instead moved further south to threaten Hu Zongnan's headquarters at Xi'an. This would force Hu to remain in Shaanxi and out of the struggle for the Central Plains.[104]

At the end of March, the Central Plains Field Army and portions of the North Jiangsu Army joined forces to besiege Fuyang. Correctly guessing that Liu Bocheng meant to ambush a relief column, the GMD sent an overwhelming force to lift the siege. Liu cancelled the campaign and withdrew his army before they became trapped. However, the GMD decision to commit so many troops exposed other portions of the Longhai Railroad to a Communist attack. As a result, while the Central Plains Field Army lifted the siege of Fuyang and withdrew, Chen Geng slipped behind the GMD to recapture Luoyang. This time it would be permanent and the damage to the GMD even more severe. After recapturing the city, Chen left it in the hands of local forces and moved his army into southwest Henan, as per the Secretariat's order in the wake of the first battle of Luoyang.

After the capture of Luoyang, Mao ordered Liu and Deng to combine forces with Cheng Geng and draw the GMD armies into west Henan. Since they were not able to draw GMD forces in the Central Plains into a decisive battle, the Communists hoped to at least draw them away from the Huaihai area.[105] However, Mao was now having second thoughts about Su Yu's crossing of the Yangtze, and the thought of potentially losing three full-strength columns because of impatience led him to postpone the venture until the summer. Furthermore, Mao recognized that the main obstacle was Qiu Qingquan's Reorganized 5th Corps, which not only blocked the way south but had also weathered the "two Chens" best attempts to draw it into battle. Thus, Mao decided that Su's army would have to join the fight in the Central Plains before it could enter south China.[106]

For this new plan, the CMC again reorganized the Central Plains order of battle. Chen Shiju was to move east with two columns – his 10th Column was with Chen Geng, so Mao felt that it was better to leave the unit there instead of moving it – and join Su Yu's Army in the Huaihai region. Su was also given control of the Central Plains Field Army's 1st and 11th Columns, which Liu Bocheng had left behind in east Henan and Anhui after the Fuyang Campaign. The Secretariat planned for these seven columns – with the Shandong Army providing support by tying down GMD forces in Shandong[107] – to destroy the 5th Corps in June and July, thus opening a path to the Yangtze River. If this period of time was not sufficient, Mao planned to return the 10th Column to Chen Shiju's command and try again in the fall after the rainy season. At the same time, the Secretariat also reconfigured the Central Plains Bureau to include both Chen Yi and Su Yu in the chain of command. Chen also became the deputy commander of the Central Plains Military District, while Chen Geng's Army was formally integrated into the Central Plains Field Army, raising its total strength to seven columns.

During this time, the Secretariat and CMC also reunited. Following Peng Dehuai's decisive victory over Hu Zongnan in Yichuan, Mao decided that the rump Secretariat/CMC was no longer required to serve as bait in north Shaanxi. In fact, Mao estimated that Hu's elite units were all gone and his remaining 23 brigades were overstretched and weak.[108] In addition, Xu Xiangqian, who had taken command of a force consisting of local units of the old SHSH Military District, had conducted a series of bold operations against Yan Xishan beginning in December 1947. This culminated in the capture of Yuncheng and Linfen, leaving Yan with only Taiyuan still in his possession. With Hu and Yan both crippled, Mao, Zhou, and Ren decided to move east and join Liu Shaoqi and Zhu De at Xibaipo in mid-April 1948. Although the restoration of the Secretariat as a whole was a significant political victory in itself, the most symbolic gesture occurred a few weeks later on April 28 when the Northwest Field Army recaptured Yan'an. It was now clear that the war had come full circle since Chiang unleashed the Strong Point Offensive in 1947.

While the war had reached its turning point with the Central Plains Offensive, the GMD army remained a formidable obstacle. Although outmaneuvered and outfought at many junctures, it still guarded the road to south China. However, the Communist counterattack had demonstrated that Chiang's Strong Point Offensive had failed completely. Liu and Deng's operations in the Central Plains had also affected the entire strategic situation by forcing Nanjing to strip its defenses in Manchuria, Shandong, and north China. This in turn allowed the Communists to turn the tables in those regions and resume offensive operations. Liu Bocheng remarked that the GMD had lost the initiative and now they would have to fight on the Communists' terms. He used a traditional Chinese saying, "chasing the deer in the Central Plains," to not only refer to the seesaw nature of the fighting but to also underline the decisive importance of that region in the age-old struggle for power in China.

Despite Mao's wish to carry the war into south China, the second half of 1948 would continue to see intense combat in the Central Plains. His generals had convinced him, once again, that an audacious thrust south would have to wait until GMD defenses could be further weakened. However, despite their strategic advantage, the Communists were entering a dangerous period. They needed to look no further than their adversaries to realize that gaining territory or moving forward without annihilating the enemy's armed forces was a recipe for disaster. In a way, the strategic situation had almost completely reversed. While the GMD braced for the coming tide, the Communists now had to be concerned about securing certain theaters of operations, such as northeast China or Shanxi, so that they could employ their full strength for fighting a decisive battle on the Central Plains or crossing the Yangtze River.

Either way, neither the Communists nor the GMD envisioned fighting the final major battles or deciding the war in 1948. The GMD hoped that a strategic defense could help them regain the initiative and eventually allow them to resume the offensive. The CCP, on the other hand, looked to a series of shaping operations to improve their position in the long-term and prepare for another counteroffensive. However, this was not meant to be because the later half of 1948 and the first month of 1949 would, in fact, see the battles that would virtually end the war.

5　Three crucibles of victory

By the summer of 1948, the Third Chinese Civil War had reached its final phase. While the Communist army prepared to wage decisive battles and so-called "battles of annihilation" in northeast China and the Central Plains, the newly reunified Secretariat/CMC also looked ahead to the implications of these operations, unprecedented as they would be in scale and importance. One primary concern was command and control as the armies were growing larger and more geographically dispersed. In the beginning of the year, Mao circulated a directive entitled "On Setting up a System of Reports," which highlighted the need for the regional forces to be accountable to the center and ordered that "the Party's leading bodies at all levels must correct bad habits of neither asking the higher level for prior instructions nor submitting reports afterwards."[1] He also reminded "leaders of field armies and military areas of their obligation to submit reports and requests for instructions on matter of strategy when necessary."[2] While it was common policy for the regional commanders to get approval from Mao and the CMC before they undertook major campaigns, there had been numerous occasions when they did not wait for a reply or moved without orders.

On the surface Mao's concern might appear simply a reassertion of Marxist-Leninist control, but there was sound military logic behind it, namely that of unity of command and effort. The Communists had learned its importance first hand during 1946 with the Shandong and Central China Field Armies, as well as seeing how it affected their adversaries. This was likely part of the reason why the numerous layers of bureaucracy within the army were slowly being eliminated to be replaced by a formal system of field armies, columns, and divisions. On the other hand, Mao's reminders also may have derived from a fear that the separation of the Secretariat had confused matters and, now reunited, Mao and the high command wanted to reassert a clear chain of command for the campaign season.

The Secretariat was also making political moves that would drastically affect the war. The most significant was the formation of a CCP proto-state to directly oppose Nanjing – a de jure challenge in addition to the preexisting de facto one. However, instead of staking the claim that the CCP should control the entire country, they founded the North China People's Government on August 17 to govern only the liberated areas. By the end of the year, this new administration would largely replace the separate Communist military and political regional organs. Mao laid down the following stipulations that had to be met before the CCP could claim control over China:

> After the bogus National Assembly elects Chiang Kai-shek president later in the year and he is even more thoroughly discredited, after we score bigger victories and expand our territories, preferably after the capture of one or two of the country's largest cities, and after northeastern China, northern China, [Shandong], northern [Jiangsu], [Henan], [Hubei] and [Anhui] are all linked together in one contiguous area, it will be necessary to establish the Central People's Government. This time will probably be in 1949.[3]

He also saw the war continuing at least another three years before the Communists could claim final victory over the GMD.[4]

Consequently, the Communist looked to 1948 to be a year of strategic shaping operations in which they would engage in protracted campaigns with multiple stages. In the Central Plains, the two field armies there looked for opportunities to damage Gu Zhutong and Bai Chongxi's armies enough to clear a path for a Yangtze River crossing. Although Mao had postponed the operation in the spring, the creation of bases in south China was still a priority for 1948. Doing so was, of course, contingent on whether they could sufficiently weaken the GMD defenses in the Central Plains. As for winning the war in north China, the Secretariat believed that only by securing northeast China and transferring the Northeast Field Army south, could they tip the balance of power north of the Yangtze River. Thus, the Communists looked to pin down, harass, and wear out the GMD armies in the Central Plains, while simultaneously destroying all of Chiang's forces in north and northeast China. An unthinkable objective only a year earlier, even in 1948 it bordered on unrealistic. However, in seeking such a situation, the Communists unwittingly set the stage for a series of climactic battles that would end the war sooner than anyone on either side had ever imagined.

Before the storm: shaping operations in the Central Plains

In June, Mao and the CMC planned another offensive against the GMD forces based in Xuzhou, to pave the way for the long anticipated Yangtze River Campaign. According to Zhu De, the Reorganized 5th and 18th Corps was the most dangerous forces in the Central Plains.[5] For the first campaign of the summer, the Communists focused on destroying Qiu Qingquan's Reorganized 5th Corps. The main effort would be Su Yu's army, which had been held back from crossing the Yangtze for this very purpose. On his left flank, the Central Plains Field Army would block Bai Chongxi's main element, Hu Lian's Reorganized 18th Corps while on the right flank, the Shandong Field Army would fix the forces of the Xuzhou HQ in Shandong by attacking the Xuzhou-Ji'nan railroad.[6]

To engage Hu Lian, Liu and Deng split their army into two parts – the East and West Armies – and planned the Wandong Campaign. The East Army, consisting of three columns under 3rd Column commander Chen Xilian, would make a feint at Zhumadian and Queshan on the Beiping-Hankou Railroad, to draw Hu Lian in that direction. In the meantime, the West Army, also consisting of three columns and local troops under Chen Geng, prepared to ambush any forces Bai dispatched from Nanyang. After Chen Xilian began his attacks on May 25, Bai responded by sending his deputy commander, Zhang Zhen, with three divisions. However, Zhang realized he was walking into a trap and escaped from the Communist encirclement on May 31, only one day before the West Army launched a general attack. In the end, the Central Plains Field Army managed to destroy a division and the 183rd Brigade, a victory well short of their original goal. However, as with many of these campaigns, these maneuvers had succeeded in the main task of creating a diversion and, in this case, prevented Bai from interfering with Su Yu's operation against Qiu.

As soon as Su Yu's 1st Army debouched into southwest Shandong, Qiu Qingquan immediately ordered his corps to assemble at Shangqiu to prevent the Communists from moving any further south. Unable to get around Qiu's force, Mao and the CMC ordered Su to remain in place and wait until the GMD dispersed before he again sought battle.[7] As a result, Chen Shiju, whose army was supposed to work with Su, moved west instead to assist the Wandong Campaign. However, Liu ended the campaign before Chen could arrive. To try to provoke the GMD, Su directed Chen to attack Kaifeng, which was only guarded by a regular brigade and a handful of local troops. While he did the 1st Army and the Central Plains Field Army were to block Qiu Qingquan and Hu Lian, respectively, from interfering. Chen employed two columns to besiege Kaifeng on June 17. Despite making some progress, Qiu's mounting pressure on the 1st Army and Chen's inability to take the final strongpoints at Kaifeng convinced Su to call off the operation. Qiu reached the city on June 27, but by then the Communists had disappeared.

Chiang, however, was not satisfied with simply lifting the siege. He immediately ordered his forces to pursue Chen Shiju's army. He attached two divisions from Liu Ruming's 4th Pacification Zone to Qiu's force as well as formed the 7th Army out of two divisions to intercept Chen Shiju. With the GMD armies now out in the open, Mao ordered Chen and Su to combine their forces to destroy the 7th Army while the Central Plains Field Army maintained its blocking operations against Hu Lian.[8] At that time, Liu Bocheng was resting and resupplying his forces, but he immediately reactivated them to draw Hu to battle. On June 27, Su's 1st Army surrounded the 75th Division, one of the units of the 7th Army, in northwest Suixian. Chen Shiju deployed to block Qiu in the north and allow Su time to destroy his quarry.

However, pressure from Qiu and reinforcements dispatched from the Xuzhou HQ – including Huang Baitao's 25th Division and the 3rd Rapid Reaction Team from Shandong – overwhelmed Chen Shiju's lines. This forced Su to intensify operations in his sector to destroy the 75th Division. By July 2, he completed his task, but by then the 25th Division was only six miles away. Rather than abandon the battlefield and the recently captured equipment, Su decided to stay and engage the 25th Division. While he encircled and isolated Huang's force, Su requested Liu Bocheng block Hu Lian's army for another week. On July 5, he began a general attack against Huang but made little impression on the defenses. In light of this failure and of the fact that Hu Lian had slipped past Liu's blocking force and was now threatening Su's rear, Su withdrew on July 8. However, Qiu made the 1st Army pay for overstaying its welcome by inflicting serious casualties on the Communists as they attempted to evacuate their wounded.[9]

The results of the first summer campaigns in the Central Plains failed to produce the tactical or strategic conditions for a late summer crossing of the Yangtze River. Liu and the Central Plains Field Army did manage to capture Xiangyang on July 14, which drew Bai away from the critical Huaihai region, but Su had been unable to defeat the Xuzhou HQ in a large-scale battle. His campaign had, however, caused unexpected effects in Shandong. Originally, Xu's Shandong Army was only supposed to support the efforts in the Central Plains battlefield by seizing Taian and then withdrawing when the GMD reinforcements arrived. However, the GMD did not retake Taian and instead shifted their forces south to respond to Su and Chen Shiju's operations. As a result, Xu saw an opportunity to cause more problems for the GMD's defense network in Shandong.

On July 4, Mao approved the Shandong Field Army's plan to attack Yanzhou, a city on the Tianjin-Pukou Railroad. At that time, Su was fighting Huang Baitao's 25th Division in east Henan, and Mao wanted to fix the Xuzhou HQ to prevent them from dispatching any more reinforcements into the Central Plains.[10] On July 12, Xu began a general attack on Yanzhou, which was defended by the Reorganized 12th Division. Originally planned as a ten-day siege, the battle lasted less than 24 hours. Xu's forces destroyed the division and captured its commander, Huo Shouyi. Wang Yaowu sent the 84th Division to relieve the city, but the rapid fall of Yanzhou allowed Xu to ambush this force with his entire army. However, while the Shandong Field Army inflicted heavy casualties on the 84th Division, the reinforcements escaped encirclement and managed to escape back to Ji'nan on July 15.

After this success, Mao wanted Xu to consider attacking Ji'nan during his next campaign. The Secretariat reasoned that threatening Ji'nan could force Qiu Qingquan and Huang Baitao into Shandong, which would assist Su's next campaign in the Central Plains.[11] Since Su had withdrawn his forces to rest and reorganize after the East Henan Campaign, his 1st Army was available to support the Shandong Army's attack. Su dispatched Chen Shiju and four columns to southwest Shandong to support Xu and deployed the rest of his army to menace the Longhai railroad.[12] The original plan called for the attack on Ji'nan to begin in the latter half of July, but the CMC changed the focus of the campaign to draw out and destroy Qiu's Reorganized 5th Corps, rather than capturing the city.[13] However, Su argued that they should try to capture the city.[14] On August 12, Mao compromised by making both objectives the goal of the campaign.[15]

As the Communists prepared to launch their attack on Ji'nan, the GMD also reconfigured its strategy. Chiang dramatically reorganized his Central Plains forces in an effort to orient them towards field battle rather than sector defense. In June, he restored to active duty Liu Zhi, who had been removed after the Dingtao Campaign, by appointing him commander of the Xuzhou HQ. This allowed the former

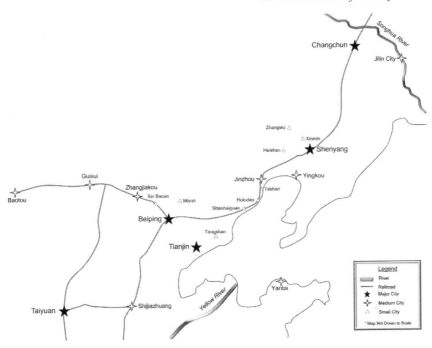

Figure 5.1 1948: The Liaoshen and Beiping Campaigns.

commander, Gu Zhutong, to return to Nanjing to focus full time on his duties as commander of the army headquarters and chief-of-staff. Under Liu Zhi was another failed commander, Du Yuming, who served concurrently as deputy commander at Xuzhou and commander of the new 2nd Army (see below). However, Du assumed most of the tactical and strategic duties for the headquarters, making him the virtual commander-in-chief while Qiu Qingquan commanded the 2nd Army.

In a way, Liu and Du's restoration not only reflected the failure of GMD strategy but also the dwindling pool of available talent, loyal to Chiang or otherwise. Chiang reformed his units into field armies, mirroring the configuration the Communists had taken a year prior. This included the formation of Du Yuming's 2nd Army at Shangqiu, Huang Baitao's 7th Army in Xin Anzhen, Li Mi's 13th Army at Bengbu, and Sun Yuanliang's 16th Army at Zhengzhou. Despite the new designation, most of these units were simply amalgamations of old ones and did not represent an injection of fresh manpower. Chiang also maintained the so-called Pacification Zones in Shandong, with the most important being Wang Yaowu's 2nd Pacification Zone at Ji'nan. After the defeat at Weixian, Wang had been significantly reinforced to bring his total manpower up to 110,000 men.

The new GMD strategy was a drastic change that seemed more like an act of desperation than a calculated measure. Yet the campaigns in the Central Plains during the summer did prove the GMD could weather the Communists' attacks when properly handled. For instance, the decisions and maneuvers employed by Qiu Qingquan, Huang Baitao, and Bai Chongxi showed that the GMD was now anticipating and counteracting the Communist tactic of ambushing a relief column, instead of obediently walking into the trap. The creation of GMD field armies offered a new opportunity for them to mass on Communist units, which were no longer the small, elusive guerrilla forces of yesterday. In this way, by professionalizing and transforming its army, the CCP also made it more vulnerable to conventional attack. However, the fact that the GMD made these adjustments after their adversaries had was not only an indictment of their own system, but demonstrated how successful the modernization of the Communist army had been.

Consequently, the war entered a new stage as the East China Field Army prepared to attack Ji'nan in another attempt to engage and annihilate the Reorganized 5th Corps – now the 2nd Army. The emphasis was no longer one of attaining a strategic position or gaining territory. The objective for both sides had devolved into the simple task of destroying the enemy's armed force. Consequently, the second half of 1948 would see the last phase of the war – the period of the great field battles.

The first crucible: Jinzhou and the Liaoshen Campaign

As Su Yu and Xu Shiyou planned to attack Ji'nan, Lin Biao also prepared to attack a major city, Changchun. The fall of Yingkou, Siping, and Jilin City in the first half of 1948 had reduced the GMD holdings in Manchuria to Changchun, Shenyang and the railway in the Liaoshen corridor. Lin still maintained his belief that only by capturing Changchun would the GMD forces in Shenyang be compelled to retreat. According to Zheng Tongguo, one of the deputy commanders of the Northeast HQ, Chiang had admitted as such.[16] Other factors for Lin included not wanting to leave an enemy force behind him and a desire to employ his full force on the front lines.

In effect, Lin's concept reflected a linear view of the battlefield. His mindset was also no doubt shaped by the fact that Communist forces operating behind GMD lines had been an important factor in turning the tide of the battle for Manchuria. Yet, despite these concerns, Mao continued to believe that the next campaign should focus exclusively on Jinzhou or Shanhaiguan in the Liaoshen corridor. For him, this was the only way to force the GMD army into a field battle. Despite this disagreement, both men believed that the Northeast Field Army's main task was to completely destroy Wei Lihuang's army and not let it escape. While they disagreed on the methods, both Mao and the Northeast Bureau envisioned destroying the Northeast HQ once and for all by the end of 1948.

In April, after the conclusion of the Winter Offensive, Lin began planning a general assault on Changchun. Mao still disagreed with this concept but he approved the operation. Furthermore, he ordered Yang Dezhi and the SCH Field Army to support the attack by creating a diversion south of Shanhaiguan to prevent Fu Zuoyi from interfering. Nonetheless, Mao was unhappy with the inability of Lin and his staff to "overcome the difficulties" that prevented them from attacking the Liaoshen corridor.[17] Allegedly, Mao was fully aware that forcing Lin to act when he did not want to was a difficult matter, and he did not press his luck on this occasion. In fact, the Chairman was once overheard saying that getting Lin to mount an offensive was harder than getting a cow to jump over a fence.[18] However, in this situation, the Secretariat reasoned that if Lin failed in his assault, they could then force him to carry out an attack on the Liaoshen corridor. At the same time, there would be no harm done if Lin succeeded at Changchun.

The Northeast Field Army's scheme for capturing Changchun was to conduct a phased operation. The first task was to destroy the city's outer defenses and the airfield. After that, they would wait for any GMD reinforcements. Once those were dealt with, the assault itself would begin.[19] These operations were slated to start in the middle of May. Lin underlined the importance of the battle by instructing his commanders to not let fear of casualties temper their actions.[20] As the Communists began deploying for the attack, Zheng Tongguo, who commanded the New 1st and 7th Corps at Changchun, drew in his perimeter to abandon some of his exterior strong points. However, he retained the airfield, which was his only remaining supply line. Despite this, the Communists did manage to capture and hold the airfield, although it changed hands numerous times. For the duration of the battle, Zheng would have to rely on supplies air-dropped into the city. By May 25, the Northeast Field Army completed the encirclement of the city and moved onto the next phase of their operation.[21]

Yet these initial battles confirmed Lin's worst fear, namely that defeating the Changchun garrison likely would be a drawn out, bloody affair. On May 29, he submitted a report to the CMC predicting heavy casualties.[22] In the beginning of June, Mao and Zhu ordered the Northeast Field Army to conduct further reconnaissance and submit a detailed report proposing possible courses of action, rather than launch an immediate attack.[23] The CMC eventually approved a proposal which called for a prolonged siege of Changchun for three to four months. During this period, the Northeast Field Army would reduce Changchun's defenses but at the same time look for an opportunity to draw out Liao Yaoxiang, the second deputy commander of the Northeast HQ, from Shenyang.[24]

However, the siege continued into July without producing the conditions for such a battle. Facing pressure from the CMC and diminishing results from the siege, Lin and Luo Ronghuan held a strategy meeting at Harbin. On July 20, Lin and Luo finally consented to Mao's wishes and proposed abandoning the siege in favor of seeking battle with GMD forces in Liaoning. Mao enthusiastically agreed, directing them to either attack Fan Hanjie's army at Jinzhou and Tangshan (Fan was the third deputy commander of the Northeast Bandit Pacification Headquarters) or move into Rehe to attack Fu Zuoyi and force Wei to send his forces in pursuit.[25] However, Lin did not like either of these plans, which placed him between the bulk of Wei and Fu's armies while his own forces were far from their supply bases. Claiming that he would suffer heavy casualties by attacking Jinzhou and that his supplies would be insufficient, Lin suggested attacking a series of small cities on the Beiping-Shenyang railroad while Nie's SCH Field Army attacked Datong to draw Fu west.[26] Mao agreed to this proposal, even though it watered down his original approach, and he assured Lin that Yang Dezhi could neutralize Fu.[27] At the same time, Mao continued to stress the need to prevent Wei's army from escaping south. He also harshly criticized Lin, Luo Ronghuan, and chief-of-staff Liu Yalou for using logistical problems as an excuse and for not making the necessary sacrifices to help the overall war effort.[28] Chinese secondary sources note that Mao's choice of words in this telegram make it his most severe rebuke of any high-level army commander.[29]

In the end, this brutal telegram was enough to get the proverbial "cow" to jump a fence. Lin subsequently submitted a new plan resolving to attack Jinzhou within the next month, assuaging Mao's anger and finally getting the Liaoxi-Shenyang (Liaoshen) Campaign into motion. The basic scheme was simple and familiar. Lin would divide his army into three parts: one to attack Jinzhou, one to block reinforcements from Shenyang, and the last to block Fu Zuoyi in the south.[30] In September, Mao made a bold declaration about the war and its conclusion:

> We are prepared fundamentally to overthrow the Kuomintang in about five years, counting from July 1946. This is possible. Our objective can be attained provided we destroy about 100 brigades of Kuomintang regular troops every year, or some 500 brigades over the five years.[31]

The belief that victory could be attained after another three or more years of fighting was also echoed in the writings of Liu Shaoqi and the Communist press.[32] The path to victory envisioned by the Secretariat lay in a complex sequence of events starting with northeast China. This plan called for Lin to secure Manchuria in 1948, after which he would combine forces with the SCH Field Army to destroy Fu Zuoyi in the first half of 1949. Depending on the situation in the Central Plains, the Northeast and SCH Field Armies could either help destroy the remnants of Bai Chongxi and Liu Zhi's armies, or the East China and Central Plains Field Army would cross the Yangtze River in force. Yet all of this depended on the success of the Northeast Field Army at Jinzhou.

On September 12, Lin's main element, six columns, three independent divisions, and a cavalry division deployed to attack Jinzhou. In the north, four columns and an independent division took up positions near Xinmin to prepare an ambush outside of Shenyang. In the south, the independent divisions of Cheng Zihua's HRL Military Sub-District deployed near Shanhaiguan to block any reinforcements from Beiping. Lin also left behind one column and six independent divisions to maintain the siege on Changchun. Once all these troops were in position, the Liaoshen campaign began in earnest as the Northeast Field Army began to encircle and isolate Jinzhou, Jinxi and the port of Huludao.

Deducing the Northeast Field Army's intent, Chiang ordered that the 49th Corps be airlifted from Shenyang to Jinzhou, and a larger, overland relief column organized to break the Communist encirclement. He even sent Gu Zhutong to personally travel to Shenyang on September 26 to deliver the orders by hand. Wei was able to dispatch the 47th Corps the same day, which arrived safely due to the Communists' failure to seize the two airfields near Jinzhou.[33] However, he balked at sending land-based reinforcements because he had already detected the Northeast Field Army's concentration outside of Shenyang and was anticipating an ambush. Liao Yaoxiang advocated a much more radical approach and proposed abandoning Manchuria altogether. With the Northeast Field Army concentrated in the Liaoshen corridor, Liao envisioned assembling the entire army, recapturing Yingkou, and then boarding ships to evacuate to north China.

However, Chiang quickly vetoed this plan and ordered Liao to adhere to the original plan and relieve Jinzhou by land. Liao thus reluctantly took command of the new Marching West Army (hereafter West), which consisted of the New 3rd and 6th Corps, the 71st and 49th Corps, and three cavalry divisions. They departed Shenyang on October 1. In the meantime, Chiang ordered Fu Zuoyi to form the 17th Army under Hou Jingru out of 62nd Corps and two additional divisions. Hou was to board ships in Tanggu and travel to Huludao where he would link up with the 39th Corps from Yantai, which had also taken naval transport, and the Jinxi-Huludao garrison – the 54th Corps. This made for a grand total of 11 divisions that would form the Marching East Army (hereafter East). By traveling across the Bo Sea, the East Army was able to circumvent Cheng's blocking positions south of Shanhaiguan. Chiang envisioned the East and West Armies converging on the Northeast Field Army and destroying it outside of Jinzhou.

In the meantime, on October 2, Lin and the Northeast Field Army headquarters arrived at Zhangwu, northwest of Shenyang. En route they received an intelligence report about the assembly of the West Army at Huludao.[34] Because Lin had not planned on such a strong force so close to Jinzhou – which itself had eight divisions in defense – he began to have second thoughts about the campaign. Although he considered retreat, such a move would have been devastating for the army because most of his vehicles had only carried enough fuel for a one-way trip. Lin would have to abandon most of his own heavy equipment if he were to escape.[35] This was also assuming that he could extract his army, which would be a challenge in itself with the GMD forces closing in on him from both directions. With an overwhelming majority of his army tied up at Jinzhou, Lin faced disaster.

In desperation, Lin sent a message to the CMC at 2000 hours on October 2 declaring his intent to abandon the attack on Jinzhou and instead renew his attack at Changchun. He did so without consulting either Luo Ronghuan or Liu Yalou, although he took the liberty of putting their names on the telegram. The next morning, Liu woke Luo with the news and the infuriated political commissar berated Lin about defying the will of Mao and the CMC, not to mention breaching the chain of command. Together, Liu and Luo convinced Lin to send another telegram revoking Lin's previous message before Mao had a chance to reply. They managed to send out this new telegram in time. It arrived at 1700 hours on October 3. Predictably, Mao wanted Lin to continue the attack on Jinzhou, but instead of criticizing Lin he offered two arguments. His first point was that their previous attack against Changchun had already failed and that another would probably meet the same fate. The second point was a warning against changing plans in the middle of a fight and the negative effect it would have on morale.[36] Two hours later, Mao sent another message reemphasizing the CMC's desire to attack Jinzhou, and again added that capturing Changchun would only make the inevitable attack in south Manchuria more difficult in the future.[37] Soon after,

Mao received the Northeast Bureau's retraction and at 0400 the next morning, the crisis abated. The Northeast Field Army would continue the attack on Jinzhou to the bitter end.[38]

With strategic debate over, the fate of the Northeast Field Army now hinged on the 4th Column, which was all that stood between the East Army's 11 divisions and disaster. Lin committed five columns and the majority of his armor and artillery against Jinzhou, a total of 250,000 men, in an effort to capture it as quickly as possible. In the meantime, the GMD closed in on the Communist flanks. The ambush force Lin had positioned near Shenyang was now to assume a blocking function, since Liao Yaoxiang's relief force was too large for them to destroy. Over the second week of October, the West Army pushed forward and eventually seized Zhangwu, Lin's headquarters and base of operations. At the same time, on October 10, the East Army reached Tashan and launched their first attacks against the 4th Column. This was the point of no return for the Communists. With his left flank giving ground, his center tied down at Jinzhou, and his right in danger at Tashan, there would be no escape for Lin or his army. After three years of struggle, the fate of Manchuria now hung on a single battle.

On October 14, the Northeast Field Army began its final assault on Jinzhou. After nearly 24 hours of fighting, the battered but triumphant Communist forces seized the city and captured Fan Hanjie and 90,000 enemy soldiers. It had been a bloody fight in which the Communists admitted suffering 24,000 casualties at Jinzhou alone. They also suffered heavily at Tashan during the 4th Column's desperate stand against the East Army. The incredible odds they faced during this battle made it one the most famous individual actions of the war. Amid countless instances of individual bravery occurred a see-saw fight in which some positions changed hands ten times or more. The victories at Jinzhou and Tashan were not only extraordinary achievements on their own, but they also set off a chain of events which unraveled the GMD's entire foothold in Manchuria.

On October 17, after hearing news of the Communist victory at Jinzhou, Zeng Zesheng and the 60th Corps, made up mainly of Yunnanese unaccustomed to the harsh Northeast winter, defected and abandoned their positions outside of Changchun. Their action doomed the Changchun garrison commander Zheng Tongguo, who was forced to surrender two days later. The city that had resisted Lin's best efforts in the summer simply surrendered without a shot after his capture of Jinzhou. With his northern salient gone and the majority of his army tied up in Liao's West Army, Wei stood completely isolated in Shenyang with his headquarters virtually undefended. Admitting defeat, he ordered the 52nd Corps to recapture Yingkou so that the Shenyang garrison could evacuate by sea.

In the meantime, Liao's army was still engaged with Lin's blocking force. Now, however, the tables had turned because the fall of Jinzhou meant that the bulk of the Northeast Field Army would soon be turned against him. Despite this danger, Chiang did not order Liao to retreat and join Wei at Yingkou. Instead he demanded that the East and West Armies continue with the original plan, except now they were to recapture Jinzhou instead of saving its garrison. The hope was that the GMD armies could capitalize on the Communists' disorganization and fatigue to snatch victory from the jaws of defeat. Oblivious to Chiang's plans, Mao had already ordered the Northeast Field Army to rest for 10 to 15 days and then reinforce Yingkou and the forces around Changchun – still in GMD hands when the order was written.[39] However, after learning of the GMD's plan and Changchun's surrender, Mao ordered Lin to concentrate his army on Liao Yaoxiang and destroy him.[40] Lin left two columns behind to continue holding the thoroughly demoralized East Army at Tashan and took the rest of the army north to intercept the West Army.

On October 21, the Communists methodically began to encircle the West Army. They began their attack two days later, forcing Liao to stop and form a defensive perimeter in the area of Xinmin, Xinlitun, and Heishan. As in so many other battles before this one, the GMD's decision to stop would be fatal. The West Army, which numbered 500,000 men, now manned a 120 square kilometer perimeter and were becoming surrounded and increasingly outnumbered by Communist hordes that grew by the hour. Yet the rapid march had taken its toll on the Northeast Field Army's command and control, which led Luo Ronghuan to suggest that Lin pause and reorganize his army. However, Lin smelled victory and he insisted on keeping up the pressure. In contrast to Luo's concern, Lin gave orders for every unit to attack Liao's army whenever and wherever they found it.[41] After a week of fierce fighting, the East Army was destroyed on October 28, and with it went Chiang's dreams of controlling Manchuria and keeping the Communists bottled up in the region.

The momentum of the victory at Liaoshen swept the Northeast Field Army to the outskirts of Shenyang, which was now all but defenseless. The main elements quickly surrounded the city while other units were dispatched further south to try to recapture Yingkou and shut off Wei's last escape route. On November 1, the Shenyang garrison, a total of 140,000 men, surrendered. The only GMD force north of Jinzhou to escape was the 52nd Corps, which was barely able to board ships in Yingkou before Communist forces flooded into the city. The last chapter in the Liaoshen Campaign, and indeed the larger battle for the Northeast, occurred a week later when the West Army retreated to Huludao, where it boarded ships for Tianjin. Representing the only bright point of the campaign for Nanjing, the safe retreat of the West Army preserved 140,000 troops and their equipment – but this was a miniscule figure compare to the GMD's overall losses.

The Liaoshen Campaign was a crushing strategic and tactical defeat for the GMD. In October, Communist press releases claimed to have reduced Chiang's entire, nationwide strength by at least one third, with a majority of these casualties occurring in northeast China.[42] Official PLA records cite 472,000 GMD casualties, which included 109,000 defections and 306,200 prisoners of war.[43] As these figures reflect, the scale of the battle and its consequences were immense. During the course of the three-year struggle for Manchuria, Chiang had willingly committed half a million troops to the region. He lost almost all of them during the Liaoshen Campaign. To make matters worse, many of them were his best troops, trained in Burma by US advisors and lavishly equipped during World War II with the newest Lend-Lease equipment. Lastly, the campaign completely discredited Chiang's new strategy of seeking field battles. Not only had it met with abject failure during its first run, but this most recent defeat far surpassed any previous setback.

Northeast China was now totally under the control of the CCP – a goal that the Communists had struggled to attain since the fall of 1945. They could now look forward to the Northeast and SCH Field Armies joining hands to eliminate Fu Zuoyi. The victory also had inadvertently helped solidify the Communist chain of command. Mao's vindication after Lin's moment of weakness (although driven by legitimate military concerns) not only marked a new chapter in their relationship but in Mao's relations with his generals on the whole. Mao's reputation gained luster after the Liaoshen Campaign and this would have immediate consequences for the rest of the war, not to mention casting a long shadow over the founding of the PRC and thereafter.

The second crucible: Ji'nan, Xuzhou, and the Huaihai Campaign

As the Liaoshen Campaign reached its climax, Su Yu and Xu Shiyou began their assault on Ji'nan. In many ways, the two battles had much in common: both were intended to draw out and destroy large GMD armies, as well as pacify a theater of operations. However, Ji'nan was a much larger city than Jinzhou and reinforcements were much closer, in the form of either Fu Zuoyi in Beiping or Liu Zhi in Xuzhou. Yet, just as Liaoshen was not supposed to be the last battle in northeast China – neither Changchun or Shenyang were addressed in the original

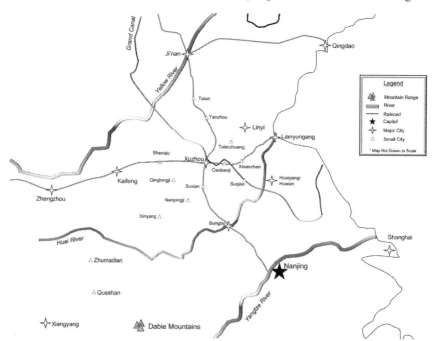

Figure 5.2 1948: The Ji'nan and Huaihai Campaigns.

campaign planning – the Ji'nan Campaign was only meant to shape the battlefield. On one hand, it would further isolate the GMD's garrisons in north China by severing the major railroads. On the other, it would help clear the path for Su Yu's army to make the long anticipated crossing of the Yangtze River.

However, the plan of attack for Ji'nan was still under debate. While the CMC and the East China Field Army agreed to the concept of attacking Ji'nan to draw out a GMD relief column, the question of how actually to assault the heavily defended city remained unanswered. The size of Ji'nan, the scale of its defenses and the strength of its garrison would require a prolonged and methodical siege. Consequently, if the Communists were serious about capturing the city, Su's blocking forces would have to hold off GMD reinforcements indefinitely. Few officers in the East China Field Army were comfortable with this prospect. Instead, they proposed to deliver only a feint on Ji'nan, rather than risk troops and time in a genuine attempt to capture the city. Therefore, Su sent a telegram to the CMC on August 28 presenting the issues of the debate and requesting guidance.[44]

Mao was not satisfied with either alternative and hedged his bets by warning against assembling the "largest possible force," lest it attract too much attention while at the same time dismissing a mere probing attack. While he agreed that ambushing the relief column was the priority, he left it up to Su whether or not to make a genuine effort to capture the city.[45] In the end, the strategic advantage of capturing Ji'nan was too much to pass up. Su also may have wanted the East China Field Army to match Nie Rongzhen's success at Shijiazhuang.

At the end of August, Su submitted his plan to capture Ji'nan and received Mao's approval the next day. For the actual assault, Su allocated 140,000 men, 44 percent of the field army, and divided it into the East and West Armies. They were to converge on the city from two directions and surround it. The West Army consisted of four columns and units from the Hebei-Shandong-Henan Military Sub-District under 10th Column commander Song Shilun. The East Army was made up of two columns and forces from the Binhai Military Subdistrict under 9th Column commander Nie Fengzhi. Su commanded the rest of the army, 180,000 men, to block enemy reinforcements from Xuzhou. He also divided that army into two parts to deploy them on opposite sides of the Grand Canal. Su commanded six columns in the east while Chen Shiju led the remaining two columns in the west. The operation was slated to begin on September 16.

While the Communists were weighing their options, the GMD were still undecided over whether to abandon territory to preserve their remaining troops. On August 27, as Su's forces moved into position, Wang Yaowu requested that the 83rd Division be airlifted into Ji'nan from Xuzhou, where it would augment his defenses. Chiang approved the request but Liu Zhi delayed the movement, believing that it would expose his own headquarters. Consequently, only one brigade of the division had arrived in Ji'nan when the battle started. On August 31, Chiang also agreed to send the 74th Division but the East China Field Army struck before he could complete the transfer. By the evening of September 17, the Communists had seized the heights east of Ji'nan and, by the next day, were shelling the airfield, rendering it inoperable. Only seven companies of the 74th Division had been airlifted into Ji'nan. From here on out, Wang would have to defend the city with the forces on hand.

On September 19, the West Army penetrated the western perimeter and cut off Wu Huawen and the 96th Corps from the rest of Ji'nan. With assistance from underground CCP members and clandestine communications, Wu was later induced to defect with his entire corps. With the airfield destroyed, almost half of his force gone, and the Communists already inside the city, Wang's once strong position now teetered on the brink of collapse. Chiang refused to let Wang abandon Ji'nan but hesitated over whether to dispatch land reinforcements or unleash his air force with concentrated carpet bombing to destroy the western part of the city, where the Communists had massed. Du Yuming advocated waiting until the East China Field Army wore itself out in the assault before dispatching reinforcements, but Chiang grew anxious and lost faith both in air strikes and in Du's calculations. As a result, he ordered the Xuzhou HQ to relieve Ji'nan by land.

Despite Chiang's commitment to a rescue, Su never got the chance for his ambush because Ji'nan fell before the reinforcements came within range. This created the one scenario the Communists had not even conceived, much less planned for. In the evening of September 23, the East and West Armies began their final assault on Ji'nan, and by dusk the next day the battle was over. Despite all fears of a prolonged siege and the contingency planning built upon that scenario, the entire Ji'nan Campaign lasted only eight days. Although the Communists admitted suffering more casualties than the defenders (26,991 versus 22,423) – almost the same figure the Northeast Field Army suffered at Jinzhou – this was expected since they were the attackers. However, the number of captured GMD troops, 61,000 men, quickly allowed them to make up their losses.[46]

The fall of Ji'nan and the annihilation of Wang Yaowu's 2nd Pacification Zone forced Nanjing to abandon north and central Shandong, leaving under their control only Qingdao and part of south Shandong. For the Communists, although the tactical gains of the Ji'nan Campaign were not as extensive as those of the Liaoshen Campaign – still ongoing even after Wang's defeat – the strategic gains were almost as significant. Securing Shandong allowed the two parts of the East China Field Army to finally join hands. They could now concentrate in the Central Plains and seek the long desired battle to clear a path to the Yangtze River.

After Ji'nan fell, Su Yu proposed employing the full strength of the East China Field Army in the so-called Huaihai Campaign. His scheme of maneuver was to have Wei Guoqing's North Jiangsu Army attack Huaian and Huaiyang, in Jiangsu, while the rest of the field army positioned itself near Suqian to ambush reinforcements from Anhui. If the GMD did not dispatch reinforcements, then Su would decide whether to end the operation or have Wei seize Lianyungang, the main port in north Jiangsu. After this, the army would rest and prepare either to cross the Yangtze River or continue operations in the Central Plains.[47] After reviewing the plan, Mao modified it so that all of the cities it mentioned, as well as the destruction of Huang Baitao's 7th Army, became primary objectives.[48] It became known as the "small" Huaihai Campaign.[49] However, it too would undergo changes as the casualty figures from the Ji'nan Campaign and reports of GMD troop transfers from Shandong to Xuzhou began filtering in. Due primarily to the casualty reports, Mao postponed the campaign until the end of October so that the East China Field Army could recuperate. He judged correctly that it would need to be at full strength to defeat Huang and Qiu's forces.[50]

The loss of Shandong and the continuing fighting in Manchuria led Nanjing to rethink radically their strategy in the Central Plains. Du Yuming proposed they abandon their garrisons on the Longhai Railroad and instead mass the army to seek a decisive battle with the East China Field Army in southwest Shandong. Liu Zhi agreed, but again, his concerns about the safety of headquarters intervened. Consequently, Liu modified Du's plan to keep Li Mi's 13th Army at Xuzhou, instead of allowing it to operate in the field. Chiang approved this final draft and ordered the campaign to begin on October 15. Soon after, the situation in Jinzhou grew critical and the entire GMD high command, including Chiang, Gu Zhutong, and Du Yuming, flew to Shenyang to meet with Wei Lihuang. Because of his past experiences in northeast China, Du remained behind to assist Wei in orchestrating the defense. With Du gone, the plan for concentrating the army and fighting a decisive battle in the Central Plains fell behind schedule. However, their moves did force the Communists to adjust their Huaihai Campaign.

On October 12, the East China Field Army decided to further postpone the campaign until October 28. Part of the reason for doing so was Mao's decision to expand again the scale of the operation. Mao now wanted the Central Plains Field Army to participate by tying down Sun Yuanliang, who, in accordance with Du's plan, was withdrawing from Zhengzhou along the Longhai Railroad towards Xuzhou. Mao also changed the East China Field Army deployments to allocate more forces to block Li Mi and Qiu Qingquan, who were now also concentrating their forces. The so-called "big" Huaihai Campaign was slated to last the rest of year, after which the two field armies would rest and prepare for still larger battles in 1949, possibly in south China.[51] Chen and Su also planned a secondary attack to eliminate GMD presence in Shandong, which primarily consisted of Feng Zhian's army at Taierzhuang.[52] At the end of October, the East China Field Army concentrated at Linyi and prepared to launch the Huaihai Campaign in the beginning of November.

As Chen Yi and Su deployed for their attack, Nanjing assumed that the Communists' next target was Xuzhou. As a result, the GMD completed the abandonment of the Longhai railroad but, instead of seeking a field battle, kept their forces in a defensive posture at Xuzhou. Chiang appointed Bai Chongxi as overall commander of both Central China and Xuzhou HQ. In the last week of October, in the wake of the GMD withdrawal, the Communists seized the Longhai railroad. After seizing Zhengzhou, Mao warned Chen Yi and Deng Xiaoping to ignore the cities and instead pursue Sun to the new Xuzhou defense line.[53] On October 27, after the East China and Central Plains Field Armies began to converge in the Huaihai area, Su proposed that they merge the armies under a single chain of command. On November 1, the CMC approved this measure, forming the Huaihai General Front Committee (hereafter called the Huaihai Committee), which consisted of Liu Bocheng, Chen Yi, Su Yu, Tan Zhenlin, and the committee's secretary, Deng Xiaoping.[54]

For the coming campaign, the East China Field Army would deliver the main attack against Huang Baitao at Xinanzhen, east of the Grand Canal in north Jiangsu, using seven columns. In support of the attack, Su employed a three-column task force to block Li Mi, who was stationed on the other side of the Grand Canal. The Shandong Army would also secure the East China Field Army's rear areas by conducting the aforementioned campaign against Feng Zhian's 3rd Pacification Zone at Taierzhuang. Lastly, Su detached two columns to the Central Plains Field Army to help block Qiu Qingquan's army at Dangshan. Liu Bocheng would focus most of his army on blocking Sun Yuanliang's powerful force.

On the night of November 6, the first shots of Huaihai Campaign rang out as elements of the East China Field Army launched their attacks. On the same day, Gu Zhutong ordered the Xuzhou HQ to contract their lines by withdrawing the 44th Corps, which was positioned on the extreme right of the GMD line, to join Huang's 7th Army at Xinanzhen. This unit was assigned to Li Yannian's 9th Pacification Zone but it had been left behind when Li deployed into the Central Plains. After the 44th Corps arrived, the plan called on Huang to relieve Li Mi's 13th Army at Caobaoji. Li Mi would then move to Xuzhou to help man the city's defenses. Due to this sudden shift, Su watched helplessly as the majority of the 7th Army escaped his trap and safely crossed the Grand Canal into Anhui. However, Huang's trailing element, the 63rd Corps was lagging, and Su resolved to destroy at least it before pursuing Huang. In the meantime, the Shandong Army induced Feng Zhian's force to surrender on November 8, thereby removing any threat to Su's rear. Their surrender also freed Xu Shiyou's army to help attack the Xuzhou defense line.

However, merely adding the Shandong Army to Su's attacking power was not enough for Mao. Instead, Mao wanted to use them to destroy Li Mi's 13th Army. At this point, the 13th Army was withdrawing to Xuzhou as per Gu's plan. Mao saw their movement as an opportunity to eliminate most of the Xuzhou Bandit Pacification Headquarters in a single battle.[55] Su, on the other hand, appears not to have been enamored with the idea of further extending his forces, and instead focused on the immediate task of destroying the 7th Army at Nianzhuang. On November 9, he began to encircle Huang's army, leaving behind only the 1st Column to mop up the 63rd Corps on the east bank of the Grand Canal. By November 11, Su succeeded in cutting off the 7th Army from the rest of the Xuzhou defense line – a task made easier by Li Mi's decision to leave Caobaji before Huang arrived. Li's premature departure did, however, prevent the Shandong Field Army from surrounding and cutting off the 13th Army.

After the Communists surrounded Huang's army, Chiang ordered Qiu Qingquan and Li Mi to lift the siege immediately. He also upgraded Li Yannian's 9th Pacification Zone and Liu Ruming's 4th Pacification Zone into the 6th and 8th Armies, respectively, using troops from Qingdao and Huludao which had survived the Ji'nan and Liaoshen Campaigns.[56] The two new armies began assembling near Bengbu and forced Liu Bocheng to have to block them as well. Already, the Central Plains Field Army had ambushed the 181st Division, which had served as a rear guard for Qiu Qingquan's withdrawal from Shangqiu. The

Communists easily destroyed it because Qiu had failed to allocate trains for the divisions. Liu then moved to Suxian to force a battle with Sun Yuanliang,[57] but only the 148th Division and a handful of second-echelon units remained in the city when he arrived. The Communists captured the town and destroyed its defenders by November 6, compelling Liu Zhi to allocate forces against the Central Plains Field Army southwest of Xuzhou, rather than using them to help the 7th Army.

As Liu and Deng attacked Suxian, the East China Field Army's 1st Column completed the destruction of the 63rd Corps and crossed the Grand Canal to assist in the encirclement of the 7th Army. Now with five of his most experienced units at hand, Su assembled a task force under Chen Shiju to assault the 7th Army. Beginning on November 11, Chen threw his forces against Huang's perimeter for three straight days, but with little to show for it. Consequently, Su temporarily called back his forces and redrew the assault plan to focus on weak points in Huang's defenses. Despite the lack of progress, Mao reaffirmed the CMC's commitment to continue the campaign. He went as far as to say that 100,000 or more casualties were acceptable.[58]

As Chen Shiju tried to bash his way through the 7th Army, the GMD relief force likewise made little headway against Su's blocking force. By November 14, Li Mi and Qiu Qingquan had advanced only six miles. Yet, despite the slow progress, the GMD had nearly broken through on multiple occasions. At some points, the defenders had to resort to bayonets and rocks. Mao, however, believed Huang's destruction was imminent and paid little mind to the desperate struggle to fend off Li and Qiu. Su fueled this belief when he cracked the 7th Armies lines and destroyed the 44th Corps on November 11. Mao therefore proposed expanding the campaign by maneuvering the North Jiangsu Army behind Li and Qiu's relief column, to cut them off from Xuzhou. This would begin the process of encircling and then destroying those armies after Su defeated the 7th Army. Although Su agreed with the plan and dispatched Wei to pursue it, the 74th Corps –reconstituted after the battle of Mengliangu – detected the North Jiangsu Army's maneuver and prevented it from accomplishing its mission.

With Su and Wei stalled, Liu, Deng, and the Central Plains Field Army also faced serious problems. Their hands were already full fending off Sun Yuanliang's army at Mengcheng. The approach of Liu Ruming and Li Yannian now threatened to overwhelm them. To assist Liu and Li in breaking through, Bai had also dispatched Huang Wei's 12th Army, a force primarily made up of Hu Lian's Reorganized 18th Corps.[59] On November 18, Mao, seemingly oblivious to the campaign's mounting problems, ordered the Central Plains Field Army to spread its forces out to engage all four armies simultaneously. Even more astounding was his idea that Liu and Deng send two columns to attack Huang Wei's rear, much like he had requested earlier when he envisioned using the North Jiangsu Army to cut off Li Mi and Qiu Qingquan's armies.[60]

At this point, the Huaihai Campaign reached a critical juncture. Mao's adjustments to the original plan had now committed his two field armies to simultaneously destroy one army (Huang Baitao's 7th Army), surround three more (Qiu Qingquan's 2nd Army, Li Mi's 13th Army, and Huang Wei's 12th Army), and block another three (Liu Ruming's 8th Army, Sun Yuanliang's 16th Army, and Li Yannian's 6th Army) – a total of seven armies. Threatening not only to overextend the Communist forces to the breaking point, if implemented Mao's plan would take them past the point of no return. To make matters worse, the Communists had not yet met any of their goals for the campaign. Su still had not defeated Huang Baitao – the purpose of the entire campaign – and the North Jiangsu Army had been foiled by the 74th Corps. In addition, the Central Plains Field Army's lack of firepower and equipment was beginning to undermine its ability to hold off Sun, Li, Liu, and Huang Wei. Therefore, the Huaihai Committee proposed abandoning all secondary efforts, i.e. attempts to surround Qiu, Li Mi, and Huang Wei's armies, and concentrate solely on the 7th Army. Afterwards, they could try to meet the other objectives Mao had laid out.[61]

The Huaihai Committee's decision was a clear repudiation of Mao's expanding vision for the campaign. It was clear that instead of accepting the limited objectives originally established, Mao now wanted to secure the Central Plains in its entirety. On November 14, he intimated as such by stating to the press that the war would be over much sooner than predicted – perhaps in only a year or more.[62] The influence of Liaoshen, especially the fact that his strategy had proved correct, no doubt played a large role in his decisions at Huaihai. It also probably played a role in his generals' willingness to accept his growing demands. Indeed, it had been Mao's decision in the first place to transform Su's "small" Huaihai into "big" Huaihai. Yet, despite Mao's grand vision and his newfound confidence, he agreed to the Huaihai Committee's plan on the evening of November 19.[63] The fact that his retraction had come only hours after Mao sent another telegram reemphasizing aggressive deployments against the GMD armies demonstrates that he was still willing to listen to reason and the counsel of his generals.

Now Su could cast his full attention on the 7th Army, while Liu and Deng could concentrate on the most immediate threats without spreading their forces thin. On November 19, the same day Mao agreed to scale back the Huaihai Campaign, Su ordered a general attack against the remnants of the 7th Army. The battle raged on for three more days, but in the end Huang's beleaguered army collapsed. At that time, Qiu Qingquan was less than seven miles away, having captured Daxujia as the last shots around Huang's headquarters in Nianzhuang faded away. With the 7th Army gone, Qiu and Li withdrew, and the first phase of the Huaihai Campaign came to an end. During this battle alone, the East China Field Army had suffered 49,000 casualties. Fortunately for them, the GMD had lost almost three times that figure – approximately 120,000 men.[64]

After the destruction of the 7th Army, Li Mi and Qiu Qingquan immediately retreated to Xuzhou to prevent Su from encircling them. As a result, the Communists focused on isolating Huang Wei's 12th Army, which meant that the Central Plains and East China Field Armies switched roles. The former would now provide the main effort and the latter would take a supporting role. At that point, Huang was preparing to seize Nanpingji, a village which possessed bridges across the Kuai River capable of bearing the weight of heavy equipment and vehicles. On November 23, the Huaihai Committee decided to abandon Nanpingji in order to draw Huang's spearhead unit, the 18th Corps across the river. Once that unit had crossed, the Central Plains Field Army planned to isolate and destroy it before the rest of Huang's army arrived. They also proposed that the East China Field Army send two or three columns to help block Li Yannian and Liu Ruming and another four to help destroy the 12th Army.[65] Despite heavy losses and exhaustion in the ranks, Su agreed to release the forces requested by the Huaihai Committee.

As these plans went into motion, Liu and Deng began their encirclement of Huang Wei. Realizing he could not link up with the Xuzhou defenses and fearing entrapment, Huang turned south to join Li Yannian and Liu Ruming. Unfortunately for the GMD, the maneuver caused a great deal of confusion, and this cost them two precious days before the army started in the right direction. However, coordination continued to be a problem and two of Huang's corps moved south independently, separated from the main body. The Communists easily annihilated these two units at Dayingji. During this time, the 110th Division defected to the Communists and even received artillery support from GMD units that thought the division was leading a new attack. By November 27, Liu and Deng had confined the 12th Army to a small defensive perimeter near Shuangduiji on the north bank of the Kuai River.

Despite successfully encircling and isolating Huang Wei, Liu and Deng realized that their army was weak compared with Huang's. To assault the 12th Army, they would have to employ the better-equipped East China Field Army columns Su had loaned them. Du Yuming, who had reassumed his position with the Xuzhou HQ after the disaster at Liaoshen, ordered an all out effort to assist Huang Wei. However, despite employing four armies to converge on Huang's position from the north and the south, the GMD simply could not break through. On October 28, Du, facing the possibility of losing the 12th Army and having the entire Xuzhou defense force encircled and isolated, proposed a general retreat south. Perhaps learning from his earlier defeat at Liaoshen, Chiang consented. On October 30, Qiu Qingquan, Li Mi, Sun Lianzhong and the Xuzhou headquarters evacuated the city.

Receiving reports of Du's flight, Su sent almost his entire remaining force – eight columns – to intercept them. By December 4, the East China Field Army had encircled and pinned down the GMD force at Qinglongji, near the Anhui-Henan border. However, this again threatened to spread the Communist forces thin. To prevent another crisis, Liu Bocheng proposed that the Huaihai Committee adopt a three-pronged policy. This entailed "consuming" Huang Wei, "pressing" Du Yuming, and "watching" Li Yannian and Liu Ruming.[66] In the beginning of December, with Du and Huang's forces surrounded and isolated, the only hope for the GMD was that Li and Liu Ruming could break through to Huang Wei. Although they ultimately failed, it was not for lack of effort; by the end of the battle, Li and Liu's armies suffered a combined 13,000 casualties.

In the meantime, with his forces trapped in north Anhui, Du discussed options with his commanders. Sun Lianzhong advocated immediately breaking out of the encirclement. While the others were lukewarm to this proposal, they deferred to Sun and divided their forces into three parts for the escape.[67] On December 6, Sun personally led his forces through the Communist siege in a tank. Although he and a contingent managed to escape to Xinyang, where he linked up with friendly forces, the rest of his 16th Army was destroyed after only two confused hours of fighting. Only a handful of survivors managed return to the original perimeter at Qinglongji. Du immediately cancelled the remaining breakout operations and resolved to move the entire force south to link up with Huang Wei.

While Su destroyed Sun's force, Liu and Deng began their final assault on the 12th Army in the early morning of December 6. After six days of unrelenting fighting, the Huaihai Committee estimated that Huang was down to 25 percent of his original strength. Yet he refused to surrender. Instead, on the night of December 15, Huang attempted a final, desperate breakout. However, with his force already weakened and the Communists closing in for the kill, it was a doomed effort. By dawn, Huang Wei's 12th Army, approximately 100,000 men, had been wiped out. This marked the end of the second stage of the Huaihai Campaign.

Already the Communists had accomplished much more than they ever imagined, even when Mao turned Su's "small" Huaihai into "big" Huaihai. They had met their primary goal of destroying Huang Baitao's 7th Army. The elimination of Huang Wei's 12th Army and Sun Lianzhong's 16th Army was an unanticipated bonus. Strategically, they had also gone far beyond their original objective of securing the Longhai Railroad, north Jiangsu and Shandong. By forcing Du's abandonment of Xuzhou and destroying the three GMD armies, they had won the Huaihai region and cleared the East China Field Army's path to the Yangtze River. However, the idea of crossing the Yangtze and setting up bases now seemed obsolete. With Li Mi, Qiu Qingquan, and Du Yuming surrounded, and Li Yannian's 7th and Liu Ruming's 8th Armies weakened and vulnerable, the Communists were on the verge of wiping out the majority of the GMD army in the Central Plains. At the same time, Lin Biao's Northeast Field Army was joining hands with the SCH Field Army to begin the Pingjin Campaign, which meant that the loss of north China was also not far behind.

In order to prevent Chiang from evacuating Fu's army by sea before Lin and Nie isolated it, Mao ordered the Huaihai Committee to delay the destruction of Du's force in Anhui.[68] Consequently, the Huaihai Committee met on December 17 as a whole entity for the first time in its existence – in fact, Su had not seen Liu Bocheng in 17 years. They met not to discuss operations but to lay out a plan for resting and replenishing their forces. As the fighting trailed off and the two sides settled in for a siege, Chiang wanted Du to break out. However, with the memory of Sun Lianzhong's disastrous attempt still fresh in Du's mind, he refused. Unfortunately for him, there would be no reinforcements or relief column. Liu Ruming and Li Yannian had both withdrawn across the Huai River after the destruction of Huang Wei's army. With a disaster looming, Li Zongren, Bai Chongxi, and the Guangxi clique forced Chiang to retire on January 21, 1949. However, before Li could assume his new duties as president, the Huaihai Campaign was over and with it went any real hope that the GMD could withstand the Communist onslaught.

On the afternoon of January 6, the East China Field Army launched its final assault on Du and his two remaining armies. Although this was probably the largest concentration of troops Su's forces had faced during the entire campaign, the effects of the siege had debilitated Li Mi and Qiu Qingquan's armies. After four hard days of combat, the Communists overran the exhausted GMD defenders and took Du Yuming prisoner. Although they suffered more than 17,000 casualties during these last assaults, the East China Field Army had inflicted 24,000 casualties on the GMD and took 177,040 prisoners of war. This brought the total GMD losses during the Huaihai Campaign to 320,335 captured, 171,151 killed or wounded, and 63,593 defections – over a half million soldiers in a single campaign.

The Huaihai Campaign was an overwhelming Communist success. Only the armies of Liu Ruming and Li Yannian, both of which were severely weakened in the fighting, stood between south China and the East China Field Army. Coming so soon on the heels of the Liaoshen Campaign, the heart of the GMD army and much of its presence north of the Yangtze River had simply disappeared. However, this did not mean the war was over or that a speedy conclusion was inevitable. Bai Chongxi still remained in Hubei and Henan and the GMD's Yangtze River defenses were still in place. Fu Zuoyi, Yan Xishan, and Hu Zongnan also still had forces in north China, although these were increasingly isolated and outnumbered. Consequently, one cannot underestimate the importance of the Huaihai Campaign both in material and moral terms. A battle which was supposed only to have created conditions for another round of campaigns had instead broken the back of the GMD cause. With Chiang removed from power and Communist armies surging to the Yangtze River, the unthinkable – a Communist state – now appeared inevitable.

The third crucible: The Pingjin Campaign

In the critical period when the end of the Liaoshen Campaign overlapped with the beginning of the Huaihai Campaign, the most pressing issue for the CMC was the timing of when Lin Biao and the Northeast Field Army would enter North China and engage Fu Zuoyi and the North China HQ. Despite the fact that Fu would soon be facing two Communist field armies, neither he nor Chiang seriously considered abandoning north China. At this time, Liaoshen had been a terrible shock to Nanjing, but with their forces still in place in the Central Plains, there was still hope the GMD could hold Beiping and north Hebei.

In May 1948, the SCH Military District absorbed what was left of the old SHSH Military District to become the North China Military District. Nie remained the commander, but the political commissar, Bo Yibo, and first deputy commander, Xu Xiangqian, were from the old SHSH Military District. The SCH Field Army correspondingly became the North China Field Army, whose commanders were interchangeable with the military district. The field army consisted of two separate armies, the 1st Army under Xu Xiangqian (formerly the SHSH Field Army) and the 2nd Army under Yang Dezhi (formerly the SCH Field Army). This effectively doubled the size of Nie's forces.

When the Liaoshen Campaign began, the North China Field Army was in the process of waging two separate campaigns in Shanxi and Rehe. Xu Xiangqian had captured Yuncheng and laid siege to Yan Xishan at Taiyuan in the fall. Yang

Dezhi's army was interdicting the rail lines between Beiping and Shanhaiguan in support of the Liaoshen Campaign. On July 23, in response to Lin's request, Nie also launched an attack on Guisui and Baotou in order to draw Fu away from the developing battle at Jinzhou.[69] In order to do so without ceasing operations in Rehe or Shanxi, Nie detached three columns away from Yang Dezhi's 2nd Army to form the 3rd Army under Yang Chengwu.

However, the immediate result of this reorganization was to create two weak armies out of a single strong one. Another consideration was the fact that columns in the North China Field Army were more equivalent to divisions, not corps like the other field armies. Thus, not only were units of the North China Field Army smaller than their counterparts in other Communist armies and in GMD armies, but, unlike the effort at Liaoshen and Huaihai, they were spread out across three fronts, instead of being concentrated on one. Despite these problems, the North China Field Army provided critical support for the other theaters by keeping Fu out of the Liaoshen corridor and isolating Yan at Taiyuan. In mid-October, Chiang recognized the inherent weakness of the North China Field Army and ordered Fu to recapture Shijiazhuang, which the Communists had left virtually undefended.

On October 27, Fu's forces coalesced at Baoding and began to move south. The CMC scrambled to repel them. Harassing the GMD forces with local troops and exploiting the ineptness of Fu's subordinates, the Communists bought time for reinforcements from the North China Field Army to arrive and man the city's defenses. After only four days of campaigning, the GMD retreated in ignominy, having not only failed to take Shijiazhuang but also having been defeated by primarily irregular troops. While this occurred, Mao and the CMC ordered Lin, who was now done with the Liaoshen Campaign, to take advantage of Fu's ill-fated sortie by capturing Shanhaiguan.[70] Lin complied and dispatched south two columns and two independent divisions in what later proved to be the first move in the Beiping-Tianjin (Pingjin) Campaign.

At this point, Mao and the CMC planned to wage three simultaneous campaigns in the North China Military District. The first two were the aforementioned attacks on Taiyuan and Guisui/Baotou. The third would be the Beiping-Tianjin (Pingjin) Campaign, in which Yang Dezhi's 2nd Army and the Northeast Field Army would cooperate to destroy Fu Zuoyi's North China HQ at Beiping and Tianjin. At that time, Fu's force consisted of four armies of more than 500,000 men deployed in a 400-mile defense line that started in Tanggu, ran through Beiping and Tianjin, and ended at Zhangjiakou. However, the order in which these campaigns should be completed, how they related to each other, and what the priority of effort should be were still under debate. The largest campaign would undoubtedly be the Pingjin Campaign, but that would not begin until at least December, after the Northeast Field Army had rested and reorganized.[71] However, as GMD losses mounted in the Huaihai Campaign, Mao and the CMC began to fear that Fu Zuoyi would escape into south China and the Communists would lose their chance to destroy him.

On November 7, Mao laid out Fu's three most likely courses of action. One, he could consolidate his defenses and stay put; two, he could take forces loyal to him and escape west towards Yan Xishan and Hu Zongnan, while the forces loyal to Chiang retreated south to Nanjing; or three, his entire force could retreat south. Preventing the last two options became the main objective of the Pingjin Campaign. By the end of the Huaihai Campaign, the Communists came to realize that Fu would choose the first option, although they still feared he might change his mind at the last moment. This concern was evident in their decisions regarding the other two campaigns in the North China Military District. On November 8, Xu Xiangqian requested an additional two columns to assault Taiyuan. Initially, the CMC agreed to transfer Yang Dezhi's 2nd Army after Yang captured Guisui. However, believing that the loss of both Guisui and Taiyuan would compel Fu to break out, Mao postponed Yang's attack until after the Northeast Field Army arrived in north China.[72]

Lin Biao and Luo Ronghuan, on the other hand, saw a different scenario unfolding. They suggested that only by leaving an escape route to the west open would Fu remain in north China long enough for the Northeast Field Army to complete its maneuver. This convinced Mao to rein in Xu and on November 16 he ordered the 1st Army to focus only on Taiyuan's outer defenses and airfield.[73] Instead of conducting three simultaneous operations, the new plan called for Nie to concentrate on capturing Zhangjiakou to prevent Fu from withdrawing to Suiyuan. Part of the impetus for this shift was the fact that the Huaihai Campaign had effectively closed the way south. To shut down the last avenue of escape, a sea evacuation from Tianjin, Mao ordered the Northeast Field Army to move up the start date of the Pingjin campaign.[74] While the Northeast Bureau cited numerous difficulties with such a maneuver – many of them similar to their earlier protests regarding the Liaoshen Campaign – Mao set the absolute deadline as November 22. By that time the Northeast Field Army would have to begin movement, ready or not.[75]

Although they were a day late, Lin Biao and the Northeast Field Army entered north China through the storied Great Wall pass at Shanhaiguan as directed. Lin, Luo, and Liu Yalou proposed that their first target should be Tangshan, but Mao disagreed because, as Tangshan was Fu's main source of coal, its loss would surely force the GMD to evacuate. Instead, Mao ordered the Northeast Field Army to immediately sever the Beiping-Tianjin rail link and eliminate Fu's last life line.[76] After settling on the primary target, the CMC next decided that Lin, who commanded the larger element, would command the campaign. To manage all the operations of the 2nd, 3rd, and Northeast Field Armies, the CMC created a joint, provisional headquarters, the Beiping-Suiyuan Front Committee under secretary Cheng Zihua.

As these issues were being resolved and the Northeast Field Army made its way into north China, on October 29 Yang Chengwu's 3rd Army began its attack on Zhangjiakou. Although Fu had planned to abandon Zhangjiakou to protect Beiping and his route to the sea, he did not consider their operation part of a new offensive. Instead he saw it as a continuation of Yang Chengwu's earlier campaign in Suiyuan. In an effort to keep his western escape route open, he dispatched the 35th Corps from Beiping and the 258th Division from Huailai to reinforce Zhangjiakou. A few days later, Yang Dezhi's 2nd Army attacked the Zhangjiakou-Beiping railroad. On December 3, the Beiping-Suiyuan Front Committee proposed that advanced units of the Northeast Field Army threaten Fu's headquarters by attacking Miyun, a city northeast of Beiping. Their intent with these operations was to confuse Fu and destroy the reinforcements he had dispatched to Zhangjiakou. However, Yang Chengwu miscalculated by positioning his ambush force to the west. Instead, the 35th Corps reacted to the attacks on Miyun by turning east straight back to Beiping. For this oversight, Yang and the 3rd Army received a serious rebuke from Mao.[77]

However, the 35th Corps was not yet safe, for even as it escaped the 3rd Army, it still had to pass through the 2nd Army. On December 7, the Communists seized Xin Baoan, but the 35th Corps easily brushed them aside and recaptured the town. However, Yang Dezhi had used this time to position a stronger blocking force further east. Fearing the loss of his best unit, Fu ordered two corps at Huailai to rescue the 35th Corps. He placed all three corps under the command of An Chunshan. After three days of limited progress, the 104th Corps, the lead unit and An's personal command, had lost 13,000 men attempting to bash through Yang Dezhi's troops. On December 11, An abandoned the effort, fearing his entire force would be surrounded and destroyed.

The dual sieges of Zhangjiakou and Xin Baoan left Fu in a quandary. Contrary to the Communists' fears, Fu still made no plans for an immediate evacuation. He assumed he still had a month or two of leeway before the Northeast Field Army arrived. His strategy was to buy time for Chiang to strengthen the Yangtze River defenses and then withdraw. Now, with his best unit trapped in Xin Baoan, his ability to control or change the course of the battle was slipping away. He also belatedly was learning that the Northeast Field Army was not resting and replenishing in Manchuria, but was already in east Hebei. Still, Fu hesitated over the decision to escape.

On December 11, Mao ordered the Northeast Field Army to isolate but not besiege Beiping, Tianjin, Tanggu, Tangshan, and other important towns in east Hebei to prevent Fu from moving to an embarkation port in overwhelming strength.[78] To this end he also ordered the 2nd Army to postpone the destruction of the 35th Corps until at least December 20, to allow Lin's forces to strengthen their hold on east Hebei.[79] By December 12, the majority of the Northeast Field Army had arrived south of the Great Wall and began moving into position. At that time, the CMC replaced the Beiping-Suiyuan Front Committee with the Pingjin General Front Committee (hereafter Pingjin Committee) consisting of Luo Ronghuan, Nie Ronghzen, and Lin Biao, who would serve as secretary.[80] Over the first half of December, the Northeast Field Army secretly surrounded Fu's army. Three columns encircled Beiping. Four columns positioned themselves between Beiping and Tianjin. Another four columns isolated Tianjin.

As this occurred, Fu began a series of secret talks with the CCP on December 14. Fu's proposal was to declare a truce during which they could send a joint telegram to the entire country announcing their mutual desire for peace. Fu hoped he could create a new united front, in which he and his army would be leading participants. On December 19, the CCP refused but, nonetheless, guaranteed Fu and his army's safety if they put down their weapons. As the negotiations stalled, Fu's position deteriorated. With Lin's forces now in position, Mao unleashed Yang Dezhi and

Yang Chengwu. On December 21, the long delayed assault against the 35th Corps at Xin Baoan began. It took only a day for the 2nd Army to overrun the defenses. Yang Chengwu took longer with Zhangjiakou, but it too fell by the afternoon of December 23. In the space of three days, Fu had not only lost his best corps and four additional divisions – a total of 60,000 men – but his only remaining road to the west as well.

The twin victories at Xin Baoan and Zhangjiakou, as well as the Northeast Field Army's presence in east Hebei, forced Fu back to the bargaining table. The peace talks resumed in January, but by that time Mao and the Secretariat had already announced to the open press their desire for an unconditional surrender of all GMD forces. Yet Fu continued to try to broker the best deal possible for himself and his troops. At the same time, the Communist armies continued to exert pressure against Fu's surrounded garrisons.

The Northeast Field Army high command had originally planned first to capture Tanggu, in order to deny Fu access to the sea. However, reconnaissance of the port's defenses revealed such an attack was impractical and would be costly. Instead, Lin and Luo resolved to attack Tianjin, which stood between Beiping and Tanggu and served the same purpose. Now that they had secured west Hebei, the Pingjin Committee also decided to move the 2nd and 3rd Armies into east Hebei, to assist with the dual sieges of Tianjin and Beiping.[81] During the period of January 8–11, Lin and Luo engaged in talks with Chen Changjie, commander of the Tianjin garrison, for a peaceful handover of the city. When they could not come to an agreement, Lin ordered a general assault to begin on January 14. Plummeting GMD morale and the Communists' overwhelming strength proved decisive and by the afternoon of the next day, Tianjin had fallen. Fu lost another 130,000 men. It looked as if his army were being taken apart limb by limb.

With all eyes now looking towards an inevitable attack on Beiping, Luo Ronghuan and Nie Rongzhen were hesitant to attack the city. Not only did they fear the destruction of priceless artifacts and historic buildings, but the Secretariat had already chosen it as their capital. No one in the CCP high command wanted to move into a city gutted by combat. For this reason, the Pingjin Committee suspended the campaign to try to reach a deal with Fu. These efforts included contacting Fu's daughter, Fu Dong, an underground member of the CCP. However, Lin Biao grew impatient and feared the talks were merely stalling tactics to allow the GMD to strengthen their defenses. Nie countered, noting that their own intelligence had shown Beiping's defenses were incomplete because the Northeast Field Army's arrival had taken Fu by surprise. Fearing Lin would act unilaterally, Nie appealed directly to the Secretariat, in effect circumventing the rest of the Pingjin Committee. His message was destroyed during the Cultural Revolution, but one of Nie's staff officers, Tang Yongjian, remembered clearly Nie's anxiety as he awaited the Secretariat's response.[82] In the end, Mao agreed with Nie and postponed a general attack indefinitely.

Despite Mao's wishes, on December 17 Lin and Luo delivered an ultimatum to Fu's representative ordering him to leave Beiping by December 21 or face attack. However, Nie secretly met with Fu's representative to request that he not deliver the ultimatum to Fu until the last moment, to give the peace initiative time to work. Instead, it was delivered to Fu Dong, who, upon reading the text, admitted it would have probably made her father fight rather than surrender. Nie then intensified the negotiations and finally made a breakthrough. Fu agreed to leave the city before December 21 and submitted to CCP demands that his army be integrated into the Communist ranks. On January 22, the Pingjin Committee entered Beiping, bringing the campaign to a peaceful end.

Fu Zuoyi's decision meant that another 250,000 troops bolstered the Communist ranks. There they would join the 232,510 captured in the earlier fighting. This, combined with battle casualties of about 30,000 men, meant the loss of another half a million men for the GMD.[83] In the space of five months, Nanjing had lost more than 1.5 million soldiers in the three campaigns of Liaoshen, Huaihai, and Pingjin. The blow was more than crippling. It was fatal. Ironically, the climax of the Pingjin Campaign provided a quiet denouement to a half-year period of massive field battles. The campaign ended not with a final assault on a beleaguered, exhausted GMD position, but with Fu Zuoyi's decision to preserve Beiping. In this way, Pingjin opened up the important precedent that the CCP deemed the "Pingjin Method." This involved offering a choice to GMD forces: a peaceful path (the Beiping method) or a military one (the Tianjin method). This was to become the pattern for the rest of the conquest of China, with most GMD units opting for the Beiping method.

In addition to establishing this pattern, the Pingjin Campaign removed the last major obstacle to the Communists' march into south China. After Pingjin, the North China Field Army moved west to assist Xu Xiangqian at Taiyuan. There, they would eliminate Yan Xishan and join Peng Dehuai's Northwest Field Army in Shaanxi to defeat Hu Zongnan. The Northeast Field Army, on the other hand, would finally get its chance to rest and reorganize before moving into the Central Plains, where it would relieve the East China Field Army. The fact that neither army had to remain behind to besiege or hold a front against the enemy contributed greatly to the disintegration of the GMD army and to expediting an end to the war. The victory at Pingjin also allowed the CCP finally to stake a real claim to being a legitimate government. With the industrial furnaces in Manchuria, the imperial capital of Beijing – restored to its original name after the GMD were ousted to reflect the fact that it was once again a capital and the Yellow River valley also under their control, the CCP had a valid political claim to a North China state. However, as events unfolded now at breakneck speed, such a move was unnecessary. By the end of 1949 the CCP would not have to "claim" anything.

According to Mao's declaration on the last day of December 1948, the party platform was now to "carry the revolution to the end." This would include recapturing all of China, not just a part of it, expelling imperialist influences, punishing war criminals, and enacting their brand of social, political, and economic reform. What the Communists demanded was actually irrelevant, for they now possessed the means and the power to carry it all out. This was the reward for having decisively defeated their enemy on the battlefield. On paper, with the armies of Bai Chongxi and Hu Zongnan still in existence, the war was not yet over, but in fact, the GMD war machine and its will to fight had reached the breaking point. Although not immediately apparent, this truth would come to fruition soon after the Communists made the last important strategic decision of the war – when and how to cross the Yangtze River.

Carrying the revolution to the end: the Yangtze River Crossing Campaign and beyond

In the spring of 1949, the CCP began to reorganize its army in anticipation of their attack on south China. From March 3 to 5, the CCP convened the Second Plenum of the 7th Congress, in which Mao proclaimed the formation of a new-look, million-man army, which for the first time officially was designated the People's Liberation Army (PLA). To reflect this transformation and the fact that most of the army would be departing their familiar theaters of operation, the Communists disposed of the regional army names. The Northwest, Central Plains, East China, and Northeast Field Armies thus became the 1st, 2nd, 3rd, and 4th Field Armies respectively.[84] Only the North China Field Army would retain its old name, as it would remain in place while the other armies marched to new areas. Columns, which had never

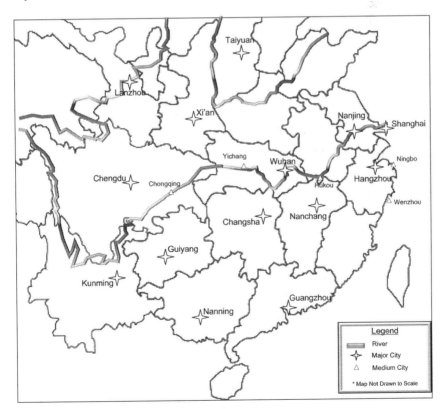

Figure 5.3 1949: Carry the revolution to the end.

been tied to a fixed number or size to begin with, were also formally replaced by corps.[85] At long last, the modern army which Zhu had envisioned in 1945 finally emerged. The party also discussed crossing the Yangtze River, preparations for which had begun as early as February 3, less than a month after the conclusion of both Huaihai and Pingjin.[86] No longer merely a probe attack to establish bases, the campaign had become a full-fledged onslaught.

After Chiang stepped down, Li Zongren had sought to come to terms with the CCP, but now that they had the upper hand, he could neither preserve GMD power nor forestall the Communists attack. More so than the Northern Expedition or any other event since the Qing conquest, events on the battlefield had eliminated the possibility of a political settlement or compromise. Nonetheless, there were still decisions to be made and battles to be fought. However, none of those waged south of the Yangtze River in 1949 would match the scale of the campaigns of 1948. As Mao and the Secretariat turned their attention towards the peace talks, the 2nd, 3rd, and 4th Field Armies quietly moved to the north bank of the Yangtze River in Jiangsu, Hubei and Anhui respectively.[87] In the meantime, the North China Field Army began its attack on Taiyuan.

While still engaged in negotiations, the CMC completed its preparations for the Yangtze River Crossing Campaign in late February. In the end, it was the Communists' unwavering intent to enter south China that prevented a truce or peace deal. Unlike Chiang in 1946, the CCP would not give in to international pressure or the temptation of a temporary peace. The first draft of the Yangtze River Crossing Campaign featured the 2nd and 3rd Field Armies crossing the Yangtze River in Jiangsu and Anhui, in late March, while the 4th Field Army engaged Bai Chongxi in north Hubei.[88] However, in March, the crossing date was pushed back to April 10 to accommodate the peace talks. The CMC also changed the plan so that the 4th Field Army deployed its full strength south of the river into Hubei, Jiangxi, and Hunan instead of seeking battle with Bai north of the river.[89]

The GMD defenses were divided between four regional commands. In the east, Tang Enbo commanded the Nanjing-Shanghai-Hangzhou (Jinghuhang) Garrison Headquarters, which included 25 corps – a total of 450,000 men. They were responsible for the defense of south Jiangsu, south Anhui, Zhejiang, and Jiangxi. In the center, Bai Chongxi's Central China Bandit Pacification Headquarters employed 15 corps, more than 250,000 men, in defense of the Yangtze River from Hukou to Yichang, with strong garrisons in Wuhan, Changsha, and Nanchang. In the west, Hu Zongnan defended Sichuan, while Ma Hongkui and Ma Bufang – the so-called "two Mas" – guarded Gansu, Ningxia and Xinjiang. The GMD hoped that this defense line, a vast crescent cutting China almost precisely in half, could stem the tide and perhaps allow Li and the new GMD government to resist or at least cause enough Communist casualties to force the CCP back to the bargaining table.

At the end of March, the CMC created the General Front Committee consisting of Deng Xiaoping, Liu Bocheng, Chen Yi, Su Yu, and Tan Zhenlin – the same members of the Huaihai Committee – to lead the Yangtze River Crossing Campaign. On March 31, Deng disseminated orders for the crossing and the exploitation operation, which he called the Nanjing-Shanghai-Hangzhou Campaign. Assuming that crossing in force would confuse and paralyze the enemy, Deng envisioned rapidly moving away from the beachhead to divide and surround the enemy forces before they could recover.[90] Deng's original plan was to cross the Yangtze in the evening of April 15, but this was postponed until to April 22 to allow more time for negotiations. The CMC expressed its willingness to push the schedule back even further if the GMD accepted more concessions.[91] However, the talks quickly broke down and the Secretariat amended their orders so that the attack would begin on April 20.[92]

In the end, the extra time afforded to the GMD did not make an appreciable difference. The Communists experienced no difficulty in crossing the river or penetrating Tang's initial defense line. As Deng recalled:

> We did not encounter fierce resistance anywhere. We made a wide, frontal crossing from scores of places, meeting with no substantial resistance in most places .... Beginning on the night of April 20, nearly all the 300,000 men crossed the river in a twenty-four hour period, plunging the enemy troops into chaos. With just one thought on their minds—breaking out of the encirclement—they fled southward helter-skelter.[93]

After establishing the bridgehead and chasing off any immediate defenders, the General Front Committee directed the exploitation phase of the campaign. This led to an astonishing sequence of events when the GMD defenses collapsed in rapid succession. By April 23, the capital of Nanjing fell without a fight after Tang's decision to abandon it and move his forces to Shanghai. Although he was able to reestablish a defense line in front of that port city, the Communists easily routed GMD forces elsewhere. By the beginning of May, the 2nd and 3rd Field Armies had captured large portions of Zhejiang, including Hangzhou, Wenzhou, Fenghua (Chiang Kaishek's hometown), and Ningbo, as well as penetrating Fujian and Jiangxi. At the same time, the 4th Field Army drove Bai away from the Yangtze and, in the process, received the defection of Zhang Zhen's 19th Army. Lin went on to capture Wuhan on May 17. With their landward flank secure, Chen and Su deployed almost the entire the 3rd Field Army against Shanghai's 200,000 defenders. This operation, the bloodiest of the entire campaign, wrapped up on May 27.

In just over a month since entering south China, the Communists claimed 400,000 enemy losses at the expense of 25,000 casualties – 17,000 of which occurred at Shanghai alone.[94] The ease at which they swept through Tang's Jinghuhang Garrision Headquarters and Bai's defenses at Hubei set an ominous precedent for the hopes of the Guangxi clique. After the conclusion of the Nanjing-Shanghai-Hangzhou Campaign, the CMC allocated sectors of responsibility to each field army to pursue the GMD and complete the conquest of south China. The 3rd Field Army was to secure the Yangtze River delta, with special attention paid to restoring the economy in Shanghai and Nanjing, and then capture Fujian in preparation for a future amphibious attack on Taiwan. The 2nd Field Army was to drive Hu Zongnan out of Sichuan and southwest China, while the 4th Field Army was assigned to south central China – Hunan, Jiangxi, Guangdong, and Guangxi.[95]

With victory close at hand, the Communists did not give Li and his fledgling government a chance to recover, nor did they offer another peace deal. After resting and reorganizing for the summer, they resumed their advance in the fall.

While the 2nd, 3rd, and 4th Field Armies crossed the Yangtze, the North China Field Army completed its siege of Taiyuan. They seized the city on April 24, officially ending decades of former warlord Yan Xishan's control over Shanxi province.[96] Yan fled to Taiwan and remained there in exile for the rest of his life. Afterwards, Peng Dehuai, who had taken command of the siege, absorbed the North China Field Army's 18th and 19th Armies (formerly Xu Xiangqian's 1st and Yang Dezhi's 2nd Armies) into his 1st Field Army. At the time, the 1st Field Army was already fighting Ma Bufang and Ma Hongkui in the Central Shaanxi Campaign. With Xu and Yang's armies under his command, Peng quickly drove the "two Mas" before him. In this sector, like the others, the battle soon became a rout and the 1st Field Army made rapid territorial gains while collecting defectors and prisoners at a prodigious rate.

On May 20, Xi'an fell, cutting off the link between Hu Zongnan and the "two Mas." On the first day of June, GMD units in Yulin defected and handed over the city to Peng. Operations continued into the late summer and fall, with Lanzhou falling on August 25 and the entirety of Ningxia by the end of September. A month later, the Second East Turkestan Republic, which had been part of the Chinese empire but had declared independence from the GMD in 1944, allegedly welcomed the 1st Field Army into its territory. This later led to the reintegration of the region into the Chinese state, where it became the province of Xinjiang.

The 2nd and 4th Field Armies made equally dramatic gains in south China during this time. On August 4, the Changsha Pacification Office, the Hunan Provincial Government, and Chen Mingren's 1st Army defected to Lin Biao, which forced Bai to retreat further south to the coastal provinces of Guangdong and Guangxi. On October 14, after engaging Bai in south Hunan and covering the 2nd Field Army's flank as it advanced into Sichuan, Lin's forces captured Guangzhou. The 4th Field Army then methodically destroyed Bai's 7th and 48th Corps, cleaving the GMD army in two. Part of it ended up in Guangxi while the rest boarded ships in Guangzhou for Hainan and Taiwan. With only 170,000 men remaining in his home province of Guangxi, Bai had no hope of holding off Lin's army. On December 4, the provincial capital of Nanning fell, and two weeks later Bai and the entire Guangxi clique evacuated the continent. The 4th Field Army settled down to consolidate their gains and prepare an amphibious operation against Hainan. They would successfully capture the island in May 1950.

In the meantime, the 2nd Field Army moved into Sichuan and Guizhou, capturing the capital of the latter, Guiyang, on November 15. By the end of the month, Liu and Deng had captured Chongqing. After surrounding Chengdu, they received the defection of the 5th, 15th, 16th, and 20th Armies, as well as the GMD garrisons in Yunnan and Xikang.[97] However, the 8th and 26th Corps in Kunming refused to surrender, which forced the 2nd Field Army to dispatch forces to Yunnan. By the end of December, both Kunming and Chengdu had fallen to Deng and Liu. This all but completed the liberation of southwest China, which allowed the Communists to move into Tibet and reclaim yet another part of the old Qing Dynasty in the following year.

While many of these operations continued into 1950, the Third Chinese Civil War came to a semi-official ending on October 1, 1949. At that time, Mao and the Central Committee had taken up residence in Beijing and announced the founding of the PRC. Although more challenges awaited, such as a resurgent GMD in Taiwan, involvement in the Cold War, and internal turmoil, the war on the continent was over. After decades of struggle, the CCP and its armed wing, the PLA, had emerged the undisputed winners of the Chinese revolution.

The period of 1948–49 stands out not only because it marked the last phase of the war, but also because of the manner in which the fighting played out. The scale of combat, casualties, and maneuvers in the space of that year were far greater than those that occurred in the previous years. For instance, the Communist casualties incurred at Ji'nan, Jinzhou, and Tianjin would have crippled the CCP earlier. But by this time, the PLA not only absorbed them – thanks partly to the large numbers of GMD soldiers changing sides after each battle – but did not balk from engaging in similar battles. In fact, it sped up the process, leading to a stunning succession of victories and creating an unstoppable momentum. The ruthless prosecution of victory from Liaoshen, Huaihai, Pingjin, and the Yangtze River was conducted with such speed and cold efficiency that one is left to wonder how the situation could have changed so radically after 1945. As previously shown, it was a difficult journey for the Communists, but one which they weathered, survived, and ultimately completed. The battles that led to the end of the war were not flukes – the CCP had earned their victory.

In the end, the battles that decided the war did not occur in Nanjing, Chongqing, Guangzhou, or any other of the GMD's traditional south Chinese strongholds. Although there was much ground to cover and a few more minor battles to be fought, any question of who would win the war ended in Jinzhou, Xuzhou, and Beiping. Despite bold talk about a Yangtze River defense line, the GMD crumbled and what was supposed to be a fight to the finish ended up as little more than a mopping-up campaign. The astounding pace of Communist operations in south China belies the level of chaos and desperation that gripped the GMD in the summer and fall of 1949. It is hard to imagine that, after so many years of fighting, Chiang's mainland regime would simply vanish with a whimper. But, contrary to expectations at the time, that is exactly what occurred.

sion

The Communists' decisive victory during the Third Chinese Civil War was a remarkable achievement. It was the CCP's ability to formulate strategy, seize the initiative, and outthink the GMD that won them the war, not GMD corruption or socioeconomic conditions. Their ability to decisively win campaigns in 1948–49 not only brought the long civil war to an end but also made that end final and lasting – an accomplishment Chiang Kaishek had never been able to attain during his term of rule. The formation of Communist strategy during the war thus represents a significant turning point in the history of the CCP, one with far-reaching implications for the study of modern Chinese history.

In the final analysis, three major themes stand out when considering Communist strategy during the war. They include the fact that the victory was not inevitable, Mao's relationship with his generals, and the final reliance on battle to end the war. These concepts are important not only because of how they undermine the basis of earlier assumptions, but because they fundamentally shaped the PRC. The Third Chinese Civil War, far from being a sideshow in a theatre of socioeconomic or political change, was the main event in China during the 20th century: the war, more than anything else, led to the end of the revolution and ushered in a new era.

Victory by design, not default

The ebb and flow of the Third Chinese Civil War was a direct reflection of the games of strategy and counterstrategy the CCP and GMD played over the course of four years. The course of events also illustrates the fact that the war hung in the balance up until the end of the three great campaigns of 1948–49. The resolution of the war hinged on a series of key decisions made at critical junctures. Although such a claim might be made about any war, it is important to recognize that it was not a single or a handful of poor decisions by Chiang that decided the war – these only expedited the final resolution. It was equally important for the Communists to make and implement the correct decisions. Because the preceding narrative has already painted the picture of the plans, decisions, and events of the war, this section will seek to illuminate, highlight, and discuss the implications of these grand strategies.

In light of the previous theories regarding the superiority of Communist guerrilla strategy and the ineptness of the GMD army, it is important to recognize that the beginning of the Third Chinese Civil War caught the CCP completely off guard. While their plan to impede the GMD progress with guerrilla bases in south China was sound, GMD maneuvers in 1945 suggested the Communist's strategies might have been useless – even had the Communists been able to complete them. Chiang's decision to change the "script" and immediately move his forces into north China by means of Allied air and naval transport derailed Mao and Zhu's strategy of an unconventional defense in the south and a conventional defense in the north. Consequently, the CCP's first real strategic decision in the war was simple and straightforward – expand throughout north China to prevent the GMD from getting a foothold in Communist territory. The haphazard manner in which the Communists carried out this decision reflects their failure to plan for that contingency. The first round in the contest had definitely gone to the GMD.

In an effort to turn the tide, the next major CCP decision was not made by Mao at all, but by his second-in-command, Liu Shaoqi. Almost overnight, Liu completely undid Mao and Zhu's pre-war plans by shifting some of their best troops into northeast China and shortening the Communist defenses in the south in an all-out bid to win Manchuria. The most important goal of Liu's strategy was to establish northeast China as a base of operations which could then supply the war effort at a national level. Not only was the whole scheme audacious and strategically clever, it enabled the Communists to seize the initiative.

Despite complications imposed on the CCP and its forces, the die were cast. This decision may very well have been the most important one of the war, even though the turning point would not come until much later, and by then the fight for the northeast had dragged on too long for the region to be decisive in itself. The true importance of Liu's "March on the North, Defend in the South" plan was that it forced Chiang and the GMD to counter this move by deploying troops to a low-priority area. Yet Chiang again proved flexible and prescient by dispatching some of his best troops in a rapid campaign to disrupt the Communist strategy.

Many observers, such as US General Albert C. Wedemeyer, viewed Chiang's decision in a harshly negative light.[1] The most common criticism was that it overextended his army needlessly. However, his move did not actually represent a logistical problem until years later when the Communists had interdicted GMD lines of communication in north China and had begun to win major victories in the Central Plains. Arthur Waldron makes a similar case in a counterfactual analysis that postulates the Communists would have formed a relatively harmless Soviet puppet-state in Manchuria, while the GMD easily could have occupied the rest of China.[2] However, Wedemeyer and Waldron assume that the Communists' defenses in north China would not have collapsed before Manchuria's manpower and industrial potential were brought to bear. As the campaigns of 1946–47 have shown, the Communists were able to fend off some of Chiang's best troops and likely would have gained the necessary time. In addition, the way Lin Biao's Northeast Field Army tipped the balance in late 1948 in north China also speaks to the wisdom of Liu Shaoqi's original vision.

Another critique of Chiang's decision to fight in Manchuria asserts that doing so exposed his best forces to a Communist army armed and aided by the Soviet Union. However, two of the most important economic and political members of the Northeast Bureau, Chen Yun and Zhang Wentian, do not mention Soviet support. The level of Soviet aid appears to have been minimal, and CCP sources not only commonly dismiss Moscow's assistance but highlight Soviet attempts to hinder CCP efforts. The Soviets did, in fact, hurt the Northeast Bureau by expropriating heavy machinery and industrial plants during their occupation. Doing so not only denied the CCP these resources later, but also painted all Communists in a bad light to the general populace. Furthermore, Communist strategy shows no inclination to count on support from Moscow during operational planning.

While Communist sources may be politically driven, there is little evidence from neutral sources to show that the Red Army did anything more than hand over Japanese weapons[3] – the same benefit Communist armies in north China received when they destroyed Japanese and Wang Jingwei regime units or captured their supply depots. The US ambassador to China, John Stuart Leighton, reported as late as October 29, 1947 that there was "little if any evidence of material assistance from Moscow."[4] Additionally, there are few instances of Soviet equipment being photographed or reported in the hands of the Communists. For example, in a propaganda picture of Mao reviewing the troops in Tiananmen Square on October 1, 1949, he rides in an American jeep and tanks in the background are Japanese Type-97s. While it was rumored that Mao strictly ordered the use of captured GMD equipment during victory processions, lest the CCP appear as pawns of Moscow, it is more likely that the Communists simply did not possess any major allotments of Soviet equipment.

If Chiang made the correct decision in 1945, then Mao made the wrong decision in responding to the GMD expedition when he ordered his ill-prepared forces to conduct a series of disastrous defensive stands. If it had not been for Lin Biao, the turning point of the war might have occurred in the spring of 1946 at Siping, with the GMD eventually grinding out a hard-fought victory against the Communists by 1947 or early 1948. As it was, Chiang was able only to win a limited victory in Manchuria and he would have to guard that front with troops that would have been better used in the "General Offensive" against the CCP's north China Liberated Areas.

Nonetheless, by the middle of 1946 Chiang clearly had the advantage and the Communists were desperate to regain the initiative. After flirting with the idea of conducting their own counteroffensive, the Communists eventually employed the so-called "mobile defense" strategy, which combined aspects of Fabian and Jominian interior-line strategy. The decision to engage in "mobile defense" has long been attributed to Mao, but this is inaccurate. In the first place, documentary evidence clearly shows that it was Mao's intent to attack rather than defend. Doing so would have resulted in a spectacular failure, as seen in Chen Yi's abortive assault in Anhui and Liu Bocheng's failure to establish bases south of the Longhai Railroad. However, it was not only Mao who wanted to launch an offensive. Chen Yi was also dedicated to the idea of attacking GMD territory, even as the Shandong and south Jiangsu fronts threatened to collapse around him. In the end, it was Mao himself who forced Chen to fight in Shandong and abandon north Jiangsu.

Those who wanted to remain on the defensive based their argument on the fact that the time was not yet right for an attack. Lin Biao, for instance, needed to rebuild his army and he fought in 1946 only to save his widely dispersed forces. Su Yu, on the other hand, argued that they could not defend what they currently held and attack GMD territory at the same time. Although Lin and Su's protests forestalled an offensive in east and central China, the attacks in west and north China went ahead as planned. As with Liu Bocheng and Chen Yi's earlier defeats, Nie's failure at Datong revealed that the Communist armies were not yet ready to conduct offensives.

Evidence that casts doubt on the claim that Mao was the sole author of the mobile defense strategy of 1946 appears in his own compositions. Although he addressed the tactical problems the Communists faced in his September 16, 1946 article, "Concentrate a Superior Force to Destroy the Enemy One by One,"[5] many of these tenets were rehashed versions of his old guerrilla warfare techniques. Although his emphasis on mass and concentration was correct, he glossed over changes in weaponry, organization, and professionalism – all of which would enable regular, standing Communist forces to perform the difficult maneuvers required in a "mobile defense." In the end, the most important strategic contribution Mao offered at this point was his approval of abandoning cities. This was critical because he had temporarily reversed this stance in 1945 to focus on capturing and holding urban centers. Revoking this directive allowed his commanders to seek battle in places of their choosing rather than having to fight over certain areas – a problem that handicapped Chiang's armies.

While Mao was mired in theory and a macro view of tactics, the Communist field generals had already begun applying advanced tactics and operational planning. For instance, at Shangdang, Liu Bocheng successfully applied the principle of attacking one target to ambush a relief column – an unprecedented Communist display of command, control, and coordination of large units. Less than a year later, Su Yu employed traditional Jominian interior-lines tactics to win seven battles in south Jiangsu and later fought skilled rearguard actions in Shandong. These examples demonstrate an understanding of conventional tactics that reveals prior education and experience, not blind adherence to a theory or party line. Far from hindering this effort, Mao facilitated it by constantly praising his commanders, avoiding micromanaging their techniques, and generally offering only strategic guidance – although there were notable exceptions late in the war, which met with mixed results (i.e. Liaoshen and Huaihai).

During this period of the war, the Communists won a few tactical victories and managed to keep their armies intact. However, the north China Liberated Areas shrank drastically from 1946 to 1947. It was at this point that Chiang made a fateful decision that changed the face of the war. Believing he had secured most of Hebei, Shanxi, and Manchuria, he embarked on the Strong Point Offensive, in which he shifted the bulk of his strength to Shandong and Shaanxi. This led to headline victories such as the capture of Yan'an and the isolation of Chen Yi's army in east

Shandong. However, this decision, even more than the expedition to northeast China, fatally overextended the GMD army. The inability of Hu Zongnan or Tang Enbo to secure either region or annihilate a Communist field army meant that the "Strong Point Offensive" was a strategic failure.

After Chiang's army wore itself out, the Communists launched their own strategic counteroffensive in the summer of 1947. In this bold attack, which involved marching a field army hundreds of miles behind enemy lines, the Communists seized the initiative. Once in their hands, they would never relinquish it, thus controlling the pace and direction of the rest of the war. For an all intents and purposes, this was the turning point. Hereafter, the GMD would never again be able to contain, much less stem, the Communist momentum. The idea for the Central Plains Counteroffensive affirmatively belongs to Mao, who proposed the counterattack in telegrams as early as the winter of 1946–47.[6]

Although the strategic counteroffensive stage began with the SHSH Field Army marching south of the Yellow River, the movement was made possible only because of the turn of events in northeast and north China. Capitalizing on Chiang's fixation with Shandong and Shaanxi, as well as Du Yuming's awkward attacks on southeast Manchuria, Lin Biao and Nie Rongzhen were also able to launch their own regional counterattacks. These fixed Chiang's troops in a series of static defensive positions and prevented their use in other regions. Indeed, a GMD army in the right place and at right time may very well have turned the tide against Peng Dehuai, Chen Yi, or Liu Bocheng. Without a strategic reserve and an obvious weak point in the center, the GMD had left themselves completely vulnerable to the Communist attack.

While it is true that Chiang unwittingly surrendered the initiative with his Strong Point Offensive, that alone was not responsible for the GMD's downfall. Indeed, Chiang was overjoyed by the thrust into the Central Plains because he thought that the SHSH Field Army would be surrounded, destroyed, or limited to irregular warfare. This hope quickly evaporated when Communist reinforcements rapidly shored up the new Central Plains region and the Shandong front collapsed. To make matters worse, the fall of Shijiazhuang exposed GMD weakness in north China just as Lin Biao's capture of Siping tipped the balance of power in northeast China. These combined factors, occurring simultaneously, spelled doom for the GMD.

With the Communists in a strong strategic position, in the summer of 1948 Mao decided to speed up the timetable of the war. Instead of a protracted affair, Mao now envisioned the war ending in two or three years by means of a series of decisive battles in the Central Plains and south China. His decision to seek battle rather than strategic position was crucial, as it prevented the GMD from reconsolidating or reforming its defenses in a meaningful way. Although this new policy pushed the Communist armies to breaking point, by refusing Chiang the chance to react Mao finally broke the pattern of strategy and counterstrategy. Mao's vision was to repeat the SHSH Field Army's crossing of the Yellow River by doing the same with the East China Field Army, except it would cross the Yangtze River into south China.

Mao called this period the "strategic offensive," in which the East China Field Army would tie down Chiang's forces south of the Yangtze River while the rest of the Communist army annihilated GMD forces north of the river. Again, Mao's generals warned against overreaching and moving too quickly. Chen Yi and Su Yu feared leaving enemy troops behind them in Shandong and Jiangsu, while Liu and Deng's army had been severely weakened by the march to and the defense of the Dabie Mountains. Like Chen and Su, Lin Biao also wanted to secure his rear areas, namely Changchun and Jilin City, before engaging in risky operations in the Liaoshen corridor. Eventually, Mao bowed to these concerns and, consequently, the GMD defenses began to unravel at an alarming pace – even more so than the most optimistic CCP estimates.

However, by the fall of 1948, the Communists were in a good position to implement Mao's strategic offensive. After a heated debate, Lin launched the Liaoshen Campaign against his own judgment and won an improbable battle. Having now secured Manchuria and Shandong, thanks to the simultaneous capture of Ji'nan, Mao wanted to launch the strategic offensive into south China as soon as possible. As this still required that the Communists defeat the GMD in the Central Plains, Mao allowed the Central Plains and East China Field Army to conduct another series of operations, starting with the Huaihai Campaign, to clear a path to the Yangtze River. Unsatisfied with the modest objectives of Su's original plan, Mao pressed for more ambitious goals. He did so even after the battle started, and at one point proposed engaging five GMD armies simultaneously, despite the relative weakness of his own force. By reaching a compromise, the Communists were able to defeat one army at a time and win a victory well beyond what they originally planned or even hoped for when the campaign began. Although they were ultimately not able to meet all of Mao's objectives during the campaign, their accomplishments proved more than sufficient not only to break through to the Yangtze River, but also to guarantee an unexpectedly speedy end to the war.

Flush with victory, Mao ruthlessly deployed the Northeast Field Army into north China. Intent on maintaining the momentum and the initiative, the Communists surprised the GMD in north China with the Pingjin Campaign. Mainly a battle of maneuvers, Pingjin ended in another GMD debacle – this time the defection of an entire army group. Now, with Manchuria, north China, and the Central Plains under Communist control, Mao's strategic offensive was not so much an attack as a pursuit and a mopping-up operation. Meeting little resistance from a broken and demoralized GMD army, the CCP captured most of continental China in less than a year, re-annexing areas that had been independent since World War II and earlier.

Mao later summed up the entire process from 1946 to 1949 in three phases: the mobile defense, the counteroffensive, and the strategic offensive. He intentionally omitted the post-World War II and "March on the North, Defend in the South" periods. As seen, the actual course of events was not as easy or clean as he described, although in a general sense he was entirely accurate. However, it is also accurate to say the Communist strategy was as fraught with disagreement, danger, miscues, serendipitous fortune, and perilous misfortune as that employed by the losing side.

With this in mind, one must then ask the question of why and how the Communist forces won. They certainly did not begin in possession of a "magic bullet" or flawless plan, as the post-World War II scramble and the collapse of the "March on the North, Defend in the South" plan demonstrated. They did not necessarily fight harder or longer, nor were Communist foot soldiers discernibly superior.

It was true that the GMD military suffered from both poor leadership and morale problems at almost all echelons.[7] They also failed fully to exploit their advantages or use mass support like the Communists did.[8] Yet in the years before 1949, many GMD units fought extremely well and were feared by the PLA's rank and file. In 1945 and 1946, Chiang's elite troops dominated the battlefield. When properly led and coordinated, the GMD were largely able to counteract most Communist maneuvers through 1947. However, the situation shifted radically in 1948 and by the end of 1949 the fight degenerated into a complete rout. While we do not see the same problems within the Communist ranks, their absence is more likely the result of lack of sources and full disclosure than of the PLA's possessing an optimal system. The difference may reside instead in the fact that because the Communists were weaker, ascribed to a strict code of party discipline, and had less to defend, they were more able to weed out incompetence and avoid making major strategic errors.

Social, economic, and political factors played a role, but they pale in comparison with critical military decisions that took place at the high levels of command. Although Chiang was certainly thinking about solidifying his political hold and his flagging economy in the beginning of 1947, he ultimately planned his General and Strong Point Offensives based on the military situation and the need for a military solution. The same was true of Mao, Liu, and Deng when they had to decide whether to commit an entire army to a one-way trip to the Dabie Mountains. The "mobile defense" phase also shows that the Communists were more than willing to sacrifice their Liberated Area administrations to save their armies. While such sacrifices may reflect a guerilla war mentality, their means and the methods were considerably different, as seen above in the discussion of "mobile defense." Lastly, the campaigns of 1948 show that battle, more than anything else, determined how and when the war would end. The decisive nature of Liaoshen, Huaihai, and Pingjin did more to coronate the CCP and exile from the continent the GMD than any reform program or political movement.

In the final analysis, the reasons the Communists triumphed are primarily those of superior leadership and an uncanny ability to seize and exploit the initiative. The long, hard road from 1927 to 1945 had produced a social-Darwinist effect on the CCP chain of command. By the beginning of the Third Chinese Civil War, only the "fittest" had survived and, despite personal quirks or issues, none of these men put themselves or their cliques over the party. All of those who did, like Zhang Guotao or Wang Ming, had long since fallen by the wayside. The effect of combat experience, often from the weaker side and in harsh conditions, also played a large role in producing extremely capable leaders. While a majority of the Communist generals had some professional military training, in the end their experiences in the Jinggang Mountains, the defense of the Jiangxi Soviet, the Long March, the Three

Years War, and the war against Japan were much more effective teachers.

Due to the fact that the Communist military leadership were all experienced combat veterans and fought exclusively on the weaker side, they knew why initiative was so important to possess and maintain. Displayed frequently at the operational and strategic levels, this knowledge was the main crux of any given campaign. Even when disagreement arose between different echelons of command, it was mainly over how to force the enemy to do something or what would be the right time to launch a counterattack, rather than a squabble over deployments or methods. Even when they lost the initiative temporarily in 1946, the CCP was still able to prevent Chiang from dictating the course of the war long enough to recover the initiative in 1947. Except for a few notable periods, Chiang rarely had the ability to choose the field of battle or force the Communists to react to him at a strategic level. This, more than any other individual factor, is probably what ultimately cost him the war.

Becoming gods: Mao and his generals

If strategy was essential in determining the course of the Third Chinese Civil War, then, by extension, the character of the men who formulated it and how they interacted with each other were equally vital. As the narrative shows, plenty of disagreement existed, but none of it crippled the army, nor did the Communists have to shuffle their chain of command in the middle of the war. The fact that CCP political and military leadership remained united and never descended into factional politics is important not only for understanding the period but also understanding the first and second generations of PRC leadership.

In terms of personnel, the high-level leadership which entered the war in 1945 was virtually identical to that which emerged in 1949. This pattern was especially true of the Secretariat, which had not only remained stable but had even survived being separated in 1947. Within this body, Mao dominated strategic and military affairs except for a few key moments when he was either sick or in negotiations. Surprisingly, strategic decision-making during such periods did not to fall Zhu De, but to Liu Shaoqi instead. Later on, despite acting as a decoy in 1947, Mao still controlled the army, although Liu and Zhu handled day-to-day operations. Overall, Mao's unwillingness to loosen his grip on the strategic control while he was in danger is notable and perhaps serves as an indicator of his future style of rule during the Great Leap Forward and the Cultural Revolution.

The reason for Mao's tight control over military and strategic affairs may have dated back to his earlier experiences with party infighting as early as 1927. During that time, Mao's theories about guerrilla warfare were mostly ignored, despite his success in the Jinggang Mountains and in defense of the Jiangxi Soviet. Additionally, in those days, the party leadership shifted strategic focus as often as they shifted personnel, which had a definite effect on the morale and capabilities of the army. These factors probably played a role in Mao's calculations during the war. His intent to maintain one consistent vision, mainly his own, and to prevent any changes mid-stride, did eventually prove decisive.

Another factor supporting Mao's dominant role in strategy was the fact that his two most senior main subordinates, Zhou Enlai and Zhu De, largely had bound their political futures to Mao and by 1945 were unwilling to oppose him – a pattern that played out for the rest of their lives. Zhou was already specializing in foreign affairs and party operations, rather than directly contributing to military strategy. Although he served as chief-of-staff of the army after the fall of Yan'an, he acted mostly as a mediator in strategic debates, throwing his support with one side or the other, rather than initiating discussions. Dick Wilson argues that Zhou benefited from the time when the Secretariat split by making himself indispensable to the Chairman, but then, as he implies earlier, Zhou had always maintained good relations with Mao.[9] Zhu, on the other hand, concentrated on the more mechanical elements of transforming and modernizing the army. For the most part, he concerned himself with industry, logistics, and procuring arms, rather than dictating how to deploy them. Thus, during the Third Chinese Civil War, both men accepted relatively minor roles in strategy.

Junior to Zhou and Zhu, but of a higher rank, was Liu Shaoqi. Liu's role as a politician and social reformer has long been discussed in Chinese and Western literature. Yet Liu rarely receives credit as a strategist, despite the role he played with the New 4th Army and in formulating the "March on the North, Defend the South" strategy. Liu's diminished reputation, especially his role in forging strategy for Manchuria in 1945, was likely due to Cultural Revolution politics. As Lin Biao and Mao took the limelight in the 1960's, Liu's "inconvenient" involvement was subtly obscured by depicting him as a lowly subordinate who was just following Mao's orders.

The existing documentary evidence, however, strongly supports the idea that Liu developed the strategy. At the very least, it was a joint effort between himself, Zhu De, and Peng Dehuai. The detail and comprehensiveness of the plan suggests either possibility. The idea that Mao had plotted out the whole scheme before departing to Chongqing is problematic. For one, the situation changed considerably between the time he left and when the plan was envisioned and implemented. Even if originally he had conceived the idea, he probably would have only provided a general vision and a few guidelines, as per his usual manner. Conversely, Liu's draft contained specific movements and contingency plans. Mao's telegrams and orders were never so detailed nor did they display the thoroughness evident in the orders the Secretariat sent to the army on September 17. Yet, as quickly as he had assumed power and played his role, Liu obediently took the backseat when Mao returned. In 1947, he did assume military functions when he teamed up with Zhu De in north China after the fall of Yan'an. However, there he contributed mostly to reshaping the north China Liberated Areas into a proto-state. Yet, despite this "disappearing act," Liu's performance at critical moments not only solidified his political and military position, but also eventually played an important role in shaping the Communists' victory.

The last member of the Secretariat, Ren Bishi, did not play much of a role in military strategy before or during the Third Chinese Civil War. In many ways, Ren remains an enigma because he died soon after the war. Much like Liu, Ren had studied in the Soviet Union and leaned heavily toward pragmatic rather than ideological solutions. He also focused on social and economic policies rather than military ones. Unlike Liu, Ren never had to stand in for Mao, but he played an important role in the party elite. As Westad notes, Ren was in the prime of his power before his death in October 1950 and with him gone, Liu lost a critical ally.[10] Yet, as a moderate, Ren likely would have been purged during the Cultural Revolution. On the other hand, because he was the number five man in the party in 1949, he might have provided enough prestige to give Liu, and to a lesser degree Deng Xiaoping and Zhou Enlai, the ability to arrest the Cultural Revolution. As attractive as that might sound, such a scenario does not take into account the man who gained the most during the Third Chinese Civil War – Mao himself.

Mao Zedong emerged from the war as the savior of the Chinese people – the man who made the Chinese finally "stand up" after years of imperialist oppression and endemic infighting. He was also the undisputed leader of the PLA, thanks to a series of critical decisions that solidified his position with his generals and the rank and file. Yet, despite PRC literature and propaganda attempts to deify Mao as a latter-day Zhuge Liang, even official sources cannot help but reveal Mao as an impatient and sometimes impractical military thinker. At the same time, however, it is clear that he was an impressive visionary who could see the end goal but sometimes failed to see all of the steps required to reach it. This picture is consistent with his post-1949 governing style.[11] Despite these flaws, Mao's strategy during the decisive phase of the war was a powerful and important influence which may well have won the war more quickly than his generals would have on their own.

Perhaps the best case study for gauging this impact is Mao's relationship with Lin Biao. Although identified as one of Mao's firmest supporters before 1971, Lin frequently criticized Mao's military strategies almost from the very start.[12] However, some sources suggest his critiques were based only on military, not political, concerns.[13] It is possible Lin's time as commandant of the Anti-Japanese University was for reeducation purposes, but he later returned to combat where he won a notable victory at the Battle of Pingxingguan. After being injured, Lin was out of active military service for almost a decade, but when the "March on the North, Defend in the South" plan went to effect, most accounts suggest that Mao handpicked Lin to lead the effort in Manchuria. Lin's subsequent independence and strategic divergence from Mao's line – not to mention Mao's tolerance – seems to underline the fact that the Chairman really did believe Lin was the best man for the job.

The tenuous relationship between Mao and the "governor-general" of northeast China continued as Lin won military victories by defying, rather than slavishly following, Mao's guidance. After all, it was Lin's strategy that had saved Linjiang, disgraced Chen Cheng, and isolated Changchun and Jilin City. Thus, it was no surprise that he greeted Mao's desire to make an "end run" to Jinzhou with little enthusiasm. Yet despite Lin's resistance, Mao won out, and the result was an unprecedented victory. The degree to which Lin's intransigence was transformed by Mao's strategic vision at Liaoshen has been downplayed and, before the release of PRC records, largely misunderstood. In the ensuing Pingjin Campaign, Lin was much more amenable, accepting Mao's orders to move south immediately and to be patient at Beiping. These paid enormous dividends and were decisions that Lin probably would not have made by of his own volition.

The Liaoshen Campaign was an important turning point in their relationship because Lin had been proved wrong in his own specialty. This deprived Lin of a degree of leverage in his dealings with the Chairman and forced him in the 1960s to become perhaps more Maoist than Mao himself. Yet at the same time Lin still showed his legendary stubbornness, as seen in his refusal to take command of the Chinese Volunteer Force during the Korean War and his desire for closer relations with Moscow. Lastly, there is the matter of his attempted coup, which remains shrouded in mystery. This action, however, may have been one of self-preservation rather than a preplanned grab for power. In the end, Lin was likely neither a staunch proponent of Mao's military theories nor was he afraid of opposing the Chairman at critical junctures. While Lin's independent streak may speak to the idea of Lin being a cynical opportunist, more importantly it reveals Mao's overriding faith in his quality subordinates – at least during the revolution.

Another important relationship in the CCP high command was between Mao and Chen Yi. Earlier in the party's history, Chen not only disagreed with Maoist strategy but even momentarily displaced Mao in the chain of command after the establishment of the Jiangxi Soviet. Additionally, not having participated in the Long March, Chen did not undergo the indoctrination process of the Yan'an decade. Instead, he fought with the guerrillas in South China and then with the New 4th Army in Central China. This resulted in a different line of strategy and an independent approach to waging the war. For instance, Chen courted businessmen and gentry while Yan'an took a hard-line against these classes. He also sought ties to Li Zongren and the Guangxi clique.[14] Yet despite these "deviations," Chen was largely in lockstep agreement with Mao and Yan'an in World War II and even more so during the Third Chinese Civil War. The fact that his adherence to Mao's policies appears natural and not contrived is an important observation.

For instance, despite the burden it placed on him, there is no evidence that Chen protested the "March on the North, Defend in the South" plan. Later on, when Mao called for a strategic counterattack in the summer of 1946, Chen was in complete agreement. It was Chen's military commander, Su Yu, who protested and eventually helped sway Mao to take up a mobile defense strategy. Rather than contention between Chen and the center, Chen's largest problem – besides the GMD – was establishing a viable chain of command within his own district. Chen was the first Communist commander to have to deal with the organizational nightmare of two separate field armies and military districts. The problem was exacerbated by Mao's habit of speaking directly to Su Yu and the Central China Field Army, rather than going through Chen. Eventually this issue was resolved when the GMD eliminated Jiangsu as a theater of operations, making the East China Field Army an entity de facto, rather than just on paper. It also served the unintended purpose of perfecting the process before other mergers took place, such as the SHSH and SCH Field Armies and the Northwest Field Army.

As for Chen's personal career, he benefited from good personal relations with Mao due to their shared love of traditional Chinese culture.[15] Not taking part in the

Long March also did not seem to harm Chen's prospects. By the end of the Third Chinese Civil War, Chen had largely divorced himself from military strategy, handing that over to Su, and focused more on state building. He eventually took on the prestigious and important role of mayor of Shanghai upon its capture in 1949 and remained an important member of the party throughout the rest of his life. Later, he served as Foreign Minister, vice chairman of the CMC, and member of the Politburo before being stripped of some of his posts during the Cultural Revolution. Passing away in 1972, Chen did not outlive Mao nor did he see the end of the Cultural Revolution. Although his reputation was damaged, as was the case with so many other high-ranking party members, he did not require a large-scale rehabilitation like Liu Shaoqi or Peng Dehuai.

The Communist commanders in the west, He Long and Peng Dehuai, maintained a different relationship with Mao, primarily because of their proximity to him until 1948. As fellow Hunan natives and born of peasant stock, one might assume that they should have been among Mao's most important associates. In fact, both of their careers ended ignominiously in the Cultural Revolution – although not because of anything they did on the battlefield. He Long started the war as commander of two under-strength regions but he led the first series of counterattacks in the west. However, as the conflict moved away from central Shanxi, his forces were allocated elsewhere and his role in strategy decreased as more important battles took place outside his area of responsibility. Peng Dehuai, on the other hand, increased his level of participation when he assumed command of Northwest Field Army in the wake of the fall of Yan'an. Although this was officially a "demotion," since Peng left his job as chief-of-staff of the PLA to take a subordinate command, it actually increased his involvement in military strategy.

Peng's role in grand strategy prior to 1947 is not clear. As one of the more high-ranking and experienced military commanders, Peng must have had an important role in the initial moves in 1945. He also may have been an important factor in rejecting negotiations with the GMD. As Westad notes, at the end of 1945, in Yan'an it was "the military commanders were in ascendance, and it was they who had Mao's ear."[16] Peng also called for a counteroffensive at the end of 1946, the only one besides Mao to take such a forward-leaning position. Whether Peng originated the idea or simply supported Mao is not clear. The decision to appoint Peng commander of the Northwest Field Army may well have resurrected his military career, dormant since the Hundred Regiments Offensive. However, Jurgen Domes argues that Peng's time as chief-of-staff improved his relationship with Mao and was important politically because it allowed him to join the Central Committee.[17] Additionally, while Peng may have opposed Mao on many occasions before 1945, they did not have any further arguments afterwards.[18] Yet Peng did not appear satisfied as a theoretician who wrote pamphlets about strategic issues and politics. Consequently, by emulating Liu Bocheng, who earlier had left the chief-of-staff post for a "demotion" to command the 129th Division at the beginning of World War II, Peng was able to share in the prestige his peers were winning on the battlefield.

Peng's political and military work thus allowed him to enter the PRC era as one of the leading figures of the PLA, despite not having participated in any of the large campaigns during 1948–49. After securing Xinjiang in early 1950, Peng took command of the Chinese People's Volunteers in Korea after Lin passed up the post and then served as Defense Minister until the fateful Lushun Conference of 1958. During that event, Peng was caught by surprise when his reproach of Mao, which was only a mild rebuke,[19] evoked a violent reaction. Instead of the close-minded dictator Mao came to be, Peng probably thought back to their Yan'an days, when he could rouse a naked Mao from bed to debate issues long into the night. Peng's miscalculation, although necessary and ultimately responsible for saving millions of lives, later led to his death at the hands of Red Guards during the Cultural Revolution.[20] However, in many ways his death enhanced his reputation in post-Mao China and underlined the fact that he was perhaps the closest of all of his peers to being a pure soldier and a dedicated servant of the state.

Unlike Lin and Peng, the next most senior commander, Liu Bocheng, did not undergo a meteoric political ascent, although militarily he was probably the most consistent and successful general in the Communist ranks. Part of the reason for his lack of political involvement was his professional training. At many points he appears to have made a conscious effort to avoid intra-party debates and power plays. For instance, his voice was conspicuously absent during the larger discussions of strategic orientation during the Jiangxi Soviet period. Liu's record after 1949 also highlights his lack of involvement in political affairs.

After the founding of the PRC, Liu remained strictly engaged in matters of training and strategy while avoiding the turmoil surrounding the Great Leap Forward and the Cultural Revolution. Because of this, he largely descended into obscurity and died peacefully at the old age of 96. Although he did suffer some criticism in the wake of the anti-rightist campaign and later for his association with his old comrade-in-arms Deng Xiaoping, this mostly manifested itself in being shuffled off to less-desirable posts. Eventually, Deng did his best to rehabilitate Liu, seeking to right some past wrongs and set the record straight in a public eulogy in the *People's Daily* after Liu's death.[21] In the end, Liu lived out his life as he thought a professional soldier should, largely apolitical and intensely focused on military affairs.

Much like Liu, Su Yu and Nie Rongzhen also tried to distance themselves from PRC politics. In many ways, those three generals comprised the core of a professional military group which focused on modernizing the army and strengthening national defense. Su's decision to command only military units and forgo political appointments, such as serving as the secretary of a regional bureau, was indicative of this behavior. Peng's removal as Defense Minister in 1958 and the installation of Lin Biao, who instituted extreme "red" measures, was a serious blow to this group's goals. However, their indispensable service during the revolution largely allowed them to survive the chaos. They were also blessed with surprising longevity, with Su living until 1984 and Nie to 1992. While Su remained a military man for his entire career, Nie branched off into the Chinese military-industrial complex where he helped build China's nuclear missile program. The complex he founded still maintains considerable economic and political clout and, in many ways, is a mini-dynasty, with Nie's descendents still playing a highly influential role in that institution.

The final figure of note to emerge from the Third Chinese Civil War was Deng Xiaoping, perhaps the most important PRC personage after Mao himself. Deng had no real military experience until he joined Liu Bocheng and the 129th Division during World War II. Yet he proved to be a quick learner and his pragmatism and efficiency made up for any lack of experience.[22] Liu Bocheng trusted Deng's opinion so much that the two became true collaborators, the ideal commander–political commissar relationship – a model that was vastly different than the Soviet archetype.[23] During the war, Liu and Deng were constantly in the center of the fighting. They would fight the first battle of the war at Shangdang and win arguably the greatest victory at Huaihai. While Liu later would concern himself only with military affairs, after the war Deng vaulted into the top tier of CCP leadership.

In many ways, the military reputation Deng had established during the Third Chinese Civil War was vital not only in allowing him to enact progressive reforms in the 1980s and 1990s, but it also potentially saved his life during the Cultural Revolution. The strength of his reputation allowed him to stand his ground when confronted by the military establishment. In the Cultural Revolution, Deng apparently fended off Lin Biao by saying, "If [Lin Biao] had his Manchuria campaign, I had my Huai-Hai campaign; [Lin] had fought from northeast China to south China, I fought from Nanking to [Chengdu]."[24] During this time, the PLA evidently protected him from the worst excesses of the Cultural Revolution, and later helped him take control of the party against a powerful array of enemies. Later on, when he was China's paramount leader, the army did not oppose him, even after he slashed their budgets and openly criticized their performance in the Sino-Vietnam War. Without his military successes, Deng might have very well disappeared from the scene soon after 1949, rather than leading China back onto the world stage as an economic power.

In the end, the events of the Third Chinese Civil War affected the CCP hierarchy not so much by changing it, but by allowing certain figures to excel and others to establish a political-military role that they might otherwise not have assumed. The data also suggests that almost all of the major Communist figures during the early years of the PRC played a role in the war and in most cases were also associated with military operations or strategy. Although we have focused primarily on those at the top, other individuals mentioned in the text also went on to significant roles in the new state. These include Ye Jianying, Chen Yun, Gao Gang, Zhang Wentian, Bo Yibo, Yang Shangkun, Rao Shaoshi, Yang Dezhi, Yang Chengwu, Chen Geng, and others. The fact that the list extends much longer speaks to the fact that this study has only scratched the surface in showing how the Third Chinese Civil War shaped the Communist hierarchy leading into the establishment of the PRC.

The importance of battle

In traditional Chinese military thought, engaging in battle with an enemy army is not necessarily a desirable outcome, or at the very least it is not the first option.

This attitude is in high contrast to Western tradition in which Clausewitizian, Napoleonic, or even ancient Greek logic determined that battle was essential to producing a final and decisive result. In the beginning of the war, the Communists and the GMD both attempted to win or gain the upper hand by maneuver, whether it was Chiang's decision to rush troops into north China or Liu Shaoqi's bid to seize northeast China. Later on, the GMD extended this tendency by trying to pacify regions through weight of numbers, in order to drive the enemy armies into other sectors. Mao followed a similar track when he sought to overextend the GMD by launching a strategic counterattack into the Central Plains. However, by the end of 1947 and through 1948, battle became the final solution. During this time the GMD looked to defeat or crush a Communist field army to redress the balance of power while the CCP sought a large-scale battle to end the war as quickly and decisively as possible. Thus, the campaigns of 1948–49, which ranked among the largest battles ever fought on the Asian mainland, were born. Not only did they virtually end the war, but they also did so with such finality that the campaigns themselves have obscured the undulating nature of fighting that occurred beforehand.

It is important to note that of the three large campaigns, Liaoshen, Huaihai, and Pingjin, only the latter aimed specifically at completely defeating a GMD regional command and pacifying a certain area. Liaoshen, for instance, was supposed to be a step towards securing northeast China with the final phase being a siege of Shenyang or another battle to finish off GMD forces in the region. However, the Northeast Field Army's improbable victory at Jinzhou and the cataclysmic defeat of Liao Yaoxiang's army completely unraveled the GMD defenses. After these events, there was no need for subtle maneuvers or tricks to gain the advantage – Shenyang collapsed after a brief fight and in less than two months, the CCP had gained total control over Manchuria.

Battle had become a means to an end in northeast China for two reasons. First, the Communists realized that it was the quickest way to free up Lin Biao's Northeast Field Army for use further south. According to the Secretariat's vision before the battle, after mopping up Fu Zuoyi in Hebei, the army would proceed to the Central Plains, where they were to support the final drive south. Second, only by eliminating Wei Lihuang's army altogether could the Communists hope to maintain the balance in other areas, especially the Central Plains. The fear of that army boarding ships and sailing to Jiangsu or linking up with Fu Zuoyi to sweep away the SCH Field Army was the most important factor in Communist planning prior to the Liaoshen Campaign. Thus, both plans for finally conquering the region centered on the idea of forcing the GMD into a large-scale battle from which they had no escape. Not only would this have been an unthinkable strategy only a few years earlier, it also went against the grain of Chinese military thought all of the way back to Sun Tzu. However, by 1948, battle was the best and only vehicle to meet all of the Communist goals – tradition or not.

The unexpected results of Liaoshen also served to further highlight how a decisive battle could end a war. As mentioned above, the campaign was originally meant to destroy the bulk of Wei's army, but no one had predicted the complete collapse and annihilation of his entire force – including the near simultaneous fall of Changchun and Shenyang. The effects of that battle probably played an important role in Mao's thinking as the Huaihai and Pingjin Campaigns unfolded. To raise the stakes from simply eliminating one army to an army group and finally a whole network of regional defenses was a considerable step. Yet this occurred in rapid succession at the end of 1948 as success engendered its own logic. Fortunately for the Communists, their gamble paid off and, as the events of 1949 showed, it was to their advantage that they sought battles and won them in such a devastating manner.

In light of these ideas, it easy to see why the Huaihai Campaign stands out in ways that its sister campaigns do not. After the founding of the People's Republic of China, "Huaihai" entered the common vernacular as a reference to completing a great task with overwhelming success. Although no longer a common saying in China today, there is still a Huaihai Street in almost every major Chinese city, not to mention numerous monuments and memorial halls dedicated to the campaign, even in places far away from where the battle took place. Although Liaoshen predated it and Pingjin, discussed below, finalized the proceedings, Huaihai was *the* great field battle of the period of great field battles. Perhaps the role it played in ushering Chiang from mainland Chinese politics, or the manner in which it exposed Shanghai and Nanjing, influenced how Huaihai was and still is regarded. The personalities involved may have also played a role in the memory of the period as the other two great field battles involved Lin Biao, whose memory was all but erased after 1971. While Deng Xiaoping's role may have also been conveniently "forgotten" during the Cultural Revolution, its importance was "recalled," along with Deng himself, after Mao's death.

Yet the most intriguing element of the Huaihai Campaign may well lie in its humble beginnings. The Liaoshen Campaign, an equally impressive undertaking, was meant to set the conditions for the final battle of Manchuria. The fact that it played out generally as scripted, despite some anxious moments and cold feet on the part of Lin Biao, also makes it pale, at least in terms of drama and suspense, in comparison with Huaihai. Another factor was that by 1948, Manchuria was a sideshow that both sides wanted to settle in order to move on and focus on more important regions. Huaihai was an entirely different matter. In its original form, it was to be the first stage within a larger strategic plan to win the vital Central Plains. Its growth from a relatively small-scale effort to isolate and destroy Huang Baitao's army into a massive operation involving the Central Plains Field Army and the forces from two GMD Bandit Pacification Headquarters was not part of the plan. The expansion of Huaihai was instead the result of the unpredictable effects of battle and success. Indeed, as the scale and numbers involved grew, so did the expectations.

While it is easy to blame Mao for overreaching and pushing his army to the brink, one must recognize that it was also this ambition that made the Huaihai Campaign decisive. Instead of settling for simple goals or taking a phased approach, Mao's decision to try to win the war in one stroke was critical to ending the conflict in 1949, instead of 1951 or 1952. Ultimately, it was the interaction between Mao and his generals – the give and take, the proposals and counterproposals – that transformed a shaping battle into an unimaginable victory. In many ways, this could have served as a parable for the entire war.

In contrast to the violent clashes which highlighted the Liaoshen and Huaihai Campaigns, Pingjin ended on a peaceful note. The defection of Fu Zuoyi's army set a new precedent for the rest of the war and, as mentioned earlier, many units and commanders followed Fu's lead. However, establishment of the precedent only could have come from the examples the Communists had already set at Liaoshen and Huaihai. As if to remind their adversary of these victories, they also made an example out of the Tianjin garrison. It is unlikely that Fu, an experienced and talented general who became famous for not backing down against the Japanese, even before the war officially began, would have submitted if he thought he had a chance to win or survive. In this way the Pingjin Campaign also shows how the idea of battle as a determiner had come full circle. The Communists had convinced their enemies of their capability at Liaoshen, Huaihai, and Tianjin. Thus, by time they surrounded Beiping the threat of combat had become a deterrent against actual combat.

Another major point that sets Pingjin apart is the sense of paralysis which the other two campaigns had cast on the usually effective Fu. Part of the reason was that his intelligence failed to recognize the speed at which Lin's Northeast Field Army entered north China. This failure resulted in a series of miscalculations when the North China Field Army launched its attack against his western flank. While Fu may have been trying to help the overall war effort by tying down Lin and Nie's armies, he only brought on a more rapid collapse by virtually folding his entire army into the Communist ranks. His inability to commit to either a western escape route, where he would have likely been destroyed along with Yan Xishan, or the sea, which would have at least given him a chance to bolster the Yangtze River defenses, ultimately caused more harm to the GMD cause than the destruction of his army in the field or in defense of Beiping. Even a suicidal stand at Beiping might have at least had the potential of slowing or severely damaging the North and Northeast China Field Armies. While this indecision may be attributable to the efficiency and effectiveness of the Communist maneuvers, part of Fu's caution was undoubtedly driven by what he had seen in Huaihai and Liaoshen.

A final consideration in regards to Pingjin is in how it symbolized what made the Communist conquest of China different from Chiang's Northern Expedition. There would be no compromise, no deals, and no potential alternate centers of power. Fu's attempts to make a deal ultimately fell on deaf ears because the Communists already had proven they could destroy him. He would not be able to disrupt the government or oppose policy the way a Guangxi clique or a Yan Xishan did during the GMD era. Only Mao, his inner circle and the CCP would rule the Chinese mainland after 1949. Thanks to the Pingjin method, their adversaries could either accept this or else face the might of the PLA. This sense of political finality was not only the ultimate legacy of Pingjin, but of the other campaigns as well.

The fact that the Third Chinese Civil War ended in a flurry of large-scale battles is not necessarily surprising in military history, but it does stand out in Chinese history. In a tradition where long wars were usually won by attrition, political intrigue, or small-scale actions, the fact that the Communist annihilated the GMD army so decisively and in such a short time is unique. This is especially true in comparison to other features of China's 20th century history, such as the indecisive nature of the Warlord era, the Northern Expedition, or World War II. The fact that the Communists could even field armies this large, not to mention be capable of engaging in such battles, is astounding, especially considering the state of their forces only a decade earlier. In the end, these factors shaped the PRC in ways that a lesser victory or a compromise would not have done.

The three topics covered in this conclusion – contingency, hierarchy, and the importance of battle – all impacted the history of modern China and the founding of the PRC. Without an adequate understanding of what the decisions were, who made them, and why, the Third Chinese Civil War loses much of its meaning and significance in the historical record. In fact, our lack of knowledge about the war itself may explain why the significance of the period has been so ignored for so long. However, our preexisting notions, namely that the victor of the war had been determined before the first shot, may be more damaging than simply admitting our ignorance. If the war indeed was determined beforehand, there really should have been no major questions, no real debate, and no decisions of consequence as to the course of the war. This is, of course, an exaggeration but it points to a disturbing pattern whereby historians marginalize the impact of human decision and war on the course of history. War is chaos and it produces unpredictable and unmanageable consequences. To think of it as just another event on a long, linear progression is a mistake that can only serve to further cloud our understanding of the past.

Even if one discounts the course of war and the role of strategy in forging its outcome, the significant shifts in terms of belief structure, loyalty, relationships, ego, etc., are immensely relevant for understanding the first and second generations of PRC leaders. Assumptions and theories regarding these men, and even the major events of the Communist era, that do not take into account what occurred during the war are problematic and likely inaccurate. The same is true when considering the importance of the battles of 1948–49 and how they fit into the greater context of modern Chinese history. Because historians label the period before 1949 as the GMD era and the time after as the Communist era, it is easy to forget how dramatic that transition really was. In many ways, the line drawn in 1949 was final and did mark two distinct eras because of the battles and the way in which the Communists won. As we gloss over the reasons why the war and events therein were important, we also risk forgetting why the Communists were able to assume control so quickly and completely after the GMD collapse.

In the end, it is not an exaggeration to say that the Third Chinese Civil War was an important turning point in Chinese history. The effects of the war are still being felt today, even as its last participants slowly pass away, leaving only imprints of past deeds and accomplishments on a system still trying to find its destiny. Buried in the West but heralded in the PRC, the Third Chinese Civil War was a time of legendary figures and titanic battles that ended a two-decade civil war and almost four decades of revolution. Even if China would not really know domestic peace until few decades later, the agonizing process of revolution and reunification that had begun in 1911 was finally over. Although political unification was only the first step, and despite the many flaws of the CCP's subsequent various programs, the critical decisions and events of 1945–49 provided the foundation from which a new, modern China could finally be built. Although that dream has only partially been realized, and in many aspects is still far off, the Communist victory in 1949 granted China an opportunity to come to terms with the modern world and move forward. Today's China may be riddled with problems and contradictions, but the guns have long stopped firing and the mark of war is largely gone from the countryside. This, in the end, is probably the most important result of the PLA's decisive victory in mainland China.

Notes

Preface

1   A Yangtze River delta dumpling stuffed with meat which literally translates into "small basket bun."

Introduction

1   Also known in Communist literature as the Liberation War. This book will utilize the more neutral title.

2   This work will use pinyin spellings unless otherwise noted.

3   For the purposes of this book, north China refers to the area north of the Yellow River from Shandong in the east to Shaanxi in the west, and central China refers to the area between the Yellow and Yangtze Rivers from Jiangsu in the east and Henan and Hubei in the west.

4   William Whitson first addressed this concept in *The Chinese High Command: A History of Communist Military Politics, 1927–71* (New York: Praeger Publishers, 1973).

5   Suzanne Pepper, *Civil War in China: The Political Struggle, 1945–1949*, Revised Edition (New York: Rowman & Littlefield Publishers, Inc., 1999); Odd Arne Westad, *Decisive Encounters: The Chinese Civil War, 1946–1950* (Stanford: Stanford University Press, 2003).

6   As the older style spelling of Chiang Kaishek is more familiar than the pinyin rendition, Jiang Jieshi, this book will use the former spelling.

7   Chiang Kaishek, *Selected Speeches and Messages in 1956* (Taipei: No Publisher Listed, 1956); Zhongyang Yanjiuyuan, ed., *Zongtong Jiang Gongshi Shi Zhounian Jinian Lunwenji* (Taibei: Zhongyang Yanjiuyuan, 1976); Chiang Kaishek, "Soviet Russia in China," in Keiji Furuya, *Chiang Kai-shek, His Life and Times*, Chun-ming Chang, trans. (New York: St John's University, 1981), p. 899; See also Li Zongren, Chiang's temporary replacement before the evacuation to Taiwan, who forwarded a similar excuse, citing poor deployment of troops after the war and the untimely disbanding of puppet troops in Te-kong Tong and Li Tsung-jen, *The Memoirs of Li Tsung-jen* (Boulder, CO: Westview Press, 1979), pp. 433–36.

8   F.F. Liu, "Defeat by Military Default," in Pichon P.Y. Loh, ed. *The Kuomintang Debacle of 1949: Conquest or Collapse?* (Boston: D.C. Heath and Company, 1965), pp. 1–6.

9   Chalmers Johnson, *Peasant Nationalism and Communist Power: The Emergence of Revolutionary China* (Stanford: Stanford University Press, 1967).

10 Mark Selden, *The Yenan Way in Revolutionary China* (Cambridge, MA: Harvard University Press, 1971); Tetsuya Kataoka, *Resistance and Revolution in China* (Berkeley, University of California Press, 1974).

11   See also Lloyd Eastman, *The Abortive Revolution: China under Nationalist Rule, 1927–1937* (Cambridge, MA: Harvard University Press, 1974); *The Seeds of Destruction: China in War and Revolution, 1947–1949* (Berkeley: University of California Press, 1984).

12   Another example of this is Barbara Tuchman, *Stilwell and the American Experience in China* (New York, Macmillan, 1970).

13   Lionel Chassin, *The Communist Conquest of China: A History of the Civil War, 1945–1949*, Timothy Osato and Louis Gelas, trans. (Cambridge: Harvard University Press, 1965 [Originally published in Paris: Payot, 1952]); William Whitson and Chen-Hsia Huang, *Civil War in China 1946–1950*, Vols. 1–2 (Washington, D.C.: Office of Military History, U.S. Army, 1967).

14   Pepper, p. 442.

15   For instance see Zheng Naicang and Wang Nan, *Su Yu Dajiang [General Su Yu]*, Second Edition (Zhengzhou: Haiyan Chubanshe, 1990); Zhao Jianping, Li Xiaochun and Kang Xiaofeng, *Luo Ruiqing* (Beijing: Zuojia Chubanshe, 1997).

16   See Junshi Kexueyuan, *Pipan Lin Biao de "Liuge Zhanshu Yuance" [Criticize Lin Biao's Six Tactical Principles]* (Beijing: Junshi Kexueyuan, 1974).

17   Beijing's Panjiayuan is still a spectacular resource with old books turning up on a daily basis. However, the rapid pace of modernization is threatening these places. In Nanjing, one of the old flea markets dealing in this type of merchandise disappeared to make way for the third largest library in the PRC.

18   Peng Meikui, *Wode Danfu Peng Dehuai [My Father, Peng Dehuai]* (Shenyang: Liaoning Renmin Chubanshe, 1997); Wang Yan, ed., *Peng Dehuai Zhuan* (Beijing: Dangdai Zhongguo Chubanshe, 1997); N.A., *Peng Dehuai – Zhengqi Zhiyan Dajiangjun [Peng Dehuai – A General of Unyielding Integrity Who Speaks Bluntly]* (http://cyc7.cycnet.com:8091/leaders/pdh/content.jsp?id=5814&s_code=1003).

19   See also a popular press magazine about Lin Biao's life which states boldly on the cover – "One cannot study the history of the party or the army without mentioning Lin Biao" ("Lin Biao Zhishu," *Zhongguo Gushi* May 2004); see also the PLA Daily, the official website of the PLA, (http://english.chinamil.com.cn/special/figures/marmore.htm).

1   Setting the stage

1   As the common translation for these units is "army", this dissertation will regard them as such. However, this character can also be translated as "corps"– the equivalent of a division in American military organization system. As both the GMD and CCP used European-style organization, this dissertation will also use that system, unless otherwise noted.

2   For instance, Mao could write telegrams under Zhu's name to both external and internal recipients, see Mao Zedong, "Two Telegrams from the Commander-in-Chief of the 18th Group Army," August 1945 in Mao Zedong, *Selected Works of Mao Tse-Tung*, (Peking: Foreign Language Press, 1969), Vol. 4, pp. 33–9.

3   This book roughly defines south China as the area between the Yangtze River in the north, the coast in the east and south and Guangxi and Hunan in the west.

4   See introduction, note 3. Additionally, while Mongolian independence was being finalized at the time, CCP territory did not extend that far north. It does not include the area northeast of modern-day Hebei which this text will regard as Manchuria or northeast China.

5   Mao Zedong, "China's Two Possible Destinies", April 23, 1945 in *Selected Works of Mao Tse-Tung*, Vol. 3, p. 202.

6   Chalmers Johnson, *Peasant Nationalism and Communist Power: The Emergence of Revolutionary China*, (Stanford: Stanford University Press, 1967).

7   Mao Zedong, "China's Two Possible Destinies," in *Selected Works of Mao Tse-Tung*, Vol. 3, p. 202.

8   Mao Zedong, "On Coalition Government," April 24, 1945 in *Selected Works of Mao Tse-Tung*, Vol. 3, pp. 258–61

9   Zhu De, "Discussing the Liberated Area Battlefield," April 25, 1945 in Zhongguo Renmin Geming Junshi Bowuguan, ed., *Zhu De Yuanshuai Fengbei Yongcun [A Perpetual Monument to Marshal Zhu De]: Zhongguo Renmin Geming Junshi Bowuguan Chenlie Wenxian Ziliaoxuan*, (Shanghai: Renmin Chubanshe, 1986), p. 247.

10 Mao Zedong, "Policy for Work in Liberated Areas for 1946" in *Selected Works of Mao Tse-Tung*, Vol. 4 p. 76; Nie, *Inside the Red Star*, pp. 509–10.

11 Zhu De, "Discussing the Liberated Area Battlefield," April 25, 1945 in *Zhu De Yuanshuai Fengbei Yongcun*, pp. 244–9.

12 Zhu De, "Views on Setting up Mortar Units and on Armaments Production," August 6, 1945 in *Selected Works of Zhu De*, (Beijing: Foreign Language Press, 1986), p. 191 (n. 183).

13 Ibid, p. 191.

14 While the actual numbers may vary depending on the country, in general terms, a mortar battery consisted of six to seven mortars while a platoon consisted of two to three mortars.

15 Mao had discussed the idea with Wang as early as July 1944; Wang Zhen Zhuan Bianxie [Compiling Team of Wang Zhen's Biography], ed., *Wang Zhen Zhuan*, Vol. 1, (Beijing: Zhongguo Dangdai Chubanshe, 1999), pp. 195–96; "Deployments for Building a Base in Western Henan," October 14, 1944 in Mao Zedong, *Mao Zedong Junshi Wenxuan*, Vol. 2, (Beijing: Junshi Kexue Chubanshe and Zhongyang Wenxian Chubanshe, 1993), pp. 731–2.

16 "Prepare to Strongly Develop the Jiangsu-Zhejiang District," November 2, 1944 in *Mao Zedong Junshi Wenxuan*, Vol. 2, pp. 733–4.

17 "Build a Northern Hunan Base and Continue to Move South," March 31, 1944 in *Mao Zedong Junshi Wenxuan*, Vol. 2, p. 759; "Mao Zedong's Directive Concerning Building a Hunan-Hubei-Jiangxi Border Base to Wang Zhen, Wang Zaidao and Others," May 4, 1945 and "CMC Directive Concerning Building a Southern Strategic Base to Wang Zhen, Wang Zaidao," June 15, 1945 in Zhongyang Dang'anguan [Central CCP Archive], ed. *Zhonggong Zhongyang Wenjian Xuanji [Selected Articles of the CCP Central Committee]*, (Beijing: Zhongyang Dang'anguan Dangxiao Chubanshe, 1991), Vol. 15, pp. 142–3.

18 "CC Directive Regarding Strategic Plan and Work Deployments in South China to the Guangdong District Party Committee," June 16, 1945 in *Zhongyang Wenjian Xuanji*, Vol. 15, pp. 145–47.

19 "CC Directive Concerning Building Bases in Central and East Henan to the Henan District Party Committee", June 18, 1945 in *Zhongyang Wenjian Xuanji*, Vol. 15, pp. 151.

20 "CMC Directive to the Guangdong District Party Committee Concerning Building the Hunan-Guangzhou-Jiangxi-Guangxi Border Base," July 15, 1945 in *Zhongyang Wenjian Xuanji*, Vol. 15, pp. 181–3.

21 "CC Directive to Hunan-Hubei-Jiangxi District Party Committee and Others Regarding the Strategic Plan for Establishing a Southern Base," June 24, 1945 in *Zhongyang Wenjian Xuanji*, Vol. 15, pp. 171–3.

22 "Mao Zedong's Directive to Wang Zhen and Wang Zaidao Concerning Present Situation and Building the Wuling Base and Other Issues," July 22, 1945 in *Zhongyang Wenjian Xuanji*, Vol. 15, pp. 186–7; "CC Directive to the Guangdong District Party Committee to Begin Long-Term Operations in the Hunan-Guangdong Border Base," August 4, 1945 in *Zhongyang Wenjian Xuanji*, Vol. 15, pp. 202–3.

23 For this book, Central Plains refers to the area between the Yellow and Yangtze Rivers, and bounded east-west by the coast and Henan.

24 "CC Directive to Zheng Lisan and Others to Develop the Henan-Anhui Base in Order to Deal with the Danger of a Future Civil War," August 4, 1945 in *Zhongyang Wenjian Xuanji*, Vol. 15, pp. 200–1.

25   The Secretariat realized that Shandong's accessibility from the sea was one potential weak spot to this rationale, but they were evidently willing to take the risk; see "CC Directive to the Shandong Subbureau Concerning Controlling the Entirety of Shandong," August 6, 1945 in *Zhongyang Wenjian Xuanji*, Vol. 15, pp. 205–6.

26   Peng Dehuai, "Speech at the 7th Congress."

27   Zhang Guotao, "Memoirs" as quoted in Whitson, p. 64.

28   Whitson, p. 70.

29   Gregor Benton, *New Fourth Army: Communist Resistance Along the Yangtze and the Huai 1938–1941*, (Berkeley: University of California Press, 1999:), pp. 364–7.

30   An Ziwen, "Ba Womende Dang Jianshe Hao [Construct Our Party Well]," *Xinhua Yuebao* (Wenzhaiban), No. 4, p. 14.

31   This process of recognizing the heir apparent was the first of its kind in the CCP and set a significant precedent. This was seen again when Mao appointed Hua Guofeng to these positions in the wake of the Cultural Revolution. The choice of Hua was strangely parallel to the selection of Liu in that Hua was himself a newcomer and was also relatively unsullied by past trangressions. However, Liu proved to be more powerful and and capable than Hua. Later on, Deng Xiaoping repeated the pattern established in the 7th Congress by appointing his understudy (first Zhao Ziyang and later Jiang Zemin) to vice chairman of the CCP and the CMC. Jiang repeated this process with Hu Jintao and Hu is now doing the same with Xi Jinping.

32   Both Ren Bishi and Yang Shangkun, secretaries of the Secretariat and the CMC respectively, played largely unrecorded roles in two powerful decision-making bodies; for a discussion about the role of the secretary both in traditional and modern China see Wei Li and Lucian W. Pye, "The Ubiquitous Role of the Mishu in Chinese Politics," *China Quarterly*, No. 132 (Dec 1992), pp. 913–36.

33   This dual structure of party and military governing bodies remains and even today, is still fused (Jiang Zemin as chairman, Hu Jintao as vice chairman) but it may well represent an interesting dilemma if the membership of these two committees is ever different. There is no direct line of subordination between the Secretariat and the CMC.

34   A judgement which makes Peng's opposition of Mao at the 1959 Lushun Conference during the Great Leap Forward even more poignant and damning for Mao.

35   For instance he wrote frequently about creating a militia to increase troop strength to relieve other units for front line service and to mobilize the masses for logistic and support functions; see Peng Dehuai, "Strengthen Local Forces," August 22, 1946, "Develop Army-Mass Relations, Develop the People's War," April 1, 1947, and "Correctly Implementing Mass Mobilization Policies," September 9, 1948, in *Peng Dehuai Junshi Wenxuan*, (http://cyc7.cycnet.com:8091/leaders/pdh/content. jsp?id=5814&s_code=1003).

36   Chahar province has since been eliminated and was absorbed into Inner Mongolia.

37   There were other units that fell under the 8th Route Army but these are not mentioned in the text to prevent confusion. These units include Yang Dezhi's 2nd Column/Hebei-Shandong-Henan Military District and separate brigades, most notably the 358th and 359th Brigades, that were at the same time also subordinate to He Long's Shanxi-Gansu-Ningxia-Hebei United Army which itself was surbordinate to the 18th Group Army. These units would soon fall under different commands and will be discussed later.

38   Chi-hsi Hu argues that Lin's criticism was in fact a subtle way of showing support without suffering the political consequences in "Mao, Lin Biao and the Fifth Encirclement Campaign," *The China Quarterly*, June 1980, pp. 252–3.

39   Nie, *Inside the Red Star*, p. 223.

40   The heart of the north China plain here refers to the highland and hinter areas and is generally equivalent to Nie's area of operations – Shanxi, Chahar, and Hebei. Most of this area was reorganized and repartitioned after the founding of the PRC.

41   According to PLA organization charts, this unit did not fall under Nie's direct control but as it operated in his area of operations, he did maintain a significant influence on its activities.

42   Suiyuan is now part of Inner Mongolia while Rehe was divided and folded into Hebei and Liaoning; "The Shanxi-Chahar-Hebei Army Should Expand into Japanese-occupied Territory," December 18, 1944 in *Mao Zedong Junshi Wenxuan*, Vol. 2, pp. 749–50.

43   Yan Xishan, 1883–1960, Shanxi Province. One of the major warlords during the 1920s, Yan dominated Shanxi Province from 1917 to 1947. During Chiang's Northern Expedition, he allied with the GMD. In 1930, he turned against Chiang, but lost in his bid for power. Thereafter, Yan remained an outsider to the GMD center of power throughout World War II and the Third Chinese Revolutionary Civil War. He eventually fled with Chiang to Taiwan and lived out the rest of his life in exile.

44   The Communists published their protests in the *People's Daily*; See "Zhu De and Peng Dehuai's Telegram to Chiang Kaishek and Hu Zongnan Protesting the GMD Army's Attack on the Shaanxi-Gansu-Ningxia Border Region," July 23, 1945 and "Zhu De and Peng Dehuai's Telegram to Chiang Kaishek and Hu Zongnan Appealing for GMD Troops Attacking the Shaanxi-Gansu-Ningxia Border Region to Retreat," August 7, 1945 in *Zhongyang Wenjian Xuanji*, Vol. 15, pp. 294–5, 207.

45   Whitson, p. 64.

46   Liu Bocheng, "Introduction the Translation of 'Combined Arms Tactics," December 11, 1946 in *Liu Bocheng Junshi Wenxuan*, (http://cyc7.cycnet.com:8091/leaders/lbc/content. jsp?id=7618 &s_code=1302); the first section of the translation was originally published in 1942.

47   Tao Hanzhang, *The Modern Chinese Interpretation of Sun Tzu's Art of War*, Yuan Shibing, trans., (New York: Sterling Publishing Co., Inc., 2000), pp. 10–12.

48   As quoted in Zhang Guotao, "Memoirs" in Whitson, p. 147.

49   Frederick C. Teiwes, "Mao and his Lieutenants," in *The Australian Journal of Chinese Affairs*, No. 19/20 (Jan–Jul 1988), p. 2.

50   These detachments were directly subordinate to a corps or army-level unit (New 4th Army) and, organizationally speaking, were equal to a European-style brigade as they was composed of two or more regiments.

51   The Dong are one of China's official minorities. Su's true heritage was not discovered until after his death when a census discovered his true roots. During his life he always regarded himself a Han Chinese.

52   Zhang had earlier led the forces which rescued some of Jimmy Doolittle's flight crews who crash landed in China after their 1942 raid on Tokyo.

2 "March on the North, Defend in the South" (August 1945–June 1946)

1   "Central Committee Decision Regarding Our Party's Responsibilities after the Japanese Surrender," August 11, 1945 and "Central Committee Guidance Regarding the Need to Strongly Seize the Traffic Lines and the Cities Along Those Lines," August 12, 1945 in *Zhongyang Wenjian Xuanji*, Vol. 15, pp. 228–31, 232–3.

2   Mao Zedong, "Decision Regarding Our Party's Responsibilities After the Japanese Surrender," August 11, 1945 in *Mao Zedong Junshi Wenxuan (Neibuben)*, (Beijing: Zhongguo Renmin Jiefangjun Zhanshi Chubanshe, 1981), pp. 268–70; "Central Committee Guidance to the Central China Bureau Regarding Deployments to Capture the Large Cities and Main Traffic Lines," August 10, 1945; and "Central Committee Guidance Regarding Preparations to Seize the Large Cities and the Main Traffic Lines Following the Soviet Declaration of War," August 10, 1945 in *Zhongyang Wenjian Xuanji*, Vol. 15, pp. 213–14, 215–16.

3   Zhu De, "First General Order of the Yan'an Headquarters," August 10, 1945 in *Zhongyang Wenjian Xuanji*, Vol. 15, pp. 217–18.

4   Initially it was the Shanxi-Henan-Hebei Military District and Field Army, but this was expanded to include Shandong on August 20.

5   Liu Han, *Luo Ronghuan Zhuan [Biography of Luo Ronghuan]*, (Beijing: Dangdai Zhongguo Chubanshe, 1997), p. 362.

6   Zhu De, "Third General Order of the Yan'an Headquarters", August 10, 1945; "Fourth General Order of the Yan'an Headquarters," August 10, 1945 in *Zhongyang Wenjian Xuanji*, Vol. 15, p. 220–2; Wang Shangrong and Huang Xinyan, *He Long Zhuan*, (Beijing: Dangdai Zhongguo Chubanshe, 1997), p. 356; "Encircle Datong and Solve the Taiyuan Question", August 16, 1945 in *Mao Zedong Junshi Wenxuan*, Vol. 3, p. 34.

7   Pukou refers to the area on the north bank of the Yangtze River across from Nanjing. Since there was no railroad bridge over the Yangtze at the time, the trains stopped at Pukou and the connection was made by ferry. The Longhai railroad is the main east-west railroad in central China, leading from Lianyungang on the Yellow Sea and running all of the way to the western border of China.

8   "Present Duties for the Army in Henan" and "Seize the Superior Position and Don't Waste the Opportunity to Attack", August 13, 1945 in *Mao Zedong Junshi Wenxuan*, Vol. 3, pp. 26–9.

9   "Central China Deployments in Preparation for Civil War," August 12, 1945 in *Mao Zedong Junshi Wenxuan*, Vol. 3, p. 4; "Central Committee Guidance to the Guangdong Party Committee Regarding Building a Hunan-Guangdong Border Base," August 11, 1945; "Central Military Committee Guidance Regarding Implementing the Central Committee's Plan to Support Operations South of the Yangtze River to the Central China Bureau," August 12, 1945; and "Mao Zedong's Guidance Regarding Present Responsibilities and War Plan to Zhang Yunyi," August 16, 1945 in *Zhongyang Wenjian Xuanji*, Vol. 15, pp. 226–7, 236–7, 241–2.

10   Zhu De, "Second General Order of the Yan'an Headquarters," August 10, 1945 in *Zhongyang Wenjian Xuanji*, Vol. 15, pp. 219; Suzanne Pepper largely overestimates the contribution of the Communist units that survived the Japanese occupation and underestimates the maneuvers that occurred right after the war and later on in September 1945 in *Civil War in China*, pp. 178–9.

11   Liu Han, pp. 363, 374; Liu Tong, *Dongbei Jiefang Zhanzheng Jishi [Record of the Liberation War in the Northeast]*, (Beijing: Dongfang Chubanshe, 1997), p. 37.

12   Liu Han, p. 374.

13   Mao Zedong, "Situation and Our Policy After the Japanese Surrender," in *Selected Works of Mao Tse-Tung*, Vol. 4, p. 17; "Expand in the Countryside, Do Not Attack the Large Cities," August 15, 1945 in *Mao Zedong Junshi Wenxuan*, Vol. 3, p. 30.

14   "Central Committee and Central Military Commission Guidance Regarding a Change in the Strategic Plan – The Present Plan is to Strive for the Small Cities and Expand the Countryside," August 22, 1945, in *Zhongyang Wenjian Xuanji*, Vol. 15, pp. 243–4.

15   Mao Zedong, "Situation and Our Policy After Victory Over Japan" in *Selected Works of Mao Tse-Tung*, Vol. 4, pp. 11–12, 22.

16   Wang Shangrong and Huang Xinyan, p. 359.

17   Ibid.

18   Nie, *Inside the Red Star*, p. 320.

19   Peng Zhen, 1902–1997, born in Shaanxi province, joined the CCP in 1923 and was arrested by the GMD seven years later. He was released in 1935 to begin organizing resistance against the Japanese in north China. During World War II, he became a close ally of Liu Shaoqi.

20   Yang Guoqing and Bai Ren, *Luo Ronghuan zai Dongbei Jiefang Zhanheng Zhong [Luo Ronghuan in the Northeast during the Liberation War]*, (Beijing: Jiefangjun Chubanshe, 1986), pp. 15–16; Liu Han, p. 375–6.

21   Shao Hua and You Hu, p. 217.

22   The region's forces were almost depleted by the transfer of Li Yunchang to the Northeast.

23 Liu Shaoqi, "Our Present Tasks and Strategic Deployment of Our Forces," September 19, 1945, in Liu Shaoqi, *Selected Works of Liu Shaoqi*, (Beijing: Foreign Language Press, 1976), p. 371.

24 Zhou Enlai and Mao Zedong, "Regarding Implementing the 'March in the North, Defend in the South' Strategic Deployments," in Zhou Enlai, *Zhou Enlai Junshi Wenxuan*, Vol. 4, (Beijing: Renmin Chubanshe, 1997), p. 1.

25 Bi Jianzhong, "Liu Shaoqi Fazhan Dongbei de Lilun he Shixian Yanjiu Shuping [Discussion of Liu Shaoqi's Development of the Northeast]" in Chen Chaochou, *Liu Shaoqi Yanjiu Shuping [Commentaries of Research on Liu Shaoqi]*, (Beijing: Zhonggong Wenxian Chubanshe, 1997), p. 216.

26 "Dispatch Nine Regiments East to the Three Provinces," August 20, 1945 in *Mao Zedong Junshi Wenxuan*, Vol. 3, p. 45; "the three provinces" here refers to the traditional administrative division of Manchuria into the three provinces of Liaoning, Jilin and Harbin. After reoccupying the region, the GMD divided it into nine provinces, perhaps, as Li Zongren implies, to allow more political appointees. Communist communication and literature use both the three and nine provinces designations. See Li Zongren, *Li Zongren Huiyilu*, (Nanning: Guangxi Renmin Chubanshe, 1986), p. 350.

27 Zheng Fengrong, "Wodang, Wojun, Kaijin Dongbei de Jige Wenti [The Various Problems of Our Party, Our Army and Entering the Northeast]" and Yao Shu, "Guanyu 'Xiangbei Fazhan, Xiangnan Fangyu Zhanlue Fangzhan de Chansheng Wenti [Regarding the Problems of the 'March on the North, Defend in the South' Strategy]" as quoted in Bi Jianzhong, "Liu Shaoqi Fazhan Dongbei de Lilun he Shixian Yanjiu Shuping" in Chen Chaochou, p. 216–17.

28 Nie, *Inside the Red Star*, pp. 517, 520.

29 Roughly equivalent to an army group.

30 Wang Xiang, *Yan Xishan yu Jinxi*, (Nanjing: Jiangsu Guji Chubanshe, 1999), pp. 256–7.

31 "Current Deployments of the GMD Army and Our Army's Present Tasks in Shanxi," August 19, 1945, *Mao Zedong Junshi Wenxuan*, Vol. 3, pp. 42–3.

32 Li Mancun, Chen Ying and Huang Yuzhang, eds., *Liu Bocheng Zhuan*, (Beijing: Dangdai Zhongguo Chubanshe, 1992), p. 325.

33 Ibid, p. 325.

34 Liu and Deng actually planned the campaign on the flight back to their sector from Yan'an on August 20.

35 Wang Zhongxing and Liu Liqin, eds., *Dierye Zhanjun [2nd Field Army]*, Revised Edition, (Beijing: Guofang Daxue Chubanshe, 1996:), p. 263.

36 Li Mancun *et al.*, p. 332.

37 "Concentrate Superior Force to Destroy Enemy One by One" in *Selected Works of Mao Tse-Tung*, Vol. 4, pp. 103–7.

38 Liu Bocheng, "Guidance on Certain Tactical Questions for the Shangdang Campaign," September 5, 1945 in Liu Bocheng, *Liu Bocheng Junshi Wenxuan*, (http://cyc7.cycnet.com:8091/leaders/lbc/content.jsp?id=7619&s_ code=1302)

39 Wang Shangrong and Huang Xinyan, p. 364.

40 Nie Rongzhen, *Nie Rongzhen Huiyilu [Memoirs of Nie Rongzhen]*, (Beijing: Jiefangjun Chubanshe, 1986:), p. 618.

41 Daniel Barbey, *MacArthur's Amphibious Navy*, (Annapolis: Naval Academy Press, 1969), p. 210.

42 Tatushi Saitoh, "Public Security Operations of the Kwantung Army in Manchuria", Unpublished Manuscript presented at the 2007 Japanese-American Military History Exchange 2007.

43 See Luo Zhanyuan and Li Binggang, "Anti-Japanese Operations and Party Leadership during the Anti-Japan War" and Li Hongwen and Wang Jing, "Summary of Operations of the Northeast Anti-Japanese United Army," in Zhonggong Zhongyang Dang

Shiziliao Zhengji Weiyuanhui and Zhonggong Zhongyang Dangshi Yanjiushi, eds. *Zhonggongdang Shiziliao [CCP Historical Material]*, Vol. 15, (Beijing: Zhonggongdang Shiziliao Chubanshe, 1987), pp. 96–127, 128–72; United States Department of State, *Foreign Relations of the United States: China 1945*, Vol. 1, (Washington D.C.: United States Government Printing Office, 1955), p. 7:214.

44　Liu Han, Luo Ronghuan Zhuan [Biography of Luo Ronghuan]. (Beijing: Dangdai Zhongguo Chubanshe, 1997), p. 376.

45　Li Yunchang, "Recalling the Hebei-Rehe-Liaoning Units Marching to the Northeast," in *Zhonggongdang Shiziliao*, Vol. 15, p. 58; Nie, *Inside the Red Star*, p. 520.

46　It is not clear where the Koreans went after this but according to Zhu De's "Sixth General Order of the Yan'an Headquarters", August 11, 1945, they were supposed to return to Korea. *Zhongyang Wenjian Xuanji*, Vol. 15, p. 223.

47　The cadre mostly came from Yan'an and the Shanxi-Suiyuan Military District. They included 10 regiments of cadre from Shanxi-Suiyuan, under Lu Zhengcao, and two Political Instruction Brigades from Yan'an. See Stephen Levine, *Anvil of Victory*, (New York: Columbia University Press, 1987), p. 103; Hu Sheng, *A Concise History of the Communist Party of China*, (Beijing: Foreign Language Press, 1994), p. 319; Wang Shangrong and Huang Xinyan, p. 363.

48　Luo instructed one commander to not take any classified material on the journey and to strictly avoid U.S. ships if at all possible; See Liu Han, Luo Ronghuan Zhuan [Biography of Luo Ronghuan], (Beijing: Dangdai Zhongguo Chubanshe, 1997), p. 377; "Complete the Sealift to the Northeast as Quick as Possible," October 15, 1945 in *Mao Zedong Junshi Wenxuan*, Vol. 3, p. 82.

49　"CMC Guidance Regarding the November Battle Deployments," November 1, 1945 in *Zhongyang Wenjian Xuanji*, Vol. 15, pp. 394–5.

50　Lin was in central Hebei in the beginning of October preparing to take over the Chahar-Rehe-Liaoning Military District, but was ordered to Shenyang in the middle of the month. While on the way, he was out of touch for the rest of the month, raising a great amount of concern in the Secretariat, who sent a series of telegrams inquiring about Lin's location. See Liu Tong, *Dongbei Jiefang Zhanzheng Jishi*, pp. 46–7.

51　Shao Hua and You Hu, p. 219.

52　"Organize the Shanxi-Chahar-Hebei 2nd Army and Annihilate the Enemy's Attack on Chengde," October 23, 1945; "Rapidly Organize a Rehe Field Army and a East Hebei Column," October 25, 1945; "Order for Cheng Zihua to Proceed to Rehe Prepare for Chiang's Attack on Chengde," October 29, 1945 in *Mao Zedong Junshi Wenxuan*, Vol. 3, pp. 80–1; Cheng Zihua, *Cheng Zihua Huiyilu [Memoirs of Cheng Zihua]*, (Beijing: Jiefangjun Chubanshe, 1987), pp. 274–5.

53　Chen Yun, "Several Points Regarding Our Work in Manchuria," November 30, 1945, in Chen Yun, *Chen Yun Wenxuan [Selected Works of Chen Yun]*, (Beijing: Renmin Chubanshe, 1984:), p. 221.; Chen saw the Soviet policy as twofold: first, they would hand over the three large cities, Shenyang, Changchun, and Harbin, and the Changchun (Zhongchang) railroad to the GMD; and second, to protect peace in the world and East Asia. For this reason, he and the rest of the CCP leadership decided to cease hoping for significant Soviet aid; Nie, *Inside the Red Star*, p. 527–28; Carroll R. Wetzel Jr., "From the Jaws of Defeat: Lin Biao and the 4th Field Army in Manchuria," unpublished dissertation, JMU, pp.: 56–63.

54　Huang Kecheng, *Huang Kecheng Zishu [Autobiographical Notes of Huang Kecheng]*, (Beijing: Renmin Chubanshe, 1994), pp. 196–7.

55　Liu Han, Luo Ronghuan Zhuan [Biography of Luo Ronghuan]. (Beijing: Dangdai Zhongguo Chubanshe, 1997), p. 400; Shao Hua and You Hu, *Lin Biao de Zheyisheng*, (Wuhan: Hubei Renmin Chubanshe, 1994), p. 220.

56　The Soviet Red Army was originally scheduled to leave in November, but would remain until March 1946, partly due to Chiang's personal request; Peng Zhen, "Our Responsibilities for Dominating the Whole Northeast," October 26, 1945, in

Peng Zhen, *Peng Zhen Wenxuan [Selected Works of Peng Zhen]*, (Beijing: Renmin Chubanshe, 1991), pp. 103–5.

57   "CC to Northeast Bureau Telegram," October 2, 1946 as quoted in Liu Tong, *Dongbei Jiefang Zhanzheng Jishi*, p. 79.

58   "Prevent the Enemy From Marching North by Destroying Him at Shanhaiguan and Jinzhou," November 1, 1945 in *Mao Zedong Junshi Wenxuan*, Vol. 3, p. 113.

59   Yang was formerly the deputy commander of the Binghai Military Sub-District but took command of the 7th Division for its mission in the northeast.

60   "[The Yang Dezhi-Su Zhenhua Column] Should Replenish in Ten Days and then March to Jinzhou-Shenyang," November 3, 1945; "Huang Kecheng and Liang Xingqie Should Advance Rapidly to Jinzhou to Annihilate the Main GMD Force," November 7, 1945 in *Mao Zedong Junshi Wenxuan*, Vol. 3, pp.119, 126.

61   Huang Kecheng, p. 194.

62   "Protect Rehe by Forming a Railroad Destruction Headquarters," November 10, 1945 in *Mao Zedong Junshi Wenxuan*, Vol. 3, pp. 128.

63   "CMC Guidance Regarding The November Battle Deployments," November 11, 1945, in *Zhongyang Wenjian Xuanji*, Vol. 15, pp. 394–5.

64   "CC Directive Regarding Preparatory Work for the Pivotal Jinzhou Battle," November 14, 1945 in *Zhongyang Wenjian Xuanji*, Vol. 15, p. 423; "Huang Kecheng and Liang Xingqie Should Strive to Find a Shortcut to Jinzhou," November 11, 1945 in *Mao Zedong Junshi Wenxuan*, Vol. 3, p. 136; Liu Tong, *Dongbei Jiefang Zhanzheng Jishi*, pp. 63–5.

65   "CMC Directive Regarding Military Deployments to Huang Kecheng and Cheng Zihua after the loss of Shanhaiguan," November 17, 1945 in *Zhongyang Wenjian Xuanji*, Vol. 15, pp. 425–6.

66   "CC Guidance Regarding the Plan for the Northeast," November 19, 1945 in *Zhongyang Wenjian Xuanji*, Vol. 15, p. 429.

67   The Zhongchang Railroad refers to the Russian-built railroad linking Dalian with Harbin; "CC Guidance to the Northeast Bureau Regarding Tasks in East and North Manchuria After Allowing [Chiang] to Enter the Cities and the Changchun Railroad," November 20, 1945 in *Zhongyang Wenjian Xuanji*, Vol. 15, p. 431.

68   Which is, of course, ironic considering his fate during the Cultural Revolution.

69   Shao Hua and You Hu, p. 222.

70   Liu Han, *Luo Ronghuan Zhuan [Biography of Luo Ronghuan]*. (Beijing: Dangdai Zhongguo Chubanshe, 1997), p. 395.

71   "Siye Zhanshi Ziliao Huibian [Compiled Fourth Field Army's Battle Record Material]" as quoted in Liu Tong, *Dongbei Jiefang Zhanzheng Jishi*, p. 97.

72   Luo Ronghuan, "Proposal Regarding Building a Northeast Base," December 13 in *Luo Ronghuan Junshi Wenxuan*, (http://cyc7.cycnet.com:8091/leaders/lrh/content.jsp?id=7324&s_code=1202); Chen Yun, "Several Points Regarding Our Work in Manchuria," November 30, 1945 in *Chen Yun Wenxuan*, p. 222.

73   "CC Guidance to the Northeast Bureau Concerning Plan of Action and Responsibilities," December 7, 1945 and "CC Directive Concerning Our Position in the Northeast and Strategic Questions to the Northeast Bureau," December 8, 1945 in *Zhongyang Wenjian Xuanji*, Vol. 15, p. 465, 474–5.

74   Peng Zhen, "Regarding Integrating the New and Old Units into the Field Army and the Deployments for Building Bases," December 8, 1945 in *Peng Zhen Wenxuan*, p. 115.

75   "CC Directive Concerning Strengthening Work in West Manchuria," December 12, 1945, in *Zhongyang Wenjian Xuanji*, Vol. 15, pp. 501–3.

76   Liu Shaoqi, "Concentrate Efforts on Building Base Areas in Eastern, Northern and Western Manchuria" in *Selected Works of Liu Shaoqi*, December 24, 1945, pp. 369–71; Mao Zedong, "Build Stable Base Areas in the Northeast," December 28, 1945, in *Selected Works of Mao Tse-Tung*, Vol. 4, pp. 81–2; Contrary to this documentary

evidence, Liu was criticized for not following Mao's directive and was painted as a supporter of Peng Zhen during the Cultural Revolution in "Chairman Mao's Successor – Deputy Supreme Commander Lin Piao" in *Current Background*, October 27, 1969, 894:16–18.

77   "Guisui, Baotou, Datong and Other Places Must Be Captured," October 22, 1945 in *Mao Zedong Junshi Wenxuan*, Vol. 3, p. 71.

78   "CMC Directive to Nie Rongzhen Regarding Cooperation with the Shanxi-Suiyuan Field Army to Protect Zhangjiakou," December 12, 1945 in *Zhongyang Wenjian Xuanji*, Vol. 15, pp. 484–85.

79   For this reason the Pinghan Campaign is also known as the Handan Campaign.

80   Li Mancun *et al.*, p. 365.

81   The portions Mao wanted Chen to attack include the Bengbu-Xuzhou-Tai'an and Dezhou sections. Geographically speaking, this would require an incredible effort from Chen's scattered forces as it would span significant parts of Shandong, Jiangsu and Anhui provinces. "Organize Part of the Field Army to Undertake the Tianjin-Pukou Campaign," October 19, 1945; "Regarding the Shandong and Central China Battle Plan," October 22, 1945; "Attack or Occupy A Few Cities to Induce a Field Battle," October 24, 1945 in *Mao Zedong Junshi Wenxuan*, pp. 65–8, 77.

82   As quoted in Liu Tong, *Huadong Jiefang Zhanzheng Jishi [Record of the Liberation War in East China]*, (Beijing: Dongfang Chubanshe, 1998), pp. 30–1.

83   "Develop Military Transportation Work to the Northwest and Northeast," November 4, 1945 in *Mao Zedong Junshi Wenxuan*, Vol. 3, p. 123.

84   "Destroy Huo Shouyi, Chen Daqing and Li Pinxian to Relieve the North and Northeast China Theaters," October 30, 1945 in *Mao Zedong Junshi Wenxuan*, Vol. 3, p. 97.

85   "Request to Change My Position as Central China MD Commander to Deputy Commander," in *Su Yu Junshi Wenxuan*, (http://cyc90.cycnet.com/leaders/suyu/content.jsp?id=11193&s_code=2303).

86   Previously these units were, respectively, the Jiangsu-Zhejiang Military District 1st Column, Central Jiangsu Military District 7th Column, the Jiangsu-Zhejiang Military District 4th Column and the New 4th Army 4th Division.

87   Wang Qinsheng, *Zhongguo Jiefang Zhanzheng*, Vol. 1, (Beijing: Jiefangjun Wenyi Chubanshe, 2000), p. 38.

88   Liu Tong, *Zhongyaun Jiefang Zhanzheng Jishi [Record of the Liberation War in the Central Plains]*, (Beijing: Dongfang Chubanshe, 2003), p. 206.

89   Nie, *Nie Rongzhen Huiyilu*, pp. 620–1.

90   Nie, *Inside the Red Star*, pp. 337–8; Wang Shangrong and Huang Xinyan, pp. 371–5.

91   Li Mancun *et al.*, p. 342.

92   "CC, CMC Directive Concerning Breaking up the GMD Large Scale Military Attack," December 12, 1945 in *Zhongyang Wenjian Xuanji*, Vol. 15, pp. 480–2.

93   Shao Hua and You Hu, p. 222.

94   Zhou Enlai, "The Past Year's Negotiations and the Prospects" in *Selected Works of Zhou Enlai*, (Beijing: Foreign Language Press, 1981), p. 285.

95   Wei Bihai, *Disiye Zhanjun Zhengzhan Jishi [War Record of the 4th Field Army]*, (Beijing: Jiefangjun Wenyi Chubanshe, 2001), p. 109.

96   Also referred to as Sipingjie.

97   Peng Zhen, "Rapidly Seize Changchun-Harbin-Qiqihaer, Control North Manchuria," March 1946, in Peng Zhen, p. 124–27, FN1; See also "Policy Regarding GMD and Bandit Local Troops," March 30, 1946 in *Mao Zedong Junshi Wenxuan*, Vol. 3, p. 156.

98   Shao Hua and You Hu, p. 225; Liu Tong, *Dongbei Jiefang Zhanzheng Jishi*, pp. 92–3.

99   Nie, *Inside the Red Star*, pp. 523–24, 536; This also contributed to the image of him in the West as a cold, depressed, and frail character.

100 This was despite the fact that it was Mao himself who ordered the capture of the Changchun and Harbin, as well as being the main proponent of the ill-fated defense at Siping.

101 Mao Zedong, "Defend Strongpoints, Control the Large, Mechanized Army and Wait for the Opportunity to Strike at the Enemy with Mobile Warfare – Telegram 1 to Lin Biao and Peng Zhen," April 6, 1946 in *Mao Zedong Junshi Wenxuan (Neibuben)*, p. 274; Shao Hua and You Hu, p. 225.

102 "Take the Whole Situation into Account, Plan for the Long Term in the Northeast," April 12, 1946 in *Mao Zedong Junshi Wenxuan*, Vol. 3, p. 163.

103 "Defend Siping and Benxi to Leverage the Peace Talks," April 13, 1946; "Quickly Annihilate the Enemy in the Northeast and Defend Our Superior Position," April 15, 1946; "Make Preparations for Any Changes in the Situation," April 18, 1946 in *Mao Zedong Junshi Wenxuan*, Vol. 3, pp. 165–66, 169.

104 John Robinson Beal, *Marshall in China*, (New York. Doubleday & Company, Inc., 1970), p. 66.

105 This included Huang Kecheng's 3rd Division (New Fourth Army), Wan Li's Column, Li Xingqie's Shandong 1st Division, Luo Huasheng's 2nd Shandong Division, two brigades and the artillery brigade from Yang Guofu's 7th Division, Deng Hua's 1st Brigade and the 359th Brigade; Liu Tong, *Dongbei Jiefang Zhanzheng Jishi*.

106 "Quickly Transfer Troops from South Manchuria to the Siping Defense," April 20, 1946; "Prepare to Attack along the Beiping-Gubeikou Line, Nankou and Other Districts," April 30, 1946; "Regarding the Proposal for the Rehe Campaign," May 3, 1946 in *Mao Zedong Junshi Wenxuan*, Vol. 3, pp. 177, 191, 204.

107 "Employ Our Entire Strength to Win Victory at Siping and Gongzhuling," April 20, 1946; "The Army at Changchun Should Immediately Split into a City Defense Unit and a Field Unit," April 21, 1946; "Defend Benxi to the Death, Strive to Last Until the Truce," April 26, 1946 in *Mao Zedong Junshi Wenxuan*, Vol. 3, pp. 175, 178.

108 Huang Kecheng, pp. 204–5.

109 Mao Zedong, "Defend Strongpoints, Control the Large, Mechanized Army and Wait for the Opportunity to Strike at the Enemy with Mobile Warfare – Telegram 7 to Lin Biao and Peng Zhen," May 19, 1946 in *Mao Zedong Junshi Wenxuan (Neibuben)*, p. 278.

110 "Military Deployments after the Retreat from Siping," May 19, 1946 in *Mao Zedong Junshi Wenxuan*, Vol. 3, p. 226.

111 Beal, p. 66.

112 Two geographical points: first, the Songhua River has two main branches, one that runs along the north edge of Harbin city and another which cuts through north Jilin province – the text here refers to the latter; second, the area between these two Songhua Rivers was part of Jilin during this time; it would be reassigned to Heilongjiang province in the Communist era; see "CC Directive to the Northeast Bureau and Lin Biao Agreeing with the Abandonment of Harbin and the Mobile/Guerrilla Warfare Plan," June 3, 1946 in *Zhongyang Wenjian Xuanji*, Vol. 16, p. 185.

113 Liu Tong, *Dongbei Jiefang Zhanzheng Jishi* [Record of the Liberation War in the Northeast]. (Beijing: Dongfang Chubanshe, 1997), p. 206.

114 Chiang Kaishek, "Communist Designs and Kuomintang Blunders," in Pichon P.Y. Loh, ed. *The Kuomintang Debacle of 1949: Conquest or Collapse?*, p. 86.

115 United States Department of State, *Foreign Relations of the United States: China 1946*, Vol. 1, (Washington D.C.: United States Government Printing Office, 1955), p. 10:581.

116 Whitson, p. 304; Wetzel, p. 159.

117 Chen Yun, pp. 230–5.

118 Whitson, p. 312.

119 Huang Kecheng, pp. 206–7.

3   The Guomindang high tide (June 1946–June 1947)

1   Jiaodong refers to the area on the west side of Jiaozhou Bay where Qingdao is located. Like Pukou, Jiaodong served as the main rail station connecting a larger city, Qingdao, with the rest of China.

2   Zhou Enlai, "Past Year's Negotiations and the Prospects," in *Selected Works of Zhou Enlai*, p. 288.

3   Liu Shaoqi, "May 4th Directive on Land Reform," in *Selected Works of Liu Shaoqi* pp. 89–90.

4   Special Correspondent, "Kongxin Zhan yu Quanxin Zhan [Empty-hearted War and Whole-hearted War]," *Guancha*, May 8, 1948, p. 13.

5   Cheng Yueh-cheng, "Three Stages of the Land Problem in Northern Kiangsu", *Economics Weekly*, Shanghai, 3:18, Oct 31, 1946 in the *Chinese Press Review*, Jan 4, 1947.

6   Levine, p. 203; Approximately 10–15% of the cultivated land had been owned by the Japanese or the Manchukuo government, as well as an undocumented amount of land to be had through revenge or *qingsuan* campaigns against land-owning collaborators.

7   See Zhang Wentian, "Build a Strong Strategic Rear Area in the Northeast," June 20, 1946 in Wei Yanru, ed., *Zhang Wentian zai Hejiang [Zhang Wentian at Hejiang]*, (Beijing: Zhonggongdang Shiziliao Chubanshe, 1990), pp. 1–8; Chen Yun, "The Situation for Building a Base in North Manchuria," April 20, 1946 in *Chen Yun Wenxuan*, pp. 225–8.

8   Liu Tong, *Dongbei Jiefang Zhanzheng*, p. 388.

9   "CC Directive Concerning Training Troops," May 1, 1945; in *Mao Zedong Junshi Wenxuan (Neibuben)*, p. 279.

10   "Central Plains MD Should Prepare to Displace Peacefully," April 30, 1946; "We Agree with the Central Plains Bureau's Plan to Deal with Chiang's Attack," May 2, 1946 in *Mao Zedong Junshi Wenxuan*, Vol. 3, pp. 189, 197; "Break out of the Central Plains Quickly and Successfully, Strive to Survive and for Victory," June 1, 1945 in *Mao Zedong Junshi Wenxuan (Neibuben)*, p. 280.

11   Mao Zedong to Liu Bocheng, Deng Xiaoping, Bo Yibo and Chen Yi, "The Strategic Plan for the Shandong and Taixing Districts after the Severance of Diplomatic Relations," June 22, 1945 in *Mao Zedong Junshi Wenxuan (Neibuben)*, pp. 284–5.

12   "Smash Chiang Kai-shek's Offensive By a War of Self-Defence," June 20, 1946 in *Selected Works of Mao Tse-Tung*, Vol. 4, p. 89; also see "Do not Fear Losing Territory and Prepare for Long-term Operations in the Northeast," May 27, 1946 in *Mao Zedong Junshi Wenxuan*, Vol. 3, p. 234.

13   "The Central China Field Army Should Prepare to Attack the Bengbu-Pukou Railway," June 26, 1946 in *Mao Zedong Junshi Wenxuan*, Vol. 3, p. 301.

14   "Proposals for Keeping the Central China Field Army's Main Strength in Central Jiangsu – Telegram 1," June 27, 1946 in *Su Yu Junshi Wenxuan*(http://cyc90.cycnet.com/leaders/suyu/content.jsp? id=11188&s_ code=2303).

15   Su Yu, "Recalling the Central Jiangsu Campaign" in Laozhanshi Shiwenji Bianweihui and Zhongguo Geming Bowuguan [Old Soldier's Historical Collection Committee and the Chinese Revolutionary Museum], eds., *Mingjiang Su Yu [Famous General Su Yu]*, (Beijing: Xinhua Chubanshe, 1986), p. 172.

16   "July 4 Telegram to Liu Bocheng, Deng Xiaoping, Chen Yi and the Central China Bureau" in *Mao Zedong Junshi Wenxuan (Neibuben)*, p. 286.

17   Zhao Yihong, *Su Yu Chuanqi [Biography of Su Yu]*, (Chengdu: Chengdu Chubanshe, 1995), pp. 169–73; Chen Zhonglong, "Discussing Su Yu's Proposal for Implementing the CMC Directive During the Central Jiangsu Campaign" and Ji Guang, "Discussing Strategic Proposal for the Central Jiangsu Campaign," in Jiangsu Sheng Xinsijun he Huazhong Kangri Genjudi Yanjiuhui and Zhongguo Gongchandang Nantongshi Weidangshi Gongzuo Weiyuanhui [Jiangsu New 4th Army and Central China Japanese

Resistance Base and CCP Nantong City Party History Work Committee], eds., *Su Yu yu Suzhong [Su Yu in Central Jiangsu]*, (Nanjing: Nanjing Daxue Chubanshe, 1995), pp. 152–6, 174–81.

18 "Raise All Guerrilla Units to Form a Guerrilla Base," July 31, 1946 in *Mao Zedong Junshi Wenxuan*, Vol. 3, p. 371.

19 "Defeating the Enemy in a Battle Close to Xuzhou Will Have a Positive Effect on the Entire War Situation," July 19, 1946 in *Mao Zedong Junshi Wenxuan*, Vol. 3, p. 352.

20 Liu Tong, *Huadong Jiefang Zhanzheng*, p. 74; "August 1 Telegram to the Central China Bureau and the CMC" in *Su Yu Junshi Wenxuan*(http://cyc90.cycnet.com/leaders/suyu/content.jsp?id=11188&s_code=2303).

21 "Su's Army Should Remain in Central Jiangsu to Improve the Situation," August 12, 1945; "Continue to Destroy the Enemy in Central Jiangsu," August 15, 1945 in *Mao Zedong Junshi Wenxuan*, Vol. 3, pp. 402, 410.

22 "Political Points of Attention After the Capture of Nantong and Haimen," August 20, 1945 in *Mao Zedong Junshi Wenxuan*, Vol. 3, p. 415.

23 Fu Kuiqing, Sun Keji and Miao Guoliang, eds, *Chen Yi Zhuan [Chronicle of Chen Yi]*, (Beijing: Dangdai Zhongguo Chubanshe, 1991), p. 343; Liu Tong, *Huadong Jiefang Zhanzheng*, pp. 104–7.

24 Reorganized Divisions refer to US-equipped and trained divisions which were roughly equivalent to a regular GMD corps. These were the strongest and most capable units in the GMD army.

25 The Guangxi clique included Bai Chongxi, who is often regarded as one of the best Chinese generals of his generation, and Li Zongren, who would replace Chiang in 1949.

26 As quoted in Fu Kuiqing *et al.*, p. 341.

27 "CMC Directive to Liu Bocheng and Others Regarding Transferring Troop and Destroying the Enemy to Aid the Central Plains Army," August 9, 1946 in *Zhongyang Wenjian Xuanji*, Vol. 15, pp. 268–9.

28 Li Mancun *et al.*, p. 353.

29 He was transferred to a political post, but his military career was not over. He would return in 1948 after his successors proved to be even worse alternatives.

30 "Battle Responsibilities of the Central China Field Army in September and October," September 4, 1946 in *Mao Zedong Junshi Wenxuan*, Vol. 3, p. 461.

31 "Proposal to Immediately Deploy the Main Strength of the Central China Field Army to Huaiyang and Huaian," September 11, 1946 in *Mao Zedong Junshi Wenxuan*, Vol. 3, p. 475.

32 "Prepare to Destroy the Enemy at Suqian, Xianan and Other Places," September 10, 1946 in *Mao Zedong Junshi Wenxuan*, Vol. 3, p. 470.

33 As quoted in Liu Tong, *Huadong Jiefang Zhanzheng*, p. 119; "Two Armies Should Cooperate to Achieve Victory," September 28, 1946 in *Mao Zedong Junshi Wenxuan*, Vol. 3, p. 500.

34 As quoted in Liu Tong, *Huadong Jiefang Zhanzheng Jishi* [Record of the Liberation War in East China]. (Beijing: Dongfang Chubanshe), pp. 125–7.

35 This region is loosely defined as the area encompassed by the Longhai railroad, which ran from the northern Jiangsu port of Lianyungang and then west through Xuzhou, Zhengzhou and Xi'an, and the two Huai's – Huaiyang and Huaian in north Jiangsu. It is also alternatively called north Jiangsu or Huaibei (as in the Huaibei Military Sub-District) in Communist literature.

36 "Fight A Few Large Battles and Develop the Situation in the Huaihai Region," August 13, 1946, "Concentrate the Central China and Shandong Field Armies in Huaibei to Destroy the Enemy Advancing East," August 15, 1946 in *Mao Zedong Junshi Wenxuan*, Vol. 3, pp. 522, 525.

37 "Deployments for Annihilating Feng Zhian and Part of the Guangxi Units," November 3, 1946; "Seek an Opportunity to Engage the 7th and 74th Divisions," November 23 in *Mao Zedong Junshi Wenxuan*, Vol. 3, p. 544.

38   "After the Juancheng Campaign, Attack to the West," November 1, 1946 in *Mao Zedong Junshi Wenxuan*, Vol. 3, p. 539.

39   "The Importance of Destroying the Enemy Attacking Shuyang," December 13, 1946 in *Mao Zedong Junshi Wenxuan*, Vol. 3, p. 575.

40   "Concentrate the Main Strength to Defeat the Enemy in South Shandong After the Great Victory at Suqian and Shuyang," December 18, 1946 in *Mao Zedong Junshi Wenxuan*, Vol. 3, p. 581.

41   Liu Tong, *Huabei Jiefang Zhanzheng*, p. 77.

42   "Prepare to Deal with the GMD Attack on Shanxi-Suiyuan and Shanxi-Chahar-Hebei," May 27, 1946; "Purchase Great Quantities of Explosives, Enact Training for Urban Warfare," May 29, 1946 in *Mao Zedong Junshi Wenxuan*, Vol. 3, pp. 237–41.

43   "Battle Deployments for Datong, Kouquan, Shuoxian, Ningwu and other Places," June 4, 1946 in *Mao Zedong Junshi Wenxuan*, Vol. 3, p. 253.

44   "Fundamental Duties of the Shanxi-Chahar-Hebei MD After the GMD Attack," June 28, 1946 in *Mao Zedong Junshi Wenxuan*, Vol. 3, pp. 305–6.

45   "Regarding Battle Deployments for Shanxi-Suiyuan," June 25, 1946 in *Mao Zedong Junshi Wenxuan*, Vol. 3, p. 299.

46   This unit was originally organized from local troops of the Taiyue Military Sub-District of the SHSH Military District after the Japanese surrender. During the Shangdang Campaign they were elevated to field army status as the Taiyue Column and after the campaign they began a regular column – the 4th Column. Wang Yuntai, ed., *Chen Geng Zhuan*, (Beijing: Zhongguo Dangdai Chubanshe, 2003), p. 314.

47   "Use the Technique of the Long-Range Raid to Capture Hongdong and Zhaocheng," August 6, 1946; "You Must Seize the Three Towns of Hongdong, Zhaocheng and Huoxian in the Shortest Possible Time," August 10, 1946 in *Mao Zedong Junshi Wenxuan*, Vol. 3, pp. 381, 398.

48   "An Opportunity to Attack the Beiping-Hankou Railroad and Battle Deployments," July 6, 1946 in *Mao Zedong Junshi Wenxuan*, Vol. 3, p. 326.

49   Yuan Dejin and Liu Zhenhua, *Huabei Jiefang Zhanzheng Jishi [A Record of the War of Liberation in North China]*, (Beijing: Renmin Chubanshe, 2003), p. 87.

50   First Capture Shuoxian and Ningwu, Afterwards Capture Shanyang and Daiyue, Do Not Alert Fu Zuoyi", June 9, 1946; "Prepare to Attack Ningwu and Other Cities," June 20, 1946 in *Mao Zedong Junshi Wenxuan*, Vol. 3, p. 261.

51   "First Attack Huairen and Other Places, Then Seek an Opportunity to Attack Datong," June 23, 1946 in *Mao Zedong Junshi Wenxuan*, Vol. 3, p. 290; Yuan Dejin and Liu Zhenhua, *Huabei Jiefang*, p. 87.

52   Yuan Dejin and Liu Zhenhua, *Huabei Jiefang*, p. 90.

53   "Battle Deployments for Destroying the Enemy Attacking Jining," September 10, 1946 in *Mao Zedong Junshi Wenxuan*, Vol. 3, p. 468.

54   See Nie Rongzhen's speech at a cadre meeting of the Shanxi-Chahar-Hebei Bureau, "Do Not Count One City or One Place as a Success or Defeat, Struggle Vigorously for Victory," September 15, 1946 in Nie Rongzhen, *Nie Rongzhen Junshi Wenxuan [Selected Military Works of Nie Rongzhen*, (Beijing: Jiefangjun Chubanshe, 1992), pp. 250–2.

55   "Destroying the Enemy's Main Strength is More Important than Defending Cities," September 18, 1946 in *Mao Zedong Junshi Wenxuan*, Vol. 3, pp. 487–8.

56   "CMC Directive to He Long for Deployments to Protect Yan'an," October 19, 1946 in *Zhonggong Zhongyang Wenjian Xuanji [Selected Articles of the CCP Central Committee]*, (Beijing: Zhonggong Zhongyang Dangxiao Chubanshe, 1992), Vol. 16: 1946–47, pp. 317–18.

57   Te-kong Tong and Li Tsung-jen, pp. 446–8.

58   "The Situation and Duties in the Northeast," July 7, 1946 in *Chen Yun Wenxuan*, pp. 229–35.

59   Xiao Jingguang, *Xiao Jingguang Huiyilu [Recollections of Xiao Jingguang]*, (Beijing: Jiefangjun Chubanshe, 1989), p. 340.

60 "You Should Concentrate the Main Force to Destroy the Enemy While He is Dispersed," October 30, 1946; "The Battle Inside the Pass Will Soon Reach its Decisive Point and Will Positively Influence the Northeast Battlefield," November 1, 1946 in *Mao Zedong Junshi Wenxuan*, Vol. 3, p. 536.

61 "Concentrate the 3rd and 4th Columns to Destroy the 91st Division", November 11, 1946; "Concentrate the Forces in South Manchuria to Delay or Destroy the Enemy Attacking North Manchuria," December 13, 1946 in *Mao Zedong Junshi Wenxuan*, Vol. 3, pp. 561, 577; Xiao Hua made a similar proposal, see Zhonggong Zhongyang Dangshi Ziliao Zhengji Weiyuanhui and Zhongguo Renmin Jiefangjun Dang'anguan [CCP Central Committee Party Historical Materials Compilation Committee and the Chinese People's Liberation Army Archive], eds., *Zhenzhong Riji*, Vol. 1, (Beijing: Zhonggong Dangshi Ziliao Chubanshe, 1987), p. 24.

62 *Zhenzhong Riji*, Vol. 1, p. 3.

63 Ibid, p. 5.

64 Ibid, p. 38.

65 "On Marshall's Statement on Leaving China," January 10, 1947 in *Selected Works of Zhou Enlai*, p. 295.

66 "Past Year's Negotiations and the Prospects," December 18, 1946 in Ibid, p. 292.

67 "Ten Major Tasks of 1947," January 1, 1947 in *Selected Works of Zhu De*, p. 203.

68 "Greet the New High Tide of the Revolution," February 1, 1947 in *Selected Works of Mao Tse-Tung*, Vol. 4, pp. 119–20, 123.

69 "Three Months Summary," October 1, 1946 in Ibid, pp. 113–14.

70 "Three Telegrams Regarding Preparation Work for the Attack," in *Peng Dehuai Junshi Wenxuan*(http://cyc7.cycnet.com:8091/leaders/pdh/content.jsp?id=5814&s_code=1003).

71 "Inflict Enemy Casualties Through Interior Lines to Change the Situation in Favor of a Switch to Exterior Lines," August 20, 1946 in *Mao Zedong Junshi Wenxuan*, Vol. 3, p. 587.

72 Chen Shiju, *Tiandi Fanfu Sannianjian* as quoted in Liu Tong, *Huadong Jiefang Zhanzheng*, p. 150.

73 "We Should Concentrate the Main Strength in Southern Shandong to Destroy the 26th Division," December 24, 1946 in *Mao Zedong Junshi Wenxuan*, Vol. 3, p. 589.

74 "The First Battle in South Shandong Should Be To Destroy the 26th Division," December 25, 1946 in *Mao Zedong Junshi Wenxuan*, Vol. 3, p. 591.

75 "Concentrate the Greatest Amount of Combat Power to Completely Destroy the Current Enemy," January 7, 1947 in *Mao Zedong Junshi Wenxuan*, Vol. 3, p. 608.

76 "You Should Increase Replenishment and Reorganization, Not Engage in Battle," January 11, 1947 in *Mao Zedong Junshi Wenxuan*, Vol. 3, p. 614.

77 Li Mancun *et al.*, p. 369.

78 "A More Advantageous Situation is to Force Qiu to Sends Forces East and Destroy Them," December 18, 1946 in *Mao Zedong Junshi Wenxuan*, Vol. 3, p. 583.

79 "Use the Recent Victory to Develop the Situation, Recapture Lost Territory and Create a Mobile Battlefield," January 18, 1947 in *Mao Zedong Junshi Wenxuan*, Vol. 3, p. 626.

80 Su Yu, "Summary of the First Stage of the Laiwu Campaign," in *Mingjiang Su Yu*, pp. 217–19.

81 "Telegram to Chen Yi, Rao Shaoshi, Su Yu and Tan Zhenlin of February 4, 1700 Hours," in *Mao Zedong Junshi Wenxuan (Neibuben)*, pp. 400–1.

82 Wang Yaowu, "Laiwu Jiangjun Beijian Ji" in Liu Tong, *Huadong Jiefang Zhanzheng*, pp. 205–6.

83 "We Can Only Patiently Wait for an Opportunity to Destroy the Enemy," May 4, 1947 in *Mao Zedong Junshi Wenxuan*, Vol. 4, p. 52.

84 "You Should Not Waste the Opportunity to Destroy the [Tang Army]," May 12, 1947 in *Mao Zedong Junshi Wenxuan*, Vol. 4, p. 70.

85 Zhang refused to be captured, despite the Communist desire to take him alive. Cornered in the cave that served as his headquarters, he died in the ensuing firefight. When his killer, Ge Zhaotian, was being berated by a Communist general, Ge Zhaotian simply replied that "I would shoot back even if he were Chiang Kaishek." However, Ge did not realize whom he had killed until years afterward when it was revealed to him by Zhang's bodyguard, who had befriended Ge during the Korean War. Zhang was buried with full honors by the Communists in recognition of his service during World War II. The GMD designated him a martyr and later claimed he committed suicide, rather than dying in battle.

86 Whitson, p. 238.

87 Peng Dehuai, *Peng Dehuai Zizhuan [Autobiography of Peng Dehuai]*, (Beijing: Jiefangjun Wenyi Chubanshe, 2002), p. 250.

88 Wang Shangrong and Huang Xinyan, p. 381.

89 Yuan Dejin and Liu Zhenhua, *Xibei Jiefang Zhanzheng Jishi*, (Beijing: Renmin Chubanshe, 2003), pp. 55–6.

90 "CMC Directive to He Long and Others Regarding Battle Deployments for the Defense of Yan'an," October 19, 1946 in *Zhongyang Wenjian Xuanji*, Vol. 16, pp. 317–18; Wang Yan, ed., *Peng Dehuai Zhuan*, (Beijing: Dangdai Zhongguo Chubanshe, 1997), p. 295.

91 "CMC's Military Deployments for the Defense of Yan'an," November 6, 1946 in *Zhongyang Wenjian Xuanji*, Vol. 16, pp. 327–8.

92 "Develop the Luliang District to Protect Yan'an and Consolidate the Taiyue [District]," November 26 1946 in *Mao Zedong Junshi Wenxuan*, Vol. 3, p. 567.

93 When first established, this army was called a "bingtuan", a generic term for army, not the more standard "yejun" or "field army"; this suggests that it was only meant to be temporary.

94 "Chen Geng and Other Units' Movement Plans," March 11, 1946 in *Mao Zedong Junshi Wenxuan*, Vol. 4, p. 7.

95 Peng Dehuai, *Peng Dehuai Zizhuan*, p. 252.

96 "Telegram to Peng Dehuai of March 27, 1947" in *Mao Zedong Junshi Wenxuan (Neibuben)*, p. 412.

97 "Telegram to Peng Dehuai of April 2, 1947"; "Telegram to Peng Dehuai and Xi Zhongxun of April 3, 1947, 0700 hours" in *Mao Zedong Junshi Wenxuan (Neibuben)*, pp. 412–13; Wang Yan, p. 310.

98 "On the Temporary Abandonment of Yenan and the Defence of the Shenxi-Kansu-Ningsia Border Region – Two Documents Issued by the Central Committee of the CCP," November 1946, April 1947 in *Selected Works of Mao Tse-Tung*, Vol. 4, pp. 129–31.

99 Hu Zhefeng, "Peng Dehuai and the Mushroom Tactic" in *Peng Dehuai Zhengqi Zhiyan Dajiangjun* (http://cyc7.cycnet.com:8091/leaders/pdh/content.jsp?id=5814&s_code=1003).

100 "April 15 Telegram to Peng Dehuai, Xi Zhongxun, Zhu De and Liu Shaoqi" in *Mao Zedong Junshi Wenxuan* (1981), p. 417.

101 Xiao Jingguang, pp. 342–47; Yu Jianting, *Chen Yun yu Dongbei de Jiefang [Chen Yun and the Liberation of the Northeast]*, (Zhongyang Wenxian Chubanshe, 1998), pp. 102–5.

102 *Zhenzhong Riji*, Vol. 1, p. 99.

103 Liu Tong, *Dongbei Jiefang Zhanzheng*, p. 315.

104 Zhongguo Renmin Jiefangjun Junshi Kexueyuan, *Zhongguo Renmin Jiefangjun Qishi Quanshi [70 Years Chronicle of the Chinese People's Liberation Army]*, (Beijing: Junshi Kexue Chubanshe, 2000), Vol. 5, Appendix 4, map 17.

105 *Zhenzhong Riji*, Vol. 1, p. 140.

106 Stuart to Secretary of State, Nanking, January 29, 1947 in Kenneth W. Rea and John C. Brewer, *The Forgotten Ambassador: The Reports of John Leighton Stuart, 1946–1949*, (Boulder, CO: Westview Press, 1981), pp. 62–3.

107 The number of GMD POWs skewed the numbers in favor of the Communists, see Liu Tong, *Dongbei Jiefang Zhanzheng*, pp. 322–3; Lin's forces also lost a significant number to cold injuries. For instance, one column suffered a total of 2,034 cold-related casualties, with 644 of these being serious, see *Zhenzhong Riji*, Vol. 1, p. 141.

108 *Zhenzhong Riji*, Vol. 1, pp. 159–60.

109 Wang Qinsheng, Vol. 1, pp. 159–60.

110 "5–5 Jueyi" in *Qunzhong*, May 14, 1947 as quoted in Liu Tong, *Dongbei Jiefang Zhanzheng*, pp. 447–8.

111 Zheng Dongguo, *Wode Rongma Shenya: Zheng Dongguo Huiyilu [My Military Record: Recollections of Zheng Dongguo]*, (Beijing: Tuanjie Chubanshe, 1992), p. 496.

112 *Zhenzhong Riji*, Vol. 1, p. 205.

113 Whitson, p. 308.

114 *Zhenzhong Riji*, Vol. 1, pp. 273–7.

115 Whitson, p. 308.

116 "China: Mongol Raid; Other Developments – Civil War," Facts on File News Digest, June 21, 1947.

117 *Zhenzhong Riji*, Vol. 1, pp. 289, 291.

118 Whitson, p. 309.

119 Liu Tong, *Dongbei Jiefang Zhanzheng*, p. 472. This figure had come dangerously close to the one Lin cited for acceptable losses during the battle.

120 *Zhenzhong Riji*, Vol. 1, p. 345.

121 *Zhongguo Renmin Jiefangjun Qishi Quanshi*, Vol. 2, p. 148.

122 "Two Conditions Under Which to Fight Large Battles of Annihilation," January 25, 1947 in *Mao Zedong Junshi Wenxuan*, Vol. 3, p. 640.

123 "You Should Start the Zhengtai Campaign Earlier in Order to Shorten the Time of the Battle," April 2, 1947 in *Mao Zedong Junshi Wenxuan*, Vol. 4, p. 20.

124 Nie, *Inside the Red Star*, p. 559.

125 Ibid., p. 561; "First Attack Weak Areas, then Attack Strong Areas; I'll Fight Mine, You Fight Yours," April 22, 1947 in *Mao Zedong Junshi Wenxuan (Neibenbu)*, p. 299.

4 The turning point (July 1947–August 1948)

1 Nie, *Inside the Red Star*, p. 558; Lin Biao had a similar assessment, see Chou Chi-p'ing, "Comrade Lin Piao in the Period of Liberation War in the Northeast," *Zhongguo Qingnian*, Apr. 16, 1960, p. 26.

2 "Sweeping Away Obstacles to National Unification," *Kuo Min Jih Pao*, July 5, 1947 in *Review of the Hong Kong Chinese Press*, 4:2; "Victory at Szepingkai," *Kuo Min Jih Pao*, July 3, 1947 in *Review of the Hong Kong Chinese Press*, 3:1; See "The "Pre-Mukden Incident" Theory," *Hwa Shiang Pao*, June 30, 1947 in *Review of the Hong Kong Chinese Press*, 1:2 and "Government to Restore Wartime System," *Wah Kiu Ya Po*, July 5, 1947 in *Review of the Hong Kong Chinese Press*, 4:2 for a counterpoint.

3 "China: Chiang; Other Developments – Civil War," Facts on File News Digest, July 12, 1947.

4 A Chinese measure of distance roughly equally to a third of a mile.

5 "CC Deployments for Liu-Deng, Chen-Su, South Shanxi and North Shaanxi," May 4, 1947 in *Zhongyang Wenjian Xuanji*, Vol. 17, p. 442; "May 8 Telegram to Liu Bocheng, Deng Xiaoping, Chen Yi and Su Yu" in *Mao Zedong Junshi Wenxuan (Neibuben)*, pp. 304–5; "Chiang's Plan to Expel Us to North of the Yellow River Will Fail," May 11, 1947 in *Mao Zedong Junshi Wenxuan*, Vol. 4, p. 68.

6 Chen Zaidao, *Chen Zaidao Huiyilu*, (Beijing: Jiefangjun Chubanshe, 1991), pp. 121–2.

7 "CC and Central Plains Bureau Guidance on Conducting Guerrilla Warfare in Hubei, Henan and Shaanxi," January 1, 1947 in *Zhongyang Wenjian Xuanji*, Vol. 16,

pp. 373–75; "The Central Plains Army is Serving an Important Strategic Function," May 28, 1947 in *Mao Zedong Junshi Wenxuan*, Vol. 4, p. 87.

8   Deng Xiaoping, "The Situation Following Our Triumphant Advance to the Central Plains and Our Future Policies and Strategy," April 25, 1948 in *Selected Works of Deng Xiaoping*, (http://english.peopledaily.com.cn/dengxp/vol1/text/a1110.html).

9   Deng Xiaoping, "In Memory of Liu Bocheng", October 21, 1986 in *Selected Works of Deng Xiaoping*, (http://english.peopledaily.com.cn/dengxp/vol3/text/c1600.html).

10 Hubei Sheng E-Xiang Bian Gemingshi Bianjibu and Hubei Sheng Junqu Zhongyuan Tuwei Zhuanti Bianzhuanshi [Hubei Province and the Jiangxi-Hunan Revolutionary Base Compilation Bureau and the Hubei Province Military District Central Plains Breakout Editorial Office], eds., *Zhongyuan Tuwei Jishi [Record of the Central Plains Breakout]*, (Beijing: Jiefangjun Chubanshe, 1992), pp. 226–7; "We Agree with Liu-Deng's Army Resting and then Crossing the Yellow River at the End of the Month," June 3, 1947 in *Mao Zedong Junshi Wenxuan*, Vol. 4, p. 91.

11 Liu Bocheng and Deng Xiaoping, "The General Order for the SHSH Field Army's Southwest Shandong Campaign," June 20, 1947 in *Liu-Deng Dajun Fengyunlu*, Vol. 1, pp. 5–7.

12 'You Should Not Lose the Opportunity to Attack the Enemy," May 12, 1947 in *Mao Zedong Junshi Wenxuan*, Vol. 4, p. 70; "Concentrate Troops to Attack and Improve the Entire Situation", May 14, 1947 in *Mao Zedong Junshi Wenxuan*, Vol. 4, p. 73.

13 "At the Current Stage, the Chen-Su-Tan and Liu-Deng Armies Should Only Cooperate on the Strategic Scale," June 1, 1947 in *Mao Zedong Junshi Wenxuan*, Vol. 4, p. 89.

14 "If You Do Not Fight You Cannot Assure Victory," June 22, 1947 in *Mao Zedong Junshi Wenxuan*, Vol. 4, p. 111.

15 "Plan for Attacking the Enemy's Deep Rear Areas Along Separate Routes," June 29, 1947 in *Mao Zedong Junshi Wenxuan*, Vol. 4, p. 113.

16 Chen-Su Da Jun Zhengzhan Jisubian Weiyuanhui, *Chen-Su Da Jun Zhengzhan Jisubian [Records of the Battles of Chen-Su Great Army]*, (Beijing: Xinhua, 1991), pp. 338–52; Also see Mao's adjustments to the plan: "Regarding Speeding Up Movements and Liu-Deng's Route", July 2, 1947 in *Mao Zedong Junshi Wenxuan*, Vol. 4, p. 119.

17 Su Yu, *Zhanzheng Huiyilu [War Memoirs]*, (Beijing: Jiefangjun Chubanshe, 1988), pp. 508–13.

18 Liu Tong, *Huadong Jiefang Zhanzheng*, p. 297.

19 "Go All Out to Disperse and Annihilate the Enemy in Central Shandong," July 12, 1947 in *Mao Zedong Junshi Wenxuan*, Vol. 4, p. 137.

20 "July 23, 1947 Telegram to Liu Bocheng, Deng Xiaoping, Chen Yi, Su Yu, Tan Zhenlin and East China," in *Mao Zedong Junshi Wenxuan (Neibuben)*, p. 306.

21 Li Mancun *et al.*, p. 388.

22 "Chen Geng's Column Will Change Directions and Cross South Over the Yellow River," July 19, 1947 in *Mao Zedong Junshi Wenxuan*, Vol. 4, p. 143.

23 "Chen Geng's Army Will Begin an Attack on Yulin in the Middle of July," June 20, 1947 in *Mao Zedong Junshi Wenxuan*, p. 107.

24 "July 23, 1947 Telegram to Liu Bocheng, Deng Xiaoping, Chen Yi, Su Yu, Tan Zhenlin and East China," in *Mao Zedong Junshi Wenxuan (Neibuben)*, p. 306.

25 "You Should Strive to Rest and Reorganize for Two Campaigns", July 30, 1947 in *Mao Zedong Junshi Wenxuan*, Vol. 4, p. 160.

26 "Su Yu Should Quickly Proceed to Yuncheng to Take Command of the Five Columns For Liu-Deng's Upcoming Campaign," August 4, 1947 in *Mao Zedong Junshi Wenxuan*, Vol. 4, p. 164.

27 "Three Points of Attention for Our Army's March South," August 12, 1947 in *Mao Zedong Junshi Wenxuan*, Vol. 4, p. 193; "Liu-Deng's Decision to March South is Completely Correct," August 10, 1947 in *Mao Zedong Junshi Wenxuan*, Vol. 4, p. 183.

28 Whitson, p. 175.

29   Deng Xiaoping, "Build Stable Base Areas in the Dabie Mountains," in *Selected Works of Deng Xiaoping*, (http://english.peopledaily.com.cn/dengxp/vol1/text/a1100.html).

30   Ibid., "Build Stable Base Areas in the Dabie Mountains."

31   Mao Zedong, "Strategy for the Second Year of the War of Liberation" in *Selected Works of Mao Tse-Tung*, Vol. 4, pp. 141–6.

32   Zhou Enlai, "A Nationwide Counter-offensive to Overthrow Chiang" in *Selected Works of Zhou Enlai*, p. 311.

33   "Make Use of our Foothold in Southwest Shandong to Break Up the Enemy's Intent of Forcing Us to [Cross North Over the Yellow River]," August 5, 1947 in *Mao Zedong Junshi Wenxuan*, Vol. 4, pp. 168–9.

34   Su Yu, *Zhanzheng Huiyilu*, pp. 574–8.

35   "Chen Yi and Su Yu Should Rapidly Relocate West," August 6, 1947 in *Mao Zedong Junshi Wenxuan*, Vol. 4, p. 177.

36   "Liu-Deng's Decision to March South is Completely Correct," August 10, 1947 in *Mao Zedong Junshi Wenxuan*, Vol. 4, p. 183.

37   "The General Intent is to Fight in GMD Territory," August 11, 1947 in *Mao Zedong Junshi Wenxuan*, Vol. 4, p. 189.

38   "The West Army Should Actively Support Liu-Deng's Operations," August 24, 1947 in *Mao Zedong Junshi Wenxuan*, Vol. 4, p. 207.

39   "Chen-Su Should Rapidly Cross South Over the Yellow River to Develop the Situation," August 29, 1947 in *Mao Zedong Junshi Wenxuan*, Vol. 4, p. 214; Liu Tong, *Huabei Jiefang Zhanzheng*, p. 329.

40   "We Agree with the Plan for the Chen-Su Army to Take Two Routes [South]," September 30, 1947 in *Mao Zedong Junshi Wenxuan*, Vol. 4, p. 277.

41   As quoted in Liu Tong, *Huadong Jiefang Zhanzheng*, pp. 362–63.

42   "The 2nd and 7th Column Should Not Presently Leave the Binghai District," September 16, 1947 in *Mao Zedong Junshi Wenxuan*, Vol. 4, p. 256.

43   "Chen Geng's Army Should Cross the Yellow River at an Earlier Time," August 9, 1947 in *Mao Zedong Junshi Wenxuan*, Vol. 4, p. 181.

44   Chen Geng, "Into West Henan" as quoted in Liu Tong, *Zhongyuan Jiefang Zhanzheng*, p. 328.

45   "After the Chen-Xie Army Crosses the Yellow River They Should Develop their Position in West Henan," August 26, 1947; "The Chen-Xie Army Should Quickly Move to Seize Shaanxian, Lingbao and Other Places," August 30, 1947 in *Mao Zedong Junshi Wenxuan*, Vol. 4, pp. 212, 222.

46   "Resolutely Form a Hubei-Henan-Shaanxi Base," September 4, 1947 in *Mao Zedong Junshi Wenxuan*, Vol. 4, p. 238.

47   "The Direction of Liu-Deng's Forthcoming Activities," August 31, 1947 in *Mao Zedong Junshi Wenxuan*, Vol. 4, p. 225.

48   Li likened his headquarters to being suspended in air – no responsibilities and no ties to reality in Te-Kong Tong, p. 312.

49   "China: Chiang; Other Developments – Civil War," *Facts on File News Digest*, July 12, 1947.

50   "Victory at Szepingkai," *Kuo Min Jih Pao*, July 3, 1947 in *Review of the Hong Kong Chinese Press*, 3:1.

51   As quoted in Liu Tong, *Dongbei Jiefang Zhanzheng*, pp. 472–3.

52   See *Zhenzhong Riji*, Vol. 1, pp. 357–9.

53   Liu Tong, *Dongbei Jiefang Zhanzheng Jishi* [Record of the Liberation War in the Northeast]. (Beijing: Dongfang Chubanshe, 1997), pp. 479–80.

54   *Zhenzhong Riji*, Vol. 1, pp. 349–51.

55   *Zhongguo Renmin Jiefangjun Qishi Quanshi*, Vol. 5, p. 181.

56   One of the nine former provinces of the GMD reorganization; it is now the eastern portion of Liaoning province.

57   *Zhongguo Renmin Jiefangjun Qishi Quanshi*, Vol. 5, p. 180.

58 Sun Zhaiwei, *Jiang Jieshi de Chong Jiang Chen Cheng [Chiang Kai-shek's Favorite General Chen Cheng]*, (Zhengzhou: Henan Renmin Chubanshe, 1990), pp. 190–2.

59 "Our Army in the Northeast Should Attack in Conjunction with the Southern Line in the Second Half of September," August 29, 1947 in *Mao Zedong Junshi Wenxuan*, Vol. 4, p. 220.

60 *Zhenzhong Riji*, Vol. 1, p. 411.

61 *Zhongguo Renmin Jiefangjun Qishi Quanshi*, Vol. 2, p. 151.

62 "After Attacking Jilin City You Should Direct the Main Attack Towards the Beiping-Liaoning, Beiping-Suiyuan Railroads," October 13, 1947 in *Mao Zedong Junshi Wenxuan*, Vol. 4, p. 305.

63 *Zhenzhong Riji*, October 19, 1947, Vol. 1, p. 430.

64 "Block the Enemy Inside the Pass, Cooperate with the Northeast Battlefield," May 8, 1947 in *Mao Zedong Junshi Wenxuan*, Vol. 4, p. 66.

65 Jin Chongji, *Zhu De Zhuan*, Revised Edition, (Beijing: Zhongyang Wenxian Chubanshe, 2000), pp. 716–19; Also see Yang Chengwu, *Yang Chengwu Huiyilu*, (Beijing: Jiefangjun Chubanshe, 1990), pp. 70–1.

66 "Telegram of Nie Rongzhen, Xiao Ke and Others Regarding Battle Deployments to the CMC," May 19, 1947 in Zhongyang Dang'anguan [Central CCP Archive], ed., *Zhongyang zai Xibaipo*, (Beijing: Zhonggong Zhongyang Dangangguan Dangxiao Chubanshe, 1997), pp. 83–4.

67 "The Orientation of the Shanxi-Chahar-Hebei's Main Strength Next Battle," June 19, 1947, in *Mao Zedong Junshi Wenxuan*, Vol. 4, p. 105.

68 Yuan Dejin, *Huabei Jiefang Zhanzheng*, p. 197.

69 Yang Dezhi, *Yang Dezhi Huiyilu [Recolllections of Yang Dezhi]*, (Beijing: Jiefangjun Chubanshe, 1992), p. 389; Yuan Dejin and Liu Zhenhua, *Huabei Jiefang Zhanzheng*, p. 197.

70 Yang Dezhi, pp. 390–1.

71 Nie, *Inside the Red Star*, p. 566.

72 Yang Dezhi, pp. 391–2.

73 Nie, *Inside the Red Star*, p. 568.

74 Nie, *Nie Rongzhen Huiyilu*, pp. 663–5.

75 "Deployments for Attacking Shijiazhuang and the Relief Column," October 23, 1947 in *Mao Zedong Junshi Wenxuan*, Vol. 4, p. 315.

76 Nie, *Inside the Red Star*, p. 572.

77 Ibid., p. 575.

78 "Telegram to Nie Rongzhen and Others Regarding the Plan for Attacking Shijiazhuang and Points of Attention," November 1, 1947 in *Selected Works of Zhu De*, p. 219.

79 As quoted in Nie, *Inside the Red Star*, p. 578.

80 Zhu De, "The Capture of Shijiazhuang: Its Significance and Our Experience and Lessons" in *Selected Works of Zhu De*, pp. 228–33.

81 "Strategy for the Second Year of the War of Liberation"; "Present Situation and Tasks" in *Selected Works of Mao Tse-Tung*, Vol. 4, pp. 145, 161.

82 "The Capture of Shijiazhuang: Its Significance and Our Experience and Lessons." in *Selected Works of Zhu De*, p. 228.

83 *Zhenzhong Riji*, October 20, 1947, Vol. 1, p. 434.

84 "The Northeast Bureau Should Use Its Entire Strength to Increase Military Production and Assist the Entire War Effort," November 13, 1947; "The Shanxi-Chahar-Hebei Field Army Should Cooperate with the Northeast Battlefield," November 17, 1947 in *Mao Zedong Junshi Wenxuan*, Vol. 4, pp. 327, 330.

85 *Zhenzhong Riji*, November 16, 1947, Vol. 1, p. 497.

86 Ibid., November 20, 1947, Vol. 1, p. 501.

87 As a side note, the temperatures near Fakui were –12 degrees Celsius during the day and –25 degrees Celsius at night; ibid., December 21, 1947, Vol. 1, p. 562.

88 Ibid., December 29, 1947, Vol. 1, p. 581.

89   "Telegram to Lin Biao, Luo Ronghuan and Liu Yalou with Copies Sent to Zhu De and Liu Shaoqi of February 7, 1948, 2000 hours," in *Mao Zedong Junshi Wenxuan (Neibuben)*, pp. 456–8.

90   As quoted in Liu Tong, *Dongbei Jiefang Zhanzheng*, p. 560.

91   "Don't Use the False Reputation Method to Win Over Defecting Troops," February 27, 1948 in *Mao Zedong Junshi Wenxuan*, Vol. 4, p. 406.

92   "Kuomintang Facing Military Crisis," *Hwa Shiang Pao*, August 13, 1947, in *Review of Hong Kong Press*, 36:2.

93   "Time for an All-Out Effort to Save Manchuria", *Kuo Min Jih Pao*, March 2, 1948 in *Review of the Hong Kong Chinese Press*, 41:1.

94   "Army Changes to Intensify Communist Suppression Campaign", *Kuo Min Jih Pao*, June 4, 1948 in *Review of the Hong Kong Chinese Press*, 103:1.

95   "On the Great Victory in the Northwest and on the New Type of Ideological Education Movement in the Liberation Army," in *Selected Works of Mao Tse-Tung*, Vol. 4, pp. 213–14.

96   "The Chen-Su and Chen-Xie Armies Should Cooperate to Attack the Beiping-Hankou Line," December 9, 1947; "Deployments for Long-term Cooperation Between the Chen-Su and Chen-Xie Armies to Support the Liu-Deng Army's Activities," December 20, 1947 in *Mao Zedong Junshi Wenxuan*, Vol. 4, pp. 341, 344.

97   "Summary of One Year of War and the Plan for the Present," July 10, 1947; "The Direction of Liu-Deng's Forthcoming Activities," August 31, 1947; "Questions Concerning the [Strategic] Direction of the East and West Army and Building," October 15, 1947 in *Mao Zedong Junshi Wenxuan*, Vol. 4, p. pp. 133–4, 225, 307–8.

98   "Route and Plan for Su Yu's Army to Cross the Yangtze River," February 2, 1947 in *Mao Zedong Junshi Wenxuan*, Vol. 4, p. 385.

99   Ibid., p. 385.

100 "Create the North Jiangsu and Shandong Armies," January 30, 1947 in *Mao Zedong Junshi Wenxuan*, Vol. 4, p. 379.

101 "Deployments After the Attack on Zizhou," March 20, 1947 in *Mao Zedong Junshi Wenxuan*, Vol. 4, p. 431.

102 "Rapidly Attack Luoyang and the Luoyang-Zhengzhou Railway," March 7, 1948 in *Mao Zedong Junshi Wenxuan*, Vol. 4, p. 415.

103 "Liu-Deng and Chen-Xie's Battle Deployments," March 22, 1948 in *Mao Zedong Junshi Wenxuan*, Vol. 4, p. 446.

104 Peng Dehuai, *Peng Dehuai Zizhuan*, p. 262.

105 "The Liu-Deng Army Will Prepare to Enter Southwest Henan and the Hanshui River Valley," April 16, 1948 in *Mao Zedong Junshi Wenxuan*, Vol. 4, p. 452–53.

106 "The Su Yu Army Will Temporarily Postpone Crossing the Yangtze River and Will Concentrate to Destroy the Enemy in the Central Plains," May 5, 1948 in *Mao Zedong Junshi Wenxuan*, Vol. 4, pp. 459–60.

107 "The Su Yu Army Will Temporarily Postpone Crossing the Yangtze River and Will Concentrate to Destroy the Enemy in the Central Plains," May 5, 1948; "The Xu-Tan Army Will Deploy the Tianjin-Pukou Railroad After Rest and Reorganization," May 7, 1948 in *Mao Zedong Junshi Wenxuan*, Vol. 4, pp. 459–60, 461.

108 Mao Zedong, "Northwest Victory and Ideological Education in the Army," March 7, 1948 in *Selected Works of Mao Tse-Tung*, p. 212.

5 Three crucibles of victory

1   Mao Zedong, "On Setting Up a System of Reports," January 7, 1948 in *Selected Works of Mao Tse-Tung*, Vol. 4, p. 178.

2   Ibid.

3   Mao Zedong, "A Circular on the Situation" in *Selected Works of Mao Tse-Tung*, Vol. 4, p. 221.

4   Mao Zedong, "The Concept of Operations for the Liaohsi-Shenyang Campaign" in *Selected Works of Mao Tse-Tung*, Vol. 4, p. 261.

5   Zhu De, "Four Talks at the War Briefing Meetings held by the Operations Bureau of the Chinese People's Liberation Army Headquarters" in *Selected Works of Zhu De*, pp. 249–50.

6   "CMC Guidance Regarding the Goals for the East China Field Army's Summer Battle," May 21, 1948 in *Zhongyang Wenjian Xuanji*, Vol. 17, pp. 163–4.

7   "Force the Enemy to Dispatch Troops in All Directions in Any Way Possible to Create an Opportunity," June 3, 1948 in *Mao Zedong Junshi Wenxuan*, Vol. 4, p. 474.

8   "Destroy One of the Enemy's Columns at the Sui-Tong-Xu Line," June 26, 1948 in *Mao Zedong Junshi Wenxuan*, Vol. 4, p. 492.

9   "Su Yu's Army Should Prepare for Another Battle Within Ten Days," July 8, 1948 in *Mao Zedong Junshi Wenxuan*, Vol. 4, p. 506; Liu Tong, *Huadong Jiefang Zhanzheng*, p. 423.

10 "The Xu-Tan Army Concentrating to Attack Yanzhou and Jining is the Best Plan," July 4, 1948 in *Mao Zedong Junshi Wenxuan*, Vol. 4, p. 498.

11 "The Xu-Tan Army Should Attack Ji'nan in Order to Disperse the Enemy," July 14, 1948 in *Mao Zedong Junshi Wenxuan*, Vol. 4, p. 514.

12 "Control the Dangshan-Huangkou Section [of the Longhai] and Menace Xuzhou," July 16, 1948 in *Mao Zedong Junshi Wenxuan*, Vol. 4, p. 525.

13 "CMC Guidance Regarding Troop Reorganization and the Next Battle," July 26, 1948 in *Zhongyang Wenjian Xuanji*, Vol. 16, p. 265.

14 "August 10, 0400 Hours Telegram to CMC, East China and Central Plains Bureau and the Shandong and North Jiangsu Armies" in *Su Yu Junshi Wenxuan*, (http://cyc90. cycnet.com/leaders/suyu/content.jsp? id=11167&s_code=2303).

15 "CMC Telegram to Su Yu and Others Regarding Questions About the Battle Plan After Resting and Reorganizing for the Rainy Season," August 12, 1948 in *Zhongyang Wenjian Xuanji*, Vol. 16, pp. 308–10.

16 As quoted in Liu Tong, p. 611.

17 "First Attack Changchun but Do Not Emphasize the Difficulties of Attacking South", April 22, 1948; "Duties for the Shanxi-Chahar-Hebei Field Army in Cooperating with the Northeast Battlefield", April 22, 1948 in *Mao Zedong Junshi Wenxuan*, Vol. 4, pp. 455, 457.

18 Westad, p. 176; see also Nie, *Inside the Red Star*, pp. 523–4.

19 *Zhenzhong Riji*, March 18, 1948, Vol. 2, p. 708.

20 Ibid, May 13, 1948, Vol. 2, p. 748.

21 Ibid, May 25, 1948, Vol. 2, p. 767.

22 As quoted in Liu Tong, *Dongbei Jiefang Zhanzheng*, p. 619.

23 "Telegram to Lin Biao, Luo Ronghuan, Liu Yalou of June 1, 1948, 0700 Hours"; "Telegram to Lin Biao, Luo Ronghuan, Liu Yalou of June 3, 1948, 1300 Hours," in *Mao Zedong Junshi Wenxuan (Neibuben)*, pp. 461, 462.

24 "Telegram to Lin Biao, Luo Ronghuan, Liu Yalou of June 7, 1948, 1500 Hours," in *Mao Zedong Junshi Wenxuan (Neibuben)*, pp. 462–4; see also "Minutes from the June 15 Cadre Meeting in Jilin: Luo Ronghuan, Liu Yalou and Xiao Jingguang's Reports," in *Zhenzhong Riji*, pp. 788–95.

25 "Telegram to Lin Biao, Luo Ronghuan, Liu Yalou of July 22, 1948, 2300 Hours"; "Telegram to Lin Biao, Luo Ronghuan, Liu Yalou of June 30, 1948," in *Mao Zedong Junshi Wenxuan (Neibuben)*, pp. 464–5, 466.

26 Liu Tong, *Dongbei Jiefang Zhanzheng*, p. 622; Shao Hua and You Hu, p. 240.

27 "Telegram to Lin Biao, Luo Ronghuan, Liu Yalou, Yang Dezhi and Luo Ruiqing of August 3, 1948, 2300 Hours" in *Mao Zedong Junshi Wenxuan (Neibuben)*, p. 466.

28 "Telegram to Lin Biao, Luo Ronghuan, Liu Yalou of August 12, 1948, 0600 Hours" in *Mao Zedong Junshi Wenxuan (Neibuben)*, pp. 468–9.

29   Liu Tong, *Dongbei Jiefang Zhanzheng Jishi* [Record of the Liberation War in the Northeast].
     (Beijing: Dongfang Chubanshe, 1997), p. 624; Shao Hua and You Hu, pp. 240–1.
30   *Zhenzhong Riji*, September 8–9, 1948, Vol. 2, p. 910.
31   "Concept of Operations for the Liaohsi-Shenyang Campaign," September 7, 1948 in
     Selected Works of Mao Tse-Tung, Vol. 4, p. 261.
32   "Allowance for the Enemy," *Hwa Shiang Pao*, August 2, 1948 in *Review of the Hong
     Kong Chinese Press*, 130:1.
33   In the original campaign directive, the Northeast Headquarters mentioned capturing
     the airfield but as Jinzhou had two, this was probably the source of the confusion.
34   *Zhenzhong Riji*, October 2, 1948, Vol. 2, p. 1012.
35   Shao Hua and You Hu, p. 241.
36   "Telegram to Lin Biao, Luo Ronghuan, Liu Yalou of October 3, 1948, 1700 Hours,"
     in *Mao Zedong Junshi Wenxuan (Neibuben)*, pp. 476–7.
37   "Telegram to Lin Biao, Luo Ronghuan, Liu Yalou of October 3, 1948, 1900 Hours,"
     in *Mao Zedong Junshi Wenxuan (Neibuben)*, pp. 477–8.
38   "Telegram to Lin Biao, Luo Ronghuan, Liu Yalou of October 4, 1948, 0400 Hours,"
     in *Mao Zedong Junshi Wenxuan (Neibuben)*, pp. 478–9.
39   "Telegram to Lin Biao, Luo Ronghuan, Liu Yalou of October 17, 0500 hours;
     "Telegram of October 18, 2300 hours"; "Telegram of October 19, 0500"; "Telegram
     of October 19, 1700," in *Mao Zedong Junshi Wenxuan (Neibuben)*, pp. 484–8.
40   "Telegram to Lin Biao, Luo Ronghuan, Liu Yalou of October 20, 1948, 0400 Hours,"
     in *Mao Zedong Junshi Wenxuan (Neibuben)*, pp. 489–90.
41   Shao Hua and You Hu, p. 252.
42   "Six Months' Time Is Up," *Hwa Shiang Pao*, Oct. 8, 1948 in *Review of the Hong Kong
     Chinese Press*, 174:2.
43   Dai Changle and Liu Lianhua, eds., *Disiye Zhanjun [Fourth Field Army]*, Revised
     Edition, (Beijing: Guofang Daxue Chubanshe, 1996), p. 231.
44   "Concentrate the Main Strength of the Field Army to Attack Ji'nan and Ambush the
     Relief: August 28, 1948 Telegram to the CMC" in *Su Yu Junshi Wenxuan*, (http://
     cyc90.cycnet.com/leaders/suyu/content.jsp?id=11193&s_code=2303).
45   "August 28, 1948, 0200 Hours Telegram to Su Yu," in *Mao Zedong Junshi Wenxuan
     (Neibuben)*, pp. 439–40.
46   Liu Tong, *Huabei Jiefang Zhanzheng*, p. 491.
47   "Proposal for the Huaihai Campaign", September 24, 1948 in *Su Yu Junshi Wenxuan*,
     (http://cyc90.cycnet.com/leaders/suyu/content.jsp?id=11193&s_code=2303).
48   "September 25, 1948 Telegram to Rao Shaoshi, Su Yu, Xu Shiyou, Tan Zhenlin, Wang
     Jianan, Liu Bocheng, Chen Yi and Li Da" in *Mao Zedong Junshi Wenxuan (Neibenbu)*,
     pp. 517–18.
49   Liu Tong, *Huabei Jiefang Zhanzheng*, p. 496.
50   "September 28, 1948 Telegram to Rao Shaoshi, Su Yu, Xu Shiyou, Tan Zhenlin, Wang
     Jianan, Liu Bocheng, Chen Yi and Li Da," in *Mao Zedong Junshi Wenxuan (Neibenbu)*,
     pp. 519–20.
51   "The Concept of Operations for the Huaihai Campaign," October 11, 1948 in *Selected
     Works of Mao Tse-Tung*, Vol. 4, pp. 279–81.
52   "Battle Plan and Deployments to Destroy Huang Baitao's Army: October 15, 1948
     Telegram to the CMC and the Central Plains Bureau," in *Su Yu Junshi Wenxuan*, (http://
     cyc90.cycnet.com/leaders/suyu/content.jsp?id=11193&s_code=2303).
53   "October 26, 1948, 0300 Hours Telegram to Su Yu, Tan Zhenlin, Chen Yi, Deng
     Xiaoping, Liu Bocheng, Deng Zihua and Li Xiannian," in *Mao Zedong Junshi
     Wenxuan (Neibenbu)*, pp. 527–8.
54   "Proposal to Unify Command for the Huaihai Campaign," October 31, 1948 in *Su Yu
     Junshi Wenxuan*, (http://cyc90.cycnet.com/leaders/suyu/content.jsp?id=11162&s_
     code=2303); despite the gesture of creating this committee, all five men would not
     meet face-to-face until after the campaign was almost complete.

55 "November 9, 1948, 1600 Hours Telegram to Su Yu, Tan Zhenlin, Chen Yi, Deng Xiaoping, Liu Bocheng, Deng Zihua and Li Xiannian," in *Mao Zedong Junshi Wenxuan (Neibuben)*, p. 535.

56 Yang Botao, *Yang Botao Huiyilu [Recollections of Yang Botao]*, (Beijing: Zhongguo Wenshi Chubanshe, 1996), pp. 167–8.

57 "November 11, 1948, 1700 Hours Telegram to Liu Bocheng, Chen Yi and Deng Xiaoping," in *Mao Zedong Junshi Wenxuan (Neibuben)*, p. 538.

58 "November 14, 1948, 2300 Hours Telegram to Liu Bocheng, Chen Yi, Deng Xiaoping, Su Yu, Chen Shiju, Zhang Zhen, Wei Guoqing, Ji Luo, Tan Zhenlin, Wang Jianan, the Central Plains Bureau and East China Bureau," in *Mao Zedong Junshi Wenxuan (Neibuben)*, pp. 544–5.

59 Bai Chongxi did not get along with Hu and thus passed him over for promotion, in favor of Huang Wei, who was also Gu Zhutong's candidate. Hu Lian served as the deputy commander of the army.

60 "November 18, 1948, 2400 Hours Telegram to Liu Bocheng, Chen Yi, Deng Xiaoping, Su Yu and Tan Zhenlin," in *Mao Zedong Junshi Wenxuan (Neibuben)*, pp. 550–1.

61 "November 19, 1948 Telegram to the CMC from Liu Bocheng, Chen Yi and Deng Xiaoping Regarding the Decision to First Defeat Huang Baitao" in Zhonggong Zhongyang Dang Shiziliao Zhengji Weiyuanhui, *Huaihai Zhanyi*, Vol. 1, (Beijing: Zhonggong Dangshi Ziliao Chubanshe, 1988), pp. 175–6.

62 "The Momentous Change in China's Military Situation," November 14, 1948 in *Selected Works of Mao Tse-Tung*, Vol. 4, pp. 287–8.

63 "CMC Telegram Regarding the East China Field Army's Responsibilities for Dealing with Li Xiannian," November 20, 1948, in *Huaihai Zhanyi*, Vol. 1, p. 179.

64 Ibid., Vol. 1, pp. 337–8.

65 "November 23, 1948 Telegram from Liu Bocheng, Chen Yi and Deng Xiaoping to Su Yu, Chen Shiju and Zhang Zhen Regarding the Deployments for Destroying Huang Wei," in *Huaihai Zhanyi*, Vol. 1, p. 189; "CMC Telegram to Liu Bocheng, Chen Yi, Deng Xiaoping Regarding Continuing the Campaign for Three to Five Months and Striving for Victory," November 23, 1948 in *Huaihai Zhanyi*, Vol. 1, pp. 193–4.

66 Li Mancun *et al.*, p. 477.

67 Qiu Weida, "The 74th Corps Destroyed for a Second Time," in Zhongguo Renmin Zhengzhi Xieshanghui Yiquanguo Weiyuanhui and Wenshi Ziliao Yanjiu Weiyuanhui [Chinese People's Political National Committee and the Historical Material Research Committee], eds. *Huaihai Zhanyi Qinliji (Yuan Guomindang Jiangling de Huiyi) [The Huaihai Campaign – A Personal Record (Original Recollections of GMD Generals)*, (Beijing: Wenshi Ziliao Chubanshe, 1983), p. 396; Qiu proposed combining their forces to break out in a single direction but he was overruled.

68 "The Concept of Operations for the Peiping-Tientsin Campaign," December 11, 1948 in *Selected Works of Mao Tse-Tung*, Vol. 4, p. 291.

69 "CMC Directive Regarding Yang Chengwu Immediately Forming a West Army to Undertake Responsibilities in Suiyuan," July 23, 1948 in *Zhongyang Wenjian Xuanji*, Vol. 17: 1948, pp. 263–64.

70 "Telegram of October 29, 1948 to Lin Biao, Luo Ronghuan, Liu Yalou," in *Mao Zedong Junshi Wenxuan (Neibuben)*, pp. 579–80.

71 "Telegram of October 31, 1948 to Lin Biao, Luo Ronghuan, Liu Yalou, Cheng Zihua, Huang Zhiyong, Northeast Bureau and North China Bureau," in *Mao Zedong Junshi Wenxuan (Neibuben)*, pp. 581–2.

72 "Yang Chengwu Should Wait Until After the Northeast Army Moves South to Attack Beiping-Tianjin Before Attacking Guisui," November 9, 1948 in *Mao Zedong Junshi Wenxuan*, Vol. 5, p. 186.

73 "Postpone the Attack on Taiyuan," November 16, 1948 in *Mao Zedong Junshi Wenxuan*, Vol. 5, p. 228.

74 "Telegram of November 16, 1948 to Lin Biao, Luo Ronghuan and Liu Yalou," in *Mao Zedong Junshi Wenxuan (Neibuben)*, pp. 582–3.

75 "Telegram of November 18, 1948, 1800 Hours to Lin Biao, Luo Ronghuan and Liu Yalou," in *Mao Zedong Junshi Wenxuan (Neibuben)*, p. 584.

76 "Telegram of November 26, 1948, 0800 Hours to Lin Biao, Luo Ronghuan and Liu Yalou," in *Mao Zedong Junshi Wenxuan (Neibuben)*, pp. 589–90.

77 "Telegram of December 7, 1948, 2000 Hours to Cheng Zihua, Huang Zhiyong, Yang Dezhi, Luo Ruiqing, Yang Chengwu, Lin Biao, Luo Ronghuan, Liu Yalou, Nie Rongzhen and Bo Yibo," in *Mao Zedong Junshi Wenxuan (Neibuben)*, pp. 604–5.

78 "Telegram of December 11, 1948, 0200 Hours to Lin Biao, Luo Ronghuan and Liu Yalou" in *Mao Zedong Junshi Wenxuan (Neibuben)*, pp. 613–14.

79 "Telegram of December 15, 1948, 0200 Hours to Yang Dezhi, Luo Ruiqing, Yang Chengwu, Lin Biao, Luo Ronghuan and Liu Yalou" in *Mao Zedong Junshi Wenxuan (Neibuben)*, p. 628.

80 As noted in Chapter 1, these three men had also made up the leadership of the 115th Division during the first years of World War II.

81 "Telegram of December 28, 1948, 2000 Hours to Lin Biao, Yang Dezhi, Luo Ruiqing and Yang Chengwu"; "Telegram of December 29, 1948, 2300 Hours to Lin Biao and Liu Yalou," in *Mao Zedong Junshi Wenxuan (Neibuben)*, p. 640.

82 Shao Hua and You Hu, pp. 263–4.

83 Dai Changle and Liu Lianhua, p. 233.

84 "CMC Directive Regarding Changing the Numeration and Order of Battle of Each Field Army," January 15, 1949 in *Zhongyang Wenjian Xuanji*, Vol. 18, p. 34.

85 The highest echelon was Field Army (now equivalent to an Army Group), followed by Army, Corps, Divisions, Brigades, Battalion, Company, and Platoon.

86 "CMC Directive Regarding the Current Military Situation and Preparing Cadre for Crossing the Yangtze River," February 3, 1949 in *Zhongyang Wenjian Xuanji*, Vol. 18, pp. 105–7.

87 "CMC Directive Regarding the 2nd and 3rd Field Armies Resting for Two Months and Then Crossing the Yangtze River to Lin Biao and Luo Ronghuan," February 8, 1949 in *Zhongyang Wenjian Xuanji*, Vol. 18: 1949, p. 117.

88 "CMC Directive Regarding Questions About the Plan to Cross the Yangtze at the End of March," February 21, 1949; "CMC Guidance Regarding the 4th Field Army First Sending Two Corps to Pressure Hankou and Pin Down Bai Chongxi's Army," February 22, 1949 in *Zhongyang Wenjian Xuanji*, Vol. 18, pp. 123–4, 125–6.

89 "CMC Guidance Regarding the Deployment of the Main Strength of the 4th Field Army," March 17, 1949 in *Zhongyang Wenjian Xuanji*, Vol. 18, p. 177.

90 "Outline Plan for the Nanjing-Shanghai-Hangzhou Campaign," March 31, 1949 in *Deng Xiaoping Selected Works*, (http://english.peopledaily.com.cn/dengxp/vol1/text/a1140.html).

91 "CMC Directive to Check the [Yangtze] River Water Level and If Postponing Will Be Disadvantageous," April 10, 1949; "CMC Directive Regarding Postponing the Yangtze River Crossing to April 22," April 11, 1949 in *Zhongyang Wenjian Xuanji*, Vol. 18, pp. 217, 219–10.

92 "Statement on the Present Situation by Mao Tse-Tung", January 14, 1949 in *Selected Works of Mao Tse-Tung*, Vol. 4, pp. 315–19; The Eight Points were: punish the war criminals, abolish the bogus constitution, abolish the bogus "constitutional authority", reorganize all reactionary troops on democratic principles, confiscate bureaucratic-capital, reform the land system, abrogate treasonable treaties, convene a political consultative conference without the participation of reactionary elements, and form a democratic coalition government to take over all powers of the reactionary Nanjing Guomindang government and of its subordinate government at all levels.

93 "From the Crossing of the Yangtze to the Capture of Shanghai", August 4, 1949 in *Deng Xiaoping Selected Works*, (http://english.peopledaily.com.cn/dengxp/vol1/text/a1160.html).

94   Ibid.
95   "CMC Deployments for the Entire Country," May 23, 1949 in *Zhongyang Wenjian Xuanji*, Vol. 18, pp. 292–3.
96   Yan himself fled to Taiwan to join Chiang Kaishek.
97   Xikang was later divided, with half becoming part of Sichuan and the other half becoming part of Xizang or Tibet.

Conclusion

1   Keith E. Eiler, ed., *Wedemeyer on War and Peace*, (Stanford: Hoover Institution Press, 1987), p. 149.
2   Arthur Waldron, "The Battle of the Northeast" in Robert Cowley, *What If?: The World's Foremost Military Historians Imagine What Might Have Been*, (New York: G.P. Putnam's Sons, 1999).
3   For instance, John Robinson Beal cites captured documents which contained complaints by Communist officers that Russia was not providing enough help, that they had harmed their cause by looting Manchuria and that Russian Marshal Rodion Yakovlevich Malinovsky had advised against providing further help to the CCP in Beal, p. 67
4   Stuart to the Secretary of State, Nanking, October 29, 1947 in Rea and Brewer, p. 149.
5   Mao Zedong, *Selected Works*, Vol. 4, pp. 103–7.
6   Some have argued that Deng Xiaoping was the first to propose this idea, see Benjamin Yang, "The Making of a Pragmatic Communist 1904–1949," *China Quarterly*, 0:135, Special Issue: Deng Xiaoping: An Assessment (Sept. 1993), p. 454.
7   "How Can the U.S. Aid China Militarily?," *Wah Kiu Ya Po*, March 5, 1948 in *Review of the Hong Kong Chinese Press*, 44:1; "Army Changes to Intensify Communist Suppression Campaign," *Kuo Min Jih Pao*, June 4, 1948 in *Review of the Hong Kong Chinese Press*, 103:1; "The Military Situation", *Hsin Sheng Wan Pao*, June 28, 1948 in *Review of the Hong Kong Chinese Press*, 108:2; F.F. Liu, pp. 1–6.
8   "Military Report to the National Assembly," *Sing Tao Jih Pao*, April 14, 1948 in *Review of the Hong Kong Chinese Press*, 69:1–2.
9   Dick Wilson, *Zhou Enlai: A Biography*, (New York: Viking, 1984), p. 173.
10   Westad, pp. 263, 325.
11   The 70/30 equation, 70% right and 30% wrong.
12   Hu Chi-hsi, pp. 250–80.
13   Frederick C. Teiwes and Warren Sun, *The Tragedy of Lin Biao: Riding the Tiger during the Cultural Revolution, 1966–1971*, (Honolulu: University of Hawaii Press, 1996), pp. 7–9; Jaap van Binneken, *The Rise and Fall of Lin Piao*, (New York: Penguin Books, 1976); Whitson, p. 58.
14   Zhonggong Jiangsu Sheng Dangshi Ziliao Zhengji Yanjiu Weiyuanhu, eds., *Suzhong Kangri Douzheng [The Anti-Japanese Base in Southern Jiangsu]*, (Beijing: Zhonggong Dangshi Ziliao Chubanshe, 1987), p. 34.
15   Percy Jucheng Fang and Lucy Guinong J. Fang, *Zhou Enlai – A Profile*, (Beijing: Foreign Language Press, 1986), pp. 123, 164.
16   Westad, pp. 59–60.
17   Jurgen Domes, *Peng Te-huai: The Man and the Image*, (London: C. Hurst & Company, 1985), pp. 40–1.
18   Domes, p. 48.
19   Domes goes into this further by presenting Peng as a populist, a man with a significant following in the masses who had to be torn down in life and death to prevent threatening other leaders, pp. 136–7.
20   Peng's memoirs are part of his failed defense against his attackers, *Peng Dehuai Zishu [Autobiographical Notes of Peng Dehuai]*, (Beijing: Renmin Chubanshe, 1981).
21   Deng Xiaoping, "In Memory of Liu Bocheng, October 21, 1986" in *Deng Xiaoping Selected Works*, Vol. 3, p. 145.

22   Evans Fordyce Carlson described him at the time as being "short, chunky and physical tough" as well as having "a mind as keen as mustard" in *Twin Stars of China*, (New York: Dodd, Mead, 1940), p. 252.

23   June Teufel Dreyer, "Deng: The Soldier", *China Quarterly*, 0:135 Special Issue: Deng Xiaoping: An Assessment (Sept 1993), p. 537; Deng was quoted as having said "We did feel inseparable in our hearts" in an unnamed official biography in Richard Evans, *Deng Xiaoping and The Making of Modern China*, (New York: Viking, 1993).

24   Red Guard pamphlet, "Yang Ch'eng-wu Hen-p'i Teng Hsiao-p'ing" [Yang Ch'eng-wu Criticizes Teng Hsiao-p'ing Severely] as quoted in Ching Hua Lee, *Deng Xiaoping: The Marxist Road to the Forbidden City*, (Princeton: The Kingston Press, Inc., 1985).

Bibliography

Archival collections or publications

Anhui Sheng Dang'anguan and Jiangsu Sheng Dang'anguan [Anhui and Jiangsu Provincial Archives], eds. *Du Jiang Zhanyi [Crossing the Yangtze River Campaign]*. Beijing: Dang'anguan Chubanshe, 1989.

Heilongjiang Sheng Dang'anguan [Heilongjiang Provincial Archive], ed. *Zhiyuan Qianxian [Supporting the Front Lines]*. Harbin (Haerbin): Heilongjiang Dang'anguan, 1984.

Jiangsu Sheng Dang'anguan: Jiefang Zhanzheng Shiqi Dang'an [Jiangsu Provincial Archive: Liberation War Period Archive]. Zhonggong Zhongyang Huazhong Fenbu [Central China Subbureau], 2101; Zhonggong Suzhongqu Weiyuanhui [Central Jiangsu District Committee], J2102; Zhonggong Huazhong Gongzuo Weiyuanhui [Central China Work Committee], 2104; Zhonggong Subeiqu Weiyuanhui [North Jiangsu District Committee], J2103.

Shandong Sheng Dang'anguan and Shandong Shehuizi Xueyuan Lishi Yanjiusuo [Shandong Provincial Archive and Shandong Social History Research School] eds. *Shandong Geming Lishi Dang'anguan Ziliao Xuanbian [Selected Material from the Shandong Revolutionary History Archive]*. Vols. 15, 16, 17. Jinan: Shandong Renmin Chubanshe, 1984.

Zhongguo Dier Lishi Dang'anguan [Second National Historical Archives of China]: Xuzhou Huizhan Dinggao, 697–701:16J-108, 702:16J-109.

Zhongyang Dang'anguan [Central CCP Archive], ed. *Jiefang Zhanzheng Shiqi: Tudi Gaige Wenjian Xuanbian [Liberation War Period: Collected Articles Concerning Land Reform]*. Zhonggong Zhongyang Dangxiao Chubanshe, 1981.

—— *Zhonggong Zhongyang Wenjian Xuanji [Selected Articles of the CCP Central Committee]*. Vol. 15: 1945. Beijing: Zhongyang Dang'anguan Dangxiao Chubanshe, 1991.

—— *Zhonggong Zhongyang Wenjian Xuanji [Selected Articles of the CCP Central Committee]*. Vol. 16: 1946–47, Vol. 17: 1948, Vol. 18: 1949. Beijing: Zhonggong Zhongyang Dangxiao Chubanshe, 1992.

—— *Zhongyang Zai Xibaipo [Central Committee at Xibaipo]*. Beijing: Zhonggong Zhongyang Dang'anguan Dangxiao Chubanshe, 1997.

Zhonggong Jiangsu Sheng Dangshi Ziliao Zhengji Yanjiu Weiyuanhu, eds. *Suzhong Kangri Douzheng [The Anti-Japanese Base in Southern Jiangsu]*. Beijing: Zhonggong Dangshi Ziliao Chubanshe, 1987.

Zhonggong Jiangsu Sheng Wei Dangshi Gongzuo Weiyuanhui and Jiangsu Sheng Dang'anju [Jiangsu Provincial Committee Party History Work Committee and the Jiangsu Provincial Archive Board], eds. *Jiangsu Dang Shiziliao*. Vols. 19, 20, 21, 24, 28. Nanjing: Jiangsu Sheng Dang'anguan, 1987.

Zhonggong Zhongyang Dangshi Ziliao Zhengji Weiyuanhui and Zhongguo Renmin Jiefangjun Dang'anguan [CCP Central Committee Party Historical Material Collection Committee and the Chinese People's Liberation Army Archive], eds. *Zhenzhong Riji (1946.11–948.11).* Vols. 1–2. Beijing: Zhonggong Dangshi Ziliao Chubanshe, 1987.

Periodicals

Dongfang Ribao.
Guancha [The Observer], Shanghai, September 1946–December 1948.
Jiefang Ribao.
Jiefangjun Ribao.
Renmin Ribao: Wushi Nian Tuwen Shujuxilie Guangpan [CD Collection of 50 Years of Pictures and Articles].
United States Consulate General (Hong Kong). *Current Background.* Hong Kong: US Consulate General, 1950–77.
—— *Index to People's Republic of China Press, Selections from People's Republic of China Magazines, and Current Background.* Hong Kong: US Consulate General 1950–53.
—— *Review of the Hong Kong Chinese Press.* No. 1–186, July 1, 1947–October 22, 1949.
—— *Selections from Chinese Mainland Press.* Hong Kong: US Consulate General, 1950–53.
United States Consulate General (Shanghai). *Chinese Press Review.* Shanghai: US Consulate General, September 1, 1945–February 15/16, 1950.

Primary Sources

An Ziwen, "Ba Womende Dang Jianshe Hao [Construct Our Party Well]," *Xinhua Yuebao* (Wenzhaiban), No. 4, p. 14–21.
Bland, Larry I., ed. *The Papers of George Catlett Marshall.* Vol. 5: The Finest Soldier January 1, 1945–January 7, 1947. Baltimore: Johns Hopkins University Press, 2003.
Bo Yibo. *Bo Yibo Wenxuan (1939–1992) [Selected Works of Bo Yibo].* Beijing: Renmin Chubanshe, 1992.
Brandt, Conrad, Benjamin Schwartz and John K. Fairbank, eds. *A Documentary History of Chinese Communism.* Cambridge, MA: Harvard University Press, 1962.
Braun, Otto. *A Comintern Agent in China, 1933–1939.* Jeane Moore, trans. Stanford: Stanford University Press, 1982.
Brewer, John C. and Kenneth W. Rea, eds. *The Forgotten Ambassador: The Reports of John Leighton Stuart, 1946–1949.* Boulder, CO: Westview Press, 1981.
Chang, Kuo-t'ao. *The Rise of the Chinese Communist Party, the Autobiography of Chang Kuo-t'ao.* Lawrence: University Press of Kansas, 1971.
Chen Geng. *Chen Geng Riji [Chen Geng's Diary].* Beijing: Zhanshi Chubanshe, 1982.
Chen-Su Dajiang Zhengzhanji Bianji Weiyuanhui [War Record of the Great Chen Yi-Su Yu Army Compilation Committee], ed. *Chen-Su Dajun Zhengzhanji [War Record of the Great Chen Yi-Su Yu Army].* Beijing: Xinhua Chubanshe, 1987.
Chen-Su Da Jun Zhengzhan Jisubian Weiyuanhui. *Chen-Su Da Jun Zhengzhan Jisubian [Records of the Battles of Chen-Su Great Army].* Beijing: Xinhua, 1991.
Chen Yi. *Chen Yi Junshi Wenxuan [Selected Military Works of Chen Yi].* Beijing: Jiefangjun Chubanshe, 1996.

Chen Yun. *Chen Yun Wenxuan (1926–1949) [Selected Works of Chen Yun]*. Beijing: Renmin Chubanshe, 1984.

Chen Zaidao. *Chen Zaidao Huiyilu [Memoirs of Chen Zaidao]*. Beijing: Jiefangjun Chubanshe, 1991.

Cheng Zihua. *Cheng Zihua Huiyilu [Memoirs of Cheng Zihua]*. Beijing: Jiefangjun Chubanshe, 1987.

Chiang Kaishek. *Selected Speeches and Messages in 1956*. Taipei: No Publisher Listed, 1956.

—— "Communist Designs and Kuomintang Blunders," in Pichon P.Y. Loh, ed. *The Kuomintang Debacle of 1949: Conquest or Collapse?* Boston: D.C. Heath and Company, 1965.

"China: Chiang; Other Developments – Civil War," *Facts on File News Digest*, July 12, 1947.

"China: Mongol Raid; Other Developments – Civil War", *Facts on File News Digest*, June 21, 1947.

Deng Xiaoping. *Selected Works of Deng Xiaoping*. Vols. 1, 2, 3. http://english.peopledaily.com.cn/dengxp/

Dong Biwu. *Dong Biwu Wenji [Selected Works of Dong Biwu]*. Beijing: Renmin Chubanshe, 1985.

Eiler, Keith E., ed. *Wedemeyer on War and Peace*. Stanford: Hoover Institution Press, 1987.

Heze Diqu Chubansheju [Heze District Publishing Bureau], ed. *Luxinan Zhanyi Xiliaoxuan [Selected Materials from the Southwest Shandong Campaign]*. Jinan: Shandong Renmin Chubanshe, 1982.

Hu Qiaomu. *Hu Qiaomu Wenxuan [Selected Works of Hu Qiaomu]*. Beijing: Renmin Chubanshe, 1992.

Huang Kecheng. *Huang Kecheng Zishu [Autobiographical Notes of Huang Kecheng]*. Beijing: Renmin Chubanshe, 1994.

Huang Yao. *Zhuangyan Dianxing: Luo Ronghuan Juan [High Quality Model Exemplar:The Collection of Luo Ronghuan*. Beijing: Jiefangjun Chubanshe, 2001.

Hubei Sheng E-Xiang Bian Gemingshi Bianjibu and Hubei Sheng Junqu Zhongyuan Tuwei Zhuanti Bianzhuanshi [Hubei Province and the Jiangxi-Hunan Revolutionary Base Compilation Bureau and the Hubei Province Military District Central Plains Breakout Editorial Office], eds. *Zhongyuan Tuwei Jishi [Record of the Central Plains Breakout]*. Beijing: Jiefangjun Chubanshe, 1992.

Hughes, Daniel J., ed. *Molkte on the Art of War: Selected Writings*. Novato, CA: Presidio Press, 1993.

Jin Chongji, Gong Xiguang and the Zhonggong Zhongyang Wenxian Yanjiushi. *Zhu De Zhuan [Biography of Zhu De]*. Revised Edition. Beijing: Zhongyang Wenxian Chubanshe, 2000.

Jin Chongji, ed. *Zhou Enlai Zhuan [Biography of Zhou Enlai]*. Vol. 2. Beijing: Zhongyang Wenxian Chubanshe, 1998.

—— ed. *Mao Zedong Zhuan [Biography of Mao Zedong] (1893–1949)*. Vol. 2. Beijing: Zhongyang Wenxian Chubanshe, 1996.

Jin Ye, ed. *Huiyi Tan Zhenlin [Recollections of Tan Zhenlin]*. Hangzhou: Zhejiang Renmin Chubanshe, 1992.

Ji'nan Shi Bowuguan, ed. *Ji'nan Zhanyi Ziliaoxuan*. Ji'nan: Shandong Renmin Chubanshe, 1979.

Kau, Ying-Mao, ed. *The People's Liberation Army and China's Nation-Building*. White Plains, NY: International Arts and Sciences Press, Inc., 1973.

Kau, Ying-Mao and John K. Leung, eds. *The Writings of Mao Zedong, 1949–1976.* Armonk, NY: M.E. Sharpe, 1986.

Lanzhou Budui Dangshi Ziliao Zhengji Weiyuanhui Bangongshi and Gansu Renmin Chubanshe Gaige Huiyilu Jishi [The Office of the Lanzhou Historical Material Committee and the Gansu People's Publishing Department of Revolutionary Recollections] eds. *Lanzhou Zhanyi [Lanzhou Campaign]. Lanzhou:* Gansu Renmin Chubanshe, 1983.

Laozhanshi Shiwenji Bianweihui and Zhongguo Geming Bowuguan [Old Soldier's Historical Collection Committee and the Chinese Revolutionary Museum], eds. *Mingjiang Su Yu [Famous General Su Yu].* Beijing: Xinhua Chubanshe, 1986.

Li Fuchun. *Li Fuchun Xuanji [Selected Works of Li Fuchun].* Beijing: Zhongguo Jihua Chubanshe, 1992.

Li Weihan. *Li Weihan Xuanji [Selected Works of Li Weihan].* Beijing: Renmin Chubanshe, 1987.

Li Xiannian. *Li Xiannian Wenxuan (1935–1988) [Selected Works of Li Xiannian].* Beijing: Renmin Chubanshe, 1989.

Li Yunchang and Selected Authors. *Xueye, Xiongfeng – Liuzai Dongbei Zhanchang de Jilu [Snow and Field, Brave Wind – Recalling the Northeast Battlefield].* Shenyang: Baishan Chubanshe, 1988.

Li Zhisui. *The Private Life of Chairman Mao.* New York: Random House, 1994.

Li Zongren. *Li Zongren Huiyilu.* Nanning: Guangxi Renmin Chubanshe, 1986.

Liao Chengzhi. *Liao Chengzhi Wenji [Selected Works of Liao Chengzhi].* Beijing: Renmin Chubanshe, 1990.

Linyi Xingbu Chuban Bangongshi, ed. [Linyi Administrative Publishing Office]. *Menglianggu Zhanyi Ziliaoxuan [Menglianggu Campaign Materials].* Jinan: Shandong Renmin Chubanshe, 1980.

Liu Bocheng. *Liu Bocheng Huiyilu [Recollections of Liu Bocheng].* Vols. 2–3. Shanghai:Shanghai Wenyi Chubanshe, 1985.

—— *Liu Bocheng Junshi Wenxuan,* http://cyc7.cycnet.com:8091/leaders/lbc/content.jsp?id=7618 &s_code=1302

Liu Qi, ed. *Liaoshen Zhanyi Qinliji (Yuan Guomindang Jiangling de Huiyi) [Liaoshen Campaign – A Personal Record (Original Recollections of GMD Generals)].* Beijing: Wenshi Ziliao Chubanshe, 1985.

Liu Shaoqi. *Selected Works of Liu Shaoqi.* Beijing: Foreign Language Press, 1976.

—— *Liu Shaoqi Wenji [Selected Works of Liu Shaoqi].* Vol. 1. Beijing: Renmin Chubanshe, 1981.

—— *Liu Shaoqi Lun Dang de Jianshe [Liao Shaoqi Discusses Party Building].* Beijing: Zhongyang Wenxian Chubanshe, 1991.

Lu Dingyi. *Lu Dingyi Wenji [Selected Works of Lu Dinyi].* Beijing: Renmin Chubanshe 1992.

Luo Ronghuan. *Luo Ronghuan Junshi Wenxuan.* http://cyc7.cycnet.com:8091/leaders/lrh/content.jsp?id=7324&s_code=1202

Ma Zhaojun, ed. *Zhongguo Renmin Jiefangjun Diyiye Zhangjun Zhengzhan Rizhi [Battle Log of the Chinese People's Liberation 1st Field Army].* Beijing: Zhongguo Renmin Jiefangjun Chubanshe, 2001.

Mao Zedong (Mao Tse-tung). *Selection of Mao-Tse-tung Works.* Vol. 2. Hong Kong: Union Research Institute 1961.

—— *Mao Tse-tung On War.* Dehra Dun: English Book Depot, 1966.

—— *Quotations from Chairman Mao Tse-tung.* Peking: Foreign Language Press 1966.

—— *Selected Military Writings of Mao Tse-tung.* Peking: Foreign Language Press, 1967.

—— *Mao Zedong Sixiang Wansui [Long Live Mao Zedong Thought]*. Peking: Foreign Language Press, 1969.

—— *On Revolution and War*. Garden City, NY: Doubleday, 1969.

—— *Selected Works of Mao Tse-Tung*. Vols. 3–4. Peking: Foreign Language Press, 1969.

—— "Mao Tse-tung's Oral Report to the Seventh Party Congress: Summary Notes (April 24, 1945)," *Chinese Law and Government* (Winter 1977–78), 10(4): 3–27.

—— *Mao Zedong Junshi Wenxuan (Neibuben) [Selected Military Writings of Mao Zedong, Internal Edition]*. Beijing: Zhongguo Renmin Jiefangjun Zhanshi Chubanshe, 1981.

—— *Mao Zedong Junshi Wenxuan [Selected Military Writings of Mao Zedong]*. Vol. 2: Anti-Japanese War Period and Vols 3, 4, 5: Liberation War Period. Beijing: Junshi Kexue Chubanshe and Zhongyang Wenxian Chubanshe, 1993.

Melby, John F. *The Mandate of Heaven: Record of a Civil War, China 1945–49*. Toronto: University of Toronto Press, 1968.

N.A., *Wenxuan yu Yanjiu* (Documents and Studies), No. 1, 1985.

Nathan, Andrew J. and Perry Link, ed. *Tiananmen Papers*. New York: Public Affairs, 2001.

Nie Rongzhen, *Nie Rongzhen Huiyilu [Recollections of Nie Rongzhen]*. Beijing: Jiefangjun Chubanshe, 1986.

—— *Inside the Red Star: Memoirs of Marshal Nie Rongzhen*. Zhong Renyi trans. Beijing: New World Press, 1988.

—— *Nie Rongzhen Junshi Wenxuan [Selected Military Works of Nie Rongzhen]*. Beijing: Jiefangjun Chubanshe, 1992.

Paddock, Paul. *China Diary: Crisis Diplomacy in Dairen*. Ames, IA: Iowa State University Press, 1977.

Peng Dehuai. *Peng Dehuai Zishu [Autobiographical Notes of Peng Dehuai]*. Beijing: Renmin Chubanshe, 1981.

—— *Memoirs of a Chinese Marshall: The Autobiographical Notes of Peng Dehuai, 1898–1974*. Zheng Longpu, trans. Beijing: Foreign Languages Press 1984.

—— *Peng Dehuai Zizhuan [Autobiography of Peng Dehuai]*. Beijing: Jiefangjun Wenyi Chubanshe, 2002.

—— *Peng Dehuai Junshi Wenxuan [Selected Military Works of Peng Dehuai]*. http://cyc7.cycnet.com:8091/leaders/pdh/content.jsp?id=5814&s_code=1003

Peng Guangqian and Zhao Haijun, eds. *Zhongguo Junshi Mingzhu Xuancui [Selections from Famous Chinese Military Texts]*. Beijing: Junshi Liaoxue Chubanshe, 2001.

Peng Meikui. *Wode Danfu Peng Dehuai [My Father, Peng Dehuai]*. Shenyang: Liaoning Renmin Chubanshe, 1997.

Peng Zhen. *Peng Zhen Wenxuan (1941–1990) [Selected Works of Peng Zhen]*. Beijing: Renmin Chubanshe, 1991.

Pi Dingjun. *Pi Dingjun Riji [Diary of Pi Dingjun]*. Beijing: Jiefangjun Chubanshe, 1986.

Ren Bishi. *Ren Bishi Xuanji [Selected Works of Ren Bishi]*. Beijing: Renmin Chubanshe, 1987.

Schram, Stuart R., ed. *[Mao Zedong's] Basic Tactics*. New York: Frederick A. Praeger, 1966.

—— *Mao Unrehearsed: Talks and Letters, 1956–71*. Harmondsworth, UK: Penguin Books, 1974.

Snow, Edgar. *Red Star Over China*. New York: Random House, 1938.

Su Yu. *Zhanzheng Huiyilu [War Memoirs]*. Beijing: Jiefangjun Chubanshe, 1988.

—— *Su Yu Junshi Wenxuan*. http://cyc90.cycnet.com/leaders/suyu/content.jsp?id=11193&s_code=2303

Suzhong Qizhan Qijie Bianxiezu [The Central Jiangsu "Seven Battles, Seven Victories" Editorial Group], ed. *Suzhong Qizhan Qijie [The Central Jiangsu Campaign – Seven Battles, Seven Victories]*. Nanjing: Jiangsu Renmin Chubanshe, 1986.

Tao Zhu. *Tao Zhu Wenji [Selected Works of Tao Zhu]*. Beijing: Renmin Chubanshe 1987.

Te-kong Tong and Li Tsung-jen. *The Memoirs of Li Tsung-jen*. Boulder, CO: Westview Press, 1979.

United States Department of State. *Foreign Relations of the United States: China 1945*. Vol. 1. Washington D.C.: United States Government Printing Office, 1955.

United States Department of State. *Foreign Relations of the United States: China 1946*. Vol. 1. Washington D.C.: United States Government Printing Office, 1955.

Xiao Jinguang. *Wang Jiaxiang Xuanji [Selected Works of Wang Jiaxiang]*. Beijing: Renmin Chubanshe, 1989.

—— *Xiao Jinguang Huiyilu [Recollections of Xiao Jinguang]*. Beijing: Jiefangjun Chubanshe, 1989.

Wang Ming. *Mao's Betrayal*. Vic Schneierson, trans. Moscow: Progress Publisher, 1975.

Wang Zhuanzhong, Xie Yulin, Ding Longjia, Gao Zhanwu and Liu Rufeng, eds. *Liu-Deng Dajun Qiang Du Huanghe Ziliaoxuan [Selected Material from the Great Liu Bocheng-Deng Xiaoping Army's Crossing of the Yellow River]*. Ji'nan: Shandong Daxue Chubanshe, 1987.

Wei Yanru, ed. *Zhang Wentian zai Hejiang [Zhang Wentian at Hejiang]*. Beijing: Zhonggongdang Shiziliao Chubanshe, 1990.

Weifang Dichu Chuban Bangongshi [Weifang District Publishing Office], ed. *Weixian Zhanyi Ziliao Xuan [Selected Material from the Weixian Campaign]*. Jinan: Shandong Renmin Chubanshe, 1982.

Wu Yuzhang. *Wu Yuzhang Wenxuan [Selected Works of Wu Yuzhang]*. Chongqing: Chongqing Chubanshe, 1987.

Xiao Jingguang. *Xiao Jingguang Huiyilu [Recollections of Xiao Jingguang]*. Beijing: Jiefangjun Chubanshe, 1989.

Xu Shiyou. *Xu Shiyou Huiyilu [Recollections of Xu Shiyou]*. Beijing: Jiefangjun Chubanshe, 1986.

Yang Botao. *Yang Botao Huiyilu [Recollections of Yang Botao]*. Beijing: Zhongguo Wenshi Chubanshe, 1996.

Yang Chengwu. *Yang Chengwu Huiyilu [Recollections of Yang Chengwu]*. Beijing: Jiefangjun Chubanshe, 1990.

Yang Dezhi. *Yang Dezhi Huiyilu [Recolllections of Yang Dezhi]*. Beijing: Jiefangjun Chubanshe, 1992.

Yang Guoning and Chen Feiqin, eds., *Liu-Deng Dajun Fengyunlu*. Vol. 1. Beijing: Renmin Ribao Chubanshe, 1983.

Yang Guoyu and Chen Feiqin, eds. *Liu-Deng Dajun Nanzheng Ji [Record of the Great Liu Bocheng-Deng Xiaoping Army's March South]*. Zhengzhou: Henan Renmin Chubanshe, 1982.

Zaozhuang Shi Chuban Bangongshi [Zaozhuang City Publishing Office], ed. *Lunan Zhanyi Ziliaoxuan [Selected Materials from the South Shandong Campaign]*. Jinan: Shandong Renmin Chubanshe, 1982.

Zeng Sheng. *Zeng Sheng Huiyilu [Recollections of Zeng Sheng]*. Beijing: Jiefangjun Chubanshe, 1991.

Zhang Wentian. *Zhang Wentian Xuanji [Selected Works of Zhang Wentian]*. Beijing: Renmin Chubanshe, 1985.

Zhang Zhizhong. *Zhang Zhizhong Huiyilu [Recollections of Zhang Zhizhong].* Beijing: Zhongguo Wenshi Chubanshe, 1985.

Zhang Zongxun. *Zhang Zongxun Huiyilu [Recollections of Zhang Zongxun].* Beijing: Jiefangjun Chubanshe, 1990.

Zhao Shigang, ed. *Chen Yun Tan Chen Yun [Chen Yun Discusses Chen Yun].* Beijing: Dangjian Duwu Chubanshe, 2001.

Zheng Dongguo. *Wode Rongma Shenya: Zheng Dongguo Huiyilu [My Military Record: Recollections of Zheng Dongguo].* Beijing: Tuanjie Chubanshe, 1992.

Zheng Weishan. *Cong Hubei dao Xibei – Yi Jiefang Zhanzheng [From Hubei to the Northwest – Recollecting the Liberation War].* Beijing: Jiefangjun Chubanshe, 1985.

Zhonggong Laiwuxian Weixuan Zhuanbu, ed. *Laiwu Zhanyi Ziliao Xuan [Selected Materials from the Laiwu Campaign].* Ji'nan: Shandong Renmin Chubanshe, 1982.

Zhonggong Shandong Sheng Weidangshi Ziliao Zhengji Yanjiu Weiyuanhui, Zhonggong Ji'nan Shi Weidangshi Ziliao Zhengji Yanjiu Weiyuanhui and Jinan Shi Bowuguan [Central Shandong Province Party Historical Research Committee Central Ji'nan City Party Historical Research Committee and Ji'nan City Museum], ed. *Ji'nan Zhanyi.* Jinan: Shandong Chubanshe, 1988.

Zhonggong Zhongyang Dangjiao Dangshi Jiaoyanshi [CCP Central Committee Party Historical Research Office], ed. *Zhonggongdang Shicankao Ziliao [Compiled Historical Data Concerning the CCP].* Vol. 6: The Third Revolutionary Civil War Period. Beijing: Renmin Chubanshe, 1979.

Zhonggong Zhongyang Dang Shiziliao Zhengji Weiyuanhui [CCP Central Committee Party Historical Material Collection Committee]. *Huaihai Zhanyi.* Vols. 1–3. Beijing: Zhonggong Dangshi Ziliao Chubanshe, 1988.

Zhonggong Zhongyang Dang Shiziliao Zhengji Weiyuanhui and Zhongguo Renmin Jiefangjun Dang'anguan [CCP Central Committee Party Historical Materials Compilation Committee and the Chinese People's Liberation Army Archive], eds. *Zhenzhong Riji.* Vols 1–2. Beijing: Zhonggongdang Shiziliao, 1987.

Zhonggong Zhongyang Dang Shiziliao Zhengji Weiyuanhui and Zhonggong Zhongyang Dangshi Yanjiushi [CCP Central Party Historical Material Committee and the CCP Central Party Historical Research Office], eds. *Zhonggongdang Shiziliao [CCP Historical Material].* Vols. 2, 10, 15, 16, 17, 19, 21, 22, 24, 26, 34. Beijing: Zhonggongdang Shiziliao Chubanshe, 1987.

Zhongguo Renmin Geming Junshi Bowuguan [Chinese People's Revolutionary Military Museum], ed. *He Long Yuanshuai Fengbei Yongcun: Zhongguo Renmin Geming Junshi Bowuguan Chenlie Wenxian Ziliaoxuan [A Perpetual Monument to Marshal He Long: Collected Materials from the Chinese People's Revolutionary Military Museum].* Shanghai: Renmin Chubanshe, 1985.

—— *Zhu De Yuanshuai Fengbei Yongcun: Zhongguo Renmin Geming Junshi Bowuguan Chenlie Wenxian Ziliaoxuan [A Perpetual Monument to Marshal Zhu De: Collected Materials from the Chinese People's Revolutionary Military Museum].* Shanghai: Renmin Chubanshe, 1986.

Zhongguo Renimn Jiefangjun Lishi Ziliao Congshu Bianshen Weiyuanhui, eds. *Xinsijun Huiyi Shiliao [New Fourth Army Documents].* Vol. 2. Beijing: Jiefangfjun Chubanshe, 1990.

Zhongguo Renmin Zhengzhi Xieshanghui Yiquanguo Weiyuanhui and Wenshi Ziliao Yanjiu Weiyuanhui [Chinese People's Political National Committee and the Historical Material Research Committee], eds. *Huaihai Zhanyi Qinliji (Yuan Guomindang Jiangling* de Huiyi) [The Huaihai Campaign – A Personal Record (Original Recollections of GMD Generals). Beijing: Wenshi Ziliao Chubanshe, 1983.

—— Pingjin Zhanyi Qinliji (Yuan Guomindang Jiangling de Huiyi) [The Pingjin Campaign – A Personal Record (Original Recollections of GMD Generals). Beijing: Wenshi Ziliao Chubanshe, 1989.

Zhongyang Chongqing Shi Weidangshi Gongzuo Weiyuanhui, Chongqing Shi Zhengxie Wenshi Ziliao Yanjiu Weiyuanhui and Hongyan Geming Jinianguan [Central Chongqing City Party Committee City Work Committee, Chongqing City Historical Material Research Committee and the Hongyang Revolutionary Memorial Hall], ed. *Chongqing Tanpan Jishi (August–October 1945).* Chongqing: Chongqing Chubanshe, 1983.

Zhongyang Yanjiuyuan, ed. *Zongtong Jiang Gongshi Shi Zhounian Jinian Lunwenji.* Taibei: Zhongyang Yanjiuyuan, 1976.

Zhongyuan Tuwei Jinian Wexuan Bianweihui. *Zhongyuan Tuwei Jinian Wenxuan (1946–1999) [Selected Works Commemorating the Central Plains Breakout].* No bibliographic data provided.

Zhou Enlai. *Selected Works of Zhou Enlai.* Beijing: Foreign Language Press, 1980.

—— *Zhou Enlai Junshi Wenxuan [Selected Military Works of Zhou Enlai].* Vols. 2–3. Beijing: Renmin Chubanshe, 1997.

Zhu De. *Selected Works of Zhu De.* Beijing: Foreign Language Press, 1986.

—— *Zhu De Xuanji [Selected Works of Zhu De].* Beijing: Renmin Chubanshe, 1986.

Official Histories

Cao Hong and Li Li. *Disanye Zhanjun [3rd Field Army].* Beijing: Guofang Daxue Chubanshe, 1996.

Cao Jianlang. *Guomindang Jun Jianshi [Concise History of the GMD Army].* Vols. 1–2. Beijing: Jiefangjun Chubanshe, 2004.

Chen Chaochou. *Liu Shaoqi Yanjiu Shuping [Commentaries of Research of Liu Shaoqi].* Beijing: Zhonggong Wenxian Chubanshe, 1997.

Chen Shaochou, Liu Chongwen and Zhonggong Zhongyang Wenxian Yanjiushi [CCP Central Committee Literature Office]. *Liu Shaoqi Nianpu [Chronicle of Liu Shaoqi].* Second Edition. Vols. 1, 2. Beijing: Zhonggong Zhongyang Wenxian Chubanshe, 1998.

Chen Shiping. *Zhongguo Yuanshuai [Chinese Marshal]: Liu Bocheng.* Beijing: Zhonggong Dangxiao Chubanshe, 1992.

Cheng Zhongyuan. *Zhang Wentian Zhuan [Biography of Zhang Wentian].* Beijing: Dangdai Zhongguo Chubanshe, 2000.

Dai Changle and Liu Lianhua, ed. *Disiye Zhanjun [Fourth Field Army].* Revised Edition. Beijing: Guofang Daxue Chubanshe, 1996.

Dai Qi and Peng Yikun. *Chen Geng Dajiang Zai Jiefang Zhanzheng Zhong [Chen Geng During the Liberation War].* Beijing: Jiefangjun Chubanshe, 1985

Fan Shuo. *Ye Jianying Zhuan [Chronicle of Ye Jianying].* Beijing: Dangdai Zhongguo Chubanshe, 1997.

Fu Kuiqing, Sun Keji and Miao Guoliang, eds. *Chen Yi Zhuan [Chronicle of Chen Yi].* Beijing: Dangdai Zhongguo Chubanshe, 1991.

Gu Baozi. *Xin Sijun Zhengzhan Jishi [War Record of the New 4th Army].* Vols. 1–2. Beijing: Jiefangjun Wenyi Chubanshe, 2001.

Guo Shengwei. *Deng Xiaoping Junshi Moulue [Deng Xiaoping's Military Strategy].* Zhongyang Wenxian Chubanshe, 2000.

Guofang Daxue [Defense University]. *A Brief History of the Chinese PLA Revolutionary War*. Beijing: Chinese People's Liberation Army Publishing House, 2001.

Hu Chiao-mu. *Thirty Years of the Communist Party of China*. Fourth Edition. Beijing: Foreign Languages Press, 1960.

Hu Qingyun. *Jiefang Zhanzheng Shiqi de Diertiao Zhanxian [The Liberation War's Second Front]*. Beijing: Guofang Daxue Chubanshe, 1999.

Hu Sheng. *A Concise History of the Communist Party of China*. Beijing: Foreign Language Press, 1994.

Hu Yongfeng and Liu Weiguo, eds. *Mao Zedong Junshi Zhihui Yishu [Mao Zedong's Art of Military Command]*. Beijing: Junshi Kexue Chubanshe, 1996.

Huang Jiren. *Jiangjun Juezhan Qizhi Zai Zhanchang [Generals Fight Decisive Battles Not Only on the Battlefield]*. Beijing: Jiefangjun Wenyi Chubanshe, 2002.

Huang Yao. *Luo Ronghuan Nianpu [Luo Ronghuan Chronicle]*. Beijing: Renmin Chubanshe, 2002.

Huang Yao and Zhang Mingzhe, eds. *Luo Ruiqing Zhuan [Chronicle of Luo Ruiqing]*. Beijing: Dangdai Zhongguo Chubanshe, 1996.

Jiang Feng and Ma Shaoqun, eds. *Yang Yong Jiangjun Zhuan [Chronicle of General Yang Yong]*. Beijing: Jiefangjun Chubanshe, 1992.

Jin Chongji and Huang Zheng, eds. *Liu Shaoqi Zhuan [Biography of Liu Shaoqi]*. Vols. 1–2. Beijing: Zhongyang Wenxian Chubanshe, 1998.

Jin Chongji and Zhonggong Zhongyang Wenxian Yanjiushi, eds. *Mao Zedong Zhuan [Biography of Mao Zedong (1893–1949)]*. Vol. 2. Beijing: Zhongyang Wenxian Chubanshe, 1996.

—— *Zhou Enlai Zhuan [Biography of Zhou Enlai]*. Vol. 2. Beijing: Zhongyang Wenxian Chubanshe, 1998.

—— *Zhu De Zhuan [Biography of Zhu De]*. Revised Edition. Beijing: Zhongyang Wenxian Chubanshe, 2000.

Junshi Kexueyuan [Military Science Institute]. *Pipan Lin Biao de "Liuge Zhanshu Yuance" [Criticizing Lin Biao's Six Tactical Principles*. Beijing: Junshi Kexueyuan, 1974.

Li Jinming. *Jinchaji Junmin Zhengzhan Jishi [War Record of the Shanxi-Chahar-Hebei Militia]*. Beijing: Jiefangjun Chubanshe, 2001.

Li Lie. *He Long Nianpu [Chronicle of He Longe]*. Beijing: Renmin Chubanshe, 1996.

Li Mancun, Chen Ying and Huang Yuzhang, eds. *Liu Bocheng Zhuan [Biography of Liu Bocheng*. Beijing: Dangdai Zhongguo Chubanshe, 1992.

Lian Youru. *Liu Bocheng yu Deng Xiaoping*. Beijing: Zhonggong Zhongyang Dangxiao Chubanshe, 1994.

Liaoshen Zhanyi Jinianguang Guanli Weiyuanhu and Liaoshen Juezhan Bianshen Xiaozu, eds. *Liaoshen Juezhan [Liaoshen: The Decisive Battle]*. Beijing: Renmin Chubanshe, 1992.

Liu Han. *Luo Ronghuan Zhuan [Biography of Luo Ronghuan]*. Beijing: Dangdai Zhongguo Chubanshe, 1997.

Liu Han, Huang Yao, Li Weimin, Pan Tianjia, Yang Guoqing, Bai Ren and Li Zhijing. *Luo Ronghuan Yuanshuai [Marshal Luo Ronghuan]*. Beijing: Jiefangjun Chubanshe, 1987.

Liu Jixian. *Lun Mao Zedong Junshi Sixiang [Discussing Mao Zedong's Military Thought]*. Beijing: Zhonggong Zhongyang Dangxiao Chubanshe, 2003.

Liu Shufa. *Chen Yi Nianpu [Chronicle of Chen Yi]*. Vol. 1. Beijing: Renmin Chubanshe 1998.

Liu Tianye, Xia Daoyuan, Fan Shushen, eds. *Li Tianyou Jiangjun Zhuan [Biography of Li Tianyou]*. Beijing: Jiefangjun Chubanshe, 1993.

Nanjing Junqu Disanye Zhanjun Zhanshi Bianjishi [Nanjing Military District Editorial Office of the War Record of the 3rd Field Army]. *Zhongguo Renmin Jiefangjun Disanye Zhanjun Zhanshi [War Record of the Chinese People's Liberation Army 3rd Field Army].* Nanjing: Jiefangjun Chubanshe, 1996.

Pan Shiying. *Dangdai Zhongguo Junshi Sixiang Jingyao [Contemporary Chinese Military Thought].* Beijing: Jiefangjun Chubanshe, 1992.

Shui Gong. *Zhongguo Yuanshuai [Chinese Marshal]: He Long.* Beijing: Zhonggong Dangxiao Chubanshe, 1995.

Sun Ebing and Shu Qiujin, eds. *Zhongguo Renmin Jiefang Jun Gaoji Jiangling Zhuan [Biographies of Chinese People's Liberation Army High Ranking Generals].* Vols. 1–12. Beijing: Jiefangjun Chubanshe, 2006.

Wang Daoping. *Zhenhan Shijie de Dajuezhan [A Decisive War that Shook the World].* Beijing: Jiefangjun Chubanshe, 1990.

Wang Dikang, Zhu Yuepeng, Liu Daoxin, Na Zhiyuan and Zhang Wenrong, eds. *Disi Yezhanjun Nanzheng Jishi [Record of the 4th Field Army in South China].* Beijing, Jiefangjun Chubanshe, 1993.

Wang Shangrong and Huang Xinyan. *He Long Zhuan [Biography of He Long].* Beijing: Dangdai Zhongguo Chubanshe, 1997.

Wang Yan, ed. *Peng Dehuai Zhuan [Biography of Peng Dehuai].* Beijing: Dangdai Zhongguo Chubanshe, 1997.

Wang Yongchun, ed. *Baqianli Lu Zhui Qiongkou: Chen Geng Bingtuan Nanzheng Qinliji [Personal Recollections of Cheng Geng's Army in South China].* Beijing: Junshi Kexue Chubanshe, 2003.

Wang Yuntai, ed. *Chen Geng Zhuan [Biography of Cheng Geng].* Beijing: Zhongguo Dangdai Chubanshe, 2003.

Wang Zhen Zhuan Bianxie [Compiling Team of the Biography of Wang Zhen]. *Wang Zhen Zhuan [Biography of Wang Zhen].* Vol. 1. Beijing: Zhongguo Dangdai Chubanshe, 1999.

Wang Zhongxing and Liu Liqin, eds. *Dierye Zhanjun [2nd Field Army].* Revised Edition. Beijing: Guofang Daxue Chubanshe, 1996.

Wei Bihai. *Balujun Yiyiwu Shi Zhengzhan Jishi [War Record of the 8th Route Army's 115th Division].* Beijing: Jiefangjun Wenyi Chubanshe, 2001.

—— *Disiye Zhanjun Zhengzhan Jishi [War Record of the 4th Field Army].* Beijing: Jiefangjun Wenyi Chubanshe, 2001.

Xinhuo Liaoyuan Editorial Division. *Jiefangjun Jiangling Zhuan [Biographies of PLA Generals].* Vols. 1–7. Beijing: PLA Press, 1988.

Xu Fenglan and Zheng Efei. *Chen Geng Jiangjun Zhuan [Biography of General Chen Geng].* Beijing: Jiefangjun Chubanshe, 1988.

Yang Guoqing and Bai Ren. *Luo Ronghuan zai Dongbei Jiefang Zhanzheng Zhong [Luo Ronghuan in the Northeast during the Liberation War].* Beijing: Jiefangjun Chubanshe, 1986.

Yang Wanqing and Liu Chunyan. *Liu Yalou Jiangjun Zhuan [Biography of General Liu Yalou].* Beijing: Zhonggong Dangshi Chubanshe, 1995.

Yu Jianting. *Chen Yun yu Dongbei de Jiefang [Chen Yun and the Liberation of the Northeast].* Beijing: Zhongyang Wenxian Chubanshe, 1998.

Zhai Weijia and Cao Hong. *Zhongguo Xiongshi: Disiye Zhanjun [China's Mighty Army: The 4th Field Army].* Beijing: Zhonggong Dangshi Chubanshe, 1996.

Zhang Lin and Ma Zhangzhi. *Zhongguo Yuanshuai: Xu Xiangqian [Chinese Marshal: Xu Xiangqian].* Beijing: Zhonggong Dangxiao Chubanshe, 1995.

Zhang Shiming. *Zhuangyan Dianxin [High Quality Exemplar]: Liu Bocheng*. Beijing: Zhongyang Wenxian Chubanshe, 2001.

—— *Zhuangyan Dianxin [High Quality Exemplar]: Nie Rongzhen*. Beijing: Zhongyang Wenxian Chubanshe, 2001.

Zhang Weiliang. *Hebei Jiefangzhan Zhengshi [History of Hebei During the Liberation War]*. Beijing: Jiefangjun Chubanshe, 2002.

Zhonggong Zhongyang Wenxian Yanjiushi. *Zhu De Nianpu [Chronicle of Zhu De]*. Beijing: Renmin Chubanshe, 1986.

—— *Mao Zedong Nianpu [Chronicle of Mao Zedong]*. Beijing: Zhongyang Wenxian Chubanshe, 1989.

—— *Zhou Enlai Nianpu (1898–1949) [Chronicle of Zhou Enlai]*. Revised Edition. Beijing: Zhongyang Wenxian Chubanshe, 1998.

Zhongguo Renmin Jiefangjun Junshi Kexueyuan. *Zhongguo Renmin Jiefangjun Dashiji (1927–1982) [The Great History of the China's People's Liberation Army]*. Beijing: Junshi Kexue Chubanshe, 1984.

—— *Zhongguo Renmin Jiefangjun Qishi Quanshi [70 Years Chronicle of the Chinese People's Liberation Army]*. Vols. 2, 5. Beijing: Junshi Kexue Chubanshe, 2000.

Zhu Ying. *Su Yu Zhuan [Biography of Su Yu]*. Beijing: Dangdai Zhongguo Chubanshe, 2000.

Secondary Sources

Apter, David E. and Tony Saich. *Revolutionary Discourse in Mao's Republic*. Cambridge, MA: Harvard University Press, 1994.

Barbey, Daniel. *MacArthur's Amphibious Navy*. Annapolis: Naval Academy Press, 1969.

Barnett, A. Doak. "Multiple Factors," in Pichon P.Y. Loh, ed. *The Kuomintang Debacle of 1949: Conquest or Collapse?* Boston: D.C. Heath and Company, 1965, pp. 7–13.

Beal, John Robinson. *Marshall in China*. New York: Doubleday & Company, Inc., 1970.

Becker, Jasper. *Hungry Ghosts: Mao's Secret Famine*. New York: The Free Press, 1996.

Benton, Gregor. *New Fourth Army: Communist Resistance Along the Yangtze and the Huai 1938–1941*. Berkeley: University of California Press, 1999.

van Binneken, Jaap. *The Rise and Fall of Lin Piao*. New York: Penguin Books, 1976.

Boorman, Scott A. *The Protracted Game: A Wei-Chi Interpretation of Maoist Revolutionary Strategy*. New York: Oxford University Press, 1969.

Carlson, Evans Fordyce. *Twin Stars of China*. New York: Dodd, Mead, 1940.

Chai Hongxia. *Su Yu*. Beijing: Zuojia Chubanshe, 1997.

Chassin, Lionel. *The Communist Conquest of China: A History of the Civil War, 1945–1949*. Timothy Osato and Louis Gelas, trans. Cambridge, MA: Harvard University Press, 1965.

Chen Jian. *China's Road to the Korean War: The Making of the Sino-American Confrontation*. New York: Columbia University Press, 1994.

—— *Mao's China and the Cold War*. Chapel Hill: University of North Carolina Press, 2001.

Chen, King C., ed. *The Foreign Policy of China*. Roseland, NJ: Seton Hall University Press, 1972.

Chen Yu, ed. *36 Strategists of the People's Republic of China*. Shanghai: Shanghai Wenyi Chubanshe, 2002.

Cheng Siyuan. *Bai Chongxi Zhuan [Biography of Bai Chongxi*. Beijing: Huayi Chubanshe, 1995.

Chou Chi-p'ing, "Comrade Lin Piao in the Period of Liberation War in the Northeast," *Zhongguo Qingnian (Chinese Youth)*, April 16, 1960, p. 26.

von Clausewitz, Carl. *On War*. Michael Howard and Peter Paret, trans., eds. Princeton: Princeton University Press, 1984.

Clubb, Edmund O. "Chiang Kai-shek's Waterloo: The Battle for Hwai[Huai]-Hai," *Pacific Historical Review*, 25:4, November 1956.

Coor, Gerard H. *The Chinese Red Army: Campaigns and Politics Since 1949*. New York: Schocken Books, 1974.

Dai Qing. *Wild Lilies*. Nancy Liu and Lawrence R. Sullivan, trans. Armonk, NY: M.E. Sharpe, 1994.

Dan Xiufa. *Mao Zedong Yu Zhou Enlai*. Beijing: Beijing Chubanshe, 1998.

Deng Liqun. *Mao Zedong Junshi Zhanluejia [Mao Zedong Military Strategist]*. Beijing: Zhongyang Minzu Daxue Chubanshe, 2004.

Domes, Jurgen. *Peng Te-huai: The Man and the Image*. London: C. Hurst & Company, 1985.

Dong Dianwen. *Juezhan Liaoshen [Liaoshen: The Decisive Battle]*. Shenyang: Liaoning Renmin Chubanshe, 1998.

—— *Tingjin Dongbei [Advancing into Northeast]*. Shenyang: Liaoning Renmin Chubanshe, 1998.

Dreyer, Edward L. *China at War*. London: Longman Group Ltd, 1995.

Dreyer, June Teufel. "Deng: The Soldier," *China Quarterly*, 0:135 Special Issue: Deng Xiaoping: An Assessment (Sept 1993), pp. 536–40.

Eastmann, Lloyd. *Seeds of Destruction: Nationalist China in War and Revolution, 1937–1949*. Stanford: Stanford University Press, 1984.

—— *The Abortive Revolution: China Under Nationalist Rule, 1927–1937*. Cambridge: Harvard University Press, 1990.

Elliott-Bateman, Michael. *Defeat in the East: The Mark of Mao Tse-tung on War*. London: Oxford University Press, 1967.

Erbaugh, Mary S. "Secret History of the Hakkas: The Chinese Revolution as a Hakka Enterprise," *China Quarterly*, No. 132, (Dec. 1992), pp. 937–68.

Evans, Richard. *Deng Xiaoping and The Making of Modern China*. New York: Viking, 1993.

Fang, Percy Jucheng and Lucy Guinong J. Fang. *Zhou Enlai – A Profile*. Beijing: Foreign Language Press, 1986.

Fang Zhu. *Gun Barrel Politics: Party-Army Relations in Mao's China*. Boulder, CO: Westview Press, 1998.

Fraser, Angus M. *The People's Liberation Army: Communist China's Armed Forces*. New York: Crane, Russak & Company, 1973.

Fu Jianwen. *Balujun Yierjiu Shi Zhengzhan Jishi [War Record of the 8th Route Army's 129th Division]*. Beijing: Jiefangjun Wenyi Chubanshe, 2001.

Fu Jing, Tie Jun and Xuan Cun. *Siye 1949 [The Fourth Field Army, 1949]*. Jinan: Huanghe Chubanshe, 2001.

Furuya, Keiji. *Chiang Kai-shek His Life and Times*. Chun-ming Chang, trans. New York: St John's University, 1981.

Gao Qing and Zeng Qingke. *Huang Kecheng*. Beijing: Zuojia Chubanshe, 1997.

Graf, David A. *Medieval Chinese Warfare, 300–900*. New York: Routledge, 2002.

Griffith, Samuel B. *The Chinese People's Liberation Army*. New York: McGraw-Hill Book Company, 1967.

Gurtov, Melvin and Byong Moo Hwang. *China Under Threat: The Politics of Strategy and Diplomacy*. Baltimore: Johns Hopkins University Press, 1980.

Handel, Michael I. *Masters of War: Sun Tzu, Clausewitz, and Jomini*. Portland, OR: Frank Cass, 1992.

Hanson, Victor Davis. *Western Way of War: The Infantry Battle in Classical Greece*. Berkeley: University of California Press, 2000.

—— *Carnage and Culture: Landmark Battles in the Rise of Western Power*. New York: Doubleday, 2001.

He Dong and Chen Mingxian. *Beiping Heping Jiefang Kaimo [The Peaceful Liberation of Beiping from the Beginning to the End]*. Beijing: Jiefangjun Chubanshe, 1958.

Hu, Chi-hsi "Mao, Lin Biao and the Fifth Encirclement Campaign," *China Quarterly*, June 1980, pp. 250–80.

Jencks, Harlan W. *From Muskets to Missiles: Politics and Professionalism in the Chinese Army, 1945–1981*. Boulder, CO: Westview Press, 1982.

Jiang Hongbin. *Chen Yi – Cong Shijiazi Dao Yuanshuai [Chen Yi From Man of the World to Marshal]*. Shanghai: Shanghai Renmin Chubanshe, 1992.

Jiangsu Sheng Xinsijun he Huazhong Kangri Genjudi Yanjiuhui and Zhongguo Gongchandang Nantongshi Weidangshi Gongzuo Weiyuanhui [Jiangsu New 4th Army and Central China Japanese Resistance Base and CCP Nantong City Party History Work Committee], eds. *Su Yu yu Suzhong [Su Yu in Central Jiangsu]*. Nanjing: Nanjing Daxue Chubanshe, 1995.

Jin Ye, Hu Jucheng, Hu Zhaocai. *Xu Shiyou Zhuan*. Shanghai: Shanghai Renmin Chubanshe, 2000.

Johnson, Chalmers. *Peasant Nationalism and Communist Power: The Emergence of Revolutionary China*. Stanford: Stanford University Press, 1967.

Johnston, Alastair Iain. *Cultural Realism: Strategic Culture and Grand Strategy in Chinese History*. Princeton, NJ: Princeton University Press, 1995.

—— "Thinking About Strategic Culture," *International Security*, 19:4 (Spring 1995), pp. 32–64.

Jones, Archer. *Elements of Military Strategy: An Historical Approach*. Westport, CT: Praeger, 1996.

Kampen, Thomas. "Wang Jiaxiang, Mao Zedong and the 'Triumph of Mao Zedong-Thought' (1935–1945)," *Modern Asian Studies*, 23:4, 1989, pp. 705–27.

Kataoka, Tetsuya. *Resistance and Revolution in China*. Berkeley, University of California Press, 1974.

Keegan, John. *History of Warfare*. New York: Knopf, 1993.

Kierman, Jr., Frank A. and John K. Fairbank, ed. *Chinese Ways in Warfare*. Cambridge, MA: Harvard University Press, 1974.

Laqueur, Walter. *Guerrilla: A Historical and Critical Study*. Boston: Little, Brown and Company, 1976.

Lary, Diana and Stephen MacKinnon. *Scars of War: The Impact of Warfare on Modern China*. Toronto: University of British Columbia Press, 2001.

Lee, Ching Hua. *Deng Xiaoping: The Marxist Road to the Forbidden City*. Princeton: The Kingston Press, Inc., 1985.

Leng Jiefu. *Dujiang Zhanyi [The Yangtze River Crossing Campaign]*. Fuzhou: Fujian Renmin Chubanshe, 1985.

Leng Jiefu and Beijing Guangbao Xueyuan [Beijing Broadcasting College]. *Huaihai Zhanyi [The Huaihai Campaign]*. Fuzhou: Fujian Renmin Chubanshe, 1982.

Lescot, Patrick. *Before Mao*. New York: HarperCollins Books, 2004.

Levine, Stephen. *Anvil of Victory*. New York: Columbia University Press, 1987.

Lewis, Mark Edward. *Sanctioned Violence in Ancient China*. Albany: State University of New York Press, 1990.

Li Jianguo. *Huaihai Zhanyi Yanjiu [Research on the Huaihai Campaign]*. Changsha: Hunan Renmin Chubanshe, 2002.

Li Shixin. *Lin Biao de Junlu Shengya [Lin Biao's Military Life]*. Hohot: Nei Menggu Renmin Chubanshe, no date.

Li Xinzhi and Wang Yuezong, eds. *Weida de Shijian, Guanghui de Sixiang [Great Events, Glorious Thought]*. Beijing: Hualing Chubanshe, 1990.

Li Yu and Wen Ming. *Yiye Shi Da Zhuli Chuanqi [Biographies of Ten Important Figures in the 1st Field Army]*. Jinan: Huanghe Chubanshe, 2000.

Liang Hsi-huey. *Sino-German Connection: Alexander von Falkenhausen between China and Germany 1900–1941*. Assen: Van Gorcum, 1978.

Liao Gailong. *Quanguo Jiefang Zhanzheng Jianshi [History of the Liberation War in the Entire Country]*. Shanghai: Shanghai Renmin Chubanshe, 1984.

Liu Bocheng Yuanshuai Jiuju Chenlieguan Choujian Lingdao Xiaozu and Liu Bocheng Yuanshui Yanjiu Congshu Bianjishi [Controlling Group of the Effort to Establish Marshal Liu Bocheng's Ancestral Home Exhibition Hall and the Editorial Office of the Research on Marshal Liu Bocheng Volume], eds. *Liu Bocheng Yuanshuai Yanjiu [Research on Marshal Liu Bocheng]*. Vols. 1–2. Chongqing: Chongqing Chubanshe, 1987.

Liu, F.F. "Defeat by Military Default," in Pichon P.Y. Loh, ed. *The Kuomintang Debacle of 1949: Conquest or Collapse?* Boston: D.C. Heath and Company, 1965, pp. 1–6.

Liu Huamian and Dan Xiufa. *Mao Zedong Junshi Bianzhengfa Sixiang Yanjiu [Introduction to Research on the Dialectics of Mao Zedong Military Thought]*. Wuhan: Hubei Renmin Chubanshe, 1984.

Liu Jianwei. *Zongheng Tianxia: Disiye Zhanjun Zhengzhan Jishi [History of the 4th Field Army]*. Beijing: Huaxia Chubanshe, 2002.

Liu Tianhe. *Xiao Jingguang*. Beijing: Zuojia Chubanshe, 1997.

Liu Tong. *Dongbei Jiefang Zhanzheng Jishi [Record of the Liberation War in the Northeast]*. Beijing: Dongfang Chubanshe, 1997.

—— *Huadong Jiefang Zhanzheng Jishi [Record of the Liberation War in East China]*. Beijing: Dongfang Chubanshe, 1998.

—— *Zhongyaun Jiefang Zhanzheng Jishi [Record of the Liberation War in the Central Plains]*. Beijing: Dongfang Chubanshe, 2003.

Loh, Pichon P.Y., ed. *The Kuomintang Debacle of 1949: Conquest or Collapse?* Boston: D.C. Heath and Company, 1965.

Meisner, Maurice. *Mao's China and After*. New York: Free Press, 1999.

Mu Xin. *Chen Geng Dajiang [General Cheng Geng]*. Beijing: Xinhua Chubanshe, 1985.

Nelson, Harvey. *Chinese Military System: An Organizational Study of the Chinese People's Liberation Army*. 2nd ed. Boulder, CO: Westview Press, 1981.

N.A. *Peng Dehuai Zhengqi Zhiyan Dajiangjun [Peng Dehuai – A General of Unyielding Integrity Who Speaks Bluntly]*. http://cyc7.cycnet.com:8091/leaders/pdh/content. jsp?id=5814&s_code=1003

Pepper, Suzanne. *Civil War in China: The Political Struggle, 1945–1949*. Revised Edition. New York: Rowman & Littlefield Publishers, Inc., 1999.

Rice, Edward. *Mao's Way*. Berkeley: University of California Press, 1972.

Said, Edward. *Orientalism*, New York: Vintage Books, 1994.

Saitoh, Tatushi. "Public Security Operations of the Kwantung Army in Manchuria." Unpublished Manuscript presented at the 2007 Japanese-American Military History Exchange, 2007.

Sawyer, Ralph D., ed. *Seven Military Classics of China*. Boulder, CO: Westview Press 1993.

—— *The Tao of War*. Boulder, CO: Westview, 1999.

Schram, Stuart R. *The Political Thought of Mao Zedong*. New York: Praeger, 1969.

—— *The Thought of Mao Tse-tung*. New York: Cambridge University Press, 1989.

Selden, Mark. *The Yenan Way in Revolutionary China*. Cambridge, MA: Harvard University Press, 1971.

Shang Jinsuo and Pang Changfu. *Mao Zedong Junshi Sixiang Yanjiu [Research on Mao Zedong's Military Thought]*. Kaifeng: Hebei Renmin Chubanshe, 1985.

Shao Hua and You Hu. *Lin Biao de Zheyisheng [Lin Biao's Life]*. Wuhan: Hubei Chubanshe, 1994.

Shao Weizheng, Wang Pu and Liu Jianying. *Zhongguo Renmin Jiefangjun Shijian Renwulu [Record of Critical Events and People in the History of the PLA]*.Shanghai: Shanghai Renmin Chubanshe, 1988.

Shi Zhenhong. *Weizhen Huadong [The Great Shock in East China]*. Beijing: Changzheng Chubanshe, 2000.

Stueck, William. *The Wedemeyer Mission: American Politics and Foreign Policy during the Cold War*. Athens, GA: The University of Georgia Press, 1984.

Sun Shuyan. *The Long March: The True History of Communist China's Founding Myth*. New York: Doubleday, 2006.

Sun Tunfan. *Zhongguo Gongchandang Lishi Jiangyi [Teaching Materials on the History of the Chinese Communist Party]*. Vol. 2. Jinan: Shandong Renmin Chubanshe, 1983.

Sun Zhaiwei. *Jiang Jieshi de Chong Jiang Chen Cheng [Chiang Kai-shek's Favorite General Chen Cheng]*. Zhengzhou: Henan Renmin Chubanshe, 1990.

Tang Tsou. *America's Failure in China, 1941–50*. Chicago: The University of Chicago Press, 1963.

Tao Hanzhang. *The Modern Chinese Interpretation of Sun Tzu's Art of War*. Yuan Shibing, trans. New York: Sterling Publishing Co., Inc., 2000.

Teiwes, Frederick C. "Mao and his Lieutenants," *The Australian Journal of Chinese Affairs*, No. 19/20 (Jan–Jul 1988), pp. 1–88.

Teiwes, Frederick C. and Warren Sun. *The Tragedy of Lin Biao: Riding the Tiger During the Cultural Revolution, 1966–1971*. Honolulu: University of Hawaii Press, 1996.

Tuchman, Barbara. *Stilwell and the American Experience in China*. New York: Macmillan, 1970.

Waldron, Arthur. *The Great Wall: From History to Myth*. New York: Cambridge University Press 1990.

—— "The Battle of the Northeast," in Robert Cowley, *What If?: The World's Foremost Military Historians Imagine What Might Have Been*. New York: G.P. Putnam's Sons, 1999.

Wang Chaoguang. *Zhonghua Minguo Shi (Cong Kangzhan Shengli dao Neizhan Baofa Qianhou) [The History of Republican China (From Victory in the War of Resistance to the Beginning of the Civil War)]*. 3rd Edition. Beijing: Zhonghua Shuju, 2000.

Wang Fusheng and Wang Fan. *Mao Zedong yu He Long*. Beijing: Beijing Chubanshe, 1998.

Wang Hongyun and Zheng Jian. *Nie Rongzhen yu Fu Zuoyi*. Beijing: Huawen Chubanshe, 1999.

Wang Meizhi and Zhao Jing. *Chen Geng*. Beijing: Zuojia Chubanshe, 1997.

Wang Qinsheng. *Zhongguo Jiefang Zhanzheng [China's Liberation War]*. Beijing: Jiefangjun Wenyi Chubanshe, 2000.

Wang Shigen. *Liu-Deng Dajun Tingjin Dabieshan [The Liu Bocheng-Deng Xiaoping Army's March to the Dabie Mountains]*. Shanghai: Shanghai Renmin Chubanshe, 1987.

Wang Xiang. *Yan Xishan yu Jinxi [Yan Xishan and Western Shanxi]*. Nanjing: Jiangsu Guji Chubanshe, 1999.

Wang Zhenhua. *Yan Xishan Zhuan [Biography of Yan Xishan]*. Vol. 2. Beijing: Tuanjie Chubanshe, 1998.

Wei Bai. *Sanye Shida Dujiang Zhuanqi [History of the 3rd Field Army's Crossing the Yangtze]*. Ji'nan: Huanghe Chubanshe, 1999.

Wei Li and Lucian W. Pye. "The Ubiquitous Role of the Mishu in Chinese Politics," *China Quarterly*, No. 132 (Dec 1992), pp. 913–36.

Wen Si, ed. *Wo Suozhidao de Du Yuming [The Du Yuming I Knew]*. Beijing: Zhongguo Wenshi Chubanshe, 2003.

—— *Wo Suozhidao de Hu Zongnan [The Hu Zongnan I Knew]*. Beijing: Zhongguo Wenshi Chubanshe, 2003.

—— *Wo Suozhidao de Yan Xishan. [The Yan Xishan I Knew]* Beijing: Zhongguo Wenshi Chubanshe, 2003.

Westad, Odd Arne. *Decisive Encounters: The Chinese Civil War, 1946–1950*. Stanford: Stanford University Press, 2003.

Wetzel, Carroll R. Jr. *From the Jaws of Defeat: Lin Biao and the 4th Field Army in Manchuria*. Unpublished dissertation, JMU.

Whiting, Allen S. "The Use of Force in Foreign Policy by the People's Republic of China," *The Annals of American Academy of Political and Social Science*, 402, pp. 55–66.

Whitson, William W. *The Chinese High Command: A History of Communist Military Politics, 1927–71*. New York: Praeger Publishers, 1973.

Whitson, William W. and Chen-Hsia Huang. *Civil War in China, 1946–1950*. Vols. 1–2. Washington, D.C.: Office of Military History, US Army, 1967.

Wilson, Dick. *Zhou Enlai: A Biography*. New York: Viking, 1984.

Woodward, Dennis. "Political Power and Gun Barrels – The Role of the PLA," in Bill Brugger, *China: The Impact of the Cultural Revolution*. New York: Barnes & Noble Books, 1978, pp. 71–94.

Wortzel, Larry M. *Dictionary of Contemporary Chinese Military History*. Westport, CT: Greenwood Press, 1999.

Yang, Benjamin. "The Zunyi Conference as One Step in Mao's Rise to Power: A Survey of Historical Studies of the Chinese Communist Party," *China Quarterly*, No. 106 (June 1986), pp. 235–71.

—— "The Making of a Pragmatic Communist, 1904–1949," *China Quarterly*, 0:135, Special Issue: Deng Xiaoping: An Assessment (Sept. 1993), p. 444–56.

Yang Guoyu, Chen Feiqin and Wang Zhuanhong, eds. *Deng Xiaoping Ershiba Nianjian [Twenty Years Record of Deng Xiaoping]*. Beijing: Zhongguo Zhuoyue Chubanshe, 1989.

Yang Guoyu, Chen Feiqin, Li Anming and Wang Wei. *Liu Bocheng Junshi Shengya [Liu Bocheng's Military Life]*. Beijing: Zhongguo Qingnian Chubanshe, 1982.

Yick, Joseph K.S. *Making Urban Revolution in China: The CCP–GMD Struggle for Beiping-Tianjin 1945–1949*. London: M.E. Sharpe, 1995.

Yuan Dejin. *Mao Zedong yu Chen Yi*. Beijing: Beijing Chubanshe, 1998.

Yuan Dejin and Liu Zhenhua. *Huabei Jiefang Zhanzheng Jishi [A Record of the War of Liberation in North China]*. Beijing: Renmin Chubanshe, 2003.

—— *Xibei Jiefang Zhanzheng Jishi [A Record of the War of Liberation in the Northwest]*. Beijing: Renmin Chubanshe, 2003.

Zeng Fanguang. *Zhongguo Geming Shibiaojie [A Record of Significant Events of the Chinese Revolution].* Changsha: Hunan Renmin Chubanshe, 1988.

Zhang Ping, Yang Jun, Lu Ying and Qiao Xizhang. *Jiefang Zhanzheng Shihua [Significant Events of the Liberation War].* Beijing: Zhongguo Qingnian Chubanshe, 1987.

Zhao Jianping, Li Xiaochun and Kang Xiaofeng. *Luo Ruiqing.* Beijing: Zuojia Chubanshe, 1997.

Zhao Qinxuan. *Shenyang 1948.* Beijing: Junshi Kexue Chubanshe, 1997.

Zhao Yihong. *Su Yu Chuanqi [Biography of Su Yu].* Chengdu: Chengdu Chubanshe, 1995.

Zheng Bo and Xiao Sike. *Dajiang Huang Kecheng [General Huang Kecheng].* Beijing: Jiefangjun Wenyi Chubanshe, 2000.

Zheng Naicang and Wang Nan. *Su Yu Dajiang [General Su Yu].* Second Edition. Zhengzhou: Haiyan Chubanshe, 1990.

Zhengxie Jilin Shi Weiyuanhui Wenxhiziliao Yanjiu Weiyuanhui Bangongshi [Office of the Jilin City Political Committee's Historical Material Research Committee], ed. *Changchun Qiyi Jishi [Record of the Changchun Garrison Defection].* Jilin: Jilin Wenshi Chubanshe, 1987.

Zhengzhou Shi Huaihai Zhanyi Shi, ed. *Huaihai Zhanyi Shi [History of the Huaihai Campaign].* Shanghai: Shanghai Renmin Chubanshe, 1987.

Zhong Zhaoyun. *Baizhan Jiangxing [A General of a Hundred Battles]: Liu Yalou.* Beijing: Jiefangjun Wenyi Chubanshe, 1996.

Zhongguo Renmin Jiefangjun Ji'nan Junqu Zhengshibu and Ji'nan Zhanyi Zhong Wu Huawen Qiyi Bianxie [Chinese People's Liberation Army Ji'nan Military District Political Office and "Wu Huawen's Defection during the Ji'nan Campaign" Editorial Group], eds. *Ji'nan Zhanyi zhong Wu Huawen Qiyi [The Wu Huawen Uprising during the Ji'nan Campaign].* Ji'nan: Shandong Renmin Chubanshe, 1987.

Zhongguo Renmin Zhengzhi Xieshanghuiyi Quanguo Weiyuanhui and Wenshi Ziliao Yanjiu Weiyuanhui, eds. *Fu Zuoyi Jiangjun [General Fu Zuoyi].* Beijing: Zhongguo Wenshi Chubanshe, 1993.

Zhongguo Xiandai Gemingshi Ziliao Congkan. *Disanci Guonei Geming Zhanzheng Gaikuang [Summary of the Third Revolutionary Civil War].* Revised Edition. Beijing: Renmin Chubanshe, 1983 (orig. 1954).

Zhu Jianhua. *Dongbei Jiefang Zhengshi [History of the Liberation of Northeast China].* Harbin: Heilongjiang Renmin Chubanshe, 1987.

Index

115th Division 9–11
120th Division 11
129th Division 11–12, 17
18th Group Army 2, 5, 9
1st Field Army 132
1st Front Army 10
2nd Field Army 132
2nd Front Army 8
2nd Pacification District/Zone 50, 116
4th Field Army 131–2
4th Front Army 6, 12
5th Division 4
5th Encirclement Campaign 9, 14
8th Route Army 2, 4–5, 8–9, 12
Anhui, debate over attack on 42–3, 45–7
April 12th Incident 6–7, 12
Autumn Offensive 87–8, 91, 94

Bai Chongxi 85, 97–8; evacuation of
    132; and Huaihai Campaign 117; and
    overthrow of Chiang Kaishek 122; in
    Yangtze River Crossing campaign 131
battles of annihilation 25, 71, 90–1, 103
Beijing (Beiping): American headquarters
    in 33; renamed by CCP 128; seized by
    GMD 19
Beiping Campaign 107
Beiping-Suiyuan Front Committee 125–6
Binghai Detachment 18
Bo Yibo 123, 147

Cai Ao 6
CCP (Chinese Communist Party): 7th
    Congress 1–3, 5, 10–11; 1945–46
    counterattack 51; administration of
    northeast 27–8; bid for the northeast
    20–1, 26–7; defections to GMD 86–7;
    evolution of strategy 38; leadership
    of 6, 14–15, 141; losses at First

Battle of Siping 37; outlawed 74;
    professionalization of army 108; reasons
    for victory 134–5, 140–1; relations with
    Moscow 136; reorganization of army
    103, 129; response to General Offensive
    44; Second Plenum of 7th Congress
    129; separation of forces 56; size of 1–2;
    strategic position of 3, 73; truce with
    GMD 34
Central China Field Army: in Central
    Jiangsu Campaign 43, 45–8; eliminated
    in General Offensive 50; organization
    of 32
Central Committee of CCP: move into
    Beijing 133; structure of 6
Central Jiangsu Campaign 45, 47
Central Plains Bureau 77, 97, 101, 174–5
Central Plains Counteroffensive 94, 97,
    101, 138
Central Plains Field Army: capture of
    Xiangyang 106; in Central Plains
    counteroffensive 83, 85, 97–100;
    formation of 81; in Huaihai Campaign
    118–19, 121; renamed 2nd Field Army
    129; in Wandong Campaign 105
Central Plains Military District: attacked
    by GMD 41; formation of 24, 32
Changchun: captured by Du Yuming
    37; CCP siege of 109–10; first CCP
    takeover of 36; in Three Large Cities
    strategy 28
Chen Cheng: in Autumn Offensive 88;
    campaigns in Northeast 87; in Winter
    Offensive 94–6
Chen Geng 52–3, 99; in Central Plains
    counteroffensive 84; in Central Plains
    offensive 98; in defense of Yan'an 63; in
    Shanxi 52–3; see also "two Chens"
Chen Linda 95

Chen Shiju 78, 99, 106; breaching chain of command 56–7; in Chen-Tang Army 78, 83; in Huaihai Campaign 119; in Strong Point Offensive 60; *see also* "two Chens"

Chen-Tang Army 78, 80

Chen-Xie Army 84, 94

Chen Xilian 104

Chen Yi: attack on Xuzhou 18; in Central Plains counteroffensive 75–6, 78, 82–3, 98, 101; in East China Military District 48–9; in General Front Committee 130; and Huaihai Campaign 117; move to Shandong 24; in New 4th Army 13–14; in North Jiangsu Campaign 50; and push south 98; relations with Mao 144–5; response to General Offensive 43, 45–6; at Shandong 32–3, 37, 47–8; in Shandong 32–3, 37; and Strong Point Offensive 56–9; in Yangtze River Crossing campaign 131

Chen Yun: after victory 147; in Northeast Bureau 20, 29; promotion of 38; strategy of 54; and Summer Offensive 66, 71; and Three Large Cities Strategy 30

Cheng Zihua 20, 87, 110

Chengde 33, 35, 40, 53–4, 94

Chiang Kaishek: agreement to Marshall truce 37; attack on liberated areas 31–2; attack on Manchuria 26; betrayal of CCP 6; criticisms of 135–6; drafting of new constitution 54; interference with chain of command 111–12, 116, 118; intervention in Autumn Offensive 91; and October 10 Agreement 25; proposal for disputed areas 40; reaction to loss of Siping 96; relationship with Mao Zedong 2; removed as President 122; reorganization of Central Plains forces 106; strategy of 33; and Strong Point Offensive 56, 74; wartime alliances 3

China, map of 1

Chongqing, GMD provisional capital 7, 19

Chongqing Military Academy 12

CMC (Central Military Committee of CCP) 17; cutting ties with GMD 17; defense of Shanhaiguan 28; elected at 7th Congress 8; and fall of Yan'an 53, 64; instructions for northeast 18–19; lines of report 2; reunion with Secretariat 101

column, definition of 10

conventional warfare 7, 25–6, 29–30

Cultural Revolution 35, 141–3, 145–6

Dabie Mountains 76, 80–2, 84, 97, 139–40

Daixian 52

Datong, in Four Cities Three Railroad strategy 50, 52–3, 92

Deng Hua 86

Deng Xiaoping: in 115th Division 12; after victory 147; background of 7, 10, 12–13; and Central Plains counteroffensive 76–7, 80; in Dabie Mountains 81–2, 100; in General Front Committee 130; in Huaihai Campaign 117, 119–21, 149; rise to power 35; in Shandang Campaign 23; and Strong Point Offensive 58; and Wandong Campaign 104; in Yangtze River Crossing campaign 131–2

Dingtao Campaign 106

Du Yuming: and 2nd Army 107; attack on Chengde 33; attack on Jinzhou 29–30; attack on Shanhaiguan 28–9; and defense of Ji'nan 116; First Battle of Siping 34–6; First Battle of Siping 34–6; in General Offensive 54–5; and Huaihai Campaign 117, 121–2; pursuit of NDUA 37; replaced by Chen Cheng 86; Second Battle of Siping 71, 74; in Strong Point Offensive 66–9; and Summer Offensive 70; at Xuzhou 107

East Army (CCP): formation of 82; and Ji'nan Campaign 115; in Shandong 83–5; in Wandong Campaign 104–5

East Army (GMD) 111–13

East China Field Army: attack on Ji'nan 108; in Huaihai Campaign 117–19, 121–2; renamed 3rd Field Army 129; in "Second Year" strategy 82; separation of 98; in Shandong 62; in Strong Point Offensive 60–2; structure of 58–9

East China Military District 24, 31, 48–51, 56–8, 78, 99

East Henan Campaign 106

East Shaanxi Army 84

East Turkestan 132

Fan Hanjie 83–4, 98

Feng Zhian 33, 47–50, 78, 117–18

First United Front 7, 11–12

Four Cities, Three Railroads strategy 50

Fu Dong 127–8

Fu Zuoyi: after Huaihai Campaign 123; attack on Shijiazhuang 124; attacks on Chengde and Jining 33; and defense of Jinzhou 111; in General Offensive 51–2;

military disposition against Yan'an 11; and Pingjin Campaign 126–8; promotion of 54; in Shanxi 18, 22, 53; and Suiyan Campaign 31; surrender of 128, 150

Gao Shuxun 31
General Front Committee 130–1
General Mobilization Bill 74
General Offensive 40–1, 43–4, 47, 49–51, 53–6, 73, 136
Great Britain 3
Gu Zhutong 60–2, 65, 85, 96, 99, 107, 110, 117–18, 176
Guangdong: CCP forces in 4; fall of 132
guerrilla warfare 3, 6–7, 42, 44, 85, 141
Guomindang (GMD): 1945 advance of 19; advance on Shandong 24; defections to CCP 23–4, 31, 33, 37, 59, 63, 95, 112, 116, 121, 131–2, 139; defense against Yangtze River Crossing 130; estimates of casualties at Siping 36–7; High Command 2; high point of success 72–3; implications of Liaoshen Campaign for 113–14; position in Northeast 87; reaction to Zhu De's General Orders 19; truce with CCP 34

Handan Campaign 31
Hao Pengjuan 33
He Long: in Central Plains counteroffensive 84; defense of Jining 33; defense of Yan'an 63; relations with Mao 145; in Shanxi 18, 51–2; and Suiyuan Campaign 31
He Yingchin 96
He Yingduo 63
Hebei: and 8th Route Amry 2; attack on by Li Yunchang 26; defended by SCH Military District 22
Hebei-Rehe-Liaoning (HRL) 18, 20
Henan-Shanxi Military District 84
Hongqiao, battle of 13–14
Hou Jingru 111
Hu Lian 83, 104–6, 119
Hu Zongnan 11, 44, 47, 51–3, 62–3, 84–5, 100, 123, 128, 130, 132, 138, 195; in Central Plains counteroffensive 84–5, 100; in final phase of war 130, 132; in General Offensive 44, 47, 51–3; military disposition against Yan'an 11; in Strong Point Offensive 62–5, 138
Huaihai Campaign 114, 116–20, 122–5, 139, 148–9
Huaihai Committee 117, 120–2, 130

Huaiyang 47–8, 116
Huang Baitao 105, 107, 116, 118, 120
Huang Kecheng: in 3rd Division 14, 20; and defense of Shanhaiguan 28; on the northeast 27; at Siping 34, 36
Huangpu Military Academy 7, 9–10, 13
Hunan 4
Hundred Regiments Campaign 7, 42–3

Japan: surrender of 1, 16; withdrawal from China 5
Jiangsu 2, 8
Jiangxi 4–5, 32, 130–1
Jiangxi Soviet 2, 8–9, 11–13, 85, 144
Ji'nan Campaign 114, 115–17
Jinggang Mountains 6, 9, 13–14, 140–1
Jinzhou: captured by Du Yuming 33; captured by Lin Biao 111–12, 148; captured by Zeng Kelin 26; defense of 28–9

Laiwu Campaign 59–60
Li Da 76
Li Lisan 28
Li Mi 107, 117–22
Li Tianyou 86, 96
Li Wen 91–2
Li Xiannian: in Central Plains 24, 32, 51, 77; escape to Shaanxi 47; in New 4th Army 4, 14; and response to General Offensive 41–2, 44
Li Xianzhou 59–60
Li Yannian: in General Offensive 47–9; in Huaihai Campaign 119–21
Li Yunchang: attack on northeast 18, 20, 26; and defense of Shanhaiguan 28; in NPDUA 27
Li Zongren: repels SCH Field Army 91; and Shanxi campaign 54; and Zhengtai Campaign 72
Liang Xinqie 28
Liao Yaoxiang 109, 111–13, 148
Liaodong Military Sub-District 54–6, 66, 68–70
Liaoning 18, 22, 28
Liaoshen Campaign 107, 108–11, 113–14, 116, 118, 123–5, 128, 139, 144, 148–9
Liaoshen corridor 86–8, 94, 97, 108–9, 111, 124, 139
Liberated Areas: attacked by GMD 19–20; creation of 2; defense of 3–4, 19, 26; expansion of 16–17; reduced in Strong Point Offensive 61; split in General Offensive 55

Lin Biao: in 115th Division 9–10; attack on Changchun 108; attack on Fu Zuoyi 123; attack on Jinzhou 110–12; attack on Jinzhou 110–12; attack on Liao Yaoxiang 113; attack on Liao Yaoxiang 113; authority in Manchuria 38, 41; in Autumn Offensive 87–8; in Central Plains counteroffensive 86; criticism of 34–5; death of 35; and defense of Jinzhou 29–30; and defense of Shanhaiguan 29; and First Battle of Siping 35–6, 86; in General Offensive 55; in Liaoshen Campaign 149; in NPDUA 27, 34; in Pingjin Campaign 125, 127; relations with Mao 143–4; strategic debates with Mao 88, 108–10; strategy of 137, 143; in Strong Point Offensive 66–9; in Summer Offensive 69–71, 76; and Third Battle of Siping 96; and Three Large Cities Strategy 34; and Winter Offensive 94–5; in Yangtze River Crossing campaign 132

Linjiang 55, 66–9

Linyi: in General Offensive 47–9; HQ of Shandong Field Army 24; and Strong Point Offensive 57

Liu Bocheng: after victory 146; capture of Xianyang 106; in Central Plains counteroffensive 76–9; commanding 129th Division 12; in Dabie Mountains 76–8, 80–1; and defense of Shanhaiguan 28; in General Front Committee 130; in Huaihai Campaign 118–21; in Huaxian Campaign 49; and Longhai Campaign 46; and officer development 25; and Pinghan Campaign 31; and Shandang Campaign 23–4; and Strong Point Offensive 57–8; tactics of 137; victory at Dingtao 47; and Wandong Campaign 104; in Yangtze River Crossing campaign 132

Liu Ruming 47–8, 50, 58, 79, 105, 119–22

Liu Shaoqi: areas of authority 89; in CCP Secretariat 6–8; land reform proposals of 40–1; prediction of end of war 110; strategy of 20–2, 29–30, 135, 142

Liu Zhi: commander at Xuzhou 106–7, 115; in General Offensive 44–5, 47; and Huaihai Campaign 117, 119

Long March 2, 6, 8–14, 140, 144–5

Longhai Campaign 46–7

Lu Zhengcao 10, 18, 27

Luo Binghui 14

Luo Lirong 91–2

Luo Ronghuan: in 115th Division 9, 11; and attack on Beiping 127; and attack on Changchun 109; move into Manchuria 20, 24; and Pingjin Campaign 125; promotion of 38; relations with Lin Biao 36, 111, 113; secretary of HRL 20–1; tasks in Shandong 11, 13, 18; and Three Large Cities Strategy 30

Luo Ruiqing 89

Ma Liwu 57, 61

Manchuria 19–20, 26–7

Mao Zedong: approves attack on Yan Xishan 23; and attack on Beiping 127; and attack on Jinzhou 111–12; attitude to GMD 19; and campaign in northeast 30; and Central Jiangsu Campaign 46; and Central Plains counteroffensive 75–9, 82, 85; confrontation with Zhang Guotao 9; control over CCP strategy 141–2; criticisms of 136; and defense of Siping 35–6; and fall of Yan'an 65–6; in General Offensive 54; in Huaihai Campaign 116–17, 119–20; illness 29; implications of Liaoshen Campaign for 114; and Ji'nan Campaign 115; move into Beijing 133; and October 10 Agreement 25; organizational role of 6; prediction of end of war 110; prestige of 143; and push into south China 98, 100–2; relations with Chen Yi 14, 144; relations with Chiang Kaishek 2; relations with Lin Biao 9–10, 27, 143; relations with Liu Bocheng 12; response to General Offensive 41–2; retreat from Yan'an 64; speech to 7th Congress 3, 21–2; strategic debates with Lin Biao 88, 108–10; strategy of 4–5, 7, 19, 25, 42–3, 55–6, 137–9; in Strong Point Offensive 61

Mao Zedong Thought 30, 35

"March in the North, Defend in the South" 21, 25–7, 38–9, 42, 48, 135, 139–40, 142–4

Marching East Army *see* East Army (GMD)

Marching West Army *see* West Army (GMD)

Marshall, George C., 33

Marshall truce 37, 39–40

Menglijanggu 61, 74, 78, 119

mobile defense strategy 3, 33, 136–7, 139–40, 144

mobile warfare 3, 25, 42

Nanchang Uprising 6, 10–12
Nanjing-Shanghai-Hangzhou Campaign
    130–1
Nanma, Battle of 78
NDUA (Northeast Democratic United
    Army) 36–7, 54; in Autumn Offensive
    87–8; becomes Northeast Field Army
    96; defeats by Du Yuming 35–8;
    formation of 34; in General Offensive
    54, 66, 68; strength of 36; in Strong
    Point Offensive 66–8; in Summer
    Offensive 69–71, 86; in Winter
    Offensive 94–5; *see also* NPDUA
New 4th Army 2, 142; 1st Division 4;
    attack on Xuzhou 18; defense against
    GMD 5; overlooked in history 13; at
    Shandong 21, 24; transformed into
    Shandong Field Army 32
New 4th Army Incident 2, 5, 8, 13–14, 24
New 8th GMD Corps 31
Nie Fengzhi 115
Nie Rongzhen: in 115th Division 9–10;
    after victory 146–7; and attack on
    Beiping 127; in counteroffensive 86, 88;
    criticism of Lin Biao 35; at Datong 137;
    in General Offensive 50–1; and North
    China Field Army 123–4; and officer
    development 25; at Qingfengdian 90–2;
    reorganization of SCH 22; in Shanxi
    53; at Shijiazhuang 93; and Suiyuan
    Campaign 31; and Zhengtai Campaign
    71–2
North Baoding Campaign 90
North China Field Army 123–4, 128–30,
    132, 150
North China People's Government 103
North Henan Campaign 76–7
North Jiangsu Army 98, 100, 116, 119–20
North Jiangsu Campaign 50
North Shanxi Campaign 51
North Shanxi Field Army 51–3
Northeast Administrative Committee
    (NAC) 41
Northeast Anti-Japanese United Army
    26
Northeast Bandit Suppression
    Headquarters 96, 98
Northeast Bureau: and abandonment
    of Liaodong 56; and Battle of Siping
    86; formation of 20, 27; and General
    Offensive 54; land policies of 41; retreat
    from cities 29–30, 37; and Summer
    Offensive 69–71; and Three Large Cities
    Strategy 28, 34

Northeast Bureau, Du Yuming's strategy
    against 36
Northeast Field Army: attack on GMD
    West Army 113; attack on Jinzhou
    110–12, 148; at Changchun 109;
    formation of 96; in Pingjin Campaign
    125–6; renamed 4th Field Army 129;
    role in victory 135; tasks of 108
Northern Expedition 6–7, 9–10, 12, 14,
    130, 151
Northwest Field Army: and fall of Yan'an
    65, 79; in North Henan Campaign 76;
    recapture of Yan'an 101; renamed 1st
    Field Army 129; in Shaanxi 85, 100,
    128
NPDUA (Northeast People's Democratic
    United Army) 27–30, 34; *see also*
    NDUA

October 10 Agreement 25–6
Ou Zhen 59–60

Peng Dehuai: in CMC 8–9; commands of
    9; defense of Yan'an 63–4; and "March
    on North" strategy 22; and Northwest
    Field Army 99–101; relations with Mao
    145; strategy of 142, 145–6; in Strong
    Point Offensive 65; supplanting Zhang
    Guotao 6; supporting counterattacks 56;
    and Yangtze River Crossing campaign
    132
Peng E 96
Peng Xuefeng 14
Peng Yubin 23
Peng Zhen: and Battle of Siping 86; in
    CCP northeast strategy 26; demotion
    of 38; meeting with Lin Biao 36; in
    Northeast Bureau 20, 27–8; and Three
    Large Cities Strategy 28, 30, 35; Three
    Large Cities Strategy 29
People's Liberation Army (PLA):
    foundation of 129; predecessors of 6;
    victory in civil war 133
Pinghan Campaign 24, 28, 31, 162
Pingjin Campaign 122–5, 128, 139, 143,
    148–50
Pingjin Committee 126–8
Pingxingguan, battle of 10, 143
Potsdam Declaration 17
PRC (People's Republic of China):
    foundation of 133; shaped by
    revolutionary war 151–2
Pu Yi 16

Qingfengdian 89, 91–2, 94
Qiu Qingquan: in Central Jiangsu
  Campaign 45; in Central Plains
  counteroffensive 101; defeats West
  Army 83; in Huaihai Campaign 117–20;
  and Wandong Campaign 105

Rao Shushi 14
Red Army 7, 11; *see also* PLA
Red Army Japanese Resistance University
  10–11
Ren Bishi 6, 142–3

SCH (Shanxi-Chahar-Hebei) Field Army:
  attack on Changchun 108; formation
  of 89; merges with North China Field
  Army 123; at Qingfendian 89–92; at
  Shijiazhuang 93
SCH (Shanxi-Chahar-Hebei) Military
  District: command of 10–11; in
  General Offensive 54; and "March on
  North" strategy 22; merged with 115th
  Division 18; merger with SHSH 123;
  reorganization of 9
Second United Front 2, 7, 10–11, 14, 17,
  41
Secretariat of CCP: counteroffensive
  strategy 83; defence of Liberated Areas
  26; policy change of 40; responsibilities
  of 6; reunion with CMC 101; split into
  two parts 64
Seven Battles, Seven Victories *see* Central
  Jiangsu Campaign
Shaanxi 10, 44, 47, 62, 85; Chiang's
  fixation with 138; Northwest Field
  Army in 85, 100; Strong Point Offensive
  in 62
Shandong 2, 11, 18, 47
Shandong Army 98–9, 101, 106, 118
Shandong Field Army 18, 33, 46
Shandong Military District 24
Shandong Military Subdistrict 11
Shangdang Campaign 23–4, 26
Shanhaiguan 26, 28–9
Shanxi 11, 18, 32
Shanxi-Suiyuan Field Army 63–4
Shanxi-Suiyuan Military District 11
Shenyang 26, 34, 148
Shi Zebo 23
Shijiazhuang 89–94, 124
SHSH (Shanxi-Henan-Shandong-Hebei)
  Field Army/Military District: in Central
  Plains counterattack 76, 79, 84; in
  Dabie Mountains 76–7, 80–1, 84; and

defense of Yan'an 63; fighting during
  ceasefire in 33; in General Offensive
  52; in Longhai Campaign 46–7; merger
  with SCH 123; in Pinghan Campaign
  24; reputation of 49; in Shandang
  Campaign 23; strategic location of 22–3;
  and Strong Point Offensive 58–9; tasks
  in Henan and Shanxi 18; victories over
  GMD 31
Siping: CCP seizure of 34; First Battle of
  35–7, 39, 54, 66; Second Battle of 70–1,
  86–7, 93, 97; Third Battle of 94–7, 138
South Shandong Campaign 57
Southern Detachment 4
Southwest Shandong Campaign 77–9, 82
Soviet Red Army 18, 26, 28
Soviet Union: occupation of northeast
  China 20; recognition of CCP 3; support
  for CCP 19, 136
strategic offensive 98, 139
Strong Point Offensive 56; conception of
  56; gains and losses 61; outcome of 66,
  74, 101, 137–8; second component of
  62
Su Yu: after victory 146; and Central
  China Military District 58; in Central
  Jiangsu Campaign 47; in Central Plains
  offensive 78, 80, 83, 98, 101; in East
  China Military District 48–9; in General
  Front Committee 130; and General
  Offensive 43–6; in Huaihai Campaign
  118, 120–1; and Ji'nan Campaign
  114–16; in North Jiangsu Campaign 50;
  and push south 98, 100; relations with
  Chen Yi 82; and Strong Point Offensive
  56, 59–61; tactics of 137; and Wandong
  Campaign 105–6; in Yangtze River
  Crossing campaign 131
Suiyuan Campaign 25, 31
Suizhong 29
Summer Offensive 69–70, 73, 76, 78, 86
Sun Lianzhong: and Autumn Offensive
  90–1; and final phase of war 121–2; and
  Pinghan Campaign 24, 31; promotion
  of 54; in Shanxi 22, 53; and Zhengtai
  Campaign 72
Sun Liren 66–8, 87
Sun Tzu 12, 148
Sun Yatsen 10, 12
Sun Yuanliang 107, 117, 119–20

Taiwan 131–3
Taiyuan Pacification Command 72
Tan Zhenlin 48, 58, 85, 117, 130

Tang Enbo: in Central Plains counterattack 78, 83; in General Offensive 45, 47, 49; in Strong Point Offensive 60–1, 138; in Yangtze River Crossing campaign 130–1
Tang Liang 78
Teh Wang, Prince 16
Three Attacks, Four Defenses 66, 69
Three Large Cities Strategy 28–30, 34–5, 38
Tianjin, CCP conquest of 127, 150
Tibet 133
"two Chens", 99–101
"two Mas", 63, 130, 132
"two Wangs", 49, 58

United Defense Army 11, 13, 63–4, 84

Wandong Campaign 104–5
Wang Jingjiu 49, 58, 60–1, 79; *see also* "two Wangs"
Wang Jingwei 16, 32–3
Wang Shitai 63
Wang Yaowu 50, 59–60, 99, 106, 115–16
Wang Zhonglian 49, 76; *see also* "two Wangs"
Wedemeyer, Albert C., 135
Wei Guoqing 98, 116, 176
Wei Lihuang 95–6, 98, 112–13, 117
West Army (CCP): capture of Xuchang 98; formation of 82; at Ji'nan 115–16
West Army (GMD) 111–13
Winter Offensive 94, 96, 108
Work Committee 64
Wu Huawei 31–2
Wu Huawen 116
Wu Kehua 37–8

Xi'an, fall of 132
Xi'an Pacification Command 62
Xiao Hua 20
Xiao Jingguang 66, 68–9, 71
Xiao Ke 22, 27–8, 35, 53–5, 68
Xie Fuzhi 84
Xin Baoan 126–7
Xu Guangda 63
Xu Shiyou 82–5, 98–9, 106, 114, 118
Xu Xiangqian 12–13, 101, 123, 125, 128, 132
Xue Yue 44, 46, 48–9, 57, 74
Xuzhou, CCP offensive against 104, 106
Xuzhou Bandit Suppression Headquarters 99
Xuzhou Pacification Command 44, 46–7, 49, 58

Yan Xishan: advance on Shanxi 18, 22–3, 52–3; in Central Plains counteroffensive 84, 101; military disposition against Yan'an 11; at Taiyuan 128
Yan'an: 7th Congress of CCP 1–2; Artillery School 4; blockade of by GMD 11; defense of 63–4; fall of 62, 64–5, 137; recapture of 101
Yang Chengwu, in Shanxi 53–4
Yang Dezhi: and 2nd Column 10; and attack on Changchun 108; defense of Yan'an 63; and North China Field Army 123–4; in Pingjin Campaign 126; in SCH Military District 10, 89–91; at Shijiazhuang 93; and Zhengtai Campaign 71
Yang Guofu 28–9
Yang Shangkun 8, 147
Yangshanji 79–80
Yangtze River Crossing Campaign 129–30
Ye Fei 47–8
Ye Jianying 8, 147
Yellow River, geography of 76–7

Zeng Kelin 20, 22, 26
Zeng Zesheng 112
Zhang Aiping 14
Zhang Dingcheng 14, 32
Zhang Guotao 6, 9–10, 12–13, 140
Zhang Lingfu 61
Zhang Xueliang 11
Zhang Yunyi 56–7
Zhang Zhen 105, 131
Zhang Zongxun 63–4
Zhangjiakou 21, 31, 53–5, 63, 94, 124–7
Zhao Boshou 72
Zhejiang 4
Zheng Dongguo 69
Zheng Lisan 32
Zheng Tongguo 36, 108–9, 112
Zheng Weisan 44
Zhengtai Campaign 71–3, 89, 92
Zhengzhou Pacification Command 44, 47, 49, 57, 59
Zhou Enlai: in CCP Secretariat 6–7; defense of Yan'an 64; estimation of General Offensive 55; and nationwide offensive 82; negotiations with GMD 35; negotiations with Marshall in Shanghai 43; and peace talks with GMD 19; support of Mao 142
Zhou Junming 45
Zhou Shidi 51–2

Zhu De: areas of authority 89; and attack on Shijiazhuang 92; background of 6; in CCP Secretariat 6; commands of 9; communication with GMD 19; defeated by Liu Bocheng 12; First General Order 17; and "March on North" strategy 22; modernization of PLA 4; and officer development 25; reorganization of NPDUA 27; Second General Order 18; and Shijiazhuang 93; strategy of 3, 6–7, 142

Zibo 60

zongdui see column

Zunyi Conference 8, 13